In the spirit of:
Medjugorje, The 90's

THE HIDDEN CHILD
OF MEDJUGORJE

Sister Emmanuel

From: Our Lady
Queen of Peace
To: You †

To the Child Jesus

To little Li

To all the children immolated
on the altar of our troubles and idols,
for they sustain the world.

CONTENTS

Appendix 1

Appendix 2

The most recent statement from the Vatican

Appendix 3

PREFACE

Throughout time, man has been in quest of security, of peace, and of happiness; however, rare are those who divine that their quest is in reality a quest for God.

In her new book, The Hidden Child of Medjugorje, Sister Emmanuel brings a precious contribution to the understanding of this aspiration. As the pages are turned, this book reveals itself to be a guide. It enables us to reach an end which is none other than the Hidden Child, the Child Jesus. In the apparitions of Medjugorje, this Divine Child hides Himself so well in His Mother that at first sight, one pays Him no attention. But whoever finds the Mother, finds the Son. Thus will it be for all who read this book.

In her previous work, *Medjugorje, the 90's*,[1] (which became in a very short time a best-seller translated into more than twenty languages), the author gave life to the messages of the Our Lady. Countless are those who have been captivated by the spiritual richness of The Nineties and by the tenderness of the Queen of Peace who emerges from its pages. The reading of this book has excited in them a great desire to come to Medjugorje as a pilgrim. There is no doubt that The Hidden Child of Medjugorje will become a best-seller in its turn, all for the glory of God.

Sister Emmanuel shows in this work the same talent. By relying on simple examples, taken from real life, she shows the reader how the supernatural can intervene in the life of each person. Reading this we are submerged in joy and we are seized by a new ardor to run toward sanctity. One starts to love God with more fervor and with a greater desire for intimacy with Him, whatever the concerns and difficulties which overwhelm us.

---

[1] Published, as revised, under the title Medjugorje, Triumph of the Heart.

This book is not a mystery novel you read on a train. It is comparable to a mosaic in which each element is unique and precious. In reading about each authentic event that it reports, we feel our hearts penetrated, through prayer and meditation, by the grace which emanates from it.

This reading opens in us a door to the Divine—that place where the supernatural is made completely natural and where the miraculous is revealed to be normal. It is in this way that God desires to manifest His love to us. The reader should not be astonished that, at times, the author describes extraordinary events and miracles because they reveal to us God's omnipotence. To hold that against her would be to wrong God.

Is not the Old Testament steeped in the marvels of God? And Jesus, did He not begin His public ministry with a miracle during a wedding in Cana? The miracles are an integral part of His effort to bring people to faith. They confirm the truth of His words and are the incomparable seal of His divine mandate.

Today it is not any different. Miracles help us to believe in the fatherly tenderness of God and to place our confidence in Him. This is how Sister Emmanuel draws us into Medjugorje.

During missions we have had together in Asia, Australia, and America, I have seen for myself to what extent she invests herself in order to lead souls to God. During great Marian Conferences, I have seen her address thousands of people, sharing with enthusiasm and conviction the messages of the Queen of Peace. Immediately afterwards, I have seen her spend hours listening, with maternal solicitude, to those who entrust their needs to her; and even at midnight she is still not tired! It is her love for the Gospa and for souls that gives her this strength. It is this same love that pushed her to write The Hidden Child, in which she encourages us to place all of our trust in God, especially in our present trials and those to come.

Taking into account all of the authentic Marian apparitions in the last few decades, with the eyes of faith we see that the Mother of God desires only one thing: to spare the world from self-destruction. She longs to introduce humanity to a new Eden. In Fatima, for example, the Queen of the Rosary calls this new time the Triumph of Her Immaculate

Heart. In the same spirit, the great French mystic, Marthe Robin, spoke of the New Pentecost of Love that Jesus promised.

A great number of believers are waiting for this intervention from God, through His merciful love. This hope is linked to the return of the Lord, according to the very words of the Mother of God to Saint Faustina: "I gave the Savior to the world; as for you, you have to speak to the world about His great mercy and prepare the world for His second coming" (Diary of Sr. Faustina, Paragraph 635).

However, in order to render us capable of returning to God with our whole being, the Lord's second coming will be preceded by an inevitable, purifying trial. Our Lady comes to our aid through her presence, through her words, and sometimes even through her tears to prepare us for the interior and exterior trials. She asks us to pray with the heart, to renounce our egoism and to make a sincere confession in order to reconcile with God and our neighbor. Thus we are established in love—free from all prejudice in our relationships without exception. She teaches us also how to adore Jesus and receive Him with a pure heart.

Sister Emmanuel has written The Hidden Child of Medjugorje for us. She helps us to make this teaching practical in our every day lives. Don't miss reading this book. We will discover through these pages how to better fulfill our vocation: to be entirely love.

Father Paul Maria Sigl[2]
Rome, March 20, 2006, on the solemnity of Saint Joseph

---

[2] Father Paul Maria Sigl is the cofounder and spiritual guide of the community "Family of Mary" in Slovakia. His ministry was closely linked to Monsignor Paul Maria Hnilica, SJ, who ordained him a priest in Fatima on December 8, 1992. Fr. Paul travels throughout the world preaching retreats and speaking at Marian conferences. For information, write to: Family of Mary, Via Ombra 1, 64010 Civitella del Tronto, Italy. E-mail: familiemariens@web.de

Neither the author nor the publisher of this book intends to preempt the judgment of the Church as to the authenticity of the apparitions of Mary at Medjugorje or the other phenomena described herein. The book contains only the personal opinions of the author, based on her own experiences and the testimony of those who have been witnesses to the events in that village and elsewhere. Both author and publisher will subject their opinions concerning the apparitions and other phenomena to the discernment of the Church as soon as any formal pronouncement on these events is made.

WARNING:

This book is a page-turner, but you should not turn its pages too quickly. It will entertain you, but its purpose is not to entertain. Do not sit down with the idea of reading it from cover to cover. Instead, savor each chapter separately, not going on to the next until you have pondered its message for you. You will benefit only if you open your heart—not just your mind—to these messages.

BRIEF SUMMARY OF THE HISTORY OF MEDJUGORJE

On June 24, 1981, a beautiful afternoon in summer, two adolescents from the village of Bijakovici[3] are chatting while strolling along the rocky hill of Podbrdo, which looks over their village. A conversation of young people their age.

One of them, Ivanka Ivankovic, age sixteen, suddenly notices a light over the hill, at around two hundred meters from them. She looks and perceives a shining silhouette of light which hovers over the ground. Astounded, she becomes quiet and stares at the light. The silhouette takes the form of a young woman. Then she exclaims, "Mirjana, look! it's the Gospa[4] !" Mirjana Dragičević, sure that Ivanka is joking, doesn't even take the trouble of looking in the direction which her friend indicates to her.

"C'mon", she says, in a mocking tone, "the Gospa" is appearing to us? - to us? - are you kidding me?"

Ivanka is convinced, but she does not insist, and they continue their walk. A third young girl joins them. It is Milka Pavlovic, who asks their help in gathering her goats. They go along, then come back to the same place. All three see the silhouette and fall to their knees.

Their friend Vicka Ivankovic is just passing by. "Look in the sky," they say to her. Vicka makes fun of them without even looking towards the hill, takes off her shoes and runs away. On the way, she meets Ivan Dragicevic, age sixteen, and his friend Ivan Ivankovic. She recounts to them the words of her friends. They decide to go back and see what is happening. As they arrive at the foot of the hill, they, too, see the silhouette and Ivan Dragicevic, frightened, flees home at full speed.

---

[3] Area which is part of the parish of Medjugorje.
[4] *Gospa* is the Croatian term for the *Lady*.

The next day, four of the children feel moved inside to return to the same place at the same time. Vicka goes to find her friends, Marija Pavlovic, sister of Milka, and the little Jakov Colo, age ten. On this second day, the six young ones see the Blessed Mother, and the definitive group of six seers is formed. Milka and Ivan Ivankovic have not been moved to return there and have never seen "the Lady" again. From that day on, the Gospa appears to the six chosen ones at 5:40 PM each day.

According to their testimony, she appears to be sixteen, she has black hair and blue eyes, and she is of an inexpressible beauty. She presented herself as the Queen of Peace and of Reconciliation. She comes to bring us closer to the heart of God by showing us the path of Peace. She invites us all to sainthood and for that gives us some very simple means, within the reach of all.

Our Lady has promised to each of the seers that she will confide in him/her 10 secrets. To this day, three of the seers, Ivanka, Mirjana, and Jakov, have received their 10 secrets and no longer have daily apparitions. They see the Virgin once a year. Vicka, Marija, and Ivan have only received nine secrets and still see Our Lady each day.

According to Mirjana, each seer has to choose a priest in order to reveal his or her secrets. For her part, she has chosen Father Petar Ljubicic, a Franciscan. Ten days before the realization of the secret, the seer will have to fast on bread and water with the chosen priest, and, on the seventh day, she will reveal the secret to the priest who will publicize it to the world three days before its realization.

In July of 1981, the Blessed Mother also promised that she would leave on the hill a permanent sign, visible by all and indestructible.

On the 25th of each month, Our Lady gives to Marija a message destined for the world. Marija transmits it to a Franciscan of the parish of Saint James. Then it is translated and published in all languages.[5]

---

[5] www.medjugorje.hr or www.childrenofmedjugorje.com

Since 1987, the Blessed Mother has shown herself to Marijana every second day of the month and prays with her for the unbelievers. This apparition is now open to all. Sometimes, Our Lady gives at this time a message to Mirjana for the public.

Twenty-five to thirty million pilgrims, including priests, bishops, and cardinals, have come to Medjugorje since the beginning of the apparitions.

The six seers are all now married.

Ivanka Ivankovic married Rajko Elez on December 28, 1986. They have three children: Kristina, Josip, and Ivan.

Mirjana Dragicevic married Marko Soldo on September 16, 1989. They live in Medjugorje with their two daughters: Veronika and Marija.

Marija Pavlovic married Paolo Lunetti on September 8, 1993. They live in Monza, in Italy, with their four sons: Michaele, Francesco Maria, Marco, and Giovanni.

Jakov Colo married Annalisa Barozzi on April 11, 1993. They live in Medjugorje. They have three children: Arijanna Marija, David Emmanuele, and Myriam.

Ivan Dragicevic married Laureen Murphy on October 23, 1994 and lives most of the time in the United States. They have three children: Kristina Marija, Mikaela, and Daniel.

Vicka Ivankovic married Mario Mijatovic on January 26, 2002. They live in Gradac, near Medjugorje, with their two children: Marija-Sofija and Ante.

My children, don't you recognize the signs of the times? Do you not speak of them? Come follow me. As a mother I call you! (To Mirjana, April 2, 2006)

1

WHO IS THE HIDDEN CHILD?

June 1981

It was around three o'clock and the burning sun began its curved descent. In Herzegovina, everyone knows that during the summer solstice it is wiser to remain inside and take a nap rather than to brave the heat.

However on that day, on the side of the hill, stood a woman. It was bizarre. It was as if she wanted to hide the child she was holding! She had wrapped him in linens, as women from the Orient do, and she was covering his face with a light veil. He was so tiny he must have been a newborn! And the woman? Was she the big sister or the mother of the child? She looked so young—hardly fifteen or sixteen. Fascinated, several youngsters stared at her. They didn't know her. She was definitely not from their village, although she resembled a young girl from their country with her beautiful black hair and radiant complexion. At times she would lift the veil that covered the child's face, as if to reveal her secret, and she would fan him with the flap of her coat but then quickly cover him again. Her attitude astounded those watching. They wondered, "What is so special about this child that she treats him like this?"

The adolescents took shelter from the sun under an oak tree. Stunned, they continued to watched the scene which seemed to have come from another world. Unfortunately, the young woman was too far up the hill for the baby's features to be clearly seen. She tried in vain to signal them to approach her, but there was no way. They were frozen, too scared to move. They would not budge.

Later that evening, the hidden child was almost forgotten. It was his mother who was the subject of conversation in the village. How could the local peasants that night in Bijakovici have suspected, even for a second, that, from that moment onwards their lives would never be the same again? It was too late! The hidden child and his mother had already begun to revolutionize this remote little Hercegovinian village. The past was gone! From now on, it would be the littlest of the little ones who would lead the dance. He, at whose name "every knee shall bow in heaven and on earth and under the earth,"[2] will lead it with His Mother! It is He—our true leader—who sends His Mother to prepare humanity for His Second Coming. It is He who, hidden in Mary and in all the tabernacles of the world, comes in a divine way to lead the world.

Countless books had been published on the Mother. A book on the Child was needed, a book that would give a little glimpse of His active presence both in and out of Medjugorje.[3]

Six months after the first apparition on the Hill, the Child Jesus came again to show Himself to the visionaries; this time He was wrapped in the golden veil of His Mother. It was Christmas! On the evening of December 25, 1981, the youngsters finally saw the Child-God face to face, and this God was a baby, an infant only a few hours old! And what was He doing? He was playing hide-and-seek with His Mother's veil! He knew that the young visionaries needed to smile. They were so rigid and awkward in the face of the Divine!

The man of today, who is restless, anxious, and sick, needs to play with the Child Jesus in order to be healed. He needs to play with God so he can revive himself. In order to conquer the powers of evil which destroy us from the inside and which threaten our world, we need weapons other than those of this world. We need the Child-God.

For example, in a great European city, satanic sects multiplied so fast in the 1990s that the city authorities decided to create an anti-Satanic

---

[2] Ph 2:10.

[3] It is not by chance that Our Lady appeared on June 24th, the Feast of Saint John the Baptist, he who called attention to Jesus hidden in the bosom of the people! Actually, Mary comes also as a precursor, to prepare the people for the second coming of Christ. This gesture of covering and uncovering the face of the Child indicated the purpose of her visits: to reveal to our blind world the hidden Child!

task force. For that, they needed to appoint a man exceptionally smart and capable of eradicating them one by one. They found an adequate and reliable man who had the proven experience to take on the position. So far the story sounds pleasant, but the reality of it revealed something else. The elected officer was none other than one of the most high-ranking Satanists!

Yes, we need weapons other than those of this world, in order to defeat the Evil One, because he has power for a little while longer.[4] We need an Innocent Child, so that Satan's empire will collapse: God has always pitted innocence against evil, and He knows why.

In this book, which proceeds step-by-step, I have tried to provide you, Dear Readers, with simple tools to help you experience something of that Child-God. You will find here various images, rich with testimonies and concrete facts. I hope that each of you may find keys for your own life and nourishment for your soul.

Here are some examples:

* If one day we are in prison for the sake of Jesus, and we find ourselves too weak to remember our prayers, there is a key in Chapter 14 entitled, "An Unknown Tongue."

* Or if we one day lack food, there is a good recipe in Chapter 75, "The God of Multiplication."

* And if one day money does not exist on earth, Chapter 78 will show a way out, "The Storehouses of Divine Providence."

* And if one day we have no more medicine, a good place to find it in Chapter 52, "Oh Good Saint Joseph."

* And if one day the waves of evil submerge us, hope can be found in Chapter 70, "Operation Jericho."

* And if one day we are afraid of death, some comfort is in Chapter 50, "Heaven Within Reach."

* If there is a fear of the future, a sure path is set out in Chapter 20, "The Rosary, or the Soviets."

* If one day forgiving seems impossible, there is a solution in Chapter 46, "Finding the Child."

---

[4] 1 Jn 5:19

* And if one day despair strikes our heart, a proven recourse is in Chapter 76, "Marthe Robin – An Anti- Suicide Angel."

Some of the testimonies in this book are not directly linked to Medjugorje, but I have selected them according to one common criterion: they reveal to us the secret power of Christ and help us to enter into a deep communion with Him. For the hidden Child of Medjugorje is, all-in-all, the Innocence of God, under whatever aspect He may manifest Himself. He is the Almighty God who is, and was, and will always be, a Child.

"Dear Children! Invoke the name of my Son. Receive Him in your heart. Only in the name of my Son will you experience true happiness and true peace in your heart. Only in this way will you come to know the love of God and spread it further. I am calling you to be my apostles." (To Mirjana, March 18, 2000)

2

VERONICA'S BLUE EYES

Margate, South Africa, August 9, 1998

Veronica could not sleep. She wondered if the strange flame that burned in her heart would keep her awake until dawn. Fortunately, Alex, her husband, had settled into a deep slumber. Spontaneously, Veronica began to pray to Jesus. Actually, in the sincerity of her heart, she began speaking to Him, because she did not use written prayers, only those that effortlessly sprang to her lips. Even when she recited the "Our Father," she did it with so much intensity that it sounded as if she had invented it herself!

It was still dark when Veronica decided to get up and sit in her living room. She chose her favorite armchair facing the Crucifix. Relaxing in it, she gave free reign to her heart. She offered every joy and every tear to Jesus, who was the sole witness of her intimate life. Veronica loved Jesus beyond all things. Her greatest joy was to entrust to Him all of her daily affairs, all her dear ones, this situation or that, and then to question Him: "Jesus, what do you think of this situation? How can I help you with it Jesus?"

Veronica didn't mark the time. She had no idea how long she had been praying when suddenly something unusual seized her. Her face felt like it was on fire, and she experienced a dazzling light. It became more and more brilliant with each passing second. "What is going on?" she wondered.

Totally Blind

Veronica had been born in South Africa to a fervent and strict Catholic family of eight children. Every morning the entire household went to Mass, and each night they attended Vespers at their local parish. Most importantly, they prayed the Rosary together. On Sundays, they attended an African Mass, where the rhythmic dancing and inspired songs seemed to stop time in its tracks. No one in the family discussed piety. This way of life was already integrated into their home, like eating, sleeping, or working. Yet from birth Veronica had had a heavy cross to carry: a retinal detachment affected both of her eyes, leaving her almost totally blind. As a child, she had no sight from her left eye, while her right eye allowed her to see the world through a kind of dark grey veil.

Veronica was a bank clerk, until 1956, when she married Alex, a financial director of a large clothing retailer. They had four children. Alex was like an angel coming down from Heaven for her! A companion sent by God to be by her side and to keep her as a precious treasure! Alex belonged to the race of husbands who know how to give their spouses that calm and tender love they themselves draw from the heart of God. It wasn't until 1977 that Veronica became completely blind. But what beauty she still radiated!

A Name No One Could Pronounce!

That night, an intense light shone on Veronica and her heart began to beat uncontrollably. After a moment of fright she realized that there was a man standing in front of her, and that he was Jesus! Whether it was an apparition or a vision, it did not matter. Jesus was standing there, all in white! Veronica could see Him, with his long hair and blue eyes, his arms extended downwards, palms facing her. Jesus was bathed in such an encompassing light that she couldn't see anything but Him. He said: "Come! Get up and pray with me!"

Jesus showed her a little village surrounded by hills. She saw a church, two steeples topped with crosses and three arched entrances. Jesus led her inside, where she saw several glass windows. One window struck her particularly. It was of Our Lady of the Annunciation and Veronica felt puzzled by what she was seeing. Before 1977 she had taken a trip to Israel, Lourdes and Fatima with Alex. But this place felt so different.

"Jesus, I do not know this place!" she said to Him. Jesus smiled, and looking at her, He said: "Medjugorje! There I will give you the light and show you the way!" Then, just as He had come, He disappeared.

Overwhelmed and grappling with what had just happened to her, Veronica found herself in complete darkness again. As she questioned herself, Alex joined her in prayer. He found her in tears but quickly realized they were tears of joy! He looked at her with tenderness and asked, "Are you okay?"

"Alex, Jesus spoke to me. He said that we have to go to Medjugorje, to walk with Him and pray. He said that there, He will give me the light and will show me the way.

"What?!" Alex exclaimed. "Medjugorje?" Alex asked her to repeat the name.

She could hear the confusion in his voice, but she could only say again, "Medjugorje."

He had her repeat the name twice more, and stared at her and then at his hands, fumbling for understanding, mulling over the strange name. They could not imagine where this place could be. Baffled, Alex grabbed a pencil and asked Veronica for a precise description. He drew the village and the church as she depicted it.

Over the next few days, they approached all the travel agents they could find in their area but each one was more ignorant than the previous. To them, the peculiar name was a complete enigma. Nobody had the slightest idea of where it could be. This name, almost impossible to pronounce, was not shown on any map or mentioned in tourist brochures. Alex encountered failure after failure, but, two weeks later, a friend telephoned them and his voice was full of enthusiasm: "I have just returned from a fantastic pilgrimage! It was in a tiny village in Bosnia-Herzegovina, where Our Lady is appearing to some teenagers. You have to go there, it's fabulous! The place is called Medjugorje."

Alex nearly lost his breath. "Medjugorje?"

The man explained how to get visas. After traversing huge mountains of administrative problems, Alex and Veronica finally obtained their visas and boarded a plane to Croatia. They had only one target on their radar screen: to obey what Jesus had asked of Veronica.

Reaching Medjugorje, the couple rented a car and started exploring the village. Alex refrained from speaking, while focusing on their new environment. All of a sudden he exclaimed: "Veronica, this is it! We're here! The church, the two steeples, the big mountain with the cross on top! I feel like I know this village. It's exactly as you described it!"

In the car they behaved like two excited children. Each detail came alive to Veronica as Alex depicted the village for her. She let each element sink deeply into her heart. Each new aspect was a confirmation of her vision, each one like a kiss from Jesus to her soul. Her dear Jesus had not deceived her! For two days, hanging onto Alex's arm, she walked everywhere in Medjugorje, participating in all the programs offered by the parish. They listened in awe to the testimony of Mira Ostojic and her family, with whom they stayed. These were people who lived Our Lady's messages with all their hearts.

On the third day of their pilgrimage Mira took them to see Vicka, one of the visionaries who was then speaking to pilgrims from all over the world. Alex tried to protect Veronica from the crowd which pressed hard against the little staircase from where Vicka was speaking. But they found themselves like two prisoners in the crowd, incapable of moving left or right. When Vicka arrived and began to pray, all eyes were fixed on her, with the shortest people on tip-toes and craning their necks in the hope of catching a glimpse of her.

Alex whispered a basic description of the scene to Veronica. All of a sudden he stopped. Something unexpected was happening:

"Veronica, Vicka is looking at you! She's smiling at you!"

"She's smiling at me? Oh, if only I could see her!"

"She's coming down the stairs. She's looking at you! She's walking toward us!"

"Oh Alex, if only I could see her too, it would be so beautiful!" She repeated.

All of a sudden Veronica felt a hand resting on her eyes. Rooted in place by surprise, her whole being listened to the beautiful voice that was praying in a strange language. It was the same voice that had spoken only a moment ago. It was Vicka! Vicka had come from her staircase to pray for her, for her stunning blue eyes! The whole crowd breathlessly wondered what would happen next. After a long moment of prayer, Vicka finally took her hands off Veronica's eyes, and Veronica felt life coming back to her right eye.

"I can see!," she exclaimed.

Vicka simply bent down, kissed her and smiled. "What a beautiful smile," Veronica thought, filled with the Holy Spirit and overjoyed! Vicka's face was the first thing she saw with her new sight. But the vision was short lived because Vicka took Veronica in her arms and embraced her with such tenderness that Veronica felt she was touching a piece of Heaven, a little bit of Mary's heart that was flowing through her little servant, Vicka. Alex wept with joy.

How amazing it was for him, rambling down the road back to the church, after having led Veronica by the arm for years wherever they went. The news of Veronica's sight being restored spread like wildfire on a windy summer day. That evening after Mass, Father Slavko asked Veronica to come to the pulpit and pray the Magnificat in front of the packed church.[5] How appropriate for Veronica to be chosen, for she herself had become a living Magnificat. She thanked God incessantly for allowing her to see again. She never expected such a healing! But, Jesus never gives a physical healing without also touching the whole person one way or the other. All His gifts are directed toward the greatest healing there is: the healing of the soul, which remains for eternity.

Veronica pondered in her heart, over and over again, the words she had received the night in Margate: "There I will give you the light and show you the way."

The way?

After the healing of her eye, a new path opened up for Alex and Veronica. Out of gratitude to God, they set themselves to work, piecing together all the broken hearts in South Africa who did not yet know His love. That same year, I asked them to collaborate with us, to be our little "Children of Medjugorje" antenna in the depths of Africa. But I didn't

---

[5] The story of Veronica's healing was published in the magazine "Glas Mira" (Zagreb, 1999).

foresee the astounding effect they would have in their country. They went way beyond all expectations! Without any previous training as missionaries, with only limited local means and many sleepless nights, they gave themselves, body and soul, to make known what had changed their lives. Thanks to them, the messages of Medjugorje have entered thousands of homes, saved lives, revived faith that had been petering out or even dying, enkindled hope, and sowed joy all over!

Apostles of the Latter Times

In Medjugorje, Our Lady has her little prophets. Throughout my 17 years of mission at her service, I have noticed similar traits in each of them that cannot be denied: they are humble and simple, totally free from public opinion, and they are constantly chewing on the Word of God and the messages of Our Lady. No stumbling block can stop them, and, surprisingly enough, it seems that they are being internally guided as to what they should pray for. As a result, they are granted almost all of the intentions they bring before the Lord! This is the little army of Our Lady, her "special commandos" who infiltrate everywhere. While the 'big shots' of this world often have to ask other 'big shots' to pull strings for them, these little prophets do not worry about a thing. They simply walk side by side with the angels and saints, and miraculously doors open for them![6]

---

[6] These apostles from the Gospa remind us of "the Apostles of the latter times" described by Saint Louis de Montfort in his prophetic book True Devotion to Mary. Here are three sections:

[54] "In the eyes of the world they will be little and poor and, like the heel, lowly in the eyes of all, down-trodden and crushed as is the heel by the other parts of the body. But in compensation for this they will be rich in God's graces, which will be abundantly bestowed on them by Mary. They will be great and exalted before God in holiness. They will be superior to all creatures by their great zeal and so strongly will they be supported by divine assistance that, in union with Mary, they will crush the head of Satan with their heel, that is, their humility, and bring victory to Jesus Christ".

[58] "They will be true apostles of the latter times to whom the Lord of Hosts will give eloquence and strength to work wonders and carry off glorious spoils from his enemies. They will sleep without gold or silver and, more important still, without concern in the midst of other priests, ecclesiastics and clerics. Yet they will have the silver wings of the dove enabling them to go wherever the Holy Spirit calls them, filled as they are with the resolve to seek the glory of God and the salvation of souls. Wherever they preach, they will leave behind them nothing but the gold of love, which is the fulfilment of the whole law".

The sun never sets without Veronica having a little anecdote to tell. It's like she's directly connected to heaven: "The Lord did this or that for that person, in that situation," she would say. When she sees a priest who has not taken his vocation seriously, she immediately becomes his spiritual mother. She doesn't stop shaking God and all His saints until the priest breaks down, weeps over his sins and starts again on the right path. If she sees a teenager stuck in depression, drugs, or perversion, the Lord whispers to her the cause of the trouble. The teenager instantly becomes her adopted son. She tenderly carries him within her heart, praying like Moses on the mountain or like the prophets who never leave God in peace. Then she manages to have a little chat with the young person, who ends up coming back to life! Veronica knows how to touch God in His heart, that's her secret!

The eyes of Veronica look like two aquamarine stones of a blue even purer than that of the Mediterranean Sea under the July sun.[7] Why did Jesus only heal her right eye? Probably out of Mercy! One day Veronica confided in me that, in a way, she preferred to be blind rather than to see, because seeing can be such a distraction for the heart!

---

[59] "Lastly, we know they will be true disciples of Jesus Christ, imitating his poverty, his humility, his contempt of the world and his love. They will point out the narrow way to God in pure truth according to the holy Gospel, and not according to the maxims of the world. Their hearts will not be troubled, nor will they show favour to anyone; they will not spare or heed or fear any man, however powerful he may be. They will have the two-edged sword of the word of God in their mouths and the blood-stained standard of the Cross on their shoulders. They will carry the crucifix in their right hand and the rosary in their left, and the holy names of Jesus and Mary on their heart. The simplicity and self-sacrifice of Jesus will be reflected in their whole behaviour.

"Such are the great men who are to come. By the will of God Mary is to prepare them to extend his rule over the impious and unbelievers. But when and how will this come about? Only God knows".

[7] See the photograph.

There are so many ugly things around nowadays! I guess Jesus took this into account: He kept the left eye for Himself so Veronica could contemplate Him from the inside and draw strength from Him. He restored the other eye's sight to share with Veronica the misery of the world, and so she can in turn offer it to God.[8]

---

[8] The healing of only one of Veronica's eyes calls to mind a similar incident in the ministry of St. Pio (Padre Pio). A construction worker working on an annex to the friary at San Giovanni Rotondo was badly injured in a dynamite explosion. His sightless left eye remained, but his right eye socket was empty. Padre Pio visited him one night through bilocation and restored sight to the empty socket! It made a believer of the doctor, who had been an atheist! When the worker asked Padre Pio about medical treatment to try to restore sight in his left eye, Padre Pio advised against it, saying that "we have the grace which we have asked for." See, John A. Schug, A Padre Pio Profile, 42-44 (St. Bede's Publications 1987). As for the dangers to the soul which come from sight, another tale of Padre Pio is illustrative. One of the residents of San Giovanni Rotondo had been blind since he was twelve. Padre Pio once asked him whether he would like to see again. He replied that he would like to do so only if it would be good for his soul and the welfare of other people. Padre Pio said to him: "You know very well that the eyes are the windows of our bodies. The dangers come always through our eyes." Accordingly, he told Padre Pio that he was happy to remain blind, and Padre Pio many times told him that it was good for him that he did not see the bad things of the world. See id. at 138.

"Dear Children! .... If you do not pray, you shall not be able to recognize my love and the plans which God has for this parish and for each individual. Pray that Satan does not entice you with his pride and deceptive strength. I am with you and I want you to believe me that I love you." (November 25, 1987)

3

GIVE THE CROWN BACK TO THE KING!

There was a conflict in my friend's heart. Catherine, 60, an Irish mother of two, a grandmother and a pillar of her parish, had decided long ago to be guided by the Holy Spirit. However, her personality was so strong that it sometimes caused her to balk at God's instructions. No matter what! The Divine often contradicts our human ways and one does not change God.

The Lord sometimes spoke to Catherine at night through her dreams. One particular night, she was counting on a peaceful night's sleep, but the message she received caused her stomach to churn. It was midsummer, and she had negotiated a three-day break to go on a spiritual retreat attended, also, by many of the diocesan priests. She needed the time to unwind, but the Lord had now assigned to her a very delicate, even embarrassing, mission!

She called her spiritual director, Sister Marina: "Marina, the Lord woke me up at 3:00 a.m. last night. He said, 'Go find Father Simon in the diocese and tell him to take the crown off his head and give it back to the King, lest it be tarnished!' What am I supposed to do?"

"You have to go tell him!"

Fr. Simon belonged to a religious Order, and his opinion was greatly respected in the town. Worried, Catherine pondered about it, was concerned and took a long time to consider her options before deciding: "No, I'm not going to tell him! Who am I to deliver a message like that to a priest?"

A few nights later, the Lord woke her up again: "Didn't I ask you to go to Fr. Simon and tell him to take the crown off his head and give it back to the King, lest it be tarnished!?"

Catherine called Sr. Marina again for advice. Sr. Marina's answer was the same: "Do it!"

"I can't. How am going I to tell him? He won't believe me anyway!"

"We'll see if he believes you or not. Nevertheless, you have to go!"

A few nights later, the Lord woke Catherine up at 3:00 a.m. for the third time. This time the voice was more insistent: "When I ask you to go, you must go! If you don't, I will send someone else."

So Catherine finally decided to go. She called Fr. Simon and made an appointment for Confession with him that evening. "What's wrong?" he asked.

"It's very important; I'll tell you when I confess my sins," she answered without any further explanation.

She met Fr. Simon in the sacristy and made her Confession. While still under the seal of Confession, she delivered the message, point blank, without any fluff. "There! That's what the Lord told me to tell you. I'm concerned you won't believe it, but here it is, and you can do with it what you want."

A week later, some friends told Catherine that they went to a Mass of Christ the King at a hotel downtown, and Fr. Simon had a magnificent crown displayed on his chasuble! She also heard that Father was a changed man. People were saying that he must have had some kind of powerful encounter with God, because he had become more friendly and approachable, and was celebrating Mass differently.

Then in January, Sr. Marina called Catherine: "You won't believe this," she said. "Fr. Simon dropped dead at the altar right after he gave the sign of peace!"

His premature death had a great impact in the diocese! One morning shortly after the funeral, Catherine entered the church and found little Bennie scrubbing the floor. They greeted one another and chatted like old friends: "What a loss for the diocese," said Bennie, "especially since he had changed so much recently. Did you notice?"

"Oh yes!"

Catherine liked Bennie a lot. She was the most humble woman in town, always ready to serve anyone. She was simple and pure like a spring.

"Catherine," she whispered, "I'm going to tell you something, but it's a secret."

"Go ahead. I won't tell a soul."

So Bernnie, checking that no one could hear, said, "Last summer I heard a voice in my heart saying: 'Go find Fr. Simon and tell him to take the crown off his head and give it back to the King, lest it be tarnished!' I knew that it was Jesus talking to me...."

Astounded, but careful not to give away her own secret, Catherine asked, "So, what happened?"

"I said, 'No way!' I was scared to death! I said: 'Who? Me? Do something like that? But Jesus, you know I can't do that, he's a priest and look at me! No, Jesus, I'm sorry, but you'll have to find somebody else!' Then I went to see the leader of the Charismatic Prayer Group, just to see what he'd say, but he didn't believe me."

"What happened then? Did Jesus ask you again?"

"No, he must have found somebody else."

"Dear Children! ... I desire to draw you ever closer to Jesus and to His wounded heart, that you might be able to comprehend the immeasurable love which gave itself for each one of you. Therefore, dear children, pray that from your heart would flow a fountain of love to every person, both to the one who hates you and to the one who despises you. That way you will be able through Jesus' love to overcome all the misery in this world of sorrows, which is without hope for those who do not know Jesus. I am with you and I love you with the immeasurable love of Jesus. Thank you for all your sacrifices and prayers. Pray so I might be able to help you still more. Your prayers are necessary to me." (November 25, 1991)

4

MY FUTURE IN THE PLANETS?

India, fall 1972

The man looked at me sternly. The tip of his sallow white beard was tied with a black rubber band, a custom one often sees in the overcrowded districts of Delhi. It was the month of September, when the monsoon had passed and the air was becoming less stuffy. From the room opening onto the alley, the sound of children playing outside could be heard, as well as the echo of hoofs: it was the nonchalant gait of the sacred, but nonetheless famished, cows that ambled down the street along the shanties. Seated in the lotus position, on sheets that no doubt had been white years ago, the man spoke in a monotonous tone, as if reading a boring administrative document. And yet, the document he was holding in his hands was the Book of My Life!

I Made a Deal With God

As a "good Catholic" of those days, I knew the Gospel well, the Epistles not very well, and the Old Testament even less. As far as wanting to fulfil God's plan for my life, this idea was completely foreign to me. What's worse was the idea had no chance of reaching my heart because, unconsciously, I had created strong antibodies against it. Since the age of 17, I had been of the view that I was better off making my own choices in life and deciding for myself what direction to take. I thought if I let God take care of it, my life would turn into martyrdom, and I would sink into a deep depression.

Why did I think that? Because it seemed that each time someone mentioned "God's will," it was due to a personal or natural catastrophe that had just taken place. People would say things like, "Oh how sad, she's not even 30 and she's already a widow, with young children…but it was God's will for her" or, " Lets pray for this kind man, who has a terminal disease and only two months left to live. Let's pray he has the courage to say 'yes' to this test, since it is God's will for his life." Or, "What a pity this child was born disabled, with no hearing or sight. What a cross for his parents! But, it is God's will and they must accept it!" I couldn't stand 'the will of God'! Throughout my childhood, I don't think I ever once heard the slightest link between happiness and God's will.

If a couple is in love and swimming in happiness, why not speak about the beautiful plan God has for them? Why do we wait for a catastrophe to hit them before mentioning the will of God?

At the age of 20, I was searching for my calling, amidst darkness and suffering. Why was I on this earth? I had absolutely no idea! Of course, the splendour of Christianity fascinated me, and the person of Christ allowed me to envision infinite dimensions and the potential for extraordinary happiness. But I could not see how to concretely fuse this with my life as a student or how to connect myself to this splendour that I could only get glimpses of, a splendour indeed more real than the sun, but still elusive to my closed heart which was stuck in the dark of night.

I revelled in the life stories of the Apostles and the first Christians, as told in the Acts of the Apostles. Their faith could move mountains and they could declare without shame, "it has seemed good to the Holy Spirit and to us to . . . .,"[9] because the living power of the Holy

---

[9] Acts 15:28.

Spirit assisted them in every circumstance. At their hands, miracles and wonders happened. Of course, they also had to face ordeals at times, but they bore those trials with joy and, in the end, love prevailed. When reading these stories, in the midst of my darkness, I could feel a little flame vibrating in the depths of my heart. I wanted to be like the Apostles! It was as if, for first time, I had connected with the life for which I was designed from head to toe. Adventure, love, passion, joy, the tangible manifestation of Heaven! Yes! That's what I wanted! So I offered God a deal, hoping to shake Him and motivate Him with these words:

"Lord, where are these apostles today? Where are they, these new witnesses, so filled with You that people collect around them like bees in a hive with the hope of only brushing against their shadow to be healed? This 'Philip,' who was taken away by the Holy Spirit to evangelize and baptize a pagan passing by on the street; this 'Paul,' whose fiery words brought millions of Jews to the Faith; and this 'Peter,' who bestowed a 'super-dose' of the Holy Spirit upon ignorant pagans through his speeches! Lord, this is the Christian life I am looking for, and I promise that on the day You show me such apostles, I will drop everything and I will follow them!"

Well, God has his own timings and maybe I had to experience my own misery before I could be open to His plan.

The *Book of My Life* in Sanskrit

On arriving at the house of the Hindu man that September morning in 1972, I had no idea of the impact that this visit would have on me. He had been highly recommended to me by a Minister of the Punjab State who told me: "If you want to work closely with the Ministry of Trade and import our handicrafts to France, we need to verify that this arrangement is really inscribed in your astral chart. Otherwise, the project won't succeed and we may as well forget it. I have a highly respected friend in the old district of Delhi who has worked at the White House for the President of the United States, and also for Mrs. Indira Gandhi. He has exceptional gifts and, as you probably know, many international leaders seek the advice of Hindu astrologers to better run their countries better."

My plan had been to import to Paris beautiful arts and crafts manufactured in India, so that I could live in India for long periods of time. I was 24 at the time; I needed to make a professional decision, and was seduced by the prospect of having my chart read.

So I agreed, and the Minister came with me to the home of the Hindu astrologer. I had hardly arrived before the man asked me the date, time and place of my birth. Then, on a piece of paper, he drew strange signs that didn't look anything like any of the astral charts I'd seen in Europe. (While in boarding school, I had been initiated from the early age of 15 to the practices of astrology as well as to the Ouija board. Some of my classmates would not take one step in life without first consulting the stars or tarot cards, or without asking the spirits who manifested themselves during our sessions of Ouija board. Of course, neither our parents nor the Sisters of this good Catholic boarding school knew what was happening behind the curtain, during our free time.)

The man wasn't smiling, and I could feel a strange sort of evilness.[10] The naive enthusiasm that had caused me to consult with him quickly dwindled away and concern grew. The man took his paper and got up. "I'll be right back," he told me, "I am going to get the book of your life from my library."

He came back holding a bunch of old, yellowish papers, poorly bound. "This book was written in Sanskrit a long, long time ago," he said. "I have always had it in my library. I have been keeping it for you. I knew you would be coming. I will read it to you. It is the book of your life."

I looked with suspicion at the strange, antique object, and I glanced at my Minister with a question in my eyes: "The book of my life?"

"Yes," he nodded.

Then, from the Sanskrit texts, the astrologer began to draw for me a timeline of the major events in my past life, year after year, since my birth. He mentioned my family's economic and social situation,

---

[10] This hatred was very real. See the Introduction to Malachi Martin's book Hostage to the Devil (Harper San Francisco 1992): "The essence of Satanist worship is hate. For the Fallen Archangel now embodies a full hatred of being, as such. Hatred of life, love, beauty, happiness, truth—of all that makes existence the greatest possible good."

the order my brothers and sisters were born in, and my grandfather's social status. He also reviewed my childhood diseases (that even I was ignorant of at the time) as well as my education level, my IQ, my emotional life, and my spiritual quest. He described some key people who had played an important role in my life. Then, he came to my 24th year. As he continued, his words became a prophecy of my future. For example, I was to become very rich, and live in a city by the sea.

I became more and more uncomfortable. The man had a piercing, metallic look with no warmth emanating from him. Rather, he had an ugliness that came from hatred in his eyes. He spoke of intimate times in my life as if dictating mathematical equations. He explained each element, each event in my life according to the position and the trajectory of the stars. For example, he said something like, "If you chose this direction for your studies, it was because Mars was coming closer to Jupiter. And at this other time, Saturn was turning this way and the Big Dipper that way, and this is why you were attracted to such and such person at that particular moment." In short, this professional astrologer led me to understand that the course of my life depended on the positioning of the stars and planets. As he reached my 30th year, after having described the next six years of my future, the man he stood up and said: "Well, this volume ends here. I am going to get Volume II of your life from my library."

I had had enough. Profiting from the interruption, I decided to stand up to go.

"No!" I said to him. "That's enough. I don't need to know the rest of my life! Thank you, we're leaving!"

The Minister was surprised with my decision and mumbled something to his friend about foreigners who don't always appreciate the richness of the Hindu culture.

The sun was at its highest when I emerged from the house. It penetrated the crowded alley below, and the shock of its light quickly forced me back to reality. But I could feel that I was not the same anymore. As hard as I tried to convince myself that what I had just experienced was nothing, 'forget it – its not important', the more uneasy I felt and peace had completely vanished from my heart. The man had injected me with a dose of subtle poison and anxiety was now welling up inside me. When I finally reunited with my friends in New Delhi, who were like my second family, I broke down in tears. Neither their friendship, nor their words of comfort helped to yank this poisoned dart from my punctured heart.

Why was I so devastated? Despite the briefness of the meeting, the man had made me an orphan: I had lost my Heavenly Father. Before then, I had believed in Him. He was my Creator, my Source, my Root, my Origin. I believed that He had created me out of love. I believed that He held the world in His hands and that Love would prevail. I knew that my true abode was with Him. And then, this astrologer had brilliantly convinced me that none of this was true, and that my life was the result of totally impersonal planetary events. I saw myself as being at the mercy of the planets—of which I knew nothing—of those big, cold, faraway and inaccessible things; inside I felt like ice. The astrologer mentioned with accuracy, the important events of my life, linking them to the planets and the stars; therefore, how could my future possibly be drawn from the freedom of my heart? The man had put upon me a yoke that revolted me and scared me. I didn't want it, but I didn't have a choice. I was a prisoner of fate.

Back in France, I resumed my activities but, little by little, day by day, I could feel my inner self deteriorating. Normally I had a rather positive nature but now a secret cancer gnawed at my hope. Strange symptoms began to surface. For example, at night, I would wake up and start uttering words of hate against one person or another, without any reason. I lost my appetite and my body weakened. But most of all, an indefinable suffering clawed at my heart, and in the still silence of the night, this pain became intolerable. After nine months of living in this black hole, I crossed the line that separates life from death and the thought of suicide became an obsession.

By 5 o'clock, I Will No Longer Exist

One day in June 1973, my sister, Marie-Pia, came to visit me. However hard I tried to hide my feelings from her, she understood my state of distress and she told me: "Emmanuelle, tomorrow is Pentecost. Come with me, I've found a fabulous prayer group. They are having a big meeting to celebrate the Holy Spirit! Come. The Holy Spirit will do something for you!"

THE HIDDEN CHILD OF MEDJUGORJE

"Your Holy Spirit is very nice, but he can't do anything for me!" Disconcerted, my sister left, but not before giving me details of where the meeting would be held.

That night was hell. I felt like I was being lacerated and crushed from the inside. In the morning, I couldn't face living anymore. The idea of dragging myself through every hour of the day had become unbearable, so, unable to face life anymore, I said one last prayer to God. It was short but sincere: "My Lord, You see, I cannot survive another day. So I am telling You, I won't make it past 5:00 o'clock tonight. I am warning You, it's over!"

When I got up, rather than pace aimlessly around my apartment, I decided to go out and find my sister. When I reached Assumption Street, in the 16th precinct of Paris, I found about thirty people who seemed as if they were from another world. Marie-Pia was right. This group was fantastic: their joy, their freedom, their warm love, their laughter! Immediately, a thought blinked in my mind: "Here they are!" Yes, here they were, the first Christians, those apostles that I had wished for so long to meet face to face!

But, it was too late! I saw them, as if in a movie: there was an impassable abyss between us. As for me, I was already on the other side, in this valley of spiritual death where no helpful arm could reach anymore. I had already signed my execution warrant and felt locked inside. I knew I would end my life at 5 o'clock. As for them, they were in the light, good for them!

I followed my sister everywhere like a puppy dog, and I couldn't control the flow of my tears anymore. Everyone noticed, but I couldn't help it. They prayed like angels but the response that came to my mind was a negative word that echoed each of their praises: "Lord, our entire lives will not suffice to praise you!" they claimed with overflowing joy. – "My life has lasted long enough!", was the response in my mind.

"Walking Towards Death"

After lunch there was another gathering where everyone burst into spontaneous prayer. It was 3:30 p.m. and my end was approaching. I had told God—five o'clock. Filled with total despair, I sat in the middle of the group like a robot, not paying attention to their prayers.

37

Around 4:00 p.m., a woman arrived and joined the group. She was very late and had missed most of the program. Her name was Andrée Thomae. I didn't notice her, but among the thirty or so Catholics participating that day, she was the only Protestant. She had hardly arrived when she began to fidget in her chair. She knew something was wrong with someone in the room. The Lord had given her a light, and she felt obliged to bring it out for all to see, despite being afraid she would be derided because of the enormity of the message she was given to speak out. She was not sure that the group would accept what the Lord had shown her.

Prostrated like a poor wretch, head down, I was pulled out of my dark hole by a thundering voice coming from the group. Among the beautiful prayers, her message struck like a thunderbolt! The tone was dramatic. Andrée could not hold it in any longer and proclaimed with authority what the Lord had revealed to her:

"Brothers and Sisters, there is a person among us who is walking to her death. This person has let the Enemy deceive her, and she has done what displeases God. She has practiced Ouija board and divination, and Satan has bound her. But Christ has the power to deliver her from the hands of the Enemy and to give her life back to her. She can come to us and we will pray for her in the power of Jesus' name."

The assembly was shocked. As for me, since the first words of the message were "a person is walking to her death," my heart started pounding in my chest. It was obviously about me! I wondered, "Did God show this woman, whom I've never met, the state of my soul? And what does she mean by 'she has done what displeases God'?"

It was my turn to fidget in my seat. I felt urged from the inside to run to this woman, and I couldn't wait for the prayer time to end! It was 4.30 p.m. when the last song finally ended, and I immediately rushed over to the woman I didn't know.

"Madam, you spoke about a person who was walking to her death." Like an authentic messenger of God, Andrée welcomed me with no fuss, no unnecessary politeness. She went straight to the point. Like the apostles, she was conscious that the situation was not in her hands, but in God's, and that a precious life was at stake.

"Ah, you're the one! Good, come over here. What have you done? You went to the Enemy's camp! You went to see astrologers and soothsayers, didn't you? And you have questioned the spirits of the dead! You have practiced Ouija board!"

"Yes, I have done that since my teenage years, with my friends. I didn't know that..."

"But it is written in the Bible! God has warned His people many times. All this is an abomination in His eyes! – Do you believe in Christ?"

"Yes, I am Christian."

"Good, wait here and I will call two or three more to pray with me over you. I don't want to do this alone. Christ has said, "Where two or three are gathered in my name, there am I in the midst of them."[11]

"Jesus Has the Power to Undo Your Bonds"

It was June. She led me outside to the beautiful flower garden of the Sisters of the Assumption. There was a bench there. Seeing how exhausted I was, she made me sit down, but she remained standing with her friends, who encircled me. I found myself in the most incredible situation and it became even stranger when they suddenly began to sing in tongues! I wondered where I had landed, at the mercy of crazy people!

Andrée orchestrated the process with the hand of a master and asked me the question of trust that would determine if victory was possible: "You put yourself in the clutches of the Enemy. He is binding you and is torturing you. His goal is to kill you. But Jesus has defeated him on the Cross. *Do you believe that today, Jesus has the power to undo your bonds, so that you can be free to walk in the light?"*

I was amazed at the question. I looked at Andrée, such a simple woman, poor apparently, who probably weighed over 200 pounds, yet she had the faith of a child, ready to move mountains. I was 25 years old and this was the first time that I had heard anyone speak about Jesus like that. A Jesus who could do some good for me? And *right now, today?* Just like it happened in the Gospels?

---

[11] Mt 18:20.

"Yes, I believe!" My voice was weak because, in truth, I wished to believe more than I actually believed.

"Good! We're going to do a prayer of deliverance. The demons that you accepted into your life are going to be chased away by the power of Jesus' Name."

I had no idea at the time what this language meant - it was all new to me. I imagined my heart was like a room into which I had let the destroyers enter; and these destroyers would flee as soon as we invoked the name of Jesus.

"You know, Andrée, even if Jesus sets me free, I will still prefer to die because the demons have done so much damage in my heart. I cannot take this suffering anymore."

Andrée couldn't be so easily defeated. She was a seasoned evangelist! "But if you believe that Jesus has the power to chase away the demons who have hurt you, don't you, also, believe that he has the power to heal you?"

Her words helped me to discover another aspect of Jesus' nature. He could heal me? And now? What a poor idea I had of Him up to then. For me He was definitely a Saviour, but a Saviour who had saved the whole of humanity in the past, who was personally not around for me today. Suddenly, he began to resemble the Jesus from the Gospels, the one who freed the Samaritan woman, and the one who healed the blind man at a specific place, at a specific hour. He was my personal Saviour, who was really alive that very day!

"Yes, I believe He can heal me!"

"And you commit to stop practicing all those abominations? Because you have to be careful! If you were to do it again, things would get much worse for you![12] Listen...." She began to read Deuteronomy, Chapter 18, verses 9 to 14:

"When you come into the land which the Lord your God gives you, you shall not learn to follow the abominable practices of those nations. There shall not be found among you any one who burns his son or his daughter as an offering, any one who practices divination, a soothsayer,

---

[12] Cf. Mt 12:43-46.

or an augur, or a sorcerer, or a charmer, or a medium, or a wizard, or a necromancer. For whoever does these things is an abomination to the Lord; and because of these abominable practices the Lord your God is driving them out before you. You shall be blameless before the Lord your God. For these nations, which you are about to dispossess, give heed to soothsayers and to diviners; but as for you, the Lord your God has not allowed you so to do."

She continued to explain to me the meaning of each verse. She was so straightforward and clear. She barely had the vocabulary to express herself, yet when it came to the wisdom of the Lord, she had an astonishing spiritual intelligence.

"You can count on me," I told her. "I won't make the same mistake twice!"

There was no time to waste. Andrée and her friends began by blessing the Lord in joy and trust. Then Andrée interceded with power for the sinner that I was. And she commanded the demons (which she named one by one) to leave me. She also broke the tie of malediction that the Hindu astrologer of Delhi had imposed on me and that was inexorably crushing me. Then, after more praises and blessings, silence. It was over.

"There, we're finished," she told me. "You can join the group for the Mass. But continue to praise the Lord and to place yourself under His Precious Blood. You need His protection!"

I will never forget the precise instant when I rose from the bench. During the prayer, I had experienced no jolt, no new emotion, nothing. But as soon as I got up, I realized that my suffering had disappeared! My deadly anguish had disappeared! I kept putting my hand over my heart again and again, like someone in search of his wallet or glasses. *My suffering—gone! Jesus had really come.... He had done His work as Saviour and given me life again!*

On my watch, the hands pointed to exactly 5.00 p.m.

I had made an appointment with Death at 5.00 p.m., but when the time came it was the Living God who came to me, not Death. My poor, ruined existence was taken into the arms of Life. I could feel the Good Shepherd close to me. He had descended into my squalid ditch and had lifted me out of it by taking my deadly wounds onto His own body. I felt His life flowing in me like a torrent of delight. All of my being was bathed in the joy of resurrection!

Jesus, My Greatest Friend

That night, I gave my life to God saying: "Lord, I had planned to die today. But You, You took my death on Yourself and You gave me Your life. Therefore my Lord, the rest of my life on earth is entirely Yours. Take it!"

During the Mass, I was laughing with joy! At the end, the shepherd of the group offered some of us to come forward to be infused with the Holy Spirit. A small team prayed over each person. All I could do was repeat to Jesus that my life was all for Him; and under the blessed hands of my wonderful brothers and sisters, I opened my heart to the Holy Spirit. Then He touched an extremely ill place inside me, where my spiritual blindness rested. I received a penetrating light, clear as crystal: the Will of God is life; my own will can only bring death. It was inescapable!

If before that I had not trusted the will of God and stayed away from it, as if it were an avalanche of misfortune, here it appeared to me that it was totally the opposite. I would cherish it and search for it with all my being, because His will was Life! That night, a Holy fear came upon me, the fear of not doing the will of God. The Holy Spirit had given me access to His treasures, to His seven gifts. In particular the one we call "the holy fear of God." It was the fear of displeasing the one we love!

That night, I slept like a newborn baby on her mother's heart and, from that day on, a new life began for me. My happiness was so great that as I went through the streets of Paris on my motorbike, I jumped up and down on the seat with joy! Jesus had become my best friend, and I would consult with Him about anything and everything, for any decision I had to make, and He guided me.

A Pristine Interior Cleaning

I often visited Andrée, who was caring for the deliverance and evangelization of people in the poorest precincts of Paris, especially among the prostitutes. With Paul, her husband, she belonged to a very lively Pentecostal Church, and both of them liked to "sneak in" among us Catholics, in a true desire of being "united in Christ." They lived in such a scant and tiny place that Andrée hardly had any room to move around her kitchen. But for me, it was like a patch of Paradise! She knew the Bible so well. For every situation she would mention a verse: "Christ said…, Paul said…, Moses said…," and she would shower my heart with rays of light from the Bible. My soul was then satisfied and my heart was filled with these fireworks; I would depart filled with a joy able to move mountains.

Very soon after my "deliverance," she explained to me, in her own way, what really happened to me in India, with this astrologer. I had always been surprised by the things he knew. How could he be reading my past in an old book? How could he have the book of my life in his library?

"You let yourself be deceived by the Enemy," Andrée told me. "He lied to you all the way through, and you, you could not see that because you didn't know God's Word very well! Yet God has warned His people!" Then, she made me understand a key Chapter in the Bible: Deuteronomy 18. It is about the prophets. Though I was a Catholic, I had never read it myself or heard it in Mass.

"You see," she added, "through your ignorance you went to the Enemy, you went to his camp, you sided with his abominations. He used them to bind you! The astrologer was his instrument.[13] It was easy for him to act against you because you were open to his lies. You shouldn't have been so naive! How many young people go over to the soothsayers, the astrologers, and become obsessed, depressed

---

[13] The goal of the Hindu astrologer was Emmanuel's possession by Satan. For descriptions of what such possession entails and the difficulty of exorcising a possessed person, see Malachi Martin's, Hostage to the Devil, and Gabrielle Amorth's, An Exorcist Tells His Story (Ignatius Press 1999).

and suicidal![14]   The book he held was actually only a support for his divination. He received information from Satan and pretended to read. You're not going to believe that a Hindu wrote the book of your life in Sanskrit a thousand years ago are you? But Satan knows your past. He is an angel. For him it is easy! He doesn't know your future, but he is intelligent and he can make intelligent guesses based on your past and your present."

"What he said to you was false.[15] His word is a word of death that leads to death. His plan was to kill you from the inside. Through his word he cast a spell on you and you were not free anymore. It was Christ who undid your bonds when we invoked his Holy Name and his Precious Blood over you. Christ has the words of Eternal Life, and, if you keep His word, He abides in you. If the lies of this soothsayer come back to your mind to disturb you or to anguish you, reject them and confess with conviction that you belong to Christ. Praise the Holy Name of Jesus, and put yourself under his Precious Blood. The Enemy will flee."

---

[14] Many people enter into the world of the occult through a desire to learn their personal future. Among the evil practices which falsely promise such knowledge are astrology, palmistry (reading lines on one's hand), and divination through devices such as Tarot cards, the Ouija board, or the crystal ball. Others seek to commune with the dead through séances. And some attempt to practice "black magic" through witchcraft, voodoo, or Satanic rituals including the "Black Mass." While the spiritual dangers attending some practices are obvious, in other cases they are not. For an expose of the roots and place of Yoga in the Hindu religion, and the possible spiritual dangers to Catholics of practicing Yoga, see Joel S. Peter's article, "Yoga & Christianity," in the New Oxford Review (February 2006).

Wholly apart from traditional occult practices, new philosophies and practices characteristic of the "New Age" in which we now live are of great concern to the Vatican. See the study published jointly by the Pontifical Councils for Culture and for Interreligious Dialogue, titled Jesus Christ, the Bearer of the Water of Life: A Christian Reflection on the New Age. (available on the Vatican's website, www.vatican.va; also in Origins, vol. 32, no. 35 (February 13, 2003)) Among the characteristic points of New Age thinking are: 1) much credence is given to the mediation of various spiritual entities; 2) humans are capable of ascending to invisible higher spheres and of controlling their own lives beyond death; and 3) there is held to be a 'perennial knowledge' which predates and is superior to all religions and cultures. Id. at §2.3.3. Practitioners of New Age philosophies may attempt to attune themselves to the universal spirit, or to engage in "astral travel," through such devices as transcendental meditation, channelling, the enneagram, crystals, and "vortices" in nature. An appendix to the joint study contains a bibliography and a glossary of terms.

[15] She was right. None of the astrologer's predictions turned out to be right after Andrée severed the tie that was holding me prisoner. In short, the Chief of Lies really had lied, and my Savior had a much better plan!

With Andrée, my discoveries about Christ's power and about demonology were, in a way, experiential. I later read the Gospels and the lives of the Saints with a new eye; I was now able to touch them, to recognize them in my every day life. Jesus had become alive!

On the day after my deliverance, I spoke to Andrée and Paul about my brother Bruno who, too, suffered from deadly anguish, because, like me, he had gone down the wrong path and had done silly things. She agreed to pray for him and to take care of his case. With my sister Marie-Pia, we then concocted a plan in two phases: first my sister was to write him a letter, informing him that she had discovered people who prayed as the early Christians, and that he would be astounded to meet them. As for me, after he had received that letter, I would call him "out of the blue" and tell him the same thing, and that my own life had taken a turn for the better toward complete happiness. It worked! Faced with the possibility of something good, my brother accepted the deal without any resistance. The next day, I introduced Bruno to Andrée and Paul. That day my brother went through a profound conversion, and he became attached to Christ with all his heart and has not let go of Him since. He, also, benefited from a pristine interior cleanup, thanks to the good care of our dear Andrée. He, also, realized that Jesus was really a truly living Savior! From that point on, there were three of us to take care of the rest of the family. The Lord has blessed abundantly our initiatives as new converts by untying the knots one by one… those old family knots so deeply rooted, so difficult to expose to the light and to undo.

We have been saved by the Mercy of God. After having tasted the bitter fruit of darkness, having cursed the day we were born, and having come so close to death, we give thanks today to the One Who—by shedding His Blood on the Cross—leads us from death into life. *

---

* See book: Ransomed From Darkness, The New Age, Christian Faith and the Battle for Souls, by Moira Noonan: an extraordinary autobiography of a woman who became adept at numerous New Age practices, from Native American shamanism to Reiki, and clairvoyance to hypnotherapy, but later was converted to Catholicism in part through her experiences at Medjugorje. North Bay Books 2005, US$15. See the link from www.Amazon.com to receive the book: http://www.amazon.com/Ransomed-Darkness-Christian-Faith-Battle/dp/0972520074

"Dear Children! Open your hearts and let Jesus guide you. For many people it seems to be hard and yet it is so easy! You don't have to be afraid because you know that Jesus will never leave you, and you know that he leads you to salvation."   (August 11, 1986)

5

A CHILD WILL LEAD THEM

What games did Jesus play as a child? In their writings, mystics often tell us that when they were little, the Child Jesus used to come to play with them, and they thought that everybody could see Him. That was the case for Georgette Faniel,[16] who spent hours with Him from the time she was five. The evangelization of children by children is one of the most spectacular aspects of the mystical realm. They have a candor worthy of the Fathers of the Church, but they're so much easier to understand.

I feel compelled at this point to quote a few titbits of conversations between the Child Jesus and young Van, 14, from Vietnam.[17]

Van: "By the way, Jesus, when you were on Earth, did you ever eat fish? Did you eat food like I eat?"

Jesus: "Of course, I ate food like yours. Sometimes I ate meat, sometimes fish, other times vegetables, but Mary had a way of preparing dishes that were really appetizing; it wasn't at all like what you eat!"

Van: "Can you tell Mary to teach me, so that, when I have to cook, I'll know how to prepare delicious meals too? What about you, Jesus, do you know how to cook?"

---

[16] See Chapter "Story of Another Soul," in Medjugorje, Triumph of the Heart, page 74.

[17] Excerpts from "L'Amour me connaît," Le Sarment Fayard, Paris. Msgr. Nguyen Van Thuan champions the cause for the beatification of Van. See Oeuvres complètes de Marcel Van, and Quel est ton secret, petit Van ?, St Paul/Les Amis de Van, Versailles. Marie Michel, Van ou l'enfant aux mains vides, Jubilé Sarment, 1999. Information on Van can be obtained from m-a-j@wanadoo.fr and amisdevan@aol.com; marcelvan.canalblog.com. Ph: +33-148-56-22-88.

Jesus: "Yes, I know how. When I was little I always stayed close to my Mother, because I loved her so much. When I was close to her, my intention was always to help her understand divine things. Mary loved me very much, and usually I knew how to do everything she did."

Van: "Little Jesus, I've wanted to ask you something for a long time. Please answer me, ok? People say that when you were growing up, you never laughed or cried, that you were calm and behaved even when you were hungry, and that you let your mom do whatever she wanted with you. Is it true?"

Jesus: "First of all, my little Van, you have to understand that according to my divine nature, I am the second person of the Holy Trinity and therefore, I am one with the Father and the Holy Spirit. But, as a human, I had all the weaknesses of a child. The only difference was that I didn't have any imperfection as you do. I wasn't greedy or rowdy like you. I did cry on occasions, but as soon as Mary comforted me, I understood. And besides, if a kid never laughed, he would cause his family to lose joy. In those days, I just acted like any other kid. When relatives brought cake for me, I took it gratefully and enjoyed it.

Jesus: "God the Father never let my family go hungry or run out of water, not even for a single meal. And Mary knew how to plan, but even more, she trusted in her real Father in Heaven. With me, she acted like a mother, but with God the Father, her heart was open like a child's. If she needed something, she just looked up to Heaven, and simply and sincerely asked God the Father. Her simplicity and sincerity were so pleasing to God that Mary was granted everything she asked, just as she told you before. For example, when she ran out of flour for bread, she simply spoke to her Father and said: 'Father, today, your little one and your children are in need!' Then she would be more specific saying, 'They're out of flour, salt,' etc. After that she would remain as peaceful as usual. The true Father in Heaven would not wait a second to grant her prayer. But he always did it in a very natural way, without relying on spectacular miracles."

Van: "Little Jesus, did you wear sandals in those days?"

Jesus: "Yes, but they didn't look like the ones they make nowadays. They looked a lot like those that Vietnamese farmers wear. My sandals weren't fancy; they were just plain, like my clothes too."

Van: "Oh Jesus, grant that all my faults and my bad habits may burn in the fire of your love. My beloved Jesus, grant that all my sin may burn in your love, even those I haven't committed yet."

Jesus: "My little brother, first you have to accept all the inconveniences I send your way. That would please me more than if you fasted for a hundred years. Even dying on the cross as I did wouldn't be better than the mortification that I want to teach you here; meaning obedience. The best mortification is obedience."

Jesus: "It is thanks to Mary that souls are able to be united to my love in an infinite and durable way. My little friend, don't ever forget this: You must love my Mother as I love you. You must think of the souls who love me as clean fresh air that allows my love to breathe and to live in the world. If this healthy air didn't exist in the world, my love couldn't live in it; it would suffocate."

The Child Jesus was taking little steps toward Van with his Mother by his side...

Van: "Mother, wouldn't it be quicker if you carried him in your arms?"

Mary: "Yes it would, but little Jesus doesn't mind struggling for a few steps out of love for you."

Van: "Tell me, Jesus, has your reign of love begun to spread throughout the world yet?"

Jesus: "Yes, it has, and the starting point of that growth is France itself. It is your Sister Therese,[18] who is the universal apostle for all the other apostles of my love. It was from there that my Kingdom of Love began to expand and continues to grow. And you, too, Van, as you write down what I am telling you, you are contributing to this task, just as I told you earlier. There are many more apostles you don't know. They, too, work in secret, one after the other, in succession, to establish the reign of my love in the world."

Jesus: "Listen to me carefully, Van, I love you very much. I am particularly fond of children and I'm so happy to be their friend. If they wish to find me, it's very easy. They just have to observe their own way of behaving. I have promised the Kingdom of Heaven to

---

[18] Referring to Saint Thérèse of the Child Jesus, who also personally taught little Van.

children without strings attached. If I had demanded of them that they fast, or imposed on them a discipline or mortification, how would the newborn that dies right after baptism go to heaven? Van, merciful love has reserved a delightful portion for the children. They need do nothing more than embrace it. The world kills the souls of children under my very eyes, but what can I do? Van, have you listened carefully? Children must be extracted from the darkness of the world. Woe to you, oh, world! If your children weren't here as hosts to Divine Love, you would be destroyed by God's justice.

Jesus: "Van, everything about children pleases me: a word, a smile, even a tear in a moment of sadness—all that pleases me. But sadly, Van, now children seem to want to compete with adults in the way they act."

Van: "You talk too much, Jesus; your tongue never quits. How many times did you miss an opportunity to be silent, not even letting me pray in peace? And then how dare you point out all my shortcomings? Ok then, I'm going to tell Mary on you; I will tell her that you never stop talking everywhere, without...."

Jesus: "What are you talking about, Van? You don't remember, not long ago, when I didn't say a word for over two months and you went all teary-eyed to complain sometimes to Mary, sometimes to Sister Therese...."

Jesus: "Van, do you love me? Why did you laugh last night when you were meditating on my crying in the manger? When I was born, I found myself in exactly the same situation as any other baby. I suffered from cold and sadness. If you had been there at that time to talk to me, I probably wouldn't have cried. If I could have heard some words of love, like now, I'm sure I wouldn't have felt the cold."

This Is Our Leader

Not too many people noticed the gift that the Gospa was preparing for us at the dawn of the third millennium. Naturally, all the friends of Medjugorje were expecting a word, a guiding motto to show us how to live this new chapter in history to the best of our ability. We knew she was going to equip us with the right gear to be able to jump into the unknown. And she didn't let us down! The very day when Pope

John Paul II inaugurated the Great Jubilee Year by opening the Bronze Gate of St. Peter's in Rome, the Gospa was appearing in Medjugorje, dressed in gold and, according to the visionaries, inexpressibly beaming with joy. Carrying the Child Jesus in her arms, she asked us to put Him in the first place in our lives. But that's not all. She referred to Him as "our Leader"; the one who will lead us on the path to salvation. Will a child really be our leader? Can it be a child who will walk ahead of us and lead us on a safe path, protect us and provide food for us? Will it be a tiny one who fights for us? Yes, exactly! That's exactly what our Mother meant. There's no mistake about it—it wasn't an obscure message.

According to the prophecies which announced the birth and identity of the Messiah, Isaiah had a vision that "a little child shall lead them."[19] In Hebrew, this verse from the Bible actually reads "little boy" *(na'ar qaton)*. In following verses, Isaiah described the child playing on an asp's pit and in the adder's den,[20] and there the child is a *Yonek*, meaning "weaned"—He is a breastfed infant.

This is our Shepherd, the Leader the Gospa introduces to us for the third millennium!

Maybe we have not yet taken seriously the meaning of Jesus' words: "Let the children come to me, do not hinder them; for to such belongs the kingdom of God. Truly, I say to you, whoever does not receive the kingdom of God like a child shall not enter it."[21] What are those childhood traits that make God "melt" like this? Each one of us can find his own answer to that question. For me, I think it is innocence. God is so deeply affected by a child's innocence that he blindly pours out all that He has – all that He is.

What maternal genius the Gospa shows us! This newborn that she is holding out for us, at the threshold of the third millennium, with such overflowing joy—this is innocence par excellence. He is indeed the leader we need because like ocean waves breaking against a cliff, the waves of evil break against the cliff of innocence.

---

[19] Is 11:6

[20] Is 11:8

[21] Mk 10:14-15

He frolics with our asps and our adders. For our generation which is afraid to welcome life, for our society which kills children by the thousands, a child was needed in order for us to heal. The Child Jesus assumes the task of healing our generation, and, as we welcome the Child Jesus from the hands of Mary, we welcome our healer. He is so little—only He can slip down into the frightening, bottomless regions of our godless world to flush out all rejection of life and instill His lasting joy. It is mind-boggling to see the miracles the Child Jesus does, the healings and the liberations when He is received and embraced. This child is dynamite!

"Dear Children! This is a time of grace. Little children today in a special way, with the little Jesus whom I hold in my embrace, I am giving you the possibility to decide for peace. Through your 'yes' to peace and your decision for God, a new possibility for peace is opened. Only in this way, little children, will this century be for you a time of peace and well being. Therefore, put the little newborn Jesus in the first place in your life and He will lead you on the way to salvation." *(January 25, 2000)*

6

CHILD JESUS, MY GOD, MY CHILD!

At the beginning of 2000, I visited Denver, Colorado. During a Marian Conference I asked the congregation to observe a few minutes of deep, recollected silence, inviting all those present to receive the Child Jesus in their arms from Mary's hands. The idea was, of course, to open their hearts to the coming of the Child. In addition to that, they could imagine his little body in their arms, pressed against their hearts, and express their love for him.

Valery, a woman in her forties, shared with me what she experienced during that brief mediation:

"When Sister Emmanuel came to our parish, she spoke about Christ and how we can welcome Him as a child. This struck me as a new idea, because I had always thought of Christ as an adult. I also pictured him on the Cross: Christ Crucified. Sister invited the congregation to close their eyes and to imagine themselves holding the Child Jesus tightly against their hearts, and to speak with him. The congregation was moved by this experience."

"Thirty years ago, I was 16 and pregnant. Though I had no intention of keeping the child, I kept him to term intending to give him up for adoption. Several years later I married, but was never able to have children. That son was my only child, and I had abandoned him! Since that day, my life had been like a void. I felt emptiness in my heart that would not stop bleeding!"

"When I held the Child Jesus, as Sister asked that day, He became real for me. He was no longer on the Cross, but in my arms. We were bonding just like a mom holding her baby in her arms. Then another feeling came over me while I was holding Him. All of a sudden I felt the weight of His body! He was letting me hold Him and it took my breath away, I was able to adore Him without saying a word. But that wasn't all!"

"While holding the Child Jesus, I felt again the pain of separation from my son. Overwhelmed, I began to cry. Yes, I felt the weight of Baby Jesus but I also felt my son Peter's body lying in my arms. Only twice had I held him as a baby. This was very liberating for me. I was going through the process of a deep healing, healing of the void within. Jesus was filling it."

"I have to tell you, also, that my son and I reconnected when he was 19. He's 33 now and suffering from abandonment. Sister mentioned the suffering and effect on a child when he does not have the experience of being held and warmly embraced in someone's arms. As I was rocking Baby Jesus and my own son, I had the feeling that the spiritual healing taking place in me was also taking place in my son Peter."

"After that day of prayer, I called my son on the phone to tell him about my encounter with Baby Jesus as I held Him in my arms. He listened quietly, and when I was done he simply whispered, "Mom, I love you!" He had never said that to me before. That had to be a spiritual healing!"

"Long ago I prayed the whole rosary every day. But I had stopped. I have started again as before, but Mary's inspiration, the way she speaks to my heart during the mysteries, takes me through the experience of everything she lived herself in those days. Now these things are within me. She is continuing the healing process! I know that God works through her in our lives. I am so grateful to Him! How healing, to welcome Jesus as a child!"

When I spoke to Valery again, a year later, she had blossomed as a woman. The Child Jesus had removed the bereavement veil from her heart and restored her identity as a woman. He has given back to her the dignity of motherhood.

I Saw the Window Closing

Another time, as I was finishing a presentation on Baby Jesus for pilgrims in Medjugorje, a woman came up to me in tears. She was so emotional that she could barely speak and had to struggle to give this testimony:

"I'm almost 60. I was married young, but could never have children. It ruined my life. My husband refused to adopt. I kept hoping against all odds for a baby. As the years passed, I saw the window of opportunity to have a child closing and then disappear. Sister, you cannot imagine how I suffered! But, today, today (choking back so many tears, she had to stop to catch her breath), I've received my child! And please, believe me! I will take good care of Him!"

This hopeful woman had understood the message and put it into practice immediately. Baby Jesus had used her suffering to carve out for Himself a little manger in the bottom of her heart to snuggle in.

The Hidden Child of Medjugorje wants to dwell in our lives and is searching for little mangers in which to rest. However, just as in Bethlehem, He's not invited by many! People have no time or space for Him. Yet, He's not demanding; all He needs is a handful of hay or a little piece of straw to come rest within us. At the same time, He seeks to multiply His dwelling places, and this is why He is attracted to each one of our hearts and each one of our families. He dreams of being able to curl up in every corner of the world, even in the most loathsome places, because He has a burning desire to sow there His salvation and peace. How would it be possible for a Savior not to have a burning desire to save? To each his own passion, and Jesus' passion is Salvation!

The Child and the University Professor

Jesus' childish ways are sometimes surprising. Here's an example: A priest visiting Medjugorje was telling me how the Baby Jesus was the least of his concerns. Being such a brilliant university professor, he had more important things to occupy his mind! Nevertheless, he had a very unique experience when he was invited to take the Baby Jesus in his arms at one of our meetings:

"After I imagined receiving Baby Jesus in my arms, I found myself ill at ease and embarrassed. I thought to myself, 'Now what am I supposed to do with this?' I was upset. I really didn't know how to get rid of it! After waging this ridiculous battle in my mind for a few minutes, I felt the tiny hand of a child caressing my neck. I turned to see who was there—no one! At that moment my heart began to melt and I immediately understood what was going on. A surge of tenderness, one that I had never felt in my whole life, swept over me. The touch of the child lasted only a few seconds, but it was a turning point for me—I am no longer the same. Baby Jesus is now constantly with me, and his presence makes me melt inside. I have to say, I really needed that!"

A Therapist Who Doesn't Suspect Our Malady

Health care practiced by Baby Jesus, the therapist, has a major advantage. It works undetected, like magic. When we are in pain and decide to consult a doctor, we have to make an appointment, and sometimes wait forever. We must describe our ailment the best we can, undergo tests, spend money, take medications, endure their side effects, and finally hope that all of this will bear good fruit and better health.

With the Child Jesus, it's a whole different process. He surrenders Himself to our embrace without suspecting for a second the malady that afflicts us; He's too little for that. His unconditional trust in us propels unknown surges of love from the depths of our being. The child comes and unlooses our deepest affection and heals us by appealing to the best in us with His mere presence. Or, He simply comes and plays with us. As He's too little to talk, He communicates by playing games. How many fences and blockages fall away? How many stones are rolled off our tombs in this way! When the hardship of our existence traps our hearts in stifling straits, how liberating it is to be able to laugh at the little things with the Child!

When the Hidden Child of Medjugorje finally showed his face to the six visionaries, He played with them! Marija tells of how he laughed with them, playing peek-a-boo behind his Mother's veil: "We were tense, stiff and distant," she says. "He wanted to loosen us up." The visionaries had no idea that God could be so simple, so accessible. Vicka tells how sometimes, at Christmas, He opens His eyes and marvels at each person present in the room as if discovering the world, He, the Creator of all things!

Mother Yvonne-Aimée de Malestroit, a French mystic, said that one evening, coming back into her room, she found the Child Jesus nestled on her bed playing with a scarf He had snatched from her closet and looking at her with the sparkling eyes of a little rascal.[22] In the few seconds of this silent scene, the Child had healed the wounds of this sister's heart that had been afflicted by attacks from the Enemy. The oppression weighing on her soul was lifted! The vise in which her heart was squeezed had vanished! With one smile, the Child had swept all the sadness away and restored the taste of Heaven to her!

That's Our Leader! Are we happy with our politicians? Our presidents? Our judges? Our bosses, or with anyone who claims to govern our modern world? Each time I ask people these questions, they sigh a resounding 'NO!' But so what? We have our King and Leader in this Child Jesus whom the Gospa is giving to us. His face doesn't show up on our TV screens and we don't hear his voice on our CD's. We don't see Him riding up and down the avenues of our big cities sitting in the back of a limo, and He doesn't make the front page of our daily newspapers. However, he promises to lead those who have accorded Him the first place in their lives, through His Mother, on the way of holiness. This procession exists in the secret intimacy of our hearts, without need for publicity, and it will never lead us astray because Jesus is the only Leader who has shed His blood for us; the only One who always keeps His word.

---

[22] From Yvonne-Aimée de Jésus, by Fr. Paul Labutte. De Guibert, France. See photo album.

"Dear Children! .... I invite you to open yourselves and to live, taking the saints as an example. The Mother Church has chosen them that they may be an inspiration for your daily life." (October 25, 1994)

7

PADRE PIO IN MEDJUGORJE?

Chicago, October 2000

Sister Briege McKenna[23] was the host of a major Marian weekend organized by Kathleen Long. Since I was on the list of speakers, my small American team showed up with their cameras, hoping to make a few TV shows about Medjugorje with Sr. Briege, who usually doesn't mind. After the interview, Sr. Briege began to pray for me and quickly received a precise image and said to me: "I see your house in Medjugorje and someone's walking around inside." I perked-up, a little worried, since normally the house is locked up when we're out of town. I wondered who could be walking around like that. But, Sr. Briege continued: "It's Padre Pio. He's holding Baby Jesus in his arms and he's handing him over to you." Sr. Briege didn't know that we had named our house Bethlehem and that the Child Jesus reigns there as our beloved King![24]

Hearing Sr. Briege speak about Padre Pio in this way, Denis Nolan was surprised and forced into a quick interior combat—he would have to re-examine a few of his ideas about Padre Pio. A few months before,

---

[23] Sr. Briege McKenna is an Irish nun with the Poor Clares. She has a ministry of evangelization and healing prayers throughout the world especially ministering to priests. Contact details: P.O. Box 1559, Palm Harbour, Fl 34682, USA. www.sisterbriege.com

[24] Sr. Briege always amazes me with this unique gift. In May of 1981, during the great international meeting of priests in Rome, just one month before the apparitions started in Medjugorje, she prayed over a Franciscan priest from the region of Medjugorje, Fr. Tomislav Vlasic. While praying for him, she saw the Church of St. James and the services going on.

Denis had made me hide a picture of Padre Pio in the bottom of a drawer when I had wanted to set it out. He said the reason was because he had no affection for Padre Pio, whose thick, furled brow made him afraid. The vision of Sr. Briege touched him and he immediately adopted Padre Pio as one of our active "Heavenly supporters"!

The day following the meeting in Chicago, we ended up at Notre Dame University, in Indiana, where I was scheduled to record a cassette on Baby Jesus. We put this event under Padre Pio's care as we were curious to see his concern for us in action, as soon as we had a chance. I admit that I was a little nervous since I had already made one disastrous attempt at recording this theme a month earlier. There was no anointing! So, this time, Padre Pio's powerful help would be a necessity, especially for such a delicate and great theme. It turned out that, at the last minute, the room we reserved for the gathering at the University was no longer available. It was closed due to fall break! Giving up the project was out of the question since a group of students anxiously awaited learning about Baby Jesus. Their evening was already set aside for this event! So, we huddled in a tight circle, like a football team plotting its next play, and began to call on Heaven for help. For sure, Padre Pio would come to our rescue. After all, Sr. Briege saw him "walking around in my house with Baby Jesus!" With confidence, we solicited his help; he had to be both quick and powerful.

Along came a student who stopped and began to stare at me. Wide eyed and totally surprised to see me he exclaimed: "Sister, you're here! I can't believe it! I had a dream last night that you came to my house to give a talk. I thought I was losing my mind because I was sure you were in Medjugorje. I can't believe you're really here at Notre Dame!" Hearing that we were left out on the street for the talk, he invited all of us to his house. And so we were rescued, in the nick of time. Thank you, Padre Pio!

As we walked up to the door of the house, we all stopped, stunned! The house was called "Padre Pio House"! And the first thing we saw when we walked in the door was the bust of, you guessed it: Padre Pio! He obviously had been expecting us and seemed to be saying: "Come on in, don't be afraid. I've opened the door for you! I'll help you!"

The recording was completed in peace.[25] Padre Pio sticks to his word. He is a good reference to keep in mind for Medjugorje projects! It seems that this humble Capuchin, faithful friend of St. Francis, may have a soft spot for this parish—a Franciscan parish, chosen by the Mother of God![26]

---

[25] Listen to the CD on Baby Jesus, available from Children of Medjugorje, see the appendix at the end of the book for more information.

[26] Those who want to venerate Padre Pio in Medjugorje, may do so in the yellow building behind St. James where a big bronze statue of Padre is on display.

"Dear children! .... God is peace itself. Therefore, approach Him through your personal prayer and live peace in your heart. In this way peace will flow from your hearts like a river into the whole world. Do not talk about peace, but make peace." *(February 25, 1991)*

8

FIRST, PEACE IN MY HEART

Michael! –I've known him for ten years and have spent hours with him in our recording studio. As a fine musician and audio editor, he worked until 2005 for Children of Medjugorje, the English-speaking branch of *Les Enfants de Medjugorje*.[27] Michael is a very charismatic person! His faith in Divine Providence earns him the admiration of his family and friends. I even suspect that Michael may have obtained from Heaven certain things God Himself had not planned to grant him! After all, didn't Jesus say: "Therefore, I tell you, whatever you have asked in prayer, believe that you have received it, and it will be yours."?[28] In every circumstance, Michael normally lives in joy. One day he told his mother, Cathy: "You and Dad must have conceived me in a moment of happiness and you must have carried me with joy, because I'm always happy!"

Michael visits Medjugorje once in a while, and each time it gives a boost to his spiritual life and that of his family.[29] Michael, also, has his secrets. Whether he prays at Fr. Slavko's grave or on Apparition Hill, he always comes back with a smile on his face. We can tell that he's been enriched with a new light about God and that he will soon put it into practice. Then he will pass it on to his wife and children, so that this new gift from God will not remain inert.

---

[27] Children of Medjugorje is now located in Denver. Phone number: 877-647-6335. (877-MIR-MEDJ) Email: pray@childrenofmedjugorje.com. Mailing Address: P.O. Box 18430, Denver, CO 80218-0430, USA;

[28] Mk 11:24.

[29] Michael and his wife Annie have four children, and are hoping for many more!

During the University of Notre Dame's 2003 spring break, he came to Medjugorje, struggling with an inner conflict. He found himself overwhelmed and paralyzed by all kinds of worries. He cried out to God, begging Him to keep his head above water. Those several days of combat, waged under the Gospa's mantle, marked a major turn in Michael's life. I believe that what he received was a most providential key for those who are chronically besieged with worry, as most of us are!

Michael told me this story in a letter a few months after his trip to Medjugorje:

South Bend, fall 2003

"My pilgrimage to Medjugorje last March changed my life. Right from the start, the Gospa showed me that I had to pray to have peace in my soul. I realized then that in the past, even if I prayed, even if I believed and received the blessings of many miracles, I still did not have inner peace. I found it difficult to pray with love and to live what I was saying. Therefore, during the rest of the pilgrimage, I put all of my personal intentions aside and prayed only to obtain peace in my soul. This helped my prayer flow more easily. I didn't have to struggle, thinking about the words I was saying."

"Back in the U.S., I tried to hold on to what I had learned in Medjugorje. But all my daily concerns sprang back into my prayers. I became distracted again, finding myself praying for things other than peace. I found myself asking, 'What should I do about this or that?' My prayer became heavier and heavier – again I was losing inner peace! Two months later, my wife received the Sacrament of Confirmation, and during the Mass we experienced an amazing outpouring of the Holy Spirit. In a very special way, this grace opened my heart to Jesus, who spoke to me very clearly. I felt as if He were looking me straight in the eye, to keep my attention and to keep my clumsy prayers from getting in the way."

"This is what He made me understand: 'Michael, your only task in prayer is to ask for peace in your heart. I will take care of these other things you're worried about. By doing this, you will become an instrument with which I will bring peace to the world. From now on, just pray to have peace in your heart, as my Mother taught you in Medjugorje.[30] I will provide for the rest.'"

"The next day, my mom was telling us that we are sometimes called to pray for particular intentions. She told us the story of a nun who Jesus spoke to about spiritual matters. Jesus had asked her to stop praying for her family and to pray for other intentions instead. After she had obediently prayed for a year as Jesus had asked, she noticed that unbelievable blessings were falling upon her family. Just because she had given up her own intentions in order to pray for what Jesus had asked of her. Listening to this, I clearly understood the seriousness of what Jesus had said to me. My prayer life changed. Though my peace may be disturbed at times, I often manage to regain it and hold on to it in my heart, as I pray for peace and nothing but peace. God has amply blessed everything else that once weighed my prayer life down." Michael strives to stay the course—his mere presence is a consolation for many.

The Gospa teaches us that our task is to pray with her for peace—but that doesn't amount to much unless we pray with the right disposition! Her message has been clear since the beginning of the apparitions: We must first ensure that we are personally in the peace of God (possessing the shalom, the fullness) and that we do not pray out of frustration or fear. To be worried primarily about anything but peace would be a disorder, because God sees the rest and provides for it.

Vicka Speaks

At a time when the smell of war still lingered in the air, I asked Vicka how peace could be preserved. Vicka said: "Our lady never talked about war. We had a war here (1992-1995), but Our Lady never gave me personally any message about the coming of that war. But, it was visible on her face, and in her demeanor and the way she presented herself. She was carrying a lot of pain. Little by little, war came. She never scared us with talk of the war breaking out or said that we should

---

[30] "Dear children, give me your problems and your worries. Thus, your hearts will be freed for prayer. And pray for my intentions." (to the prayer group, winter 1990). Listen to CD 'Touch your Heavenly Mother". See the appendix at the end of the book for more information.

prepare for it in this way or that way. Rather, before the war, she told us so many times (as she is doing now) that wars can be prevented with fasting and prayer. So we must avoid those wars by helping her through our fasting and prayer!"

Then I asked, "Vicka, at the school of Our Lady, did you learn how to receive true peace, I mean divine peace as opposed to human peace?

Vicka said, "As she has already taught us, the first thing to do is to rid our hearts of anything negative—to cleanse it from any speck of negativity. Then, we should ask her for the grace of Peace. When I ask the Gospa to give me true peace and serenity, if I ask from the heart, she gives it to me. All we have to do is ask—as long as we ask with confidence and love! And also ask to be changed! Peace does not come to us merely because we use the word 'peace.' You see, today, there are so many people who say, 'I want peace, I want peace!' Those are just words. We must say, 'I want to change! I want to cleanse my heart!' Then, following this inner purification, peace will come to our hearts."

Dear Children! God sends me to you out of love, that I may help you understand that without Him there is not future or joy and, above all, there is no eternal salvation. Little Children, I call on you to leave sin and accept prayer at all times, so that through prayer you may come to know the meaning for your life." (April 25, 1997)

9

FR. SLAVKO'S WORDS OF WISDOM

Do you know the man about whom the Gospa boldly spoke to the entire world? With the message above, the Gospa honored her apostle. Didn't he tirelessly stand up for her in front of the world? And as Jesus said, "I tell you, every one who acknowledges me before men, the Son of Man will acknowledge before the angels of God."[31]

The day after Father Slavko Barbariæ's death, Our Lady gave the message of the 25th. I'll never forget that moment when we, the small group of translators, read the message received by Marija before it was sent around the world. Marija's eyes were all red with tears, but she was laughing as she repeated, "Slavko u nebu! Slavko u nebu!" ("Slavko's in heaven!"). Here is the message:

"Dear children! Today when Heaven is near to you in a special way, I call you to prayer so that through prayer you place God in the first place. Little children, today I am near you and I bless each of you with my motherly blessing, so that you have the strength and love for all the people you meet in your earthly life and that you can give God's love. I rejoice with you and I desire to tell you that your brother Slavko has been born into Heaven and he intercedes for you. Thank you for having responded to my call." (November 25, 2000)

Except for John Paul II, the Gospa had never mentioned anyone by name in her official messages, but she did for her child Slavko! Rare are

---

[31] Lk 12:10.

the departed souls who have been blessed with such a Heavenly "birth announcement," distributed to millions of friends in just a few hours!

What Are You Saving Your Energy For?

I would like to share with you a few of Fr. Slavko's words that reflect so well his personality, his determination and also his humor. In 1987, our friend Kate was about to climb up the steps to the rectory with him, when he paused a moment to listen to what a few aging and rather plump American women were talking about at the bottom of the stairs. Seemingly amused, he asked Kate if she had heard what they were sharing.

"No, Father, I didn't pay attention," she replied.

"Well, each one of them was explaining to the others how to preserve their physical strength. One does her laundry in such a way that she uses only a certain amount of strength; another does her cooking in a special way so that she doesn't spend energy; and the third her shopping. They were competing to see which one could expend the least energy possible." Then he added mischievously, "I wonder what they'll do with all that energy when they lie in their graves! You see, for me, when I'm dead, I hope that no matter how they put me through the press and the wringer they won't squeeze a drop of energy out of me!" He skipped up the stairs four steps a time and turned to ask: "What about you?"

That's a good question for all of us!

A Little Humor About Fasting

Fr. Slavko was an expert on fasting. No one in the village had ever fasted or helped others to fast like he did. For my part, I suffered from the after effects of severe viral hepatitis that prevented me from fasting. After seven years in Medjugorje, and many failed attempts, I complained to the Gospa: "Mother, you send me around the world to spread your messages but you don't grant me the grace of fasting myself! How can I talk to your children about fasting if I don't do it myself? I don't want to be a hypocrite. If you want me as your apostle, you have to grant me this blessing!"

She responded quickly. One Friday in November, I received the grace to fast. I felt no adverse effect of fasting with bread and water. The battle was won! Naïve as I was, I expressed my joy to Fr. Slavko, "Father, Father, guess what! I have been blessed with the grace of fasting! That's it—now I can fast!"

He looked at me over his glasses and said: "So, Sister Emmanuel! When the Gospa asks you for something, you actually wait to receive the grace before you do it?? Maaa…!"

I swallowed hard to down this dose of "Slavkonian spirituality". Nevertheless, I felt the need to make an attempt to justify myself somewhat, "I've been trying for seven years! Every time I tried, I was drained of all my strength and had to stay in bed or sit; I couldn't stand on my feet. I was so out of breath that I couldn't speak!"

His eyes lit up as he joyfully exclaimed: "You couldn't speak? But, that's very interesting! You're giving me a good idea. I'm going to recommend to a lot of men to have their wives fast! There'll be more peace in their marriages!"

We both burst out laughing….

Do You Know How We Lose Peace?

Fr. Slavko did not speak in a vacuum, but passed on the teachings that he had himself acquired through his own life experience and from his own spiritual struggles. During his last visit to the Cenacle Community, Fr. Slavko spoke to the young ex-drug addicts, whom he considered his spiritual children. He always gave them the best of himself. All of these boys had relentlessly suffered from the lack of peace in their families. Fr. Slavko said to them: "Do you know how we lose peace? When we begin to see only one aspect of a person—an aspect that we don't like—ignoring the whole person. Then criticism enters our hearts. We forget everything else. By focusing solely on the one thing that upsets us, we are blinded. Even if this fault, or bad habit, or even sin is real, when we get fixated on it, we lose sight of the beauty of life in that person, of what he may have done in the past, what he has given, suffered, etc. We are locked in a limited and distorted awareness of the person because we have become the prisoner of that one little thing."

"Then, we lose gratitude, and without gratitude, we can't have peace. Gratitude opens the door to peace. If someone comes to your home and all you express to him is praise and gratitude for all he's done and all his efforts, it will be very difficult for him to sustain any resentment toward you. You have already paved the way for peace and reconciliation! It's so easy in relationships to let ourselves get disturbed by a personality trait that appears insurmountable! Why can't we see beyond that point? We have put on blinders that obstruct our vision! When that happens, we should say: 'I am destroying peace!'"

"The basic decision we have to make is to always be grateful and to have a sharp eye out for what others do for us, for what God does for us, and even what God does for us through others. Am I upset today because it's raining? Bogu hvala (thanks be to God), the rain's disrupting my plans, but maybe God sent it to prepare the earth that will feed us next summer. I have to broaden my outlook on things and let grace spring out where it must. My inner peace will always be restored by my gratitude."

A Few Sunsets Too Many

The Lord gave me an extraordinary sign toward the end of the year 2000. Seeing the end of the Great Jubilee approaching, I decided to visit with Fr. Slavko. I thought it would be a good idea to forgive one another for all the clashes, or misunderstandings that may have tarnished our friendship, in order that we might take full advantage of the Mercy offered by the Jubilee. All I needed to do was to make an appointment.

Once a decision like that is made, it is very important to act before the sun sets. I made the mistake of letting several sunsets go by. One night, however, I received a light that left me with sudden insight. I had a dream where I sat at a large table. Around the table was nothing but joyful conversations. Fr. Slavko was sitting across from me. Among all the guests, his face was transfigured and beaming with celestial joy. I was staring at him, fascinated by the beauty and the love that radiated from him. He looked at me as if trying to share with me the great happiness that emanated from him. I woke up so overwhelmed by this flash from Heaven that I said aloud: "That's how we should be with one another all the time!"

The next day, Fr. Slavko was gone....

I give thanks to God for hearing my intention and for taking me through that appointment as a foretaste of His mercy and His glory.

Some people lament the void left in Medjugorje by Fr. Slavko's departure and seem to say: "I missed my chance to meet this remarkable priest! Now, it's too late!" But what would Fr. Slavko do in such a situation? As he liked to say: "I've received a special grace: when the day is done, I've forgotten all about it." He never looked back and did not fear the future but lived in the present.

One day a pilgrim made the mistake of telling Fr. Slavko: "Father, you should get some rest." He was often upset by this kind of comment; expressing his frustration with a waving hand, he replied: "I'll get rest in heaven!"

Now, I like to kid with him beyond the veil, and ask him: "Slavko, are you really getting any rest now?" Because, since his death, he has never been so active! He has never left Medjugorje. Now he has a twenty-four hour open door policy. No more standing in line. Saints in Heaven treat us as if each one of us was the only person in the world.

He Suffered in Silence

Where does the power of his intercessions that we see today come from? Why was he born in Heaven so soon after his death on earth?

Fr. Slavko suffered in silence, and it was extremely rare for him to let any sign of it show, even to his closest friends. Towards the end, he often liked to visit Marija, because her company felt like family. She had an insider's knowledge of the wrenching heartbreaks he endured. To open up to Marija was, for Fr. Slavko, a little like dropping his burden at the foot of the Gospa and abandoning it to her maternal care.

In a casual conversation with a friend of mine, a few months before his "Heavenly birth," he confided: "I am crucified!"

He, nevertheless, continued to preach gratitude toward God during the last days of his life in Medjugorje. As he celebrated Mass for a group of German pilgrims the morning of his death, he said to them: "We always complain! We would like to be somewhere else, in a different time, in Jesus' time for example, so that we might love Him, touch Him and believe in Him…. But, we must be convinced that God has chosen what is best for us and that, if there had been a better time or a better place for us, if there had been an era or a location better suited for us, He would have put us there, because He could have."

"Dear Children! Today I wish to tell you to always pray before your work and at the end of your work. If you do that God will bless you and your work. These days you have been praying too little and working a lot. Therefore, pray, because in prayer you will find rest." (July 5, 1984)

10

HIJACKING THE MISSION

Blinded by Jealousy

One day, Fr. Slavko mentioned how we can harm God's work without even knowing it. I can still hear him say: "When we receive from God the gift of helping others and begin to use it, we run the risk of becoming too attached to our work. Say, for example, that we have a ministry, an organization, a Peace Center, a charity of one kind or another that truly comes from God, but now we find out that someone else has received a similar gift and that he, too, is doing a lot of good. We even realize that the person is doing better than we are, and we begin to feel bad. We let jealousy invade us. It torments us and turns into an actual illness. Instead of rejoicing at the good being done, we become sad and frustrated, just because this goodness isn't coming out of our own work. We make such a mountain out of it that we even end up seeing that person as a threat against us, and we consider sabotaging his work.[32] We start saying bad things about him, and making negative comments about his ministry. We try to make it clear that we are the one doing the good works. This can make us lose peace to the point where we are no longer able to carry out the good works to which we are committed."

---

[32] Cf. Lk 9:49-50.

"That's how, after all of our good intentions and accomplishing excellent results, we can end up damaging God's work and even sadden God Himself. The only way to prevent this is by seeking only God and His glory in everything we do, without involving our own agenda; by being aware of our tendency to claim God's gifts as our own and confessing it; by detaching ourselves from our actions and the fruits they bear, because they don't belong to us. To avoid wrecking a good mission, let's examine our hearts and ensure that we are truly free—ready for God to withdraw our ability to do good works at any moment, if that is His holy will."

During his missions around the world, Fr. Slavko had observed many such cases within Marian groups. In his homilies, he knew what he was talking about. He was, also, a man of silence. He kept many confidences about spiritual battles or storms involving the Gospa's children in his heart. He took them, wrapped up in his prayer, on his morning excursions to the mountain, where he interceded for all. Fortunately, all of these intentions were buried with him. It is helpful to stay alert in order to purify our way of serving God.

Jesus spoke those wonderful words to St. Mechtilde: "Everyone who honors the gifts I have bestowed on others will reap the same merits and the same glory. If one bride's adornment seems more radiant than another's, the one can acquire the same beauty by drawing near her with a loving heart."[33]

Blinded by Self Will

Vicka is firm when it comes to the plan of Our Lady for the world, and Our Lady is firm when it comes to the desires of the Father. It seems that this firmness is sometimes missing in our own hearts and that we are also lacking the virtue of the holy fear of God that is its pedestal.

Vicka occasionally receives indications from Our Lady about some new communities, particularly those in Brazil, where they are blooming abundantly. "Aleanza Misericordia" is such a community that, though

---

[33] To Saint Mechtilde of Hackeborn, Germany (13th century).

quite new, has already had magnificent results among street kids and young adults left to fend for themselves. Fr. Antonello, a priest originally from Italy, is the founder of that community. Well-equipped with spiritual gifts that are so necessary to carry out such a mission, Fr. Antonello draws much of his inspiration from Medjugorje. With the unexpected collaboration of Divine Providence, he happened to see Vicka, who, to his great surprise, wanted to meet him as soon as possible. She began to talk to him about his community before he had said a word. Actually, the Gospa had given Vicka some information to pass on to him.

With Fr. Antonello's OK, I'd like to emphasize some important points in this message. Securely seated in a chair of the "apparition room" in her house that morning, Vicka spoke to him: "The Madonna told me to tell you that this charity work is the will of the Father who is in Heaven. He wants it."

"Isn't that what you tell everyone who comes and asks your opinion on starting a charitable project, Vicka?," the priest replied, somewhat distrustfully.

Taken aback, Vicka continued: "No, the Madonna told me to tell you this, and what I'm saying now is for you! The Gospa, also, said that you must act only when, together, you see that what you're about to do is the will of the Heavenly Father and not just because one of you gets the desire to do something and claims that it's God's will. The Madonna has told me to tell you that many communities are at first born from a true desire of the Father, truly from God. But, unfortunately, too often, men take control of the works and don't leave room for the Heavenly Father to act. They get wrapped up in so many things that they no longer take the time to ask the Father for guidance, or to pray in order to discern whether the decisions they make are in accord with God's design. That's why God abandons those projects; they stop thriving and eventually die. As for your concerns, these are works that God desires and the Madonna blesses them."

Our Lady couldn't be clearer than that! No one can presume to be immune to straying in this way, because everything that comes from the Father sends Satan into such a rage that he will make all attempts to snare those who wish to listen and follow the instructions they receive in prayer.

What would have become of the Church had John Paul II not been, first and foremost, a man of prayer, a great listener, and poor in spirit, constantly aware of the fact that the ship he steered was not his own. Swamped by work as he was, he knew how to preserve the essential: His personal and intimate ties with the Holy Trinity. His friends, for example, tell of the time when they arrived somewhere and were offered a warm meal before bed. Everybody was around the table, except one of the guests: John Paul II! Everyone went out looking for him and found him in the chapel, kneeling in front of one of the Stations of the Cross. "Ah, right! Today's Friday," someone said. They had noticed that every Friday, the Pope never went to bed without first praying a lengthy Way of the Cross. "I draw my strength from it," he said. That evening, when he was done, he reappeared, visibly re-energized, to bid his friends goodnight.

"Dear Children!…. May Holy Confession be your first act of conversion and then, dear children, decide for holiness." (November 25, 1998)

11

THE BAR OR THE CHURCH?

Dublin, Ireland, 1998

Lynn was at the end of her rope. She couldn't go on much longer. Her marriage gasped for air, and she had been suffering martyrdom. Her husband was an alcoholic—she had tried in vain to alleviate his addiction. The situation seemed no longer manageable. She continually begged Our Lady to put a stop to the tragedy, but nothing was happening, and she was on the brink!

One evening a friend showed up unexpectedly and said: "Lynn, why don't you go to Medjugorje with Leo? You will see, Our Lady will do something for you. There are unbelievable graces over there!"

A glimmer of hope was born in Lynn's heart, and she decided to go to Medjugorje, even if that meant using up what little savings she had. She approached Leo about it, but he categorically dismissed the idea. He couldn't understand why he should go to Medjugorje since he'd much rather be in a bar than in a church. But Lynn wasn't ready to give up. She definitely would not go without him. She devised an unusual offer: "I'll go to the church and you can go to the bars—the bars in Medjugorje!" After a period of time, she finally convinced him, and off they went! Once in Medjugorje, Lynn pleaded to the Gospa for her husband's conversion, asking that he be next to her in church some day.

Late in the evening of the third day, Leo stepped out of a bar and found himself wandering the streets of Medjugorje, completely lost. Not a soul was around for him to ask directions. Eventually, he came across a man pacing up and down as if waiting for someone. "Hey, I'm lost!" said Leo. "What are these things?"

"These things? Well, these are confessionals."

"Confessionals? What about you? What are you doing here?"

"I'm a priest—a priest next to confessionals—get the picture?"

"Yeah, well, I guess ... I guess that could be a sign for me to go to confession, huh?"

For the first time since he was a child, Leo made his confession, and the Blood of Christ flowed over the precious soul of this man so aware of his littleness in front of God.

In 2001, three years later, the couple returned to Medjugorje to give thanks, because, since the absolution he received that night, Leo had not touched a drop of alcohol!

What is so marvellous about Medjugorje is the royal freedom with which Mary operates. No matter what, she stays by our side, dispensing her heavenly gifts to all who come to her. If a new book aimed at destroying Medjugorje gets published, her maternal care never wavers, always healing and comforting! If she reads in a magazine that she has never appeared in Medjugorje, she's here that same evening, relentless, praying with Ivan, Marija and Vicka.[34]

If she hears from some people that one has to be cautious about signs, she still continues to obey her Son who has given her to us as a mother. She knows that a mother is, above all, a heart that gives signs of love; she just adds more! She also knows that the Enemy saturates the world with his signs of death, tormenting us at every turn. As a mom, she will not stand by and watch without intervening, without assisting those in danger!

One evening, a little girl of eight from France saw Our Lady at the Blue Cross during an apparition with Ivan. Why was this little girl chosen? Why not, after all, it is our Queen's prerogative! Thousands

---

[34] Amidst the waves of attacks against Medjugorje, we have to keep smiling. One reader helps us along with these words: "Since there's no effect without a cause, only two hypotheses stand: Either this organized scam has led thousands of people to conversion (which would pose a serious theological and metaphysical problem), or those conversions can be attributed to some unknown acts of Divine origin, which by pure coincidence are occurring since the very first day this swindle operation began!" As the humorist Alphonse Allais said: "Shakespeare never existed. The works attributed to him were written by an impostor whose name, incidentally, just happened to be Shakespeare."

didn't get to see her that evening. Why? It was our Queen's prerogative! Either way, Mary is spreading goodness around, targeting each individual need.

I am thankful to our Mother Church for leaving us free to believe that Mary does appear in Medjugorje. Yes, I believe that Mary places herself within our reach and performs extraordinary works in Medjugorje.

Dearest Gospa, please continue to appear for a long time! You told us that "at each of my visits, I spread the reign of my Immaculate Heart a little further and Satan loses a little of his power." How many Leos are there left for you to help? We beseech you to keep appearing until the triumph of your Immaculate Heart!

Dear Children! One must invite people to go to confession, each month, especially the first Saturday. I invite people to frequent confession. Do what I have told you. There are numerous people who do not observe it. Monthly confession will be a remedy for the Church in the West. One must convey this message to the West." (August 6, 1982)

12

NOTHING TO CONFESS?

Some people are endowed with a very special spiritual antenna. This gift works in them throughout the day and sometimes even wakes them up at night. Kathleen Long struggles with this very gift as she is constantly challenged by the Holy Spirit.

Kathleen invited me to speak at a Marian Conference in Chicago. I can still hear the long story she told me the night before the conference, in the coziness of her dining room, while she was still recovering from the shock of events that she had just endured. Kathleen is a stable Irish woman, blessed with solid common sense. She speaks straight from the heart. The Irish blood flowing in her veins makes her an adventurer who would stop for anything except the Lord Himself! Recurring health and family problems have scarred her heart, but it was with this lovable and resilient clay that the Lord fashioned for Himself an apostle and a prophet.[35] Kathleen's small house is filled with a breath of prayer and the presence of angels. That is not surprising, since one of the rooms, the one I slept in the night of our discussion, was also the room that Jakov Colo, the visionary, had slept in during his missions in the United States. Our Lady has appeared to him several times in that room.

Kathleen's eyes filled with tears as she recounted the story of the spiritual marathon she had endured over the previous weeks. Once again and without warning, the Spirit of the Lord had given her an

---

[35] In 1990, Kathleen founded the Center for Peace inspired by Medjugorje. She had no funds or anyone's support, which allowed the Divine Mercy to act unhindered. As St. Paul said, "For when I am weak, then I am strong." (2 Co 12:10).

urgent assignment. She related the story to me, as follows. "I live in the U.S. but my homeland is Ireland. I go back there occasionally to visit my family. That's what I did last month. I had hardly returned to the States when I went to Georgia for a three-day seminar to improve my computer skills. The first night there, I woke up at 3:00 a.m. hearing this: 'I want you to go back home.' I answered, 'I can't go Lord—I just got back from being home!" But, He replied, "You have to go back right now!"

Kathleen couldn't get back to sleep again. The thought of going back to Ireland seemed so ridiculous. She said out loud, "I was just there after a long absence, and I'm going back in June!" She waited until 7:00 a.m. to get up after four hours of solid interior combat. Before she set her feet on the floor, she knew in her heart that she must return to Ireland. Before breakfast, she announced to her assistant, Cloe: "I have to go back to Ireland. I have to!"

"What? But, you just got here!" said Cloe, shocked. "It can't wait. Please get a ticket for me to go from Atlanta to Chicago; from there I'll get a flight to Dublin."

Once in Chicago, Kathleen called her folks in Ireland. They told her that everything was fine there. One night went by and on Saturday morning, she called again. Still nothing to get alarmed about! So, she went to Mass and during Consecration, she heard the same voice insisting: "You must go home immediately!"

However, from the other side of the Atlantic Ocean, her sister Barbara was telling her she had lost her mind: "What do you want to come home for? Don't be ridiculous? You're coming in June." "It'll be nice then and we'll go out and have a good time together!"

The next day Kathleen flew to Ireland and showed up at Barbara's door. "What are you doing here?" exclaimed Barbara.

"I'm here, that's all. Just wanted to be sure everyone was OK. By the way, what time is Mass tomorrow?"

"You don't have to go to Mass. You just relax!"

Kathleen's sister hadn't been to church for a long time, and she was a little touchy about the subject of religion.

The next morning after Mass, Kathleen grabbed the priest. "Father John, would you come to the house to meet with my sister?"

"Why do you want me to see her?"

"Oh, can you just come? You can give her the sacrament of the sick. She has a bad case of the flu. And you could hear her confession. You can tell her I invited you for coffee or something like that, OK?"

"OK, I'll try, but I know Barbara, and she'll be very suspicious if I show up just like that, just to say hello!" Two days went by…. No priest. Kathleen tried again insisting that he should come, keeping the Anointing of the Sick and Confession in mind.

"Why is it so important," he asked, "and how am I going to pull it off?"

They sat down trying to keep each other calm. "Don't worry about what to say once you get there, Fr. John, just come, and the Lord will take care of the rest. I know for a fact that the Lord is handling this personally."

Fr. John finally showed up. "Oh! Barbara, how are you? Actually, I came to see Kathleen. I heard she was back from the States!" Then, seeing Kathleen: "Hello, Kathleen! Did you come back for any particular reason?"

"I just wanted to come spend a week with my family. By the way, it's beautiful to be able to go to Mass here with the Blessed Sacrament exposed!"

Barbara interrupted: "You know, Father John, my sister Kathleen is one of those religious nuts who invented religion."

"Really? How did that happen? Don't you have the same mother?"

Kathleen cut in: "Of course we do. By the way, Father John, since you're here, why don't you give the Anointing of the Sick to my sister? She's just getting over a bad case of flu."

Fr. John, turning to Barbara, asked, "Would you like it?"

Barbara inquired what the Anointing of the Sick was all about. "Hmmm, if it's just to give me strength and to keep the flu from coming back, why not!"

So, Fr. John gave her the anointing, and then Kathleen, in a casual and detached way, suggested: "While you're at it, Fr. John, why don't you hear her confession?"

That didn't slip by Barbara unnoticed. She was so embarrassed! She said, "But I have no sin to confess! I never set foot outside the house, I don't hurt anyone. I just take care of my family!" Nevertheless, she ended up having her confession heard, thanks to Fr. John's skillful cooperation. She later admitted to Kathleen that she hadn't gone to church a single time in thirteen years. Her husband never went, and eventually she ended up adopting his atheist views. It's so much easier to let things slide! No more Masses; no more Confession!

After Barbara had received the sacraments, Kathleen felt a deep peace in her heart and decided to return to the States that same week. On the eve of Ash Wednesday, three days after her return, she received a phone call from Ireland—her sister had died suddenly of a heart attack in her sleep. She was 59 and the mother of eight children.

Kathleen used to ask her, "Barbara, how can you go to sleep at night without confession? What if the Lord decided to call you back in the middle of the night? Invariably, Barbara would answer, "Hmmm, I never think about that...."

The Confession of Faustina

A few decades ago in Poland, a great Saint was afflicted with severe tuberculosis. What she experienced during that time can shed some light on the great sacrament of Mercy. Because of her illness, Sister Faustina Kowalska had not been able to go to Confession for over three weeks. She wept out of repentance for her sins and certain spiritual trials she was enduring. But, fortunately, as she herself wrote:

"This afternoon, Father Andrasz came into my room and sat down to hear my confession. Beforehand, we did not exchange a single word. I was delighted because I was extremely anxious to go to confession. As usual, I unveiled my whole soul. Father gave a reply to each little detail. I felt unusually happy to be able to say everything as I did. For penance, he gave me the Litany of the Holy Name of Jesus. When I wanted to tell him of the difficulty I have in saying this litany, he rose and began to give me absolution. Suddenly his figure became diffused with a great light, and I saw that it was not Father A., but Jesus. His garments were bright as snow, and He disappeared immediately. At first, I was a little uneasy, but after a while, a kind of peace entered my soul; and I took note of the fact that Jesus heard the confession in the same way that confessors do; and yet something was wondrously transpiring in my heart during this confession ...."[36]

Since Christ had nominated Sister Faustina as "secretary of His Mercy," He revealed to her what escapes our senses, and what He himself feels, when we receive a Sacrament. Through the revelations reported in her diary, Sr. Faustina effectively takes us beyond the veil, and leads us into God's thoughts—His feelings, His desires and His sorrows. We are so unaware of them. What joy it would be for us to plunge into such treasures, deep into the innermost being of God. He desires nothing more than to let us enter into Him and discover Him! Here's one of the most beautiful passages on the Sacrament of Confession as seen from the heart of Jesus:

"Today, the Lord said to me, 'Daughter, when you go to confession, to this fountain of My mercy, the Blood and Water which come forth from My Heart always flow down upon your soul and ennoble it. Every time you go to confession, immerse yourself entirely in my mercy with great trust, so that I may pour the bounty of My grace upon your soul. When you approach the confessional, know this, that I Myself am waiting there for you. I am only hidden by the priest, but I myself act in your soul. Here, the misery of the soul meets the God of mercy. Tell souls that, from this fount of mercy, souls draw graces solely with the vessel of trust. If their trust is great, there is no limit to My generosity. The torrents of grace inundate humble souls. The proud remain always in poverty and misery, because my grace turns away from them to humble souls.'"[37]

---

[36] Divine Mercy in My Soul: The Diary of Sister M. Faustina Kowalska, §817 (Marian Press 1987).

[37] Diary §1602. When he was Cardinal of Krakow, the future Pope John-Paul II brought Sister Faustina's writings out of the vaults where they had been put away by mistake and left for years. Now is the time to read and reread these works that, along with the messages from Medjugorje, are God-sent nourishment for our generation, which is misled, but thirsty for God. Jesus himself told Sr. Faustina: "In the Old Covenant I sent prophets wielding thunderbolts to my people. Today I am sending you with My mercy to the people of the whole world. I do not want to punish aching mankind, but I desire to heal it, pressing it to My merciful heart. I use punishment when they themselves force Me to do so; My hand is reluctant to take hold of the sword of justice. Before the Day of Justice, I am sending the Day of Mercy." (Diary § 1588) Listen to CD 'The Divine Mercy Chaplet'. See the appendix at the end of the book for more information.

"Dear Children! ... I invite you all to decide for God so that from day to day you will discover His will in prayer. I desire, dear children, to call all of you to a full conversion, so that you will have joy in your hearts." (June 25, 1990)

13

LET'S GO AND SEE THE CRAZY OLD LADY!

When I was a little girl, every summer my parents used to invite to our home a couple who always brought joy to us, the six Maillard children. They had earned the honorary titles of "Uncle John and Auntie Sonia." He was the perfect ivory-tower philosopher,[38] capable of reciting by heart entire chapters from Aristotle, while being totally incapable of cooking an egg for himself. She was a painter from Denmark and, together, they formed the most dissimilar couple you could think of, at least so it seemed to us children.

What brought delight to us in those days were the stories of Uncle John. We only had to press him a little—"Tell us the story of...."—and there he was, retelling with astonishing precision, word for word, phrase by phrase, in the exact order, the same exact story he had told during his last stay! He did not mind at all, as he could not recall that we had heard all of his stories before. Among the "edifying" stories, which communicated an undeniable anointing of the Holy Spirit, there were also a few jokes—always the same four!

Every summer, one of us was in charge of saying: "Uncle John, Uncle John, tell us a joke!" Then we would get ready to die laughing, because, in a very unique tone of voice that my brothers could imitate with such skill, he would tell us again the same four jokes, in the same order, and laugh like a child while violently shaking the chair he was

---

[38] A disciple of Msgr. Guyka and of the great theologian Fr. Garrigou Lagrange, OP, Jean Daujat was also an intimate friend of Jacques Maritain.

sitting on. My dad would wink at us and my mother would stifle a chuckle, indicating we were going too far. To tell the truth, Uncle John's jokes were a little old, and not really that funny, but we loved the whole routine.

Since 1940, John and Sonia had frequented the home of Marthe Robin.[39] Regularly, during their retreat at her *Foyer de Charité*, or on other occasions, they spoke with her at length. Sonia's first experience with Marthe was a positive but difficult lesson in humility. World War I was barely over, and she had signed up with her husband for a retreat at Marthe's Center. The Foyer was just opening in a country exhausted by war. Participants could converse with Marthe for only a few minutes in her little farm house in "La Plaine" (a region just above Châteauneuf-de-Galaure). Father Finet, co-founder of the Retreat Center, would introduce people one by one or two by two, in the minuscule bedroom, dark as a cave, where Marthe lived, bedridden.

When Sonia paid her first visit to Marthe, she and John introduced themselves and exchanged the usual greetings with Marthe. Then suddenly Marthe asked, "Mrs. Daujat, did you sleep well last night?" Sonia replied, "Oh yes, Marthe, thank you! I slept very well!"

"Why are you telling me you slept very well, when you did not sleep at all? You spent the entire night with back pain, turning and tossing, saying: 'What a horrible mattress! What a poor hostel this is!'"

Silence ensued. "Well, ah….," an ever-refined Sonia quietly uttered.

"Please, promise me you will fetch Miss Diane at the Foyer and ask her to change your mattress. Make sure she gives you an excellent one. You need your rest!" That event turned out to be the beginning of a long and profound friendship!

The Trio from Lyon

Something of a very different nature happened years later in Châteauneuf. Uncle John would relate the story to us, filled with the

---

[39] Marthe Robin (1902 – 1981), great French mystic. She founded the Foyer de Charité with Fr. Georges Finet. Email: foyer.de.charite@fdc-chateauneuf.com. Insights into her life and ministry can be found in Fr. Raymond Peyret's book, Marthe Robin: The Cross and the Joy (Alba House 1983).

excitement and awe of a philosopher knocked off his horse by Divine intervention.

One day in Lyon, a young man was sitting at a table with his two mistresses, around a bottle of wine, in a well-known bar of the old district. The surroundings were drab and the conversation almost non-existent. Infinite boredom had taken hold of the trio. They had done it all, they had committed again and again all possible sins, they had tried it all, tasted it all, and finally, they had run out of ideas. What could they possibly come up with to inject a little excitement into their lives?

"I have an idea!" the man burst out, his eyes suddenly lit with evil pleasure. "Why not go together and see that crazy old lady?!"

"What crazy old lady?" asked one of the two women."

"You know, the crazy one from Châteauneuf, the one who is always locked up in the dark!"

"Ah, you mean the 'mystic'? People say she carries the stigmata."

"My foot! I bet it's just a trick to make money!"

"I love that idea!" said the other woman, "but we need a tight plan here, it's very hard to approach her."

"Don't worry, I know someone who's been there. The plan is simple: we will sign up for a retreat, and on the second day, they'll ask us who wants to go and see Marthe. So we'll just put our names down, and of course we'll play the 'pious' types…."

"No problem there!"

"…and we'll say we have an important question for her, and the three of us have to see her, the three of us together. And once we're in the room, we'll just have the time of our lives mocking her, insulting her, cursing her the worst way possible, the worst she ever would have heard! Gee, she's going to remember us for the rest of her life! And of course afterwards, we'll tell it all to the newspapers!" And the three of them cackled in advance at the mean trick they were about to play.

Three weeks later, our three scoundrels pretended to be little doves. They were quietly eating their lunches among all the other retreat participants in Châteauneuf-de-Galaure, when their names were called:

"It is your turn to go and see Marthe. Be ready at 3:00 p.m. by the front door. Father Finet will drive you there."

However, they were not aware of an important detail concerning the rules of the Foyer: Marthe always asked to know in advance the list of the people who wished to see her. In certain cases, she signaled that a request could not be fulfilled, in the case, for example, of a journalist who was carrying a hidden camera, or a joker who wanted to do damage to the reputation of the Center. She prayed at length for each guest.

Our threesome from Lyon arrived at Marthe's waiting-room. They sat in front of the empty wood-burning stove while the old grandfather clock ticked away the seconds and minutes. The atmosphere was somehow different; they were not as cocky as they were in the bar in Lyon, but... not to worry, their plan was perfect! It was bound to work!

A woman came out of Marthe's bedroom; her eyes were filled with tears.... "Go on, hurry, this is your turn!" summoned Father Finet, pushing them gently into the dark bedroom, while pointing out with a flashlight where they should sit.

Before they had realized where they were, and before they even had found their chairs, Marthe was already speaking to them: "Go on, go on, have a good laugh! That's all I deserve!"

Dead silence in the room. Our trio is speechless. Seconds go by, time is hanging heavy.

"But, Madam, we, uh...."

"Go on, go on, don't be afraid, tell me all that is burdening your heart, I know what a sinner I am, I deserve it!"

The man, seized by the eeriness of the moment, tries to catch his breath and utters in a shaky voice: "But Madam, we don't want to say anything to you, we did not come here to make fun of you...."

"Yes you did. Remember that evening, March 4th in Lyon, in a famous bar of the old district! You were wondering what to do next, and you decided to come to see "the crazy old lady of Châteauneuf," to make fun of her...."

The trio become totally speechless. The fear created by the shock penetrates them right down to their bones. Even their ability to think is suspended; they lower their heads, stupefied, dumb.... They had gotten it all wrong, they had lost, they did not know…. And then slowly, their proud attitude was replaced by a gentle and fragile opening of their hearts. And Marthe continued to speak to them, saving the situation from disaster.

The man and his two mistresses stay for over an hour, listening to Marthe. Her immense love for all beings slowly wins them over, and they are not trying to hide anymore. She seems to know everything about them, but what's most surprising about her is that she seems to love them the way they are, the way a mother loves. She even seems to look at herself as being beneath them. She shows them an infinite respect and she presents to them the splendor of God's project for their lives as Christians. She seems to completely dismiss the fact that their lives of debauchery so far has not prepared them to hear such pure, such sublime words! She expounds on the beauty of life for those who love God, and on the splendor of the soul that is profoundly united with Jesus. They are transported by her enthusiasm.

On that day, at the insignificant little farm of La Drôme, love wins a beautiful victory over hatred. When our three friends leave Marthe's house, with the Mistral wind blowing on their faces, they are transfigured, they stumble with joy. They seem to have travelled very, very far, into another world.

The fruits of that visit: one friar and two nuns.

"Dear children! Today I call you to open yourselves to prayer. May prayer become joy for you. Renew prayer in your families and form prayer groups. In this way, you will experience joy in prayer and togetherness. All those who pray and are members of prayer groups are open to God's will in their hearts and joyfully witness God's love. " (September 25, 2000)

14

AN UNKNOWN TONGUE

That evening, as on all other Thursdays, the Crypt of St. Sulpice Church in Paris was filled to capacity. Pierre Goursat, founder of the *Emmanuel Prayer Group*, had had a stroke of genius in selecting this strategic spot, in the heart of the Latin Quarter, to gather the members of the prayer group—ever increasing in number. We were then in 1975, and, since 1973, Paris had been witnessing the remarkable spiritual hatching called the "Charismatic Renewal." Pierre, the leader, had me sit on his left side so that I could make a short exhortation during the prayer time. To his right was Suzanne, who would keep things under control (as the assembly was open to all) and also read some Bible passages throughout the prayer time.

In the assembly, two unknown men took their seats. One was dressed in black. Nobody paid attention to them, since the prayers had already started and joy resounded throughout the Crypt in praise and songs. Then came time for spontaneous prayers and quiet time to listen to the Holy Spirit. All of a sudden, a very strong emotion came over me. Something had been put into my heart, and I had no clue of what it was. It was obviously not for me alone, but for the whole assembly. I started to sweat and my heart was pounding: I knew I had to deliver a message, but I didn't know what I had to say. I understood that I would have to open my mouth and jump right in, but, because of my shyness, I waited a few seconds. I sensed that I would feel no peace until I had delivered the message. In a case like this, the hardest part is uttering that first sound—the beginning of the first word—because after that, the Holy Spirit takes over and does the rest.

That night, it was a song that came forth from my lips, in an unknown tongue. A deep silence seized the assembly. Pierre turned to me: "Did you understand what you sang?"

"No... but I felt the very strong presence of Mary."

Five minutes later, Suzanne opened her mouth. Out came a discourse, also in an unknown language. Once again, there was a profound silence in the assembly. Strangely, there was no one who could interpret those two messages. What a pity! St. Paul, the great Apostle, would not have liked that; he was so intent that the whole assembly should understand the words spoken in tongues so they could be edified.[40]

The prayer finished an hour later. We exchanged warm goodbyes and little by little the Crypt emptied of people. As I was ready to leave, a man came up to me. It was the man in black, somebody I had never met before, obviously a newcomer.

"Miss, where did you learn to speak Syriac-Aramean?"

"Uh, excuse me? Syriac....?" I was laughing, but he was not laughing at all.

"You spoke perfect Syriac-Aramean. Where did you learn that?"

"Father," I said still laughing (I thought he was a monk), "I have never learned that language and I didn't even know it existed!"

"Come on Miss. You sang in that language less than an hour ago, and with a perfect accent, I might add. There is a guttural sound that no European can pronounce, but you pronounced it perfectly. And on top of that, you avoided a very subtle grammatical error at the beginning of your sentence."

"Ah, I see.... You mean during the prayer time?"

"Yes."

"It was a song in tongues. When someone sings in tongues, he does not always understand what is being said."

"You did not understand the meaning of your words?"

---

[40] 1 Co 14:13-28.

"No, not a word! However, I really felt the presence of the Mother of God, but it was just a feeling."

"Miss, allow me a few more minutes. I know Syriac-Aramean very well, and I often pray in that language. What struck me is that your song was a prayer to Mary."

"Oh, so you understood it? Then you can tell me what I sang?"

"Yes, you addressed salutations and praise to the Mother of all the people of God. Your words were very close to the Hail Mary, but you added some praises other than the classic ones like full of grace and blessed are you among women."

Then he took a piece of paper from his briefcase and started writing the song using the appropriate alphabet. I was happy to learn that Our Lady was blessed through that song and that it had been her desire to let me know that she was blessed.

It was obvious to me that I wouldn't be going home anytime soon that night. I watched as the monk grabbed Suzanne to have a word with her, since she was the one who had delivered the other message in tongues.

It was Father Louis Leloir, a Benedictine priest, Professor of Semitic Languages at the University of Louvain (Belgium), who happened to be one of the greatest specialists of Syriac-Aramean in the world. In fact, he spoke it fluently.[41] When visiting Paris, he often stayed with his friend, Fr. Jean-Marie, a priest who offered him lodging. This priest knew and appreciated our prayer meetings where charisms of the Holy Spirit were flourishing. He noted the good fruits of conversion among his parishioners. Father Leloir however was far from sharing Fr. Jean-Marie's enthusiasm and he even frowned upon what he declared as "silly nonsense that may lead simple people astray." He even reproached Fr. Leloir for being seduced by the nonsense.

He explained that according to the Desert Fathers, the greatest of all charisms are tears of compunction that lead to sincere repentance and conversion. And he advised Fr. Jean-Marie that "it would be imprudent for a soul to desire charisms other than these. This is the most precious gift from the Holy Spirit, and all should aspire to it. All

---

[41] He told about this event and our meeting in Paris in his book, "Communion," available in French, published by the Benedictine Order.

those other so-called charisms only end up distracting people from what is essential. You should really fight it—this entire new movement is a real disaster!"

Father Jean-Marie had kept his cool. He knew how to penetrate his friend's soft spot: "You are a Professor! How can you dismiss such a reality without first giving it a thorough examination? Come with me tonight to St. Sulpice Church! Just like Jesus said to His first disciples, "Come and see!"[42] You must first see, hear and touch."

So, controlling his natural aversion, Father Leloir followed his friend, dragging his feet, to the Crypt of St. Sulpice. The song in tongues turned out to be his first shock, but an even bigger shock awaited him with Suzanne's spoken message. Suzanne delivered, in ancient Hebrew, a very inspired vision of priesthood in the eyes of God. And it just happened that at that time, Father Leloir had to write an article about priesthood in a specialized magazine and he was struggling to find the missing pieces that would help him complete the article. He had pleaded with the Holy Spirit to send him some help, because he was blocked by a question concerning the two types of priesthood, the Ministerial Sacerdotal and the Royal Priesthood of the Laity.

What a surprise, then, to hear the most enlightening information on the subject, in a Hebraic language, coming from a young, French, monolingual woman! His article was done, with the answer sent from Heaven! It is worth noticing the Holy Spirit's humorous touch: Suzanne did not speak in Hungarian or in Chinese; rather, she spoke in ancient Hebrew, a language that only Father Leloir, in the whole pious assembly, could understand and memorize that night![43]

We quickly became best friends. Since then, Father Leloir has changed course. He is now proclaiming these signs of the Spirit for our times with the same intensity he had been belittling them in the past. And the Spirit has not let go of him. The day after the "St. Sulpice event," Father Leloir flew to London to speak at an ecumenical

---

[42] John 1:38-39.

[43] One could doubt this event if it weren't for the fact that Father Louis Leloir was a world renowned Professor, famous for his scientific precision in dissecting ancient languages. His friends and colleagues have heard him, more than once, relate this story. Furthermore, they saw his astonishing change of attitude toward the French Charismatic Renewal after the "St. Sulpice event."

assembly. There, it was an English Protestant Brother who gave him quite a shock. In the middle of prayer time, he heard the brother singing in tongues, in perfect ancient Latin. He was singing some kind of litanies to Our Lady! God has His own ways for ecumenism!

A Treasure for the New Times

The Holy Spirit is way ahead of us and His prayer inside us joyfully transcends the limits of our knowledge and the thickness of our wounded psyche. And so it is that even the less educated, poor in religious knowledge, can still lift to God the most sublime prayer, and even deliver a message to someone without knowing anything about that person. Speaking in tongues is a tangible sign of this, very well described in the Acts of the Apostles.[44]

It seems to me that this gift, the smallest in the family of charisms, must be developed in our preparation for the New Times. Praying in tongues re-shapes one's inner harmony and edifies him. If he goes through phases where he has lost his bearings, if he does not know anymore what to say, what to think, what to pray, then the gift of tongues comes to rescue his helplessness. If he has forgotten everything because of a physical or moral shock, or even because he was brainwashed, he is still left with this incomprehensible murmur, this budding of the Divine. He knows he is praying from the core of his being, along with the incredible Friend his soul possesses, a Friend who remembers all, and who compensates for his weakness. What a comfort it brings!

In Medjugorje, Our Lady has made known to the visionaries the type of communication from soul to soul that exists in Heaven among the blessed and how they communicate with God. Our poor human words, with all their frustrating baggage of misunderstandings, give way to an immediate and perfect understanding of the message that is being exchanged. There, everything is exposed under the splendor of Divine light. As St. Theresa of Lisieux (The Little Flower) used to say: "All will be said in a glance." Prayer in tongues is one way in which we get a little closer to this reality. Longing for Heaven, while letting the Spirit of Love pray in us, is a great gift indeed!

---

[44] And they were all filled with the Holy Spirit and began to speak in other tongues, as the Spirit gave them utterance (Acts 2:4).

"Dear Children! Do not be afraid because I am with you even if you think there is no way out and that Satan is in control. I am bringing you peace." *(July 25, 1988)*

15

THE VAGABOND OF CHÂTEAUNEUF

Andrée and Paul Thomae often reproached me for my relationship with Our Lady. As true and faithful Pentecostals, they were uneasy when they heard me invoke her in prayer. The Marian dimension was totally missing from their lives, and I fervently prayed for them to be able to taste the joy of taking their Heavenly Mother "home" one day. In this way, I prayed that by welcoming Our Lady, their hearts would be enlarged with the splendid gift that Jesus offered them from the Cross.

At that time, Marthe Robin[45] was in her last years on this earth, and in the Châteauneuf-de-Galaure House, Father Finet used to speak about Our Lady with such grace that it was almost impossible for the retreat participants not to consecrate themselves to her for the rest of their lives. Marthe had confided so much pertinent information about Our Lady to Father Finet! Every week Our Lady visited Marthe, before she entered the Passion of Christ on Thursday night, to support and encourage her.

So I suggested that Andrée try something. "Before you completely close your door to Mary," I said to her, "why don't you study the question a little bit more with some people who are very close to God, and who

---

[45] Marthe Robin was a stigmatic in France whose case for Beatification is open in Rome. Jesus asked her if He could live His Passion in her. She accepted. For over 50 years, every Thursday, Jesus asked again if He could live His Passion within her. She would answer "yes" and she entered a sorrowful ecstasy until Saturday night. She found herself in Jerusalem and could see Jesus in His Passion but she also experienced the same sufferings He endured. The unpublished accounts she gave of her experience of the Passion is very close to those of the Blessed Anne Catherine Emmerich (a stigmatic German nun who dies in 1824). Her accounts are slated to be published after she is beatified.

bring back to Christ hundreds of lukewarm believers and unbelievers every year?"

A few years passed before she made up her mind.

The day came when Paul and Andrée were in their little Renault car, on the back roads of France, going down the Rhone valley. They knew there was no time to waste. They could not be late to Châteauneuf; they had to be there by Monday night for a five-day retreat.[46] They couldn't afford the toll on the beautiful highway between Paris and Marseille. On the outskirts of the village, a man in his fifties was standing on the side of the road poorly dressed, hair in disarray—he was hitchhiking. For Paul and Andrée, it was obvious what they should do. As Christians, it didn't even cross their minds to leave a brother behind in need. The man climbed in, somber and in pain. When asked where he was going, he was not too sure; he only knew that he was looking for "the sunshine of the South...."

"Do you know Jesus?" Paul asked him.

"Well....," the man answered.

They engaged in a fraternal conversation. Seeing that the man's destination was rather hazy, Andrée offered to take him with them to the retreat. The man half-heartedly accepted the invitation. Andrée was totally ignorant of the rather strict rules concerning the sign up procedure for a retreat at Châteauneuf. She was only familiar with the large "Conventions" organized by Protestants—a different charism altogether!

They arrived late at night in Châteauneuf. The three friends were given their retreat schedule and found their rooms. After looking at the schedule, Paul and Andrée were chagrined. There was no mention of a "charismatic prayer meeting" on any one of the five days that, by the way, looked very busy. "Not to worry," they thought, "we'll simply add in one of our own." They planned the meeting for the very next morning at dawn, before the common program would even begin.

After a rather short night, they secretly gathered in one of the rooms while the first rays of light filtered through the sky. Paul and Andrée

---

[46] When he was about to open the retreat center, Father Finet had planned on doing three-day retreats. "No," Marthe told him, "one does not change a soul in three days; the retreats will be five days long."

started to bless and praise God with all their hearts, thanking Him in advance for all the graces that He had prepared for them in this Holy place, although it still seemed strange to them. But the man, perplexed, remained silent. During prayer, as it often happened, Andrée began a phrase in tongues. The message was not understandable. For her, this was all normal. She was confident that the Lord would reveal its meaning, if He so desired; they continued to praise Him.

Suddenly, the man started to cry. He couldn't hold back his tears much longer. Eventually he cracked: "Andrée, you speak Polish?"

"No! Why? Did I speak in Polish?"

"Yes! Well, no, it is more like a dialect. It is the dialect of my native village in Poland."

An electric bolt shot through Andrée, giving her goose bumps. She waited for what was coming next. But the man was choked up; he could barely utter a sound, the shock was too strong.

That was your dialect?" Andrée asked him. "Then you understood this message in tongues?"

The vagabond would never forget that morning. The extraordinary friendship which Paul and Andrée had shown him—their simplicity, their poverty of means, their poverty of expression, won his trust. The stranger opened his heart and invited them into his life of suffering, failures, and bitterness in his poor broken existence. Then he shared his secret with them:

"I used to be a priest. But I gave it all up years ago. I am a sinner....a poor sinner. I have lost everything. I have been wandering without a purpose for so long. But this morning.... Andrée, this is not you who spoke! You could not know all this about me, all those personal things in my life.... You spoke in my own dialect as if you were one of us, one from my village, and without any accent! But it was Jesus who spoke. He spoke to me like he would speak to a priest. He says that he forgives me and that he wants to give life back to me, he wants me to come back to him because his love never left me. He says that I am still a priest and he still needs me, he invites me to take his hand again so we can live together again....He needs me...."

Paul and Andrée shed silent tears. They are speechless and so incredibly happy. Isn't their unique mission in life to bring back souls to Christ?

That morning in Châteauneuf, the exchange of the sign of peace happened, most unusually, before Mass, and it was two lay people who gave the sign to the priest! Signs wet with tears!

The person in charge of the retreat very gently told them off for having added something of their own to the common program—she did not know anything about the Charismatic event that had just taken place—and she asked them to blend into the group of other retreatants in the deepest silence. As for Marthe, the founder of the Foyer, the little stigmata bearer, who prayed and offered her suffering for priests and sinners, I don't know if she saw the whole scene in spirit—as she might have—but I can just imagine her immense joy when she learned about this conversion, one on a par with that of St. Paul on the road to Damascus! My guess also is that she smiled at the thought that, to bring back to Himself His priest and son, God chose two Pentecostals in a secret gathering!

Ah, the Ecumenism from Above....

" Dear Children! My invitation that you live the messages which I am giving you is a daily one, specially, little children, because I want too draw you closer to the Heart of Jesus. Therefore, little children, I am inviting you today to the prayer of consecration to Jesus, my dear Son, so that each of you may be His. And then to the consecration of my Immaculate Heart. I want you to consecrate yourselves as parents, as families and as parishioners so that all belong to God through my Heart. Therefore, little children, pray that you may comprehend the greatness of this message which I am giving you. I do not want anything for myself, rather all for the salvation of your soul. Satan is strong and therefore you, little children, by constant prayer, press tightly against my motherly heart. Thank you for having responded to my call" (October 25, 1988)

16

CONSECRATION IN THE LAND OF THE MAFIA

It's not true that the only people to be found in Sicily belong to the Mafia! After all, as Saint Paul says, where sin increased, grace abounded all the more![47] It seems that a strong spiritual breath of renewal has been blowing on Catholics there in the last few decades:

Siracusa, October 27, 2001

A large crowd of approximately twenty thousand people gathered for an exceptional celebration. The visionary Marija Pavlovic-Lunetti was invited. The prayer groups of Mary Queen of Peace planned this initiative with great care. In fact, before "D" day, thousands of Sicilians did a Novena of prayer and fasting and were taught a catechesis. By

---

[47] Rom 5:20.

Marija's side was Father James Manjackal, from India, very well known in Europe for his preaching and his Healing Ministry. The Governor, also present, Mr. Salvatore Cuffaro, entrusted the whole Island to the Immaculate Heart of Mary. During the reading of the Act of Consecration, applause from the crowd interrupted the President four times on account of its volume. After seeing sixteen years of constant Italian presence in Medjugorje, I can easily imagine the situation! Many were crying.

After the Consecration, Our Lady appeared to Marija at 5:40 p.m., twenty minutes before Holy Mass, as usual. During the apparition, Our Lady appeared very happy. She thanked those gathered and gave the following message: "You will not regret what you have done today, nor will your children, nor your children's children!" As she was leaving, Our Lady blessed the whole crowd with the Sign of the Cross.

Since then, every October a large gathering of prayer has been organized in Syracuse to renew this Act of Consecration. In the aftermath of that first Act of Consecration, a surprising event happened:

Cetina, 53, a Sicilian mother of four, has had the gift of prophecy since she was a child. To help you situate her, her spiritual director is Father Mateo Lagrua, a very well-respected personality within the Church, who is also the spiritual director of two Cardinals.

On September 5, 2002, around midnight, while she was praying the rosary, Cetina had the vision of an island, where there was a city, and a large finger was pointing to it. She also saw Our Lady dressed in white. She was looking at the finger and was pushing it away toward the sea, so it would not point to the city anymore. The following day, September 6th, a tremendous earthquake took place. Its epicenter was under the sea, exactly at the level of Palermo. The city barely trembled. The earthquake was so powerful (5.6 on the Richter scale) that, had it happened right under the city, it would have totally destroyed it. Father Mateo said that Jesus had mercy on Sicily and that the town was spared due to the intercession of Mary. President Coffer declared on the well-known national TV channel Rai3: "We thank Our Lady for having saved Sicily from the earthquake." His declaration was then broadcast by Radio Maria throughout Italy.

Let's not forget this: that way before she appeared in Medjugorje, Our Lady had given the same message in Fatima, Portugal, asking that we consecrate to her Immaculate Heart and to the Sacred Heart of Jesus not only the people, but also the families and the parishes, even the nations! Portugal was the only country to do it as a nation, and what beautiful fruits that bore! Portugal was spared during the entire World War II! When Hitler's troops were ready to invade Portugal, Christians prayed fervently to Our Lady of Fatima. As it was, these troops received the order from Germany: Turn back!

This was in 1942, and the German Army never came back to threaten this country. Mary was watching over her treasure!

The Consecration of the World by John Paul II

There is no need to write about John Paul II's personal consecration to Mary. He personified Totus Tuus: never ceasing to walk with her, through her and in her.[48]

On May13, 1981, in St. Peter's Square, during the assassination attempt that almost cost him his life, the Holy Father had a notable and decisive experience. He realized that Mary, as his mother, was responsible for saving his life! Thirteen years later, during the Italian Episcopalian Conference gathered at St. Mary Major, he declared: "It was a maternal hand that directed the bullet...and prevented the dying Pope from crossing the threshold of death."

John Paul II went even further in recognizing that this attempt on his life was actually a grace for him! Msgr. Dziwisz, at his side in the ambulance on the way to the Gemelli Clinic, revealed that the few words uttered by the Holy Father during the journey were: "Mary, my mother. Mary, come! Mother, come!"[49]

---

[48] In his book, Crossing the Threshold of Hope, he wrote: "Totus Tuus. This phrase is not only an expression of piety, or simply an expression of devotion. It is more.... Through Saint Louis of Montfort, I came to understand that true devotion to the Mother of God is actually Christocentric, indeed it is very profoundly rooted in the Mystery of the Blessed Trinity, and the mysteries of the Incarnation and Redemption....This mature form of devotion to the Mother of God has stayed with me over the years, bearing fruit in the encyclicals Redemptoris Mater and Mulieris Dignatatem." Id. at 212-13.

[49] Carl Bernstein & Marco Politi, His Holiness, 294 (Doubleday, 1996). The Gospa appeared the next month in Medjugorje. Pure coincidence?

Observing that the attempt was made on May 13th, the anniversary of Our Lady of Fatima, John Paul II took the opportunity of his recuperation to reflect on the messages of Fatima. He asked that all of the archives of the Apparitions be brought to him, including the mysterious third secret that had not yet been revealed, in order to examine the requests of Our Lady. It was in the Gemelli Clinic that he conceived the project of answering her supplications without further delay.

The Church as a whole had not yet honored Mary's request to consecrate Russia and the whole World to her Immaculate Heart. This would require the consent and participation of all the Bishops. The Pope worked on this project with the fervor of one who had escaped death. He could feel the urgent need for the Act of Consecration to benefit of the world. Against all odds, he managed to get it all into place, and less than three years after the assassination attempt, this unique event in history at last took place under his guidance. Mary had been right: such a masterpiece required a man like John Paul II, an exceptional man who later was honored by the gathering of the Heads of State for his funeral!

In union with all the Bishops, he consecrated the entire world to the Immaculate Heart of Mary, and Russia was included, as Msgr. Paul Hnilica was in Moscow that day.[50] The Fatima visionary Lucia, who was still alive at the time, declared that this Consecration had been accepted by Heaven.

John Paul II renewed this Act of Consecration during the Holy Year, on October 8, 2000, in the presence of eighty Cardinals and one thousand five hundred Bishops, and he entrusted the entire world to Mary. Up to the moment of his death in 2005, he never ceased to invite the faithful to walk with the eyes and the heart of Mary. He encouraged them to be, with her, the Prayer Warriors our troubled generation is in such need of, and to build with her and in her the Civilization of Love.

The Little Hand of Agnes Bojaxhiu

Msgr. Paul Hnilica told me that in 1988, he asked Mother Teresa of Calcutta:

---

[50] See the chapter, "The Pravda Contained the Truth," in the book Medjugorje ,The 90's.

99

"Your apostolate with the poor is so successful! What is your secret?"

Without any hesitation she answered that this grace had come from her mother. When she was seven or eight, her mother grabbed her by the hand and took her for a long walk in a park outside the village. As she did not know the way, little Agnes could have been afraid to get lost, but the hand of her mother gave her a deep feeling of security. She let herself be guided with perfect docility. Then her mother stopped on the way and she confided to her: "My daughter, as you put your hand into mine today, during all your life I ask you to put your hand into the hand of your Mother in Heaven, the Holy Virgin Mary. With her, you will always be sure you won't get lost, and you will never take the wrong path. Never let go of Our Lady's hand!"

"Father Paolo," said Mother Teresa, "I have always followed this advice of my mother, and that is my secret! And today, as I am nearing eighty years old, I do not regret having done so!"

In fact, in the hand of Mother Teresa, reaching toward the poorest of the poor, don't we see in reality the hand of the Mother of God who joins herself to the distress of her children? What could little Agnes Bojaxhiu have done without this maternal hand?

Prayers of Consecration From Above

In Medjugorje, this maternal hand has grabbed many young people. She asked all those young people to consecrate themselves. But to consecrate themselves to what end? Religious life? Not necessarily! Whatever their state in life, their choices for the future and their place in society, Mary has reminded them first and foremost of the great gift they have received from God in baptism. She has traced for them a path to be what all baptized are already inside: priest, prophet and king!

In order to help the young people to plunge into the True Love and to live by it, the Blessed Mother has given them, through the *inner-locutionist*, Jelena Vasilj, two prayers of Consecration. Each of us can make them ours. Our Mother has created them for us; they come from Above! (November 1983)

Consecration to the Heart of Jesus

O Jesus, we know that you are meek,
That you have given your heart for us.
It was crowned with thorns by our sins.
We know that today, you still pray for us,
So we will not get lost.
Jesus, remember us if we fall into sin.
Through your most Sacred Heart,
Make us all love one other.
Cause hatred to disappear among men.
Show us your Love. All of us love you!
And we desire that you protect us,
With your heart of the Good Shepherd.
Enter into each heart, Jesus!
Knock on the door of our hearts.
Be patient and tenacious with us!
We are still locked up in ourselves,
Because we have not understood your will.
Knock continually, O Jesus, make our hearts open to you,
At least while we remember the Passion that you suffered for us.
Amen

Consecration to the Immaculate Heart of Mary

O Immaculate Heart of Mary, overflowing with goodness,
Show us your love for us.
May the flame of your heart, O Mary, descend upon all Peoples.
We love you immensely!
Impress in our hearts a true love.
May our hearts yearn for you!
O Mary, meek and humble of heart, remember us when we sin,
You know that we men are sinners.
Through your most sacred and maternal heart,
Heal us from every spiritual illness.
Make us capable of looking at the beauty of your maternal heart,
So that thus we may be converted by the flame of your heart.
Amen.

Mother of goodness

O my Mother! Mother of goodness, of love, and of mercy!
I love you immensely and I offer myself to you.
By your goodness, your love and your mercy, save me!
I wish to be yours. (I belong to you.)
I love you immensely and I wish that you would protect me.
In my Heart, O Mother of goodness,
Give me your goodness so that I may go to Heaven.
I ask you for your immense love.
Give me the grace to be able to love each person as you loved Jesus.
I offer myself entirely to you.
I desire that you be with me at each step,
Because you are full of grace.
I desire never to lose your grace, and if I come to lose it,
I'll ask you to help me find it again.
Amen

(Another prayer "dictated" by Mary to Jelena for the young people on April 19, 1984, Holy Thursday)

"Dear children! Today I want to wrap you all in my mantle and lead you all along the way of conversion. Dear children, I beseech you, surrender to the Lord your entire past, all the evil that has accumulated in your hearts. I want each one of you to be happy, but in sin nobody can be happy. Therefore, dear children, pray, and in prayer you shall realize a new way of joy. Joy will manifest in your hearts and thus you shall be joyful witnesses of that which I and My Son want from each one of you. I am blessing you. Thank you for having responded to my call. " (February 25, 1987)

17

VICKA ON HER STEPS

Consecrating a whole country is truly marvellous, but it implies some very solid individual consecrations among the people....

In Medjugorje, the Gospa herself has shaped her consecrated ones, and if she keeps some of her instruments very well hidden, she allows others to shine like beacons in the heart of the village. One of these instruments is the visionary, Vicka! In her own way, this young lady incarnates the remarkable success of the School of Mary: "When you speak, they will recognize my voice," Our Lady said to the prayer group.

While living as a simple parishioner, married with children, she fulfils her role as laity in the Church—a role held in high esteem by John Paul II and Benedict XVI; and a role ever-so prophetic for our generation.

Rare is laity so deeply consecrated from the heart to God and to Mary. Vicka finds her joy in bringing Them joy. There can be no doubt she has chosen the right path, because her joy increases every day of her life. Her life is difficult in many regards—how many times has she found herself on the brink of death! But she transforms everything that happens to her into gifts that she offers to her beloveds, Jesus and Mary. She "packages" sorrows and joys together and offers it to Jesus with gratitude. This is how she is able to convey Heaven to those who approach her. Doesn't the life of a consecrated person consist of anticipating Heaven in order to allow others to breathe it? I praise the Lord to have been so often the recipient of such a grace....

One morning I was to meet with Vicka at 8:00 a.m. When I arrived, I saw a group of Polish people in the courtyard. She motioned to me that I should wait a bit: "I will see you soon, after I speak to them," she told me. So I started praying, waiting for the group to leave, and trying to keep at bay the vision of the immense pile of work waiting for me at home. But it went on and on! Every time Vicka would finally bless a couple of people, another little group would show up. Thirty, fifty, seventy minutes went by.... Finally I lost hope and I got up to leave.

At that instant, Our Lady—in a manner of speech—grabbed me by the collar and spoke to my heart. It is not that I received a vision or an audible message, it was rather a very clear interior communication that I could translate as thus: "Stay, and watch my servant Vicka. The way she acts pleases me. Her heart is wholly in what she is doing. Watch how she welcomes each person who comes to her with joy and love. Look at her patience. She is acting the way I taught her to act, the way I would do it myself. You, you do the same."

Immediately my impatience went away. I saw, with the eyes of my heart, the scene that had been happening in front of me for the last two hours. That day, I understood a little bit better the true grace of Medjugorje and how much we need it to heal from our overly human way to be efficient. How much we need it to bear divine fruit, fruit that remains. It is Mary who cultivates the fruit trees of her Oasis of Peace and she especially cherishes the kinds who are docile to her will. Those kinds are the truly consecrated ones: they produce nothing without her, and Jesus loves to get close to them to collect their fruits.

"Dear Children! Pray and by your life give witness that you belong to me, because in these turbulent days Satan wishes to seduce as many souls as possible. Therefore, I invite you to decide for God, and He will protect you and show you what you should do and which path to take. I invite all those who have said "yes" to me to renew their consecration to my son, Jesus, and to His Heart and to me, so we can take you more intensely as instruments of peace in this unpeaceful world." (April 25, 1992)

18

I WAS JUST DRIVING BY

A little town in Ireland, May 4, 2003

It was almost midnight and Inge was still not home. Outside, the storm seemed to be intensifying. The rain was beating violently on the windows. "When will this gale ever stop?" Mechthild wondered. She began to pace nervously in the kitchen. "I should never have let Inge go out in this horrid weather," she thought to herself. Suddenly, the door bell rang.

"It can't be Inge. She has a key!" She tried to block a surge of fearand went to open the door. A gust of wind hit her in the face. Two men were standing discreetly near the doorway, embarrassed, with a paper in their hands. They were wearing uniforms, drenched in the downpour. Before they could explain the reason for their late visit, Mechthild understood. As if in a dream, she heard the muffled voices of the two men. One of the policemen asked to speak with a "member of the family." Mechthild gathered all her courage and asked them to sit down.

"What is happening? Is it Inge? Inge Braun?" "....Yes, she is my daughter."

Then she heard the words that were to pierce her heart. One of the police officers talked about a collision. "Your daughter's car probably skidded," he said. He asked Mechthild to come with him and identify the body, but Mechthild's mind was gone already; it had escaped into a universe that does not belong to this world, one that tastes like eternity. Mechthild joined her daughter in the mystery that was now the latter's home. She heard herself utter some questions automatically: "Where? How far from the junction? Where is the body?" "....I will follow you!"

Stunned, Mechthild followed the guard, still trying to convince herself, "This is not possible! Please Lord, let me wake up and make me realize this is just a nightmare! Inge is fine and will soon burst in the door, noisy and full of her usual hearty laughter!" But as though penetratinga veil, the words of the guards forced the reality to sink in.

I Ask You to Save Them

Mechthild was originally from Germany. She underwent more than her share of suffering throughout her life. Her mother was harsh with her, and from a very tender age, the male members of her family severely abused her. As a child, even though she was not baptized, she would run to the statue of Mary at the sight of one. Mystical experiences? No. But the softness and kindness of this Lady were a balm to her bleeding heart. While near her, Mechthild was able to catch her breath again before returning to face the world. The comfort was a mystery for her.

"Mary was teaching me in secret," she would later declare.

At fifteen, not able to cope with the sexual abuse, she attempted suicide. Soon afterwards, Mechthild married young, and left for Ireland, hoping to escape her damaged past. Unfortunately, her husband turned out to be an alcoholic, like her step-father. What a tunnel of darkness! The temptation to overdose on medicine was never far from her mind.

She gave birth to three children. As an adult she decided to be baptized in the Catholic faith. Thankfully, after a solid preparation, the great day of her Baptism arrived. Then her life completely changed—the joy to at last have Jesus was bearing her up. She brought up her children in the Catholic Faith.

Inge, her little one, was a difficult child from day one. She was very attached to her alcoholic father, and was therefore the most damaged by her parents' divorce. She was eight when her father left home out of the blue, without news or hope of a return. Inge never saw her dad again. She often directed her anger towards her mother, with a harshness that sometimes turned into violence. Her heart bleeding from such crises, Mechthild constantly begged Our Lady to become a better mother.

In 2001, she went to Medjugorje and there she decided to consecrate her children to the Sacred Heart of Jesus and the Immaculate Heart of Mary. She gave Our Lady charge over her children, asking her to be their mother from Heaven and watch over them from above. Mechthild was going to walk hand in hand with the Mother of God, her forever friend.

"I give them to you. From now on, they belong to you! All I ask from you is that they be saved. Even if they choose the wrong path, I pray that you will bring them back to your Son," she said.

This was a very joyous day for Mechthild! She was seized by a deep sense of peace, as if the great burden that had been on her shoulders 'till now had finally been removed. She knew in her heart that her offer had been accepted "Up-There."

Our Lady must have had lots to do because Inge was on a very dangerous slope: Drugs, alcohol abuse, late nights…The relationship between mother and daughter became infernal. When she came back from Medjugorje, Mechthild asked some of Inge's friends to approach her and to help her realize that her behavior was unhealthy. That same night, by surprise, Inge wrote a beautiful letter to her mother. She loved her mother deeply and asked her for forgiveness, for all the pain she caused. In reality, her wounded heart was desperately looking for love but it was looking in the wrong places! From that day on, a dialogue started to happen between Inge and her mother.

"Inge," Mechthild told her, "if you want to live with us, you must change! We will establish rules. You must be home before midnight and also help me around the house."[51] Then, the relationship started to

---

[51] In a message about families, transmitted by Ivan, Our Lady said: "Parents must limit their children's freedom."

improve between Mechthild and her daughter. It is true that Mechthild loved her more and more: to criticize constantly was not the right method. In prayer, Our Lady was teaching Mechthild that she could not bring up her children the way she had been brought up herself—with violence! Instead of hurting them, she had to take them into her arms.

My Love, Go to Jesus Now!

Outside the storm was abating. Mechthild thanked the guards and jumped into her car. In the I.C.U., she was reunited with the precious body she had given birth to, fed, and loved—this young body that was only 17! Inge was still breathing, but just barely. It was the end. Her coma was too deep to hope for a return. In a flood of tears, Mechthild emptied her heart out to Inge, while holding her hand. "Please, Inge, forgive me for the times I was not a good mother to you! I love you so much! I'll never forget you! If you want to go to Jesus, please go! Don't worry about us, we'll be fine! You, my love, just go and be with Jesus! He is coming for you, He is calling you. Don't be afraid! Leaving so suddenly, at 17, my love... I love you, Inge. Go in peace!"

Like a candle, Inge slowly faded away in the embrace of her mother. Mechthild felt a sword being twisted in her womb. How can one suffer so much? "Oh Lord, let me die with my child, I can't deal with this!" She cried out to God, praying that He would not allow her to drown. But a small glimmer of light crept up from deep, deep inside of her. She knew that her Little Inge was "all right." She kissed her on the forehead, putting her head gently on her daughters. She was certain that from the moment of the accident Our Lady came to get her! After all, her heart had been consecrated to the Immaculate Heart of Our Lady!

"Holy Mother, you are there with her, aren't you? You are coming to take her with you, aren't you?" she cried out.

On the day of the funeral, the Capuchin priest who was going to celebrate Mass for Inge called Mechthild. He had an urgent message for her: "Mechthild, I just heard that on the night of Inge's death, Father Richard was driving by a car accident. He told me everything. The wind was incredible! He saw a car crash that had just happened and he parked his car nearby, in case someone was injured or even near death and needed a priest. He had with him Holy Oil for the Sacrament of the Sick. He went to the cars. The young man who had been driving did not have a scratch. But the one injured was a very young girl. She was still breathing. He asked her if she wanted to receive forgiveness from Jesus for her sins. She could not speak but she was still conscious. Father Richard gave her the Anointing of the Sick. He told me that she was at peace. Then she went into a coma and…well…they took her to the hospital. Mechthild, this young girl, it was your Little Inge!"

An electric shock coursed through Mechthild, she was seized with joy. In an instant, life seized her entire body and soul. What fantastic news! Inge had been able to receive the Sacraments! The Mother of God had kept her promise in the contract between those two mothers! Mechthild had to wait until the day of the funeral to be told about this sign from the Mother of God, to be told that she had been there at the accident's site! She had sent her apostle to make little Inge elegant before God, before she would come and whisk her away herself! Mechthild knew it. She had been right to continue trusting, despite all evidence that Inge had died without the Sacraments!

It Is She Who Embraces the Ones I Embrace

In 2003, a month after Inge's death, Mechthild returned to Medjugorje. She rang our door bell and sat with us around our humble kitchen table. Her heart poured out. What a gentle light in her gaze! She told us about her conversion, the consecration of her children, and most importantly, the last months with Inge.

"In 2001, Inge asked me what I wanted for Christmas. 'I don't want anything for Christmas,' I answered her! 'All I desire is that you go to confession.' I thought that she was going to get mad at this request, but to my surprise she answered: 'OK, but not with Father Gabriel.'"

"You know Inge, you can go to any priest you want! There is a visiting priest at Saint Sophia, if you'd like. Remember that everything the priest hears during confession is secret and confidential, so don't worry, he will not tell me anything.' I asked that priest to come to the house. He invited Inge for a walk, and they went into the countryside. An hour and a half later, I saw them come back and Inge was beaming."

"But, the most beautiful gift I received was when that same priest came back and he told me how deeply he had been affected when he had heard about Inge's accident. He told me: 'You know Mechthild, priests cannot talk about the Confessions they hear. However, there is one thing I can tell you: I always forget the Confessions that I hear, but Inge's Confession, I will never be able to forget! She reviewed her entire life, starting with the moment when she remembered sinning for the first time.'"

"To think she made such a confession was for me a miracle, and the best Christmas present I could receive! I had consecrated Inge in 2001, and from that time on, I had been freed from all major worries about her. I had put her into the hands of her Heavenly Mother and in God's hands, and together They were watching over her. Strangely enough, a month before the accident, Inge had started to dramatically change. She was starting to amend her life! For example, she always kept her promise to be home before midnight. She took great care to speak nicely and to be of service. She was opening up!"

"The night of the accident, what a miracle took place! As she was leaving the house she said to me for the first time in her life: 'I love you mom!' I answered off the cuff, without looking up, 'I love you too.'"

"She turned back around and stepped in the doorway. She told me very seriously: 'But mom, this is real. I truly love you!' They were her last words, it was her last glance."

"My ex-husband was not with us in church for the funeral, of course. But Father Brian noticed a man standing outside, sobbing like a child. Not knowing who he was, Father went to him and asked: 'Are you a member of the family?' The man was so overwhelmed that he could not even answer. So Father Brian asked: 'Are you Inge's father?' And the man nodded."

"I thank God for picking Father Brian for this short but intense encounter. Here too I could see the hand of God. My ex-husband disappeared and I never saw him again. On the evening of the funeral, all of Inge's friends came to the house. They squatted around my kitchen counter and began speaking about her. They bombarded me with questions: they did not understand how Inge could have changed so much, so deeply, in such a short time."

"What did you do to help her change that much, they asked?"[52]

"It is from them that I came to know my daughter! She would talk to them about God and would show them the best of herself. Even today we cannot count all the blessings that came from Inge's death! It's amazing! These young people ask for her help, she is like a friend in Heaven for them, a friend in a high place who can obtain many graces. She is alive!"

"Since the consecrations of my children, I have noticed that my heart is drawn to the young people. The other day a young girl of 17 came to my house and said,

'Mechthild, can I ask you a question? You have a very special way of holding me in your arms. I really feel it is Our Lady who hugs through you. How do you explain that?'

'The answer is simple,' I said, 'I always ask Our Lady to use my arms, so in reality, it is Our Lady who embraces those I embrace.'"

"When I consecrated my children, I did not realize what I was doing. I didn't 'get it.' Something really strikes me now: when He took Inge back, the Lord only took back what belonged to Him. She never was mine. He had put in my trust this child, His great treasure, just for a certain time. This thought gives me such peace! Then I often say to the Lord: 'I thank you Lord for having given me Inge. Thank you for all the time I had with her!'"

"A week before the accident, I was in Medjugorje. I believe Our Lady already had a plan: she wanted to prepare me for this event. To lose a child—she knows what it is like! But from time to time, I want to cry out: 'Lord, soften this pain!' The image that gives me the most consolation is the image of Christ embracing the Cross. Because when He embraces the Cross, He embraces me!'"

---

[52] The great French mystic Marthe Robin used to say: "When the Lord is getting ready to call someone back to Him, He prepares this person unconsciously."

"Dear children! Rejoice with me! My heart is rejoicing because of Jesus and today I want to give Him to you. Dear children, I want each one of you to open your heart to Jesus and I will give Him to you with love. Dear children, I want Him to change you, to teach you and to protect you. Today I am praying in a special way for each one of you and I am presenting you to God so He will manifest Himself in you. I am calling you to sincere prayer with the heart so that every prayer of yours may be an encounter with God. In your work and in your everyday life, put God in the first place. " (December 25, 1987)

19

I TRIED ALL THE TEMPLES IN SINGAPORE

I had just left Singapore and my heart was heavy. May and I were headed to the airport. My mission had just ended after twelve intense days in Malaysia. May insisted that she would give me a ride, and I was happy to be spending my last few hours in Asia with her.

May is Chinese, from Singapore. Her face radiates light and simplicity. Her pure heart makes her a person—as Jesus said about Nathaniel—"in whom there is no guile."[53] Taking advantage of the privacy of the car, May began telling me the most touching story about her conversion. Thank God I was not the one driving—tears would have hidden the road from my eyes!

"I am of Chinese origin and so is my husband. We have two children. As Chinese, we followed the Cult of the Ancestors. God had little importance in our lives. We did not know anything about Christianity, apart from a few churches we had seen in Singapore."

"One day, my husband, even though still young, fell seriously ill. Anguish took hold of me and everything around me began to spin. I knew this was a deadly disease. Without being able to do anything, I watched him suffer as his health deteriorated, slowly, slowly.

---

[53] John 1:47.

Eventually he died. I could not stand the pain I felt inside. I told myself that maybe there was a spiritual reality that could help me understand the meaning of human life and help me get out of my despair. I decided then to go to all the temples in Singapore: Buddhist, Hindu, Tao. In each of these temples, however hard I begged and cried to the gods, my torment remained the same—unbearable."

"Then, I decided to try the Christians. I had been told they had a very good temple. I went there: it is called 'The Church of the Novena.' People constantly flock there to pray Holy hour novenas and also novenas to the Immaculate Heart of Mary. You know, Sister, we took you there the other day! While I was first standing in the Church, I heard a sentence that I did not understand very well, but it plunged so deeply into my heart that I did not have any trouble to remember it, and I often repeated it. It was, 'O my Jesus, forgive us our sins, save us from the fires of hell. Lead all souls to Heaven, especially those in most need of Thy mercy.'[54]

"When I heard this, a peace I had never known before engulfed my heart and I understood clearly that those words were true, were real and that I had to focus on them like a lighthouse in the storm. I had no clue of what those words meant, but I knew it was the truth. I then asked a Catholic to explain to me what they meant. Her words confirmed my feeling and gave me great joy and great peace. That day, the name of Jesus entered into my heart. I really met Jesus, the Christ. At last I was clutching the Living God!"

"From that day on, I started talking to Him, completely trusting, like one talks to her best friend. I asked to be instructed about Christ and my joy continually increased. Now that I have found Christ, I possess an extraordinary treasure like none other. Everyday, every hour, I thank God for having revealed His Son to me and for having saved me through Him."

"Last year, I received Baptism and so did my children. I also like very much the Mother of Jesus. She helps me raise my children! I can't believe I lived that long without Jesus and Mary. They have become everything to me."

---

[54] Prayer taught by the Angel to the Fatima visionaries, in 1917.

For May, as for all who sincerely say to Jesus, "You are everything to me," life turns into a marvelous adventure! Who else but Jesus could fill this Chinese woman's heart and make it sing, "Thou hast turned for me my mourning into dancing!"[55]

---

[55] Ps 30:12.

Dear Children! Advance against Satan by means of prayer. Satan wants to work harder now that you know he is at work. So put on the armor for battle and, with the Rosary in your hand, defeat him!" (August 8, 1985)

20

THE ROSARY OR THE SOVIETS?

Numerous are the cases in history where the Rosary has acted with power. All know its triumph in 1571 at the Battle of Lepanto, preventing the attempted Turkish invasion of Europe.[56] Here is another example, closer to us:

After World War II (1940-1945), Austria was divided into four occupied zones, with the Soviets holding the Eastern part of the country. The capital of Austria, Vienna, was also divided into four sectors. Three years went by under the Soviets' oppressive control. The Austrians could not bear it anymore. But what could 7 million Austrians do against an enemy numbering 220 million! Father Peter Pavlicek, a Franciscan priest, recalled the victory of Lepanto, where the odds were 1 against 3, yet the Turks were defeated by a Rosary procession organized by Pope Pius V.

In 1948, Fr. Pavlicek started an operation known as the Crusade of The Rosary and Repentance.[57] He asked that ten percent of all Austrians commit to praying the Rosary every day for the departure of the Soviets, and 500,000 people made their pledge. They prayed the rosary over a period of seven years. It even became a secular event. In 1955, as the Soviets still occupied part of Austria, 60,000 Catholic faithful marched through the streets of Vienna while praying, with the participation of

---

[56] See, e.g., Mary and the Moslems, available at:
www.catholic.org/featured/sheen.php?ID=1311.

[57] See, The Most Holy Rosary of the Blessed Virgin Mary, available at www.opusangelorum.org/Formation/Holyrosary.html.

some members of the government! Those members were at the same time engaged in negotiations with the occupying forces in order to liberate their country.

The negotiations concluded with a State treaty that stipulated that all the occupying troops had to leave the country. It was a unique event in post-WWII history! The treaty was signed on May 25, 1955. Back from the last round of negotiations in Moscow, the Austrian Chancellor Julius Raab declared: "God came to our rescue!"

The Soviets left the country without one drop of blood being shed (reminiscent of the victories of Joan of Arc, which also saw no bloodshed). No historians or army strategists were able to explain what made the Soviets decide to pull out of this country, which was so strategically desirable for them. It was a door to the West, with very rich soil.

The Soviet withdrawal will remain an enigma to the secular world, but Father A. William from Austria got the answer when he questioned Teresa Neumann, the famous German stigmatic, about it in 1962, three months before she died. "The truth is," she informed him, "it was because of the Rosaries said by the Austrian people!"*

The Rosary in Austria was more successful in freeing the country from the Soviet occupation than were the freedom fighters of Hungary, where 25,000 innocents lost their lives. The Rosary is more efficient than the weapons of man! Why not pray it rather than count on politicians who are more or less reliable? Isn't it urgent to stop right now the interference of the Enemy within our families, our countries, and our world? If it took 500,000 Austrians praying the rosary for seven years to finally oust the Soviets from their country, how many American people are needed today to restore their country and allow the Queen of Peace to implement her plan for peace?

I like this very simple image: When you take the Rosary out of your pocket to pray, just imagine that in fact you are taking Mary's hand. Then, do not let go of it all day long, and she will guide you![58]

* A good biography of the mystic and stigmatist Teresa Neumann, see: A Light Shone in the Darkness, by Doreen Mary Rossman (Queenship Publishing, Goleta CA.)

---

[58] Listen to the CD 'The Rosary with Medjugorje', as well as CD 'The Miracle of the Rosary – Joyful Mysteries'. See the appendix at the end of the book for more information.

Dear Children! It would be a good idea to give up television because after watching some things you are distracted and unable to pray."
(December 8, 1981)

21

THE BOX THAT CREATES A VOID

Laurence, forty years old, is very active in Holland. A Medjugorje pilgrim, she walks with God as a single person and she does not count her pain when working for Our Lady. Her personal experience is an example of how to use freedom well!

"I had not watched television for 15 years. But four months ago, I subscribed to my local cable company. My goal was to not miss big events happening in the world. After only four months I cancelled my subscription, convinced that it was the right decision to make. Why? Because I found that while watching television in the evening, I became empty. Even if I was watching a simple news program, so that later I could pray about what I saw, it didn't work—my prayer was distracted. Every time, it was the same thing: I watched for an hour and then I couldn't pray anymore, because my heart had been hardened and something in me had been disconnected from God, separated from my source. I couldn't pray regarding events in the news as my spirit was in turmoil."

"So I asked myself what was happening. And I found the answer: when I watched television, the spirit of the world entered into my heart. The moment I switched it on, I willingly plugged myself into the spirit of the world. I consciously said 'Yes' to it. Soon this spirit ate away at my insides, at what was linked to God, and I became more and more empty."

"When I decided to get rid of the television, I cancelled my subscription the very next day. As soon as I posted the letter, a great joy entered my heart. I felt immersed in a light and I felt like the Heavens agreed with my decision. So I said to Mary, 'As I am not watching the news anymore, I will dedicate this hour to praying the Rosary.'"

"Since that day, I pray an entire Rosary every evening, and I can tell I am not wasting my time at all!—while I certainly was wasting my time and my spirit when I was watching television. And because I was praying the Rosary, a great desire to fast was born inside me. I can see it clearly: when a person is disciplined in one facet of their life, they receive the strength to grow and become serious in other domains too. Praying the Rosary in the evening gave me the strength and the space to fast with bread and water just like Mother Mary asks us to do."

"I don't want to generalize—this is just my personal way to give God the first place in this area of my life. I was able to discern that, as television is now, to leave it behind is God's will for me! If a person chooses to watch television, it seems to me that great vigilance is required to be protected from the Evil One. He is so active in some programs!"

Avoid Television....

The experience of Laurence fits perfectly with the advice given by Our Lady in Medjugorje to the prayer group. She said, "Renounce all passions and all inordinate desires. Avoid television, particularly evil programs, excessive sports, the unreasonable enjoyment of food and drink, alcohol, and tobacco." (First point in the Rule of Life given to Jelena Vasilj, on June 16, 1983.)

Mary is asking us to turn off the television nine days before the great feasts like Easter, Pentecost and Christmas. She wishes that, like the Jews, families gather around the Bible and discuss the texts that concern that feast.

However, the Gospa did not forbid television. She did not ask that we throw our television sets out. As a mother, she knows that it would be too hard for some of her children. (For those who suffer from depression or excessive solitude, television is sometimes the only way for them to hear other human beings!) Also, some programs are beautiful; it is up to us to work, so that these beautiful programs increase in number!

As for the days of fasting, Our Lady said: *"If you do not have the strength to fast with bread and water, you can give up other things. It would be good to give up television, because, after certain programs, you are distracted and incapable of praying..."* (Dec. 1981) *"When you watch TV programs, your head is filled with the news, and then there is no room left for me in your heart."* (April 17, 1986)

Laurence added: "In the evening, no matter what time it is, I pray in silence for an hour before I go to bed. It is at that time that a great joy comes inside me, and all becomes orderly. Of course, it is important to have some contact with others to grow in the spiritual life, but I realize that, for me, this is only possible after I plunge myself into the presence of God through prayer. First, prayer; then comes the rest! Concretely, if I have to choose between praying and talking to someone, I give priority to prayer. That way I receive the interior freedom that is necessary so that I can be led by the Holy Spirit. It is He who shows me if I should contact someone or not."

How Many Years Did I Lose With This Television On?

Sonia, from Boston, Massachusetts, has 10 children. "I always had the TV on. It was automatic. After my conversion, I understood in my heart that Jesus was inviting me to turn it off. The decision was hard to make. But very quickly I realized that Jesus was talking to me, was guiding me in all the details of my daily life! And I thought: 'How many years did I lose with this television on, while all along Jesus was waiting for this noise to stop so he could talk to me! If only I had known!'"

Colette (USA) wrote to me: "Fifteen years ago, because of the children, we decided not to have a television at home. We have a screen so we can watch DVDs and tapes, that's all. This really cleans up the atmosphere in a big way! Especially in the States, where there are so many channels and so many stupid programs. To do without television is like giving up cigarettes or alcohol. All of a sudden, you feel clean, light, and free! And it gives you time to do other things! Take a walk, read, pray...."

As a Mother, Mary is looking for ways to introduce us to communion with God and our fellow men! As a Queen, she wishes to rule over our communication! Non-stop "communication" and communication in all ways impairs, alters or even stops real communion with others.

Dear Children, tonight your Mother is especially happy to see you. Tonight I want to ask you to give me your problems and difficulties, so that you are able to pray with more freedom and more joy, so that your prayer becomes a prayer of the heart. That is why I wish to ask you to release yourselves from your difficulties through prayer; and I will pray for you. Dear Children, I need your prayers." *(May 11, 1990)*

22

A SIGHT THAT PADRE PIO NEVER FORGOT

It was the year 1896, in the harsh province of Avellino, Italy. Little Francesco, soon to be nine, would not miss for anything the religious services that marked the lives of his fellow Christians in their hard working, peasant community. He sought solitude to say the Rosary, and to have a dialogue with God. He liked to sleep under the stars. When the weather was overcast, he appreciated the hospitality of Aunt Daria, who harbored a special place for him in her heart, and who set a room aside for him at her farm. His favorite refuge was a huge elm tree, where he spent long, reflective hours. There, he already foresaw the hard spiritual combat against the Evil One who was just beginning a long series of humiliations and attacks against little Francesco. God fascinated the soul of little Francesco, and his exceptional fervor was already bothering the powers of darkness.

One day, his father took him to Atavilla Irpina for the annual feast of San Pellegrino, a beloved and venerated martyr in that region. For the occasion, the peasants organized a huge livestock market. Little Francesco's dad, Grazio, went there in order to buy a working horse for the family. The boy was so excited he hardly slept a wink the night before the fair. Early the next morning, he and his dad set out for Irpina, taking along the family donkey for the long walk to the town. They arrived before noon, and managed to find a place inside the already packed church.

The faithful had come from all around the area. They had brought to their beloved saint as signs of love, the most picturesque of devotions—they offered him their petitions with very expressive gestures, even explosive ones! They threw up their arms to the Heavens, crying, laughing, praying. Then, with a loud clatter, they fell to their knees, as if to grab the Saint's attention with the commotion. Some offered him gigantic candles, decorated with very bright colors; others brought flowers or velvet hearts embroidered with gold. This popular display of piety was as touching as it was noisy and colorful. All the people were pressed around the altar, where the portrait of the Saint was displayed. Fortunately, Saint Pellegrino managed to find, among the cacophony, numerous people with sincere hearts, who confided in him genuine prayers of hardships, pains, hopes and desires.

Suddenly, a poor woman dressed in rags, obviously crushed under the miseries of the world, began to harangue the Saint in a loud voice. Her arms drew from under her rags a poor little being, inert and deformed. As she cried out to the Saint, the crowd, taken aback by such a monstrosity, hushed, letting the mother pour her heart out in sorrow.

The woman then thrust forward her little one and launched into a prayer as no one had ever heard. In her pleading, she used words that were rude but well-used in the Avellino dialect, a language rich in colorful expressions. Here is our pleader, openly taking her anger out on the Saint, crushing him with heart-wrenching reproaches:

"Throughout my life, I have honored you. I never missed any of your feasts! So often, I lovingly offered you candles, I brought you presents and I always trusted you for help! I always spoke well of you in the village, and this is how you thank me! You know I live alone and I have no money, and now I am with a deformed child! How am I going to take care of him? Don't you care? You can very well see I am incapable of taking care of this child! Are you going to be the one who will go out in the streets begging to support him? What kind of Saint are you anyway?!"

Her voice was getting louder and louder, and her words were interrupted with heart breaking sobs. Eventually she reached the peak, saying: "You, You are comfortable! You have everything! You are in Heaven! Things are easy for you! If this is what you call sainthood, leaving the suffering people to fend for themselves, well, then I am disgusted! You strut around in your picture frame, but when a heart is struck with sorrow, you don't lift even a finger to help! Well, thanks a lot! What an example of charity you show us! All the prayers I have said to you…. I was so stupid; I should have saved my breath! All you are capable of doing is giving me this completely deformed child…So what are you going to say to me now, huh? Maybe you are expecting me to go back to my village singing your praises? Think again!!!"

The crowd was now still. Nobody dared to utter a word. People wondered if they should feel embarrassed for the woman, or for poor San Pellegrino, who doubtless had never before been so chastised. Francesco wondered what was going to happen next. It couldn't just end like this.

The mother's voice broke down. She had yelled too much, cried too much, bled too much. In a last burst of temerity and faith, she walked up the steps to San Pellegrino's altar.

In the crowd, little Francesco was taking it all in, and with his eyes wide open, he prayed with all his might for this poor devastated mother. But his father roughly pulled him by the arm: "Come, it is time to go!"

"No, wait Daddy, wait!"

Francesco made himself as heavy as lead. His father realized that there was no way Francesco would give in. The scene continued to unravel before them. On the altar, the woman was peeling the rags from her little martyr and she lifted him up like a Host in front of the picture of the Saint, as if to show him she was not joking. Slowly, she placed him down on the altar, while saying: "Here, take him! Keep him, or give him back to me healed!" Then she moved away, determined to obtain justice. In the church, the silence was deafening, one could hear a pin drop.

"Come on Francesco, I must search for this horse!" whispered Grazio.

"No, Daddy, let me stay a little bit more!" Francesco planted his feet. He was determined to see what would happen. The woman stood there, waiting. People started talking again and soon in the church there was the noisy chatter of a feast day.

Suddenly, little Francisco opened his eyes wide: a miracle was taking place! Deep breaths of awe could be heard from the astonished pilgrims as they watched the deformed little baby begin to peacefully roll onto his side. The body of the little child, which was lifeless before like a vegetable, tried to get on to his hands and knees. His limbs straightened out and they looked normal. The noise that rose from the crowd was unbelievable. Grazio, pushed left and right by the crowd, attempted to leave, but was forced back inside by a wave of new pilgrims who wanted to get in and see what had happened. Now, the bells of the church began to give voice to this event, as the local custom demanded it when a miracle of San Pellegrino took place.

Everyone in the church could witness that the child was definitely healed. The members of his body were now in harmony. The great, the beloved, the venerated San Pellegrino had performed another miracle, under their very eyes. Touched to the core of his soul, little Francesco never really recovered from the shock. He would later become the great Padre Pio, the exceptional intercessor configured to Christ even in his flesh. Later he would recount to his dear ones that event at San Pellegrino and the enormous impact it had on his prayer life. And he would always add with gravity:

"On that day, I learned how to pray!"[59]

---

[59] Among his close ones was Padre Domenico Labellante, the trustworthy companion of Padre Pio's last twelve years. Padre Domenico himself confirmed this event to me when we met at San Giovanni Rotondo in July 2003. Numerous times, he had heard this story from Padre Pio, who loved to cite the faith of this woman as a wonderful example.

"Dear children! You are the ones responsible for the messages. The source of grace is here, but you, dear children, are the vessels which transport the gifts. Therefore, dear children, I am calling you to do your job with responsibility. Each one shall be responsible according to his own ability. Dear children, I am calling you to give the gifts to others with love and not to keep them for yourselves" (May 8, 1986)

23

HAVE YOU EVER THOUGHT OF BECOMING A PRIEST?

April 2001

In Ruzica's pension, there were sixty Canadian pilgrims hurrying toward the dining room. That night, they were going to have a farewell cake, and they would share with one another all the graces they had received during their pilgrimage. Some had experienced healings, others had received light for their path in life. Everyone anticipated a beautiful evening together! The following day, the plane would take them back to the Northwest Territories and surrounding areas, to the most frigid areas of Canada. Their stay in Medjugorje was coming to an end, and they didn't want to miss a bit of it!

Larry, the group leader, seemed satisfied. It was a decent group, no big problems or unpleasant surprises; the week had been rich in encounters, prayers, Sacraments and multiple blessings. The Gospa had worked well in many hearts, but Larry's serenity was about to be disturbed: a man came to him and whispered in his ear that he wanted to use the microphone for a while, because he had an important announcement to make to the group. It was Denis, a rather discreet man whom Larry had, frankly, hardly noticed the whole eight days.

Larry looked him up and down, barely concealing his annoyance. He had everything organized another way, and he feared the unexpected. But, the man seemed normal and levelheaded, and he was quite determined; Larry felt he had to grant his request, even as he wondered, "What could he possibly have to say that is so important?" He asked him: "Well, what's it about?"

"Don't worry," Denis replied. "Everything's fine! I'm the bishop of Yellowknife. I want to let the group know who I am and share some things about the pilgrimage."

Larry caught his breath, mute with astonishment. He started trembling and his cheeks turned a little red from embarrassment. "Yes!" he managed to get out, while forcing a smile. "Of course! I'll announce that you have something to say…this is wonderful!"

Denis walked with Larry toward the microphone, joyful and relaxed. "We have a special guest," declared Larry. "I'll let him introduce himself to you!"

"Hi! I am Bishop Denis Croteau, OMI, from the Mackenzie diocese in Northen Canada. My residence is in Yellowknife, Northwest Territories. I wish to…."

The group had been ready for almost anything, but not this flash of news! Then it exploded with joy. The applause was thundering. Some stood up and patted one another on the back, others laughed, still others cried with emotion. Larry applauded, too, all the while reliving in his head, with a certain apprehension, each of his talks, each of his attitudes towards Denis. They had had a bishop in their midst and they had not even known it!

Bishop Denis Croteau did not let the commotion go to his head. He explained why he had chosen to come incognito:

I came to Medjugorje like Msgr. Paolo Hnilica. Upon his return from Russia, in March 1984, he had met with Pope John Paul II. The Pope asked him, 'Paolo, did you go through Medjugorje?' He answered, 'No, Your Holiness.' The Pope persisted, 'Why didn't you go?' 'The Vatican advised me not to go.' The Pope made a little gesture that meant, it's Okay—forget the Vatican! Then the Holy Father added: 'Go there incognito, come back and tell me what you have seen.'"

"I live in Yellowknife, in the Northwest Territories," Bishop Croteau continued. "I have kept my distance and not mingled too much with the group for fear that I would betray my identity or blow my cover as they say in "spy" language. Why? For two reasons:

"First I had been told that priests who come to Medjugorje receive special treatment while here. And on top of that, they sit in the Sanctuary of the church and are not really part of the crowd. They are asked to work, to hear confessions, to bless the religious articles, etc. I wanted to come to Medjugorje as a regular pilgrim. I wanted to taste the full flavor of the pilgrimage as an ordinary baptized Catholic. No first class treatment. I did not want to 'live' Medjugorje from the Sanctuary, but from the pew. Easier said than done! Try to live a whole week with a group of sixty fellow-pilgrims without even once talking about who you are and what you do for a living! Even for a bishop it is no small task! I should say it is even doubly difficult!

"Try to deflect the justified questions of my roommate, Edmond, inquiring about who I was without even telling a white lie. I am afraid I would have had to abuse the sacrament of confession as my contrition wouldn't have been very sincere for such lies!

"One day, the conversation went like this:

Ed: 'Denis, what is it you do in life?'

The Bishop: 'I work for the Church, in Catholic Teaching.'

Ed: 'Ah, you teach in a Catholic school?'

The Bishop: 'No, I work at the Diocesan level.'

"Those questions were giving me just enough time to direct the conversation toward less dangerous subjects. Another day, Edmond came back at the subject:

Ed: 'Did you leave a family behind?'

The Bishop: 'No, I don't have a family.'

Ed: 'So, you are not married?'

The Bishop: 'No, I am single.'

Ed: 'Have you ever thought of becoming a priest?'

The Bishop: 'You know, since Vatican II, lay people are given ample opportunities to serve the Church in a meaningful way, without becoming priests or sisters.'

"This was like walking on a tightrope! After such a week in Medjugorje, I am convinced that I could have had a second vocation and work for the KGB!"

"The other reason I came to Medjugorje was to see for myself what it was all about and if it would be worth letting my friends organize a pilgrimage for the people of my diocese. To make that discovery, I had to live Medjugorje as a regular pilgrim. I came, I saw, and I was won over. Medjugorje is all that it is claimed to be!"

"I came here under "pressure". My little sister, Micheline, kept feeding me with information, books, and articles. She is a very determined little woman. She finally got me hooked."

"I have been a missionary priest in the Canadian North for more than forty years. I work mostly with the Dene (Indian) people and with Inuit (Eskimo). They have a great devotion to Mary. Their favorite devotion is the recitation of the Rosary. They would be in Heaven coming to Medjugorje! They would be strengthened, their faith would be rejuvenated, they would be delighted like fish in a pond and they would adopt Medjugorje."

"In closing, let me tell you how much I appreciated this experience. It has been highly spiritual. I understand now why people who come here always want to come back. It is special. It is unique. I realize that I could have been a more talkative companion, but I reached my goal. There is a price to pay for everything we want. My hope now is that one day we will be again on the same plane, the same bus heading in the same direction that is Medjugorje, where we leave part of our hearts."

One year later, Monsignor Croteau came back to Medjugorje overtly as a Bishop, with a group from his region. His sister Micheline, this time, organized the pilgrimage. At the end of this second visit, he gave the following testimony:

"What strikes me is the piety and devotion of the people, the faith and the testimonies we have received here. We have seen people of prayer, people who believe, people who live their Christian experience of faith and love. These are people on fire. It's wonderful! I have tried all sorts of things in my diocese to transform my faithful, because we live in a dysfunctional society, and I have spent thousands and thousands

127

of dollars on sessions and workshops. But, after having spent all that money, I did not accomplish ten per cent of what was accomplished here in one pilgrimage. So, you have in me someone who will heartily recommend a pilgrimage to Medjugorje!"

"The highlight for me has been hearing confessions. For a priest, it might be the best place to really know and discover what Medjugorje is all about. I can't conceive of a priest coming here and hearing confessions for an hour without being convinced—-absolutely convinced, that Heaven is at work in Medjugorje. We can touch with our finger the work of Mary and the work of God in listening to people and the way they are transformed. Some come here and are just good people, but when they leave, they are much better Christians. Others come here as sinners, and they know it (sometimes not), but by the time they leave, they know they were sinners and they know they are saved and that their sins are forgiven. The priest experiences this first hand. And if someone told me it is Satan who is at work in Medjugorje, I would say, 'Well, that's a very poor devil! I don't think he belongs to Hell, he's obviously doing the work of Heaven! I think he ought to be promoted to Heaven!'"

*Dear Children! Tonight especially I would like to invite all parents in the world to find time for their children and families. May they offer love to their children and may that love be parental and motherly love".
(July 31, 1989)*

24

THE SATURDAY NIGHT SUICIDES

The need for adoration is so powerful in the heart of man, that no one can resist it for long. True atheists or unbelievers do not exist. There are only people who turn to the wrong gods.60 As they haven't experienced yet the love of the Living God, the Real God, they search elsewhere. Everyone deep down has his own potential for adoration and he places it somewhere. If he does not adore the Living God, then his adoration will turn to a human being, an activity or a thing, and this is the tragedy of idolatry that sooner or later leads to despair.

All of us thirst. We thirst for life, for love or to be loved, we thirst for a kind of happiness that does not expire. By drinking life directly at the everlasting source in the Heart of God, we will always have bliss, even on the chaotic paths of our human existence. On the other hand, if we turn to the puny little cisterns of life to quench our thirst, they will run dry sooner or later. Then we will dry out, become angry, and die of thirst.

My psychiatrist friends have noticed a common trend in France: they see the largest number of suicides between Saturday night and Sunday morning. The emergency units are well equipped for this phenomena they call "the Saturday night virus." This is a product of the West, with its materialism pushed to the limit, a virus that attacks the gentlest and most vulnerable of all people: our young ones. This is why Our Lady comes to Medjugorje! Her heart of a mother cannot tolerate the terrible

---

[60] The Gospa does not use the word "unbeliever," but she uses instead the phrase: "those who do not yet know the love of God."

suffering of these young people, who have been broken down by despair and who would rather die than face emptiness inside. For them, she holds the keys that can get them out of their prisons. Those she has already saved, through her intervention in Medjugorje, are countless!

I can still picture the couple who approached me in the church parking lot one day and timidly asked me: "Please Sister, could you pray for our son Mark?"

"Yes, of course!," I said, seeing so much distress in their eyes. They were about to go when I dared to ask them, "Is he having problems? Is he sick?"

There was a dead silence. After a long pause, the man murmured to his wife: "Go on, I can't. You tell her."

"Well, Sister, last week my husband went into the attic to find something, and there he found our son, hanging!"

The shock hit me like a blast of fire and I couldn't utter a single word. I was totally mute! Suddenly, I could see in front of me two hearts, cut into pieces. I tried in vain to hold back my tears.

Then she added: "Sister, we came here immediately after the funeral. We could not bear staying at home. We loved him so much. We had told him again and again: 'Mark, this girl is not for you, she will leave you like she left the others before you!' But he did not listen to us. We could see he was in love and it overpowered him. When things were not good between them, he started using drugs. And Sister...."

"Sister," the father interrupted, "could you tell us where he is? Is he happy now? How do we find out?"

They left the parking lot without hearing one word from me. My heart had just cut off the sound from my mouth. But as I was holding their hands in mine, I couldn't hold back my tears any longer, and I know they felt they had been heard and understood. Fortunately, I saw them the next day in church.

Never Again!

This is the cry we utter to the Heavens when others confide in us this way. And our little cry is only a pale echo of the heart of Our Mother who sees her children dying from emptiness. She came to stop this massacre! She came to deposit in our hearts the Hidden Child she held in her arms in Bethlehem; the One who alone has the power to fulfill us, beyond our most secret desires.

Young Mark left too early. He too could have received this great gift from Mary and he could have been saved! But for the other "Marks" who are now facing the abyss, there is still time![61] There is still time for us to do something about their emptiness! Mary gives us the key in these few words: "Dear little children, put God into the first place in your lives, and you will be on a secure path with Him." (Message for the Youth Festival, 1996)

On August 2, 2005, in the midst of the Youth Festival, Our Lady came to pray for the "unbelievers" with Mirjana, as she does every month. Thousands of young people from all countries had gathered to welcome their Mother, to pray to her and to receive her blessing. The message we received after the apparition was very shocking! The situation it describes is very real, we can't deny it and we can't gloss over it! It would be good to learn this message by heart and to ask for the grace of the Holy Spirit that He takes an X-ray of our hearts. Through those divine rays, may He reveal the contents of what our hearts really contain. That way, we will be able to review our choices! We will decide to host in our hearts the True Love and not the fake one, the True Light and not the false shimmering, the world constantly puts upon us.

Mary said: "Dear Children, I came to you with open arms, so I could embrace all of you, under my mantle. I can't do it while your hearts are full of false shimmering and false idols. Purify your hearts and allow my Angels to sing in them. Then I will be able to take you under my mantle and I will give you my Son, the true peace and happiness. Do not delay my children! I thank you." (Message to Mirjana, August 2, 2005).

---

[61] In Amsterdam in 1954, Our Lady recommended to the seer Ida to say and have others say every day this prayer that she gave to her. In view of the increasing calamity of suicides (more than one an hour in France), it is something worth remembering. Prayer to Our Lady of All Nations: "Lord Jesus Christ, Son of the Father, send now your Spirit over the earth. Let the Holy Spirit live in the hearts of all Nations, that they may be preserved from degeneration, disaster and war. May the Lady of All Nations, the Blessed Virgin Mary, be our advocate. Amen." Ecclesiastic approbation : Harlem, May 31, 1996.

In view of the increased number of suicides among young people and the general poisoning of our society, Our Lady's cry became even more poignant on January 2, 2006, in her message to Mirjana: "My children! My son is born! He is here with you. What in your hearts prevents you from receiving him? What is false in them? Purify your hearts through prayer and fasting. Recognize my son and welcome him. He alone can give you true peace and true love. The path to eternal life is him, it is my son! I thank you."

Dear Children! Teach your own children because if you are not an example to them, children will fall into godlessness." *(August 25, 1989)*

25

PAULINE!

She was 18 and hadn't been baptized yet.

"Before I came to Medjugorje, I had really hit rockbottom. My parents are atheist. When I was 9, they divorced. After that, I let myself be taken in by all the evils in society. At 13, I started doing drugs. My broken family slowly reduced me to a state of fear and closing up within myself. I would go forward without feeling, without seeing, without living, like a zombie. 'Emptiness'—that is the word that describes very well my inward disposition. I threw myself into the 'pleasures of the flesh,' and I fell apart. I took refuge in my work. Last summer, I attempted to commit suicide, and when I woke up in the hospital, I realized that life was just horrible. I had no way out, no future."

"I had a Catholic friend, Alice. Her life had changed after coming back from Medjugorje, and every time she would talk to me about Mary, I could feel light coming into me. At the end of July, she called me: 'Pauline, I am going to Medjugorje and I have booked three seats—one is for you. Come!'"

"It was a shock to me, because I felt Alice's words were a calling. I immediately said 'yes.' However, I had a summer job, as an extra on a film set, and I could not quit. Also, I had no money for the trip. So I asked my dad, without much hope, because he had told me in the past that he was done helping me. But, miracle of all miracles, he immediately said 'yes' for half the amount. My mom gave me the other half. Another sign was given to me: the film studio informed me that there was to be a ten day break in the filming, just at the right time!"

"I arrived in Medjugorje on the last day of the Youth Festival. I went to the evening Adoration, then we climbed Mount Krizevac for the Mass at dawn. It was the Feast of Transfiguration. As I was climbing, I tried to experience this time with God, but I couldn't concentrate in prayer. I felt only emptiness. When I got to the top, I paced back and forth; I could not stand still. I felt so tormented inside. Finally I left the Mass before the end and went down the mountain alone. It was just like I had heavy armor around my heart. It made me suffocate and it was blocking God out. I wanted God but I could not get Him."

"I was not baptized, and at that moment I understood the importance of Baptism."

"A boy from my region, Pierick, told me, 'Pauline, you have to go to Confession!'"

"He was right. But the idea of telling all my sins to a priest stressed me out completely. I could see all of my faults and I was thinking: 'How am I going to say this? And that? It's too horrible, I can't do this!' But, I did it anyway. It was my first Confession, and I did not know one had to be baptized to receive the Sacrament! Right from the beginning, the priest seemed to perceive very clearly the immense wound that was inside me and he told me the solution: to take Mary as my mother and to become again like a little baby in her womb. What seemed to matter to him about my Confession was not to take my sins into account but rather to have me welcome the Heart of the God who was waiting for me and who was suffering with me."

"During the confession and the blessing that followed, the emptiness that had been inside of me disappeared! And I cried for joy. I was laughing! It was like all the evil that had built up inside me since the beginning was coming out of me. I could feel all the filth leaving me. After that, joy kept coming into my heart more and more every day; at last I could pray with the heart! Now, I would get up early every morning to say my prayers. I experienced the feeling of being filled for the first time. I could feel God healing me."

"In Medjugorje, I filled my open wounds with the love that Mary gave me through Our Lord. I know the road will be long and tough. 'Be strong and hold on!'—those words keep coming back to me." Now

I know that it is impossible for me to consider life without the Holy Trinity. The truth is there. It is so good to be happy!"

Pauline is being prepared for Baptism. Let us entrust to the Gospa Pauline as well as the thousands of young people who suffer today like Pauline did before she met God.

Living Water for Thousands of Young People!

Sister Briege McKenna[62] told me this very significant episode: in May 1981, she met a priest from Yugoslavia, Father Tomislav Vlasic. He asked her to pray for his parish and for his country. This was a difficult time, when the Government was strongly fighting the Church. Because he was responsible for the youth in Herzegovina, he was very sad to see how the Communists, through their alluring promises, were attracting many young Catholics and getting them to sign up. These young people would then leave the Church and join the Party.

In prayer, Sr. Briege received a vision that she described as follows: She saw a white church with two steeples. Father Tomislav was sitting in the main celebrant's chair in the church, and streams of Living Water were coming down from the altar. Many young people were coming forward, and using their hands as a cup, they were avidly drinking this water flowing from the altar. After having quenched their thirst they would go back home, and then would return to the church, bringing along with them their friends who, in turn, would happily come to the stream of Living Water and drink of it. Sr. Briege saw thousands of young people coming in this way and inviting more and more young people their age to come and drink of this water.

Father Tomislav felt consoled by this vision, as the church described by Sr. Briege was his church, the church of Medjugorje! About one month later, on June 25th, Our Lady appeared for the first time in Medjugorje, choosing six young people to be her witnesses. Since 1989, the Youth Festival has taken place every summer in Medjugorje, bringing thousands of young people who there find meaning for their lives and, in many cases, conversion of their hearts.

---

[62] See Chapter 7.

Dear Children! This evening I call you in a special way to pray for all unborn children. Pray especially for the mothers who consciously kill their children. Dear children, I am sad because so many children are being killed. Pray that there will be as few as possible of these cases in the world." *(July 21, 1982)*

26

THE TENDERNESS OF CHILDREN

The Poor and the Gifted

Adam was one of the top students in his 3rd grade class. Everything seemed to come so easily to him. One day, the teacher announced that the students would be allowed extra recess time as soon as they completed their math problems! The whole class was excited, and the students hurried to finish their assignment. But, the teacher noticed that little Freddie was lagging behind. Freddie was under heavy medication to control his convulsions, which caused him to work very slowly. No recess for him that day....

Then she saw Adam, who had just finished his assignment, heading for Freddie's table to give him a hand. Adam encouraged Freddie as he waited patiently for him to finish. The teacher felt a lump forming in her throat as she watched this eight year old perform such an act of mercy and compassion. She was witnessing mercy in action.

This is a true story that happened in March of 2001—children are good teachers! Adam didn't make Freddie wait long to come to his aid.

Our Lady tells us to "Be merciful from the heart. Perform good deeds and don't let people wait for you too long."[63] (To Mirjana, March 18, 2001)

---

[63] Similarly, St. Faustina encourages us not only to implore Divine Mercy, but to live it too. Jesus told her: "I demand from you deeds of mercy, which are to arise out of love for Me. . . . I am giving you three ways of exercising mercy toward your neighbor: the first—by deed, the second—by word, the third—by prayer. In these three degrees is contained the fullness of mercy." (Sr. Faustina's Diary, Paragraph 742)

Little Mikey

Michael and Annie (USA) have three children, and they have been living the school of Our Lady since their wedding. They express a joy that touches everyone who comes in contact with them. One day, their young four year-old son Mikey was listening to his uncle Joseph (nine years old!) telling him the story of The Little Red Hen:

The Little Red Hen found a grain of wheat and asked all the other farm animals: "Who wants to help me plant the grain of wheat? No one answered. "OK, I'll plant it myself!"

"Who will help me to water the wheat?" No one answered. "OK, I'll water it myself!"

"Who's going to help me harvest the wheat?" No reply. "Mill the wheat?" Still no answer, and so on, until comes the time to eat the bread. Of course, now, all the animals wanted to help eat it! But The Little Red Hen said, "I don't think so! Nobody came to help me cultivate the wheat, so my little chicks and I, we'll eat the bread all by ourselves!"

At this point, little Mikey interrupted the story teller vehemently: "If the Little Red Hen had been Jesus, she still would have given them her bread anyway!"

Protect My Soul, Jesus!

There was a family in the U.S. that was very close-knit and prayed together at night as the Gospa asks us to. The children were used to hearing their parents speak about Jesus as the family's best friend – The Good Shepherd they always turned to. Colin was one of their six boys, and Cathy, his mother, told us this story as a sign of how much divine protection was upon them.

One evening, as she was putting her little three year old Colin to bed, he said to her, "Mom, I hear a voice at night that says, 'Colin, your soul will go to hell!'"

"Oh, Colin," she replied, "don't listen to that. Pray to Jesus and He'll take care of you!"

"I did," he said, "and Jesus told me what to answer." Cathy then asked him what Jesus had told him. Colin replied: "Jesus told me,

'Colin, when you hear that, say, '"Jesus, keep my soul!"' Indeed, if Jesus is for us, we have nothing to worry about.[64]

She Was Smiling at Me

In Newry, Ireland, Fr. Tony, O.P., told me of the time when Ivan, the visionary, visited his parish of Saint Catherine in March of 1995. On that day, Ivan received his apparition before Mass, in the presence of 2,000 people gathered in prayer.

The next day, a twelve year-old girl, Elena, told her teacher; "I had two Masses in church yesterday!"

"Really?," asked the teacher surprised.

"Yep!," answered the little girl. Actually, Elena, who was mentally handicapped and reasoned like a five year-old, had mistaken the prayer before the apparition for a Mass. Here's what she innocently told the teacher:

"During the first Mass, Our Lady of Lourdes came, and she spoke with a man. I couldn't hear what she was saying, but she smiled at me." (Elena mentioned Our Lady of Lourdes because she, herself, had been to Lourdes with her dad who volunteered every year as a stretcher-bearer for the sick. So, "Our Lady of Lourdes" is the only name that she knew for Mary.)

The teacher reported this conversation to Elena's parents, who in turn asked their daughter to tell them what had happened. They heard the same story word for word. When they asked her what Our Lady looked like, Elena answered: "Our Lady of Lourdes had a blue-grey dress on and she had a white thing over her head. I could see her hair. She was smiling at me. There were some colored lights behind her, like Christmas lights. She was all shiny and she had something like water falling behind her."

The Dominican priest was familiar with this family and he was able to interview the little girl personally. What he received from her was the exact same story that the teacher and her parents had heard. Not a single word was added or omitted. The father explained to me that the

---

[64] Cf. Rom 8:31.

lights mentioned by Elena were probably the stars that crown Mary's head in Medjugorje.

The most marvelous fruit of this event can be seen in Elena. From that day forward, her demeanor changed drastically; she now beams with joy and has become much more open. Isn't it wonderful that, among the 2,000 people present, Our Lady chose to be seen by a handicapped child? What a beautiful example Mary left us by showing such kindness toward a precious little life that today's world would be so quick to ignore![65]

Don't Be Afraid to Have Children!

After one of Our Lady's apparitions, in August of 1984, Fr. Tomislav Vlasic, O.F.M., went to meet with a group of four Italian couples whom I know well. One of the ladies, Rita, is the one who brought back to Civitavecchia[66] from Medjugorje the famous statue that has cried tears of blood on fourteen occasions. Her daughter, a member of the Famiglia di Maria community in Rome, told me the following story:

Fr. Tomislav Vlasic[67] conveyed to them what Our Lady had just said during her apparition to the visionaries: "You have so few children! Have children! Do not be afraid to have children. Before they become your children, they are my children. Consecrate them to my Immaculate Heart."

Among the four women present, my friend Rita was in her forties and had five children already. Another woman, a gynaecologist, had been trying for a long time to have a child but to no avail. A third one was sterile, and the fourth one had been made permanently sterile through human intervention. They accepted the message and, what is extraordinary, is that the three women who had not been made sterile

---

[65] After confession, Christ gave Sr. Faustina these words: "Because you are a child, you shall remain close to My Heart. Your simplicity is more pleasing to Me than your mortifications." (Sr. Faustina's Diary, Paragraph 1617)

[66] In Civitavecchia (just outside of Rome) in 1997, a small statue of Our Lady that had been brought back from Medjugorje cried tears of blood fourteen times. The last time, she cried in the hands of Msgr. Girolamo Grillo, local Bishop. Jesus has suggested that we should read the signs of times.

[67] At that time, Fr. Tomislav Vlasic was spiritual advisor to all the visionaries, as well as to the young people of the prayer group. Our Lady spoke of him saying: "He leads you well."

by human hands all became pregnant right there, in Medjugorje, during their pilgrimage in August 1984. All three had a lot of problems with their pregnancies and were mostly confined to bed rest, but three babies were born, alive and well, and they now are the joy of their parents.

The Massacre of the Innocent....

Medjugorje, 1985.

Mirjana's daily apparitions had already ended and she was having one annual apparition every March 18th. It was probably during one of those that the following event took place. Adriana, a great friend of Medjugorje, was present with a few other people in a tiny room at Mirjana's house for her apparition. When Mirjana came out of ecstasy looking devastated, my friends asked her what had happened. Mirjana made a face that conveyed alarm and shock. Our Lady had spoken to her about the secrets, and Mirjana told them that she had witnessed some very painful scenes where even children perished.[68] In one such scene where children were victims in the drama, Mirjana asked Our Lady: "But God is good; how can He allow such things to happen?" So Our Lady explained to her that He wasn't the one doing these things, but man, who doesn't listen to God. Then she added something very important: "In the church today, as two thousand years ago in Bethlehem, the slaying of the innocent goes on. This sacrifice is connected to the sacrifice of Jesus crucified."

From the Mouth of Children

The following are jewels gleaned from the notebook pages of children who offered prayers and sacrifices to Our Lady:

---

[68] Jelena also, the visionary from the heart, has seen some difficult scenes. Some secrets were difficult to hear for some of the visionaries, and Our Lady told them that the Lord had granted them the grace to forget, that is to say that some of the things they have learned are suppressed from their memory to allow them to live a normal life not being aware of them, while still being able to carry them.

Their Prayers:

"Pray for those who are never happy." (Silouane, 9)

"Lord, use my prayer for the man who drinks the most." (Pierre, 9)

"Grant that I go to Heaven, and my sister, and my mom and daddy and my dog and my hamster, and my sister's hamster, and that I love everybody—except devils." (Dana, 7)

"Dear God. I can't wait to do my First Communion so that I can receive you in me." (Myriam, 10)

"My prayer—a big rosary bead." (Jo, 7)

Their Sacrifices:

"To clean up my cat's throw-up instead of letting my parents do it. I ate the burnt toast instead of letting the others eat them." (Marie-Reine, 12)

"I walked six miles to stop abortions." (John, 10 – USA)

"I found a dime and I gave it to a poor lady." (Myriam, 10)

Their Inspirations:

When I was in Argentina, a friend told me this story; "I explained to my six year-old, Magdalena, that my husband and I, as her parents, aren't her creators. I said that God is the only true source of life, and He had put her in our care to help her live and grow in holiness in this world—that we are like instruments of God in her life."

Two days later, I overheard her explaining all this to her cousin of the same age. This is how it came out: "Well, you know, Roberto, I'm telling you, they're not really your parents. God and Mary are your real parents. Your parents and my parents, they're just like baby-sitters!"

"Dear Children! I invite you to decide for God and He will protect you and show you what you should do and which path to take. I invite all those who have said "yes" to me to renew their consecration to my Son Jesus and to His Heart and to me so we can take you more intensely as instruments of peace in this unpeaceful world. Medjugorje is a sign to all of you and a call to pray and live the days of grace that God is giving you. Therefore, dear children, accept the call to prayer with seriousness. I am with you and your suffering is also mine.' (April 25, 1992)

27

VICKA'S WORDS OF WISDOM

The Value of Suffering

As I was writing this Chapter, Vicka, the visionary, was in great pain. For weeks, she lay in bed, unable to move or meet with the pilgrims. One day she had bent down to pick up something, and straightening herself up too quickly, she had thrown her back out and herniated two discs, leaving her in excruciating pain. She used to visit the sick tirelessly, to comfort them and share Jesus and Mary's love with them, but now, she was doing even more—sharing their distress from her sickbed. She prayed more than ever.

During the '80s, Vicka suffered acute physical pain. The Gospa often instructed her on the hidden value of suffering when it is offered to God. "Very few people understand the great value of suffering," she told Vicka. "If they only knew how many graces they could earn for themselves and for others."

It is true that our western materialism does not prepare us to accept suffering in this way; rather, we reject it or even rebel against it. Vicka likes to share these words of Mary with pilgrims: "Dear children, when you are in pain you say: *'Why me? Why couldn't this happen to someone else?' And then you think that Jesus and I are far from you. You shouldn't talk like that, my dear children. Jesus and I are always close to you!*

Instead, open your hearts and you'll understand just how much we do love you. Dear children, when you are sick, say to God: 'Lord, I thank you for the gift you are giving me.'"

Vicka knows from experience that suffering endured in this manner becomes "the path to joy."

Vicka: No Compromising His Work

Chrissey has been working with us for over five years. The visionaries have become familiar with her and she sometimes asks them interesting questions that we could also have asked.

Question: "How do you decide where you go on your missions; is it based on the invitations you receive?"

Vicka: "As you know, people constantly ask us to go see them. We receive those requests night and day! No, the important thing is to reflect in my own heart: 'What does the Gospa need of me at this time?' I receive so many invitations from countries that have material resources and I could spend all my time in America or Italy. No, I also have to listen to those who have nothing, to those in countries who face great hardships, and I tell myself: 'I will respond when the Gospa puts a sign in my heart!' I wait in peace, and sure enough, she shows me the right time, the right place, and the way she wants me to spread her messages. When a sign comes, you know it. You can feel it, it's obvious. Even if my friends push me to go where they live, I must not take that into account because friendship has nothing to do with missions. Missions are something else. You cannot decide to take trips just to please your friends. You must go with what your heart tells you in prayer, and stick to it. You have to be strong. The important thing is to move on in peace and the way God is showing you in your heart."

These words from Vicka can be a lot of help to anyone with a strong desire to be an instrument in Our Lady's plans. In fact, when conflicts surface, or pressure builds up in group efforts for a mission, a retreat, or any activity, it is a great blessing to be able to share the same goal and to be able to say together: "Now let's pray and open our hearts to receive what God has in store for us!" How are we going to put ourselves at Jesus and Mary's disposal and find out what their plans are—and not put our own plans first? When we really seek God first, our only concern is to please Him. It's really obvious. We all have experienced the fact that God blesses the efforts of those who make no compromise between His work and other priorities."

Vicka: An Example of Confidence in God

The village is quiet in winter. Pilgrims are few and that gives more time for shopkeepers and the visionaries to spend with their families around the fireplace. At the end of January, a Chinese woman named Yvonne came to live with the Community of the Beatitudes in Medjugorje. She was saying that it must be easy for the visionaries to discern God's will. "Since they see Our Lady everyday," she said, "they know how to stay on the right path. But, for us, how can we know what God wants in our lives and how can we be sure that we're right?"

We asked Vicka if she could shed some of her light on this. She gave a warm welcome to this pilgrim from China. Vicka beamed with such joy and heavenly love that she looked like she was holding a magic key to peace. Indeed, she traced a straight line that leads to happiness, but there's nothing magical about it! Vicka had a conversation with Yvonne as follows:

Vicka: "People who think themselves witty and intelligent," she said, "do things according to their own plans, not concerned with God's plan. They fail because of pride, and they have to face a multitude of obstacles to complete their projects in their quest for God."

Yvonne: "For myself, I pursue my own goals, maybe out of pride, but also because I need to know what's going to happen, step by step."

Vicka: "You know, there are a lot of people who say they want to do God's will. But in reality, when it comes to choosing a path, they choose what they like best and what gives them the most pleasure. But it isn't possible to follow God's will only sometimes, and the rest of the time follow our own feelings! Many people say: 'Lord, show me the way,' but in reality, in their heart, they haven't made the firm resolution to put God first. They continue to pick and choose with Him and they never find peace. After a while they find themselves at an impasse, and end up suffering much. Then they turn to God and cry out: 'Lord, why have you let this happen to me?' Unfortunately, those people have created their own problem! But God is merciful. When you follow

Him, He arranges everything for you. When you start out firmly intent on realizing God's plan for your own life, God sees your goodwill and hands everything down to you. God is always ready to give! And if you make a wrong turn, He is always ready to pick you up again in His arms to comfort you. But if you have to go back to the starting point because of your wrong turn, see how much time you will lose! There is no time to waste! All you need to do is ask God whatever you need and then offer yourself to receive His graces. Many people do not ask God for graces. God can be found in the heart of each person. Everybody knows, somehow, that God exists, but some avoid thinking about Him and refuse to admit that He exists."

Yvonne: Isn't it right to follow our own feelings? Don't our feelings also come from God?

Vicka: "You have to consider God's will first if you want to have this feeling of peace in your heart and inner security. You can't feel well if you have fear in your heart. You can't trust your feelings if you do not have inner harmony. Strive first to love and to be happy with yourself. When something comes from God, you have great joy, a great peace and harmony. When you feel fear, confusion and anguish, it comes from the Enemy. If your project is God's will, you'll have problems, sure, but He'll make your path smooth. When you do God's will, He gives you everything you need, and problems and hurdles end up disappearing."

Yvonne: "That seems so easy for you!"

Vicka: "Don't have great expectations. Take it one step at a time. Nothing will happen overnight! Usually, the hardest part is to get going. You have to start slowly to be able to understand and listen to God's will. Day after day, learn to listen to God's will; you'll find out that God's graces are on your side. You will receive God's graces after you start doing His will. Sometimes God wants to test us to see how strongly we really want to do His will. God wants you to choose and sometimes you'll be struggling with what attracts you and other alternatives. God gives each one of us a great gift: free will. He wants you to use your freedom and to choose. God doesn't want to force us into anything. Sometime we'll fail by making the wrong choice, but God is merciful—He expects that. As long as we show genuine efforts to follow Him, God will help us."

Yvonne: How can we come to terms with those feelings that haunt us?

Vicka: "Fear nothing—reject them and give them to God. You won't be able to pray unless you prevent those worries from penetrating your being. You know, Satan always tries to plant confusion in our hearts. So, remain conscious of Satan's presence and his actions, and never let him act in your heart! He wants to inject worries and fear into it and upset you in all kinds of ways. Simply hand all of that over to God and accept His peace. Most people have no idea how much God wants to give to us and to what extent He loves us! You have no reason to be afraid!"

What Have I Done to Help Them?

After her wedding, Vicka kept her promise to remain at her "post," speaking to pilgrims. She set for herself a schedule of alternate days to speak to them at the "blue house," her old family home. She has been delivering the messages from there since 1981, with the same enthusiasm and the same love as she did the first day!

In between pilgrim groups, while she was speaking at the "blue house," I asked her about the wave of law suits against American bishops. Vicka stated that, "Each one of us has a conscience, and it is most important to follow our own conscience, to be straight with God and with people. If I hear that a bishop has been accused of this or that, who am I to judge his conscience? No, I'm not going to judge him, but I am going to examine my own conscience and ask myself: 'For years the Gospa has been calling us to pray for priests, bishops and the Holy Father. What have I done to help them? Have I prayed for them with all my heart?' That's the question! God sees the rest. For my part, I have to help the best I can without wasting any time making comments about my priests. There are already too many words spoken and not enough prayer!"

Then I asked, "What about you, Vicka, how do you pray with the heart? What can you say to those who say, 'I can't pray from the heart; I just can't manage to open up my heart?'"

Vicka: "Each one of us has to try! You see, my experience is my own. I pray in my own way, as the Lord taught me. Praying is joyful for me because it is my answer to God. I have decided to answer to God. I have made my decision to answer! People who say they can't, it's because they don't want to for fear of having to change internally. But, in fact, the Lord is waiting for them. He is waiting for that moment when they say, simply, 'Lord, do with me what you will!' But first of all we must believe that God loves us. I know that God loves me, so I am giving myself entirely to Him. Then, when I open my heart up to Him, He moves me along. You know, all prayers are said in different ways. I pray a certain way, you pray a different way. That's true for every one of us. All that matters is that we pray from the heart; that we desire to pray from the heart. Whenever we have this desire, God is always there, ready to give!"

"Dear Children! The best fast is on bread and water. Through fasting and prayer, one can stop wars, one can suspend the laws of nature. Charity cannot replace fasting. Those who are not able to fast can sometimes replace it with prayer, charity, and confession. But everyone, except the sick, must fast". (July 21,1982)

28

TERRIFIED OF FASTING

In my Community of the Beatitudes, Br. Jean-Michel had a problem with fasting that could be described as visceral, as we all could testify. It didn't make it easier for him to be living in Medjugorje where fasting is always on everyone's mind, especially with Our Lady's frequent reminders in her messages. But Jean-Michel can speak for himself:

"The two days of the year that I used to dread the most were Ash Wednesday and Good Friday, because that's when the Church requires fasting, and I had a hard time with fasting. Nevertheless, I signed up for the five-day "Fasting and Prayer" retreat, because I knew that it was necessary for several reasons. Secretly, I was hoping to be told: 'Sorry, it's full,' but it wasn't."

"As we were getting closer and closer to the date of the retreat, my anxiety was increasing, and when D-Day arrived, I was in a state of utter panic. If anyone had just told me not to go, I would have obediently complied and with joy; but no one encouraged me in that direction. I was in such a state that I followed a pilgrim's advice and went to pray at Fr. Slavko's tomb, begging him to come to my rescue. I said: 'You're the one responsible for creating this retreat, do something!'"

"On the first day of the retreat, I decided to be submissive and to seize the grace of the moment. I wanted to live everything that was proposed without holding back. If I had known that we were going to fast for five days, I would have snapped right away. But the thought didn't even occur to me once. That was the grace of all graces! Then I climbed Apparition Hill, Podbrdo, and there I wrote a letter to Our

Lady. I explained all my worries and problems to her. I abandoned all of them to her so that I wouldn't have them on my mind during the retreat and I told her that I was offering up the week of prayer and fasting for her intentions—a swap of sorts. I was astounded to see how everything went so well, without any kind of difficulty and without even for an instant thinking of material concerns—the length of the retreat, or how difficult it was to fast. I even felt happy at the end of the retreat, because I had been able to deeply immerse myself into the mysteries of the Rosary, allowing myself the times suggested for meditation. I also was able to live the Mass more intensely, as if I was entering each room of a beautiful castle, as the preacher had taught us."

"I give thanks also for the physical healing that occurred totally unexpectedly. I had been suffering from hydrocele, a hereditary condition that causes an accumulation of serous fluid in the genital area, causing a frequent need to urinate. Before, I had to carefully watch how much I drank when leaving on a long trip and before any drawn out activity. This handicap was a real inconvenience. From the beginning of the retreat, we were encouraged to chew our bread until it turned liquid and also to drink two or three large cups of herbal tea with each meal. I was very careful to observe all the instructions in order to prevent headaches, nausea or other problems. So much so that I didn't even think of the consequences that drinking such large amounts of liquid could have had for me. The first day, I drank a total of six large cups of herbal tea, and nothing untoward happened. At the time, I didn't pay attention to it. The next day, I realized that I had gone to the bathroom only twice. Puzzled, I repeated the same thing and, again, everything was normal. I had to conclude that I no longer had a problem of hydrocele. After the retreat was over, I rushed to drink a glass of wine and a cup of coffee. The adverse effect, usually drastic, did not occur; everything was normal. Since that day, I've had no problem and I give thanks to the Lord for this unexpected healing."

"Then, I told myself: 'If I had only known, I would have gone to this retreat a long time ago!'"[69]

---

[69] Read Freed and Healed Through Fasting, by Sr. Emmanuel, or listen to the CD 'Fasting, Door to God's Power'. See the appendix at the end of the book for more information.

God Does Not Force Us

One day, I asked Vicka what to say to people who still hesitate to fast, who find it too hard. "You know," she answered, "everything we do without putting our heart into it is hard! It's even better not to do it. If I say, 'Well, today it's just too hard for me, I'm confused in my head, I'm hungry,' then it's better not to fast, because God doesn't force us. It is up to you to feel in your heart how and when you have to respond to Our Lady's request and then answer it with all of your heart!"

"Our Lady desires that we respond from the heart, but if you don't have the heart, it is better not to do it. God does not force us. If you say, 'I have a headache, I feel dizzy,' those are excuses, you see, excuses so that you don't have to respond. Our Lady wants us to purify our heart by fasting. That's the most important kind of fast. She asks you to fast with bread and water on Wednesdays and Fridays. The only way to have a good fast is to have a firm intention to fast. With a strong will, we can do anything. It's the same thing with avoiding sin. Fasting is going to purify me from my sin and from everything that troubles me. That's what pleases Mary the most. If today I fast on bread and water and right away I have all kinds of bad thoughts, hurt someone, or behave badly, then it would have been better not to fast. I have to first uproot my naughtiness before I can take a new step forward."

Two Precious Pearls

These are the instructions Jesus gave to Sister Faustina when He revealed to her how He wished the sisters of her congregation to live:

"Your purpose, and that of your companions, is to unite yourselves with Me as closely as possible.... I place in your care two pearls very precious to My heart: these are the souls of priests and religious. You will pray particularly for them; their power will come from your diminishment. You will join prayers, fasts, mortifications, labors and sufferings to My prayer, fasting, mortification, labors and sufferings, and then they will have power before my Father."[70]

---

[70] Sr. Faustina's Diary, §531.

29

RECIPES FOR FASTS

From a practical point of view, the quality of bread used for fasting makes a big difference. The best is to choose a dense and nourishing bread. If you can't find one at the store, you can make your own. It is important to drink a lot of water during days of fasting, to avoid headaches. Our Lady has not specified whether water has to be hot or cold; she hasn't given any detail. Hence, each can decide on this freely, with the heart and according to one's state of health. It is also very important to pray more during fasting days. It is needed to be able to persevere in our efforts.

Recipe for fasting bread

For 2lb. of flour, add in that order:
25 + oz. lukewarm water (about 98o F)
1tsp sugar
1tsp baker's yeast
Mix well, and then add:
2Tbs. oil; 1Tbs. salt, 1 + cup rolled oats (oat meal)

Preparation:

Mix all ingredients. Add small amounts of flour as needed, if dough is too thin.

Let stand 2 hours minimum (or all night) in a warm, even temperature location (not under 77°F) covered with a damp cloth. Place the dough (about 1 + in. thick) in a well oiled baking pan.

Let stand for 30 minutes. Place in oven pre-heated at 320° and cook 50 to 60 min.

The quality of the bread will vary mostly according to the type of flour used. Whole wheat and white flours may be mixed.

Recipe for flat rye loaves

2.2lb white flour
2.2lb whole rye flour
1Tbs vegetable oil
4 + cup water
A pinch of baking powder; a pinch of salt
1tsp sugar
1 packet (about 1/3 oz.) yeast

Preparation:

Mix yeast, one Tbs. of flour and one tsp. of sugar together, and then add it to two cups of warm water to let the yeast rise. Mix the other ingredients together and add the yeast and the rest of the water. Knead until you can form a compact and smooth ball. Divide into 20 to 25 pieces and roll them into balls. Cover them with a damp cloth and place in the refrigerator. (It will keep two to three days). To cook, spread the dough into miniature pizza crusts. Bake in the oven at maximum temperature. Serve the breads as soon as they are cooked; they loose flavor and texture as they cool.

Recipe for English bread

9 oz. white wheat flour and 9 oz. whole wheat flour
1 + tsp salt
1oz. fresh yeast
2 oz. butter
1 cup water
1 tsp lemon juice

Preparation:

Mix flour, salt, water, lemon juice. Add butter, and then yeast. Let rise 60 to 90 minutes.

Fold dough 4 or 5 times and squeeze it with your hands while digging in underneath to let air in. Form into a ball slightly flattened on the top. Let rise another 30 to 45 minutes depending on ambient temperature.

Pre-heat oven to 430° F. Brush surface with milk or one beaten egg, sprinkle with flour, and make cuts in the surface, widening each cut towards the end. Place on a sheet of parchment paper and cook 20 to 30 minutes, depending on the oven. The bread is done when it sounds hollow.

"Dear Children! I call you to make a choice. God gave you free will to choose life or death. Listen to my messages with the heart that you may become aware of what you are to do and how you will find the way to life. My children, without God you can do nothing; do not forget this even for a single moment" (March 18, 2003)

30

HOW MUCH IS YOUR SARI WORTH?

Mother Teresa of Calcutta had a way of turning people upside down with a simple word. Each day, her long hours before the Blessed Sacrament filled her soul with the living Word of God (despite the fact that she had long periods of spiritual dryness), and that Word would burst forth on the people around her throughout the day.

One day, a very rich Indian woman came to see Mother. She was draped in expensive jewels and dressed in a magnificent sari. The woman was struck by the light that emanated from Mother. She wanted that light! She truly wanted to come closer to God. Not knowing how to express her thirst, she offered to give Mother Teresa a lot of money. Mother answered her that the most important thing she could give was not her money but her heart. It was the heart that needed to be transformed!

Mother asked: "How much is the sari that you are wearing worth?" The woman thought and told her the price. It was exorbitant! "Well," said Mother, "the next time you come to see me, try to wear a less expensive sari."

"Is that all?" wondered the woman, surprised. As one might guess from reading the lives of the saints, she expected instead to be asked to make a radical change in her life. Changing the standard of her sari seemed a small thing to the woman, although her female vanity was miffed. However, she stuck to the very simple advice and made sure that next time the clothing she wore was more sober.

By that tiny move, she opened the door of her heart to God. His grace entered and took hold of her little by little, transforming other areas of her life. When she went back to Mother Teresa wearing a less flashy sari, Mother, to her surprise, told her the same thing: "Next time you come to see me, wear an even more plain sari." This pattern continued several times until finally, Mother Teresa had to insist that the woman not wear a poorer sari than her own!

Great Saints teach small things! Holiness takes humble steps. In fact, following this repeated lesson, the woman lived a great life of conversion in the footsteps of Mother Teresa, and later became a wonderful instrument of God in Calcutta.

Mother Teresa had a keen eye for knowing where people were in their hearts. The woman would not have lasted long if she had tried immediately to make a radical change. She would have given up after the first difficulty and lost the battle against discouragement. But the wisdom of this humble way, this small, incremental effort, enabled her to make everything progress in her life, according to her capacity to love at the time. Her soul was like a flower searching for the sun and opening up according to the natural speed of its cycle. Flowers forced to bloom too quickly do not last long.

The Gospa invites us all to conversion of heart through simple moves:

Which habit of mine will I change? Well, startingtoday, I am going to do something I never did in the past!

- This abandoned crucifix, covered with dust, why don't I clean it, kiss it, hang it up and put flowers near it? Every morning I will address it a few words coming from the heart.

- This $10.00 bill, I will put it in the mailbox of a mother in difficulty. She won't even know the gift comes from me! Everyday, I will give something to someone.

- It's pouring rain and I have to go shopping. Instead of complaining, I will say, "Thank you Lord for the blessing of the rain!" And from now on, I will bless the Lord for the very first obstacle I find in the morning.

- Why not call this old uncle who lost his wife and show him a little bit of warmth? From now on, I will treat him as a friend instead of ignoring him.

- Much of my time is spent watching TV or reading useless magazines. I will use it instead to pray for the dying who are scared, so that they can abandon themselves to the mercy of God, and I'll send them my Guardian Angel.

- On my way to work, I will transmit a blessing to the people driving in front of me (or sitting near me in the subway), and I will entrust their lives to the Blessed Mother.

- When I give lunch to my young children or grandchildren, I will tell them a story of Jesus taken from the Gospel, and I will help them find concrete ways to imitate Jesus during the day.

- Every night I will read a Psalm before going to sleep and I will memorize the verse that touches me most.

Something about computers fascinates me: After writing a text, the change of one word is enough to cause everything to move around and find a new place. The harmony of the text is saved as if that word had always been there. But no word is at the same place anymore. So it happens in spiritual life: if I decide to change my ways in just one area, everything will move in my heart. The little piece of sun that I introduce will touch every aspect of my life, and the fire of love will spread to one person after another. Light will win in all aspects!

"Dear children! I beseech you to take up the way of holiness beginning today. I love you and, therefore, I want you to be holy. I do not want Satan to block you on that way. Dear children, pray and accept all that God is offering you on a way which is bitter. But at the same time, God will reveal every sweetness to whomever begins to go on that way, and He will gladly answer every call of God. Do not attribute importance to petty things. Long for Heaven." *(July 25, 1987)*

31

TONIGHT, YOU ARE GOING TO DIE

Fr. Jacques woke up one morning convinced that he was going to die that evening. The feeling was so powerful that he got up, completely dazed, and began to put his affairs in order. He started with prayer, doing a serious examination of his conscience, and thinking: "This is the last one. I'd better do it well!" Deeply repentant of each sin, he had all the pieces to make a good confession. He entrusted his soul to the infinite mercy of God, in total abandonment to it.

Then he told himself: "What matters at the time of death is the love and charity we have in our heart." So he carefully met with each member of the Community. He asked them for forgiveness for any wrongdoing, offence or sin he might have committed against them. He did this sincerely and with joy, peace and affection. That day, he applied himself to conduct all his work in the Community with great love, forgetting himself and concerned only with God's glory and service to his brothers and sisters. He thought to himself: "Since it's my last day, it would be well to leave with them a good memory."

As usual, he went to the chapel for his hour of Adoration. During the whole hour, he applied himself to bringing his soul into communion with Jesus as never before. Then he put his whole heart into his celebration of Mass, which he did more slowly than usual, pronouncing each phrase and each prayer as if he had actually been looking at Jesus in front of him. He was wild with love for Jesus. He knew that this was his last

Mass. He thanked the Lord with his whole heart for the tremendous gift of Holy Orders, and better appreciated the profundity of it.

As evening drew near, he wanted to spend each minute that was left walking hand in hand with Jesus and with Mary, to whom he had confided his priesthood. Several times, he had to fight against bouts of fear when he thought that he wasn't worthy—that he had sidestepped so many graces, or that he had neglected this or that responsibility. But the more his misery came up to choke him, the more he tossed it into the abyss of God's infinite Mercy. This was the fiery furnace of which little Saint Therese said: "Even if I had committed all the crimes imaginable, I would still trust because I know that this multitude of offences are but a drop of water in this intense furnace."[71]

Then night came. He went to bed at his regular time; and fell asleep. In the morning he was surprised to find himself still on earth. Did the Lord forget to come pick him up? No, that was not possible—the Lord never forgets anything or anyone. Then, Jacques understood that the Lord must have had a different plan for him. By letting him think that his death was at hand, He just wanted to teach him a lesson:

See how passionately you prayed to Me today!

See how you filled every minute of the day with all the love that your heart could give!

See how you were able to see Me in each of your brothers and sisters and serve them with all your heart!

See how deeply you lived the Holy Sacrifice of the Mass!

See how contrite your heart felt when you presented all your sins to Me, and with what trust you so completely abandoned yourself to My mercy!

See with what generosity and joy you distributed your possessions, careful that the neediest should get the best!

See how gratefully you reviewed in your heart the gifts and graces that you have received from Me throughout your life, especially the grace of knowing Me intimately and becoming My priest!

---

[71] Last conversation with Mother Agnès, July 6, 1897.

See how seriously you applied yourself in settling your temporal affairs, especially those pushed aside and neglected for so long, which could have become hurdles for those near you!

See, finally, how quickly the meaning of material and human concerns has crumbled in your own eyes as you faced your final hour, and how poor and naked you found yourself without any recourse other than Me, your Creator and your God!

The Lord was asking Jacques to live each day this way; such was his path to holiness.

It is very beneficial to our soul to reserve at least one day a year to run through a sort of "dress rehearsal" of our own death. Father Jacques of our Community gave me that idea....

Heading Toward the Lighthouse

Blessed Charles de Foucauld[72] made a point to live everyday as if the Lord was going to take him away that particular evening. Like the sailor who steers his boat straight for the beacon that will show him the way into the harbor, fighting head winds and anything else that may send him off course, such a soul is always striving to keep its bow aimed at the light of Christ, without deviation. It takes care to set a straight course for the final leg that will take it to the port of its true home: Heaven.

This spiritual demeanor has fashioned saints, and can fashion us still today in holiness. There is a very easy test that can tell us if our spirit possesses this attitude. Let us contemplate our latest decisions. For example: I am young. My whole life lies ahead of me and I must decide now on a path to take. I decide to become a doctor. However, on the evening of my first day in med school, the Lord is going to call me home. Immediately, I will find myself under the Holy Spirit's x-ray, and my entire life will pass in front of my eyes like a movie threaded through God's projector of truth. Will I then feel proud of it, or ashamed?

---

[72] He was beatified by Pope Benedict XVI, in St. Peter's Basilica, on November 13, 2005. His life inspired the foundation of two religious orders: the Little Brothers of Jesus, and the Little Sisters of Jesus.

Certainly, the Lord doesn't expect us to put a coffin in our room, as did some of the desert fathers, to stay focused on our last destination and our true home. Nowadays, with our fragile psychology, this would more likely cause deep psychological traumas and psychiatrists would just get richer. No, the Lord has better ways for us now: He has given us His Mother who reminds us in Medjugorje: "Dear Children, do not loose sight of your true home in heaven!"

Or again: "Little children, don't forget that your life is passing by like a spring flower that is today radiant in beauty, but that tomorrow no one will remember."[73]

"Dear children, do not put so much importance on petty things—long for heaven."[74]

Prayer groups, in Medjugorje or anywhere else, are the Lord's answer for our times. In those marvellous crucibles, the Holy Spirit constantly reminds us, through one another, of the beauty and wonder of the gift of life, and the splendor of our destiny in eternity.

If I Were Carrying All the Sins of the World On My Conscience....

In her diary, St. Faustina shared an experience not unlike Fr. Jacques', one that could very well also be ours:

"In the meditation on death, I asked the Lord to deign to fill my heart with those sentiments which I will have at the moment of my death. And through God's grace I received an interior reply that I had done what was in my power and so could be at peace. At that moment, such profound gratitude to God was awakened in my soul that I burst into tears of joy like a little child. I prepared to receive Holy Communion next morning as "viaticum," and I said the prayers of the dying for my own intention. Then I heard the words: 'As you are united with Me in life, so will you be united at the moment of death.' After these words, such great trust in God's great mercy was awakened in my soul that, even if I had had the sins of the whole world, as well as the sins of all the condemned souls weighing on my conscience, I would not have doubted

---

[73] Message of March 25, 1988.

[74] Message of July 25, 1987.

God's goodness but, without hesitation, would have thrown myself into the abyss of divine mercy, which is always open to us.... O my Jesus, Life of my soul, my Life, my Savior, my sweetest Bridegroom, and at the same time my Judge, You know that in this last hour of mine, I do not count on any merit of my own, but only on Your Mercy".[75]

---

[75] Sr. Faustina's Diary §§1551-53.

"Dear Children! One more time I beseech all of you to pray and that by your prayers you will help unbelievers who do not have the grace to experience God in their hearts with a living faith." (March 18, 1989)

32

WHAT AM I SUPPOSED TO DO NOW?

Before I wrote *Medjugorje, the 90's*, I made a deal with Our Lady.

I said to her, "You seem to want this book, so, OK, I'll write it. But you know how painful it is for me to barricade myself behind my door with my notes, unable to meet the pilgrims who come knocking. So, to make up for this, I am asking two things of you for this book. First, that you will provide me with the topics and the stories for the Chapters (the only way hearts will be touched). Second, that you will use this book for unbelievers. Please put it into their hands yourself. Grant that, reading it, they lose the false peace that the world gives, and they begin to search for the Truth and become inwardly tormented, until they find God. And, please, give me a sign—show me some unbelievers who have found God through this book."

I was sure to touch a soft spot in her motherly heart since, through Mirjana, she asks us to put the unbelievers first in our prayers. Lo and behold, the book had barely been published when it began to make waves! Here is one of the first stories that came to me, and it is certainly not the least.

A woman, about fifty, stopped me on the way out of Mass in Medjugorje. "Sister, I have to talk to you. You're the only one who can help me!" (This all-too-common approach usually rubs me the wrong way, since I am definitely not the queen of discernment.)

"Actually, Sister," she continued, "I'm here because of your book! My daughter gave me your book for Christmas, but as soon as I saw that it was all about religion, I put it away in a drawer without reading any of it. I didn't know anything about God, and, to be honest, He was the furthest thing from my mind. My daughter is very devout. This wasn't her first attempt to push her beliefs on me.... I don't know why, but the other day I discovered it and started to read it. I just couldn't stop reading! All those stories—my goodness, Sister, I couldn't believe it! I read the book from cover to cover in one night. I swallowed the whole thing down in one gulp. But, Sister, afterward I didn't feel well inside, I lost my tranquillity! I couldn't get a moment of peace. I was thinking about it constantly and couldn't find any peace."

"Imagine—I didn't even believe in God, much less in the Virgin Mary, and here I was, reading this book that told me not only they exist, but they are truly active. It was like a bomb had gone off, Sister, an explosion! I couldn't sleep any more. It was constantly working on me and I thought, 'either this Sister is telling the truth and I've completely missed the boat all my life, or she's the one who's off her rocker and I'm on the right track.'"

"But, I was getting nowhere. No matter how much I tried to convince myself that you were crazy, something was telling me that those stories were genuine and that this book was showing me the truth. So, between the two of us, the crazy one had to be me! And I kept wondering if I had to start my whole life all over again. Sister, you have no idea how much I suffered, I was so sick inside, trapped. I was getting aggressive, and I couldn't eat or sleep anymore. After a few days of this turmoil, I was so exhausted that I had to stay in bed."

"My thoughts were tormenting me, so I had to find a clear answer, and I didn't dare call my daughter and look stupid! So I had the idea to do an experiment to see which one of us was crazy. I told myself, 'the Sister always talks about prayer. She says it really helps, it brings peace and works miracles. Well, let's see if that's going to work for me! I'll do exactly what she says in the book; I'm going to follow her instructions and pray for a few days. We'll see if she's telling the truth.'"

"The problem, Sister, was that I didn't know how to pray. I had never prayed in my whole life; what could I do? I was too ill to torture myself with this additional question, so I just acted as if God really existed. I called on Him and totally unloaded on Him. Oh, He heard it all that day! I didn't leave anything out! And, at the end, I said: 'There, now if you really exist, let's see you do something about all of this!'"

"You won't believe this, Sister, but He did answer! And how! My heart was filled with peace, a peace like I never imagined, something completely new and so sweet. I felt my entire being rejuvenate. Sister, I can't find the words. Can you imagine the joy and surprise that I felt? Then, I continued to speak to Him and the more I talked, the more He answered, overwhelming me with more joy and happiness. That's when I received the gift of faith. I could feel God's presence, right there!"

"As I started sleeping and eating normally again, I called my daughter and told her: 'You know that book you gave me? Well, I read it. What a shock! I've realized that everything you believe in is true. You're right, God exists! But what am I going to do now? I don't know anything; I don't even know where to start!'"

"My daughter gave me two pieces of advice: 'Read the Bible, and go to Medjugorje as soon as you can. There, you will understand the underlying foundation, and then, Sister Emmanuel will tell you what to do."

"So, here I am, Sister. I'm here—What do I do now?"

Dear Gospa, thank you—I caught your wink! You have such a tender loving way to fulfill a contract—and with so much humor!

"Dear Children! I myself invited each one of you here for I need you to spread my messages throughout the whole world". (August 23, 1983)

33

A GREAT INVITATION

During a mission in a remote village of Poland, I was invited to introduce the messages of Our Lady to a group of young people, between the ages of eighteen and twenty. They were thirsty to know more about Medjugorje, and with each message from Our Lady that I shared with them, their joy increased. Each new aspect of the events in Medjugorje ravished them. But my heart broke when I heard them say with sadness, "Too bad, we'll never be able to go there." How could they afford a passport, a plane ticket and other expenses when getting adequate nourishment was already a daily struggle? Go to Medjugorje?—It was an impossible dream!

Without thinking, I heard the words slip from my mouth: "Of course you're going! In Medjugorje, it is the Mother of God who sends out the invitations! Aren't you her children? So, she'll take care of everything, you can count on it!" The kids looked at me as if I had whacked them on the head. "Just talk to her plainly, as you would to your mother. Touch her feelings. For example: 'Mom, you've already invited millions of your children to Medjugorje so that they would change their lives. What about me? Why haven't you invited me yet? Did you forget about me? Don't you think I need a conversion? Then, please, invite me too! And since you are my mother, well, the money part, you'll take care of that too, right? I thank you ahead of time!' You talk to her like that and I don't see how her mother's heart wouldn't just melt. But remember, it all depends on how totally you trust in her love for you. OK?"

They didn't have to wait long to see the results. The following summer, I found them on the front steps of St. James Church! And each one of them couldn't wait to tell me how it all happened: how they found the money, how they obtained their visas, etc. Each story was unique. The Gospa used her imagination to touch each heart. My young Polish friends were swimming in joy!

It's true. In Medjugorje, it's the Mother of God who sends out the invitations! And since she is the mother of all people, we see the entire spectrum of races, peoples and languages, styles and walks of life from all over the world gathering for the evening Mass. All of these people are side-by-side exchanging nothing but kind greetings. Among those guests, many admit to being somewhat taken aback. "It was stronger than me," they say. "Something drove me to come to Medjugorje! I just arrived yesterday, and, to tell the truth, I don't have a clue why I'm here!"

The answer to them is clear: If you don't have a clue, don't worry. The Gospa knows. Just go with the flow and you'll find out. You'll leave a different person!

Our Lady's Barbershop

Denis Nolan testifies: "I remember, years ago, Sam Belardinella came to see me after a conference I had just given on Our Lady's apparitions in Medjugorje. 'It's easy for you to talk!', he said. 'I'm just a poor barber, I don't even earn enough to pay my income taxes each year. Where am I going to find the money for a plane ticket to Medjugorje?'"

"'Sam, just ask Our Lady,' I answered, 'and if she doesn't give you the ticket, Jesus will give it to you Himself, because He'll be so happy that someone's paying attention to her!'"

"Two weeks later, Sam came to see me with a bewildered look on his face. He was holding a letter from Mark Bavaro, in his hand. Mark Bavaro is a football player with the New York Giants, and Sam used to cut his hair when he was playing for Notre Dame. Mark had written that his wife Suzie and he wanted to go to Medjugorje, but since Suzie was pregnant, they couldn't go. In the envelope, he had placed both their rosaries with a note that said: 'Sam, could you do us a favor? Of course, I'll understand if you can't do it. I've placed in this envelope a check for $2,000. Could you and your wife go to Medjugorje and have our rosaries blessed by Our Lady?'"

"Upon his return from Medjugorje, Sam placed a statue of the Blessed Mother in his barbershop and did not allow his customers to make any trouble or improper jokes. From that day on, his shop was known as 'Our Lady's Barbershop!' Sam would admit that before his pilgrimage, given the choice between flying his pigeons and going to Mass on Sunday, he would rather fly the pigeons. But his ways have entirely changed. Over fifteen years have passed since that trip to Medjugorje and, not only does Sam go to Mass every Sunday, but he faithfully serves each morning at the 6:45 a.m. Mass!"

Our Lady knows all her guests!

All of a sudden, on June 24, 1982, to the great surprise of the locals, the little village of Medjugorje filled up with a huge crowd. The Gospa had chosen June 25th to celebrate the anniversary of the apparitions and the news spread far and wide. That day, for the first time, Ruzka Pavlovic, Marija's oldest sister, saw a crowd of foreigners mingling with Croatians. Even people from the free world, Germany, Italy, Austria, France, and America came to venerate their Gospa. Ruzka was so impressed that she tried to calculate the total number of visitors in her head. To leave a better imprint of this amazing event, she got the idea to ask her sister, "Why don't you ask the Gospa how many people came for the anniversary?"

Marija asked the question that same evening, and to her surprise, Our Lady took less than a second to give her the answer. Calmly as one would give the time of day, she answered without hesitation, "8,482 people came."[76]

Most people would file this anecdote in the Banal Events folder. On the contrary, I see it first as a message for all mothers, everywhere, and for all of us as well, because, as Marija likes to remind us, if anyone comes on a pilgrimage to Medjugorje, it is by invitation from the Gospa. Of course, there was a certain amount of preparation required to bring the trip about, but, aware of it or not, the fact that a person came to Medjugorje was the direct result of a personal invitation received from the Heavenly Mother.

---

[76] Ruzka didn't later remember the exact number, but the idea's the same.

In other words, the Gospa is very aware of whom, among her children, she has invited. She knows each one by name, why she extended the invitation to them, and what she has prepared for each one. She also knows who did not respond to her call! Can we just imagine for a moment the emotion in her mother's heart when a group arrives in Medjugorje? What joy for her to be able to distribute her Heavenly gifts to each one of those who responded to her invitation! But, what sorrow she must have when she has to unwrap some of the gifts. Indeed, some of her guests play deaf and are reported missing from her Oasis of Peace!

Ruzka laughed with so much joy as she told me the story about her question for the Gospa on June 24, 1982; she looked like a little girl proud of having pulled off a good one! Though, I'm afraid that I spoiled her excitement when I asked, "Did she also tell Marija how many of her invited guests didn't show up?"

"Dear Children! Abandon your concerns to Jesus. Listen to what he says in the Gospel, 'And who among you , through his anxiety is able to add a single hour to his life ....but seek first His kingdom and its righteousness and all things will be given to you.".   *(October 30, 1983)*

34

FLORENCE'S LEGENDARY BILLS

In the span of fifteen years, Florence de Gardelle acquired a solid reputation among the pilgrims of her native Provence, France, as well as among the families of Sivric, one of the hamlets of Medjugorje where her pilgrims stayed. They all agreed on one thing: she was amazing! She could easily hold an entire army in suspense for hours while describing the wonders of the Gospa's involvement in her life.

One day, when I was with her, I brought up the issue of the practical and financial aspects of her pilgrimages to Medjugorje. I had noticed, as a matter of fact, that many times she had allowed several destitute people to come along without paying.

"How do you do it?, " I asked her.

"The Gospa pays the bills!," she replied.

"OK, but...."

"It's different every time, and every time it's a surprise. Do you remember the message in 1983 when she said 'I have invited each one of you to this place myself'? And further, 'No one comes on a pilgrimage to Medjugorje without a personal invitation from me.'? Over the past 15 years, I've personally seen how true this is! If we, on our end, respond to her invitation, Mary will organize everything herself. All she asks for is a little, 'Yes.' As soon as that 'yes' is given, she removes all the obstacles: lack of money, time constraints, hostility of relatives, etc."

"What was the particular instance that affected you the most?"

"I'll never forget our pilgrimage in February 1996. She really showed her colors that time! For eight years, we had been bringing 8 - 10 young people, at no cost to them, from an association we know well, that is led by a priest. They were enrolled in a program that taught them construction skills and formed them spiritually. In 1996, Fr. John told me that he wanted to invite some friends of his association and I started to receive registration forms marked: 'Travel offered by Fr. John.'"

"Ten, twenty, thirty forms accumulated. I called Fr. John to point out that we would soon have about one bus full! 'No problem Florence; we'll work out the details after the trip. Don't worry!'"

"I said 'OK.' But…. The registrations were multiplying: Forty, then fifty. So I called him again and told him: 'Father, don't you think that's about enough? We're up to two full buses now. There are thirty-eight berths in each coach. With the rental fees, lodging costs….'"

"Don't worry, Florence," he said, "it's very important that each of these young people come! I have a strong feeling about that!'"

"Finally, I ended up with sixty-six registrations, and only two of those could pay their way. I told Our Lady, 'Look, this isn't my pilgrimage organization. It's yours. You invited them! Even if some of them were enticed to come along, you can't abandon your priest who has such a desire to bring these youths to you! So, it'll have to be your problem, not mine!'"

"Anyway, we left with five buses! Normally, during the trip, I show carefully chosen videos that prepare the heart. One of those is the moving testimony of Father Verlinde on the dangers of the occult and everything related to it, like false healings, the use of pendulums, Yoga, Transcendental Meditation, Oriental religions, etc. As soon as I started the video we heard a horrible noise. We stopped to check the coach and saw that one of the wheels was completely bent out of shape even though the bus had hit nothing. So, I went to the next coach, and as soon as I stuck the video in the machine, a tire blew out! I headed for the third coach, thinking that we must have a real dose of graces coming!

"As we headed home through Croatia, one of the buses broke down in the middle of nowhere. The mechanic's verdict was that it couldn't be fixed. So, the pilgrims had to be redistributed among the remaining four coaches. When we left Nice, I had been surprised to notice that the fifth bus wasn't full. But on the way back, after we were done redistributing the pilgrims, it came out just right. There wasn't a single berth left over. Our Lady had calculated just right. Of course some of us had to spend the night sitting up, since there were no more berths available, but we all made it back!"

The group of young people ended up being deeply touched by God during their pilgrimage and each one of them shared their joy with the others over the microphone."

You Will Witness Those Signs

"When it was time to pay the bills, what a surprise she had! Thanks to all the donations, undoubtedly inspired by the Blessed Virgin Mary, we were able to settle every single bill without going in the red."

"By the way, right from the beginning of those pilgrimages, I had told Our Lady: 'If some day I go into debt, I'll take it as a sign from you that it's time to quit and I'll stop immediately!' Not once, in fifteen years, did we ever go into the red. Out of the two hundred people we had on that pilgrimage, only seventy paid for their trip and expenses. The rest of them gave whatever they could."

"May God abundantly bless those who, throughout all these years, have so lovingly sent their gifts and donations! May it be returned to them a hundredfold! Thanks to them, we were able to take all those people!"[77]

"Dear children.... Only through total self-denial will you be able to recognize God's love and the signs of the times in which you live. You will then be witnesses to those signs and will begin to speak of them. I wish to lead you into that." (Message of March 18, 2006 to Mirjana)

---

[77] In 2003, Florence had to stop taking buses to Medjugorje when her husband, Bernard, became gravely ill. Florence understood that her place was now by her husband's side, drawing her strength from Mary's heart at the foot of the Cross. Fortunately, the "Nice Coaches" are still going, following a different shepherd: Marie Source de Vie, 4 rue du Chateau, BP 14 –F 76133 Saint Martin du Bec, Tel: 33 02 35 30 28 43 – Fax: 33 02 35 30 33 75. E-mail: contact@msvie. com , Web: www.msvie.com .

"Dear Children! Today, again as your Mother, I want to warn you that Satan wants to ruin everything in you; but your prayers will prevent him from succeeding. When you fill up all the empty spaces with prayer, Satan will not be able to enter your soul. Pray dear children and I will pray with you to defeat Satan. May this be a time in which all of us receive and pass on to others peace" (March 21, 1988)

35

YOUR PEACE WILL FLOW LIKE A RIVER

Medjugorje, June 1992

The Serbo-Croatian war was raging. Vicka's patio remained miserably deserted. No pilgrim dared set foot in the little village surrounded by enemy troops. The throes of war had already obliterated villages and populations in Bosnia and Herzegovina, but Vicka was more active than ever. One day I heard that she went throughout Biakovici (her village) and neighboring villages to encourage the soldiers, praying with them, blessing them and boosting their morale. Nothing would ever shake her joy—a joy that will certainly go down in Medjugorje legend. One morning, I stopped by her house and, faced with her unfailing smile, I asked her this provocative question:

"Vicka, aren't you afraid? All your brothers are fighting on the front—aren't you scared for them? You heard what they did to those villages beyond the Neretva River? They burned everything, cut the people's throats and killed the animals…. That's just five kilometers from here. Aren't you worried about your parents?"

Her eyes looked into mine, and she replied without a second's hesitation. "Sister Emmanuel, when you have God in your heart," she said, thumping her chest with her good countrywoman's hands, "when you have God's peace in your heart, what can you possibly be afraid of?"

I can still see her gaze that morning. A gentle flame of happiness radiated from her entire being in the midst of unspeakable chaos. The top one hundred books written on God's peace could not have taught me more than those words sprung from her pure heart!

Peace to Fill Our Void

Let's travel to Jerusalem for a moment. Close to Calvary, in the garden bordering the rock quarry, the tomb of The Crucified One is empty! The stone has been rolled aside and Jesus is standing there, radiant with light and glory! I am fascinated by His beauty: it's not of this world. I want that beauty. I have to have it. Like Mary of Magdala on that Easter morning, a force springs up from deep inside me and urges me to embrace Jesus. Except for the demons who have chosen to detest Him forever, no one can see Jesus' beauty without desiring His embrace.

He calls me by my name and greets me: "Peace be with you!"

He has just conquered sin and death. He has conquered my death and He is offering me His victory with a humble and immense joy. It's irresistible! Yet, no matter how hard I try to open myself up to that peace and desire to seize it with all the fibers of my being, I am blocked! I can only receive a minute amount of it! It seems that the rest of it continues to bounce off me and return to Jesus. Is my heart impenetrable?

Yes, our hearts are impenetrable! Over the years, they have been "peace-proofed" so that they repel, not just the soft rainfalls but also the heavy downpours of thunderstorms and hurricanes offering Jesus' grace!

Every time we are at Mass, we find ourselves in the presence of the same adorable, living Jesus who spoke to Mary of Magdala in the garden on Easter morning. That same Jesus comes down upon the altar at the words spoken by the priest, who at that moment, is just like another Christ, in order to live again His Passion, His Death and His Resurrection; nothing less than that! When the priest says, "The peace of the Lord be with you!," it is Jesus, Himself, who is saying that to me personally. But where's my heart at that moment? Where has it wandered off to? Why is it that coming out of church I find myself struggling again with the same conflicts, the same inner stresses, if the resurrected Jesus has handed all His peace over to me? There again, I am closed up tight! Why?

On that day in the garden, Jesus said "Shalom!" At each Mass he offers me that same Shalom again. I sure would like to know what that message contains! Actually, Jesus' Shalom doesn't have that much to do with the concept of "peace" our world has constructed. Shalom isn't the absence of conflict. It isn't the delicious feeling of relief when our enemies have finally moved on; or when the headwinds have at last died down and the belligerent waves of our storms have subsided. No, that isn't what Shalom is about. Those just give us a feeling of tranquility that can be broken any moment! Our enemies can return to attack; aggressions can start again and new trials assault us. Thank God, Christ's Shalom is something completely different: "Peace I leave to you; my peace I give you; not as the world gives do I give it to you."[78]

The first meaning of the word shalom is "completeness," or "fullness." If I am complete within myself, whole and full, then I have shalom. If I walk into a motel to book a room for the night and the attendant tells me, "Sorry, no vacancy," then I can say that the hotel has shalom. It does not have any unoccupied room; it has no void. The opposite of shalom isn't war, but void or emptiness (though wars do take place because of vacuums). When the Angel Gabriel addressed Mary as "Full of Grace," he proclaimed that she had the perfect Shalom: no space that was not occupied by God.[79]

Two thousand years later, appearing in Medjugorje, the "Mother and Queen of Peace" tells us: "Dear Children, you have emptiness within yourselves! Do not keep that emptiness, because Satan roams seeking to fill them. Dear Children, fill that emptiness with prayer."

The Queen of Peace comes to Medjugorje to heal us of our void! She knows how much emptiness tortures the human heart. Why do so many young people turn to drugs or alcohol these days? Why do some hop from partner to partner, sacrificing the precious gift of their sexuality on

---

[78] Jn 14:27.

[79] Listen to CD 'Stressed? Oppressed? Bless!'. See the appendix at the end of the book for more information.

the altar of perversion? Why do they constantly stick music in their ears, blaring, blasting their confused consciousness into fantasy worlds? The answer is clear: They cannot stand the torture of those inner voids and they're ready to grab onto anything that will help them forget, even for an instant, that they are empty! Empty of hope; empty of love; empty of direction for the future; trapped in materialism without a visible way out. Who wouldn't seize any possible escape within reach, even if it is labeled "Warning—May Prove Fatal"! When faced between the torture of emptiness, or death, some choose death.

They must be told that the Mother of God comes to Medjugorje mostly for the youth. She chose six young people from the village to heal them of emptiness. She revealed to them that, to fill them, the Creator offered them a sumptuous present: Nothing less than Himself! "Do not forget, dear children, that God gives Himself to you completely."

Saint Thomas Aquinas came up with a great formula: We are "capax Dei," or "capable of God." The Creator fashioned us in such a way that we are capable of containing Him, Him—God in all His dimensions! How bewildering is the human soul—how bottomless its depths!

The Hebrew phrase for "He created them in His image" is very difficult to express accurately. It has more to do with a concept of form than with image: we possess God's "form," His "mold." But with what do we choose to fill the immense vessels of our hearts? With a small satisfaction here and a little pleasure there. With some passing gratification that leaves us unfulfilled and in anguish. Heaven is our vocation, and our most unavoidable desire is to be filled to the brim!

How to Go from Anguish to Shalom

Here is an example that will illustrate some people's attitude:

"I'm a good Catholic. I go to Mass every Sunday, but I have no peace! Worse, I am tormented by the thought that I might get sick. I'm getting older, and the thing I hate the most is illness. I don't want to get sick! The thought of pain is repulsive to me; I don't want to suffer or to get stuck in bed; I don't want to lose my job or to be humiliated by personal nursing care procedures. So, I go to the doctor every month to make sure that my body is not preparing to surprise me!"

175

This man, as good a Catholic as he may appear to be, is, in fact behaving as a perfect pagan who doesn't know God and who suffers from emptiness. He doesn't remember the day of his baptism when he became a child of God—an heir of God. On that day, he acquired an immense fortune, since, having become a member of God's family, everything that belongs to God is also his. And conversely, everything he possesses belongs also to God. His body belongs to God. So, if his body belongs to God and it gets sick, whose problem is it? God's!

But our friend is not living his baptism. He has unconsciously severed his ties with the family; he has reclaimed his stake. He holds his destiny in his own hands, clutching it as tight as he can. When he says, "This is my body, my health; it's my life and I'm in charge....," he has in fact, without suspecting it, pushed God out of the picture, thus creating his own emptiness. God, in His humility, does not impose Himself where He is not invited. And our friend has shown Him the door: "Lord, this is my life, my health, so, if you don't mind, keep your hands off!" This is precisely where the big trap is laid. It is unconscious and therefore that much more effective. Our friend believes that his life is secure because he has taken it in his own hands, when what actually takes place is the exact opposite: he is emptying himself. God isn't welcomed in his house, and since where God is absent so also is light, our friend has opened his door to darkness. And guess who's busy in the dark? Who needs darkness to operate, for fear that his deeds may be exposed? We know who![80]

The Trickster and his angels have their private entrances and they are delighted to find in him this big, dark emptiness. They could not dream of a better place to act. They will proceed by gnawing at that poor man from the inside; they will nibble without mercy, and our friend will wonder why he is tormented. He begins to feel restless. The distress that churns in his stomach is beginning to put fear in his heart. To forget his distress, he looks for distractions, but he's not entirely unaware. He knows that, when the distractions wear out, he will have to go back to the cheap hotel that his heart, deprived of love, has become.

---

[80] "And this is the judgment, that the light has come into the world, and men loved darkness rather than light, because their deeds were evil. For every one who does evil hates the light, and does not come to the light, lest his deeds should be exposed. But he who does what is true comes to the light, that it may be clearly seen that his deeds have been wrought in God." (Jn 3:19-21)

We are at a crucial stage where a large part of the population is today, resulting in a fortune for pharmaceutical reps who sell anti-depressants, and fortune-tellers. Let's look at what the Queen of Peace is telling us:

"Dear children! I am inviting you to a complete surrender to God. Pray, little children, that Satan may not wave you about like branches in the wind. Be strong in God. Do not be anxious or worried. God himself will help you and show you the way...." (Message of May 25, 1988)

Total surrender is the only way our friend will ever find peace. Like all the solutions Jesus and his Mother propose, it's both simple and demanding. Instead of tightening his grip on his own health and material life, our friend must let go and deliver himself into God's hands. The process is easy to understand; a child knows what it means to give something to his father. But it is also demanding, because our friend is going to have to change his attitude and say: "Lord, since I am baptized and I belong to you, my body is yours. So, do with it as you will. As for me, the goal of my life is to glorify you. If you wish to be glorified by my health, then all you have to do is to make me healthy. But if you have other plans for me and wish to use some illness to purify me, then, Lord, your will be done, because, either way, what counts for me now is to glorify you!"

With this truly Christian attitude in the heart (craziness to an unbeliever), our friend becomes free. He no longer lives in a state of flux. He is above all that! Now that he has invited his Lord to carry out His divine plan in him, Jesus can flood the immense space of his open heart. He is so pleased by the invitation, that He will fill it to the brim. And so, Shalom now resides in the heart of our friend who can delight in its peace—the True Peace!

Let's now look at another example of a good "practicing" Catholic who has "everything he needs"—except peace (it has been replaced with an impalpable anguish that he cannot shake). Having become very rich, he retired and thought to himself: "Great! I have a fortune in savings, a beautiful house, a brand new car—I'm going to enjoy all that from now on. I've earned every bit of it; never got anything for free, never stole anything. I have earned everything with the sweat of my brow for forty years, it's all mine and I can do whatever I want with it."[81]

---

[81] Lk 12:15-21.

What more is there to say? He has unconsciously kept Jesus at bay, as if he had told him, "Lord, I'm taking care of my business, please keep your nose out of it!" He has created his own void in his heart, like the previous example, because Jesus sees that there's nothing for Him to do there.

However, a beautiful path leading to peace will open up in front of this man if he changes his mind and begins to pray: "Jesus, I have good news for you! You saw all my possessions? Well, you can do anything you want with them! Whatever you choose to do with my belongings, I'll be happy, because my joy is in glorifying you in everything. If you want to increase my fortune, go right ahead! But if you want to spend it for your needs and your own projects, take what you want; from now on, it's a joint account; I'll countersign all your checks!"

A flow of peace will flood this man's heart, because the risen Jesus has received his warm invitation and He will pour out His light, joy and love for him. This man is now free; he no longer fears bad news because he has put trust in his God! He is drawing peace right from the source.

There is another kind of murderous possessiveness fatal to the peace of the heart, something we develop gradually toward our loved ones, usually our children. It's so easy to become oblivious to the plan of holiness their Creator has for them, and thwart His works by projecting onto them our own ideas and our own expectations: "He's my son, he has my name; I paid for his education....!"

Should our peace fluctuate at the mercy of their choices in life, good ones and bad ones? Of course not! Consecrating a child to God or the Mother of God from his conception sets us free because this move liberates us from the burden we impose on ourselves to take the place of God for our child.

Even in the midst of painful moments that are bound to occur in any parent-child relationship, our Shalom will remain firm and unshaken if we have surrendered the fate of our children into God's hands: "Lord, here's the child you have put in my care. You are his Creator, his Shepherd and his Savior. You have placed him in our family so that we may help him grow according to your calling and become what your loving design has been for him in all eternity. Help me Lord to be loving and conscientious, to live up to my responsibility towards him, to give of myself totally and to do everything in my power to help him find his way to holiness.[82] May your Holy Spirit assist me in the formation I will provide for him. Do to him according to your good will, Lord, because this child is your child, he belongs to you. I am offering him up to you and consecrate him to you in total confidence."

Once this dedication, or consecration, has been made, we experience a deep freedom, and its twin, peace, gushes into our hearts. We could go on with a multitude of examples: our relationship with our work, with the future, with ourselves, with others, with our culture, even with our common sins. Whatever the focus, the result is always the same: The more I gain control of things, the more I lose peace and the more I surrender to God, the more I acquire peace.

Everyday at Mass, Jesus stands in front of me in the splendor of His Resurrection, burning with the desire to get hold of the voids found in my heart and fill them with Himself! His loving gaze scans the depths of my inner being and finds all the closed and carefully bolted doors, those areas of my life which He has never been able to enter, because I never invited Him. He desires them with the greatest longing. Will they remain off limits? Or will I hand Him the keys? Will His Shalom, once again today, bounce off the walls of my sealed hiding places, or am I going to recognize the time of my visitation, and open up to the glory of the Risen One?[83]

Tough to Remove Bitterness

There is a dark and dismal hiding place sealed at the bottom of the human heart that tends to resist any approach of the Risen One. Hidden in the recesses of this cave are numerous containers, of varied sizes, from which escape toxic vapors that subtly leak out in all directions. What's down there? Our bitterness! The bolted steel doors would be

---

[82] "Dear children! I rejoice because of all of you who are on the way of holiness. I beseech you, by your own testimony help those who do not know how to live in holiness. Therefore, dear children, let your family be a place where holiness is birthed. Help everyone to live in holiness, but especially your own family. Thank you for having responded to my call." (Message of July 24, 1986).

[83] "Dear children, open your hearts to my Son Jesus; let him in!" (Message to Mirjana, March 18, 1991).

understandable if those were bottles of costly fine wine, carefully put away for worthy celebrations—but bitterness? Why all the security?

It's in the nature of bitterness to be tough to remove. Like those stubborn stains that defy detergents, bitterness binds itself with insolence and resists all our efforts. Everyone has heard a relative announce, even on his death bed: "I've forgiven everybody, but not So-and-so. I'll never forgive him for what he's done to my daughter, never!"

Oh that sealed hiding place down there...who will ever prevail against it? I can still hear Fr. Daniel-Ange say in one of his homilies: "To forgive is not difficult...." Then, watching the congregation's reaction for a moment, he continued: "It's impossible!"

If Jesus, in order to offer us His peace, had to take the wrath that was hanging over our heads upon Himself, if He had to die on a Cross, He who is the source of life, to conquer our sin, even to its most despicable extremes, it is because His peace isn't of human origin. It's a grace that only God can give; a supernatural gift that no man can either manufacture or sell. Consequently, even if I give my health and my money to God, with my future and everything that I hold dear, while I hold on to bitterness toward my brother, Jesus' Shalom will bounce right off me without having a chance to enter. Sometimes I do not clearly realize that I have made this bitterness the most precious of my jewels. I hold on to it as I would an arm or a leg; I feed on it as if it were a staple of life. But it's nothing more than a poison that's destroying me!

For this poison too, the Resurrected Jesus is eager. He waits only to hear the faintest whimper out of my mouth to deliver me from it.

"O Lord, take this bitterness! I'm giving it up to you! Please come and remove it—it hurts too much. It has taken hold inside. It's a bleeding ulcer and I can't touch it! O Jesus, you drank the vinegar from the sponge the soldier held up to your lips when you were on the Cross, come and soak up the vinegar of my bitterness and let your forgiveness flow through me. I don't have mercy for everyone—please, inject yours into me."

Fr. Georges Finet, co-founder of the Foyers de Charité with Marthe Robin, used to say that "If we can't forgive, we can want to forgive. To want to forgive is already to forgive. If we can't even want to forgive, we can desire to want to forgive. To have the desire to want to forgive is forgiving!"

With his immensely big and generous heart, God watches out for any minute sign of good will on our part to pour his mercy into us. He who sought and saved all that was lost alters everything with His transforming grace—even our toughest bitterness under our armored shell is changed into a perfume. He came for the sick and the sinner. That puts me on His list! He came and dismantled the locks of my sordid cavern and He has mopped up my bitterness. I can lift up my head and look into the face of my marvelous and radiant Savior as He says, "May My Shalom be upon you!"

Vicka and the Great Gift of Peace

Some pilgrims have not hesitated to ask these questions to Vicka:

Question: "How do you acquire such peace and joy? Is it because you see the Virgin Mary?"

Vicka: "It's not as important to see Our Lady as it is to feel her inner presence. What's even more important is to put what she tells us in her messages into action. God has given me the great gift of peace. I don't have the words to express my gratitude. It's a grace that comes with Our Lady's mission as Queen of Peace. Peace has increased in me day after day because I wanted it and because I still want it; and I pray for it everyday.

Question: "What is the secret of your permanent smile and your joy?"

Vicka: "My smile and my joy? There is nothing I desire more than to realize Our Lady's desires. I am her servant. I gave her my life and I'm ready to do anything she asks me to do. This is a source of joy for me. I wish so much that everyone could feel that way and could receive the grace of transmitting the love Our Lady has for each one of us. I know that the Virgin Mary's desire is that we pass her presence on to others showing that she is among us. Every day, I know that I'm going to meet pilgrims from all corners of the world, who are suffering in all kinds of ways and who are far from God. To be able to comfort them is such a grace, I can't be sad! Every morning, as soon as I wake up, I pray this way: 'Here I am, Gospa, do with me what ever you wish!'"

We can have neither peace nor tranquillity if we let our problems get the best of us. Unfortunately, so many people get so stressed out and let themselves go to pieces over the most insignificant little things. Those who lack peace should take some time out to spend with their soul. They should also have a personal talk with God, to share with Him those things that are making them nervous and to ask Him to free them from those burdens.

Once we've found true peace, we can't loose it that easily. Sometimes people come to me and they know nothing about God. I see, with sadness, that many of them have closed their hearts to God. My greatest joy is to welcome them because then I can transmit to them the Love of God who is a Father so close to each one of us. Little by little, those people begin to long for His presence within and around them.

"Dear Children! Bless (with a Special Blessing) even those who don't believe. You can give them this Blessing from the heart to help them in their conversion. Bless everyone you meet. I give you a special grace and my desire is that you give it to others." (November 29, 1988)

36

BLESSING IN THE SUBWAY

We obviously can't expect everyone to come to Medjugorje. This is why the Gospa has devised a number of very powerful ways to touch, with her Motherly heart, those who will never be able to come, reaching them wherever they are. First there are her messages that are translated into all languages and sent out over the Internet every 25th of the month as spiritual nourishment for millions of people. Then, there are the missions of the visionaries, especially those who still receive a daily apparition (at this point Marija, Ivan and Vicka), because the Gospa visits them wherever they go. They don't need to confine themselves to Medjugorje. With the international journeys taken by the visionaries, Our Lady goes to all the countries and for some this is their first visit from Heaven!

I remember an episode that happened in the beautiful little Family House of Prayer in Craig Lodge, Scotland, where Calum MacFarlane, the founder, had invited me to give a talk about Medjugorje shortly after Marija's visit. Not far from the village, there is the ancient Marian Sanctuary of Dalmaly. For generations, people from all parts of Scotland had flocked there to plead and to open their hearts to their Heavenly Mother. Marija Pavlovic had the idea to pray a late afternoon rosary in this blessed spot. The Queen of Peace appeared to her as usual, at 6:40 p.m. Later a friend told me: "You see, there had never been any apparition of Our Lady in the sanctuary, but since Marija came here, it has become enriched, in a discreet way, by the Our Lady's visitation, and people come here more willingly."

At the beginning of the apparitions, the Gospa told the visionaries that, "If it is necessary, I will appear in every home!" Since then, on all the continents of the world, many more homes have enjoyed her motherly visitation through the presence of the visionaries. In 1988, Our Lady revealed her famous "Special Motherly Blessing," which has been widely circulating among the faithful ever since. Through this blessing, she has been able to meet a multitude of her children everywhere on earth, because those who have received it also spread it. To the extent we transmit this blessing; we become her extended hands and the carriers of peace.[84]

Shortly after I had received this blessing on Mount Krizevac during an apparition to Marija in the early '90s, the Gospa gave me several signs to encourage me to spread it freely, and I'll never forget the first one. One evening, the church in Medjugorje was overflowing and all three aisles were blocked. The crowd was so dense that I didn't think one more child could fit. I was standing half way down the central aisle, squeezed but happy to be part of this mass of people from the four corners of the world. Suddenly, I heard a slight commotion behind me. There was a man struggling to get up closer to the sanctuary, progressing inch by inch, trying not to push aside anyone. When he reached me and I was able to see his face and his entire person, I saw a picture of poverty; it was clear that this man hadn't had a full meal for sometime. He looked so lonely. His gaze and his features reflected a combination of pain and of light, the light of someone who has learned to suffer with Jesus and who's already showing some signs of His glory.

At that moment, my heart bled for him and I wondered how I could possibly help him. The man continued to move up. He passed me, his eyes fixed on the altar ahead that seemed to draw him forward. By the time he had progressed another couple of yards, the thought came to me to give him the "Special Motherly Blessing." I probably should have focused on the Mass, but I couldn't help it. I closed my eyes and with my whole being, I passed the blessing on to him, calling down upon him all the treasures from the depths of Mary's heart. When I opened my eyes, the man had stopped and stood motionless for a few

---

[84] To better understand the "Special Motherly Blessing" and its origins, read the following Chapters in Medjugorje, the 90's: Tetka's Creatures, A Silent Blessing, A Satanist on the Hill, The Cafés of Lake Como.

seconds. Then he turned around and began to scan the crowd behind him, looking for someone. When his eyes reached me, he smiled at me, a smile that came from the soul and said, "Oh, thank you Sister!" Then with the same mildness, he continued his trek toward the altar and disappeared from my sight.

Mary scored a major point in my heart that day! Now, whenever I travel by train or plane, I make a point to distribute the Special Motherly Blessing as much as I can. In large international terminals, for example, my assistant, or whoever I'm travelling with, and I assign ourselves different areas to cover: "OK, you take the right, I'll take the left!" Then we proceed slowly to bless as many people as we can, beginning with the children. Seeing us walk like that, so slowly, some people probably think we're somewhat infirm, but who cares? That won't stop us!

How Dare You Bless Me!

Sometime after the episode in St. James, my friend Karen from the United States told me what had happened to her in Rome as she was waiting for the subway train on the Termini-Vittorio Emmanuel line:

"One evening in 1991, just before midnight, I was waiting for the last train. The platform was packed after the closing of theatres, bars, restaurants, discothèques and similar places in that rough part of town. The train wasn't due for another ten minutes, so as usual, I started to bless all the people waiting on the platform with me, one by one. I was standing at one end and someone standing at the opposite end caught my attention. She looked like the incarnation of misery and a human wreck—mentally disturbed or drunk, and probably both. Her distorted face showed the grimace of evil. I started praying for her, begging God to give her His blessing in a special way. I said those exact words: 'Lord, come to her through the Special Motherly Blessing of Our Mother.'"

"I had barely finished formulating these words in my mind, when the woman began to scream in front of everyone, shouting from the other end of the platform: 'How dare you bless me!' Then she jumped up and started a mad race along the platform, pointing to me and yelling threats: 'Stop that—Stop blessing me!—Stop blessing me! She looked like a frenzied lion ready to devour his prey. I stayed calm and continued to bless her repeating the same words."

"Some people around me were asking me: 'Do you know this woman?' 'Why does she want to attack you?'"

"'Don't worry; leave her,' I replied. 'She'll be fine!'"

"It was a long platform, but the woman was moving fast in spite of several people trying to stand in her way. Everyone on the platform, and on the opposite one, fixed their eyes on her wondering what was going to happen. I could tell that some of them were terrified. As she approached me, she was spitting, cursing, howling at me like a wolf in the night without food. I don't know what would have happened to me if the Gospa hadn't protected me. At least five men came to my rescue and tried to handle the situation, but her strength was beyond human."

"I knew that God wanted to touch her with His grace, so I finished the blessing against all odds, articulating it one word at a time from my heart. As I finished the blessing, her rage subsided and strangely the scene returned to normal. It seemed like a deep liberation had taken place. When the train pulled in, filling the station with its clicking and whining metal sounds, the woman stepped into the nearest car and sat down as if nothing had happened. Her face was transformed; anger had given way to peace. I got in the same car and we looked at each other as if we were friends. When I got off at my stop, she stayed on—I never saw her again."[85]

I believe that the Gospa won another great battle that evening with her Special Motherly Blessing! She just had to press this poor child against her Mother's heart, at any cost.

---

[85] It is common to see people who have been under Satan's grip fall ill when we pray for them. Their feelings are caused by what the Enemy (their master) feels facing Christ, who conquered him from the Cross. Controlled and made aware by Satan, those people often recognize the person praying for them.

"Dear Children! Tonight also I am grateful to you in a special way for being here. Unceasingly adore the Most Blessed Sacrament of the Altar. I am always present when the faithful are adoring and at that time special graces are being received. " (March 15, 1984)

37

FEDERICO:
FOUR YEARS OLD—SIX TUMORS

Milan, November 2004

Torn apart with sorrow and anguish, Sabina no longer knew where to turn. Brain tumors would soon take her little Federico from her! Several series of exhausting radiation and chemotherapy sessions had changed nothing. Three of the six malignant tumors were inaccessible by a scalpel; any attempt to remove them would inevitably cause irreversible brain damage. The best team of doctors at the Milan Institute of Oncology was closely following the case. From the medical point of view, there was no hope left.

The boy was only four years old and seemed to be wilting into nothing. But, even though he was suffering, he didn't allow his spirits to wane. Between episodes of pain, he would tell his mother tenderly, with pure eyes: "Don't worry Mom, we'll be fine!" Sabina would then run to hide in the bathroom, the only safe refuge where she could give free reign to her tears and bouts of despair.

Sabina was no longer a believer, and she made a point to keep away from the Church. As the Gospa would say, she did not know the love of God. Her friend Laura, however, was a member of a fervent prayer group in Milan. She took Federico to heart and placed him under her spiritual wing, launching a prayer campaign for him. For nine consecutive days, each member of the group spent one hour in front of the Blessed Sacrament for the child, begging Jesus to heal him and to bring peace to his mother's heart, wounded also by the recent separation from her husband.

At the end of the novena, the disease ruthlessly persisted. The prayer group wondered if the Lord had other plans for Federico that might not include healing. Laura was not discouraged. She had another plan: An Italian missionary priest posted in Brazil, Father Antonello[86] happened to be in Milan for a few days and organized a healing Mass in St. Anthony's Church. Laura invited Sabina to come for the Mass, bringing the little one along. Sabina dragged her feet; she could hardly stomach the idea of entering a church. Finally, she agreed to go in spite of herself. She had no grand illusions: if neither faith nor hope was motivating her, despair was! "What do I have to lose?" she thought. "If it doesn't help, it can't hurt either, I guess."

As soon as Mass started, Sabina felt drawn toward the celebrants who projected joy and appeared so human and approachable. Federico was curled up on her lap, sleeping with one eye shut. The other eye was on the priest, who made him laugh during the homily. When the congregation laughed, Federico laughed even louder, not necessarily knowing why! As in Medjugorje, Fr. Antonello exposed the Blessed Sacrament on the altar after Mass, leading the assembly in Adoration. He then took the monstrance and carried it in procession through the packed church. Federico's eyes followed the priest. He couldn't figure out why he was walking around showing everyone that beautiful golden sun. Fr. Antonello took his time, blessing each section of the congregation with his huge monstrance. He begged Jesus to touch each heart and body present, just as He did 2000 years ago from the middle of crowds pressing against Him. As Father approached Sabina, he could see the little boy, thin and with no hair, cuddled against his mom. He came closer, blessed the child and placed the monstrance directly on the boy's forehead.

Sabina would never forget that moment. She didn't understand a thing about what was happening. Federico collapsed as if struck by lightning. He lay on the floor, stretched out. Panicked, she bent down to pick up her son. But, as she put her hand behind his head, she realized that he was sleeping peacefully. Sabina decided to let him sleep as long as the Adoration continued.

---

[86] Father Antonello Cadeddu, who founded the Community of The Alliance of Mercy with Father Enrico Porcu in Brazil. Web site: www.misericordia.com.br

Some time later, after the procession, Fr. Antonello began the "Tantum Ergo." The little boy woke up, opened his eyes and said: "Mom, that priest was funny! It burns where he touched me! Mom, I feel fire inside my head!"

Sabina didn't pay much attention to those childish words at first, but she began to wonder as he repeated the same thing to her several times throughout the night and the next day: "Mom, it's burning in my head—there's fire in my head!" Sabina got scared. Federico reassured her, saying, "It doesn't hurt—it just feels funny."

She quickly made an appointment to be seen at the Institute. A new cat scan was made and after the radiologist studied the pictures, and re-adjusted his glasses several times, he turned to Sabina. She noticed that he had lost all the color in his face! Sabina braced herself for the worst.

"Sabina, what did you do? Who performed surgery on your son?"

"But Doctor, he didn't have surgery."

"Sabina! This child was operated on, it's obvious!"

"But Doctor, I swear...."

"Come here, look! Look for yourself!"

The pictures clearly showed that the six tumors had completely disappeared! But they didn't just vanish magically. Where each tumor had been located, a visible scar could be seen with tiny little suture marks confirming that a highly skilled surgeon's hand had cut it out. Even the three tumors ruled absolutely inoperable had been removed from brain tissue considered too soft to withstand sutures!

In a matter of seconds, she replayed Federico's words over the last forty-eight hours since the priest's blessing: "Mom, it's burning in my head—I have a fire in my head!" It finally came clear to Sabina. The medical doctors could think whatever they wanted! As far as she was concerned, there was no doubt who the Surgeon had been: Jesus. Her Creator is the most fabulous one of all!

Today, Federico is six years old. He plays, he runs, he jumps; he makes mistakes that most boys his age do. He is in full form. From His little white host in the middle of the "golden sun," Jesus touched him. As for Sabina, her tears of grief have been replaced with tears of joy!

"I have felt Jesus alive," she says. "I have felt that He is with us and that he healed my son. Now, I thank God everyday for Federico, who has recovered all his strength. He's full of joy, full of life! Everyday, he looks up to heaven, and with his little hands, he sends kisses up to Jesus, as if they've been best friends forever! Jesus is his best friend. Me too, I thank Jesus, God the Father and the Holy Spirit for the infinite patience they've had with me. They allowed this painful trial to occur so that I would, at last, realize that They are by our side, and that we are the Church! It's up to us to keep humanity united in God's Love!"

"Dear Children! I invite each one of you to make friends with your Guardian Angel. Ask him to help you." (To Marija, November, 1987)

38

THE ANGELS OF BETHLEHEM

The Angels are underemployed! Their friends, the humans, are far from suspecting all the benefits that Angels think of bringing to them. Sometimes I pray to them with great intensity in prickly situations, and because of the fruits it produces, I promise myself every time to integrate them even more into my daily life.

One day, I was to give a talk about Medjugorje, in a church where about 2,000 people were expected. My feelings were fluctuating between the joy of sharing the messages of Our Lady and a certain apprehension in front of people who, I knew, rarely laughed at my attempts at humor. I was worried that I was going to lose my enthusiasm after the first five minutes, and then would remain a little uncomfortable.

That is when the Angels came to my mind, and I had a new idea to launch an appeal to the immense choir of Angels of Bethlehem. Everything about them was perfect for the situation: their sheer numbers, their joy, and the fact they were bearers of good tidings. So I presented them with this request: "You know the situation, therefore I pray to you, place yourselves at the side of each person, and fill the church. Take away any heaviness! When I speak, bring joy in abundance, so the atmosphere becomes light and high-spirited, and the messages go straight to everyone's heart."

After a few microphone adjustments, I went ahead and started; and what a surprise it was to see a sudden joy light up all the faces. What an encouragement! But my surprise doubled when they started laughing, even though I hadn't said anything really funny. Twenty minutes later, the whole assembly was laughing so hard and the joy was so present, that I had to whisper a little word to my troop of Angels: "Dear Angels, it's OK, you spread a real spirit of joy and I thank you! But…if they continue to laugh like this, I won't be able to continue! Could you please…uh, could you turn down the volume a bit, so I am able to deliver the message in a calmer atmosphere?"

That was a memorable evening, once more the Angels had dazzled me. What a key the Heavens hand out to us, in case the atmosphere is heavy. Appeal to the Angels of Bethlehem. Believe me, their sense of humor is delicious; don't let them be idle!

Sylvie the Protestant

Talking about angels, I had the opportunity to put them to the test, in a place that is dear to their hearts and where I was granted the grace to live with my Community for more than three years—Nazareth. At the beginning, four of us were accommodated in a tiny, three-room house where I experienced some of the most beautiful moments of my life. It was a hidden life, propitious to the manifestation of our invisible friends.

Among us was Sylvie, a Sister with a Protestant background. Having only recently converted to Catholicism, she hadn't integrated yet all the riches of our faith. For example, she absolutely could not pray to the Angels. "Protestants don't address prayers to Angels," she said. In reality, she doubted the validity of this practice.

While I often related the adventures I was sharing with my guardian Angel, pinpointing how much help I was getting from him, Sylvie was brooding over her own doubts. As her questioning became more and more critical, she decided to get an answer once and for all. So that day she tried a little experiment. Secretly she addressed this request to my guardian Angel: "If you are indeed as powerful as Sister Emmanuel claims you are, then go and tell her something on my behalf. If I see that she has understood your message, then I will believe that indeed it is possible to pray to the Angels." (The message was a reproach that she didn't dare tell me.)

She prayed this in the morning, before I left for the Italian hospital where I was working part time. Then we met at the house for lunch. I remember this as if it was yesterday: I opened the door, and before I even greeted the sisters, I said, "You'll never guess what the Lord told me this morning at the hospital!"

Five seers visit with Fr. Jozo Zovko, July 1981; (chap. 1).

Mgr. Fulton Sheen, prophet of the Holy Hour, had a secret! (chap. 82).

Dorota S. after healing, with author; (chap. 58).

Yvonne -Aimée de Malestroit. She used to recover the stolen hosts; (chap. 66).

Fr. Slavko Barbaric and newly baptized Michaele, son of Marija; (chap. 9).

Scott Black, a Protestant transformed in Medjugorje; (chap. 47).

Veronica Knox, South Africa. Her beautiful eyes were blind; (chap. 2).

Mirjana in ecstasy. Our Lady appears to her every 2nd of the month.

Mgr Denis Croteau, Canada. The adventure of a Bishop who came to Medjugorje incognito; (chap. 23).

© St. Clare Sisters, 1989

© Pilgrim2000, 21 Jan., 2006

Vicka, tirelessly visiting with the pilgrims and the sick; (chap. 17).

Sr. Briege McKenna, a special prohet for our times! She brings to the Hidden Child lots of people; (chap. 49).

© Ivan Ivankovic, 1972

Mate Sego, illiterate peasant. He received confidences from God before the Apparitions; (chap. 81).

Saint James Church, Medjugorje. In it happened thousands of conversions!

View from the house The Children of Medjugorje, where the author lives.

Hard work in the tabacco fields in Medjugorje. Our Lady put an end to it; (chap. 81).

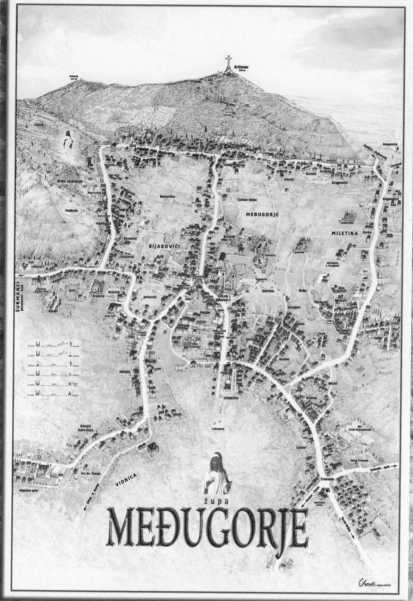

Medjugorje map in 2004.

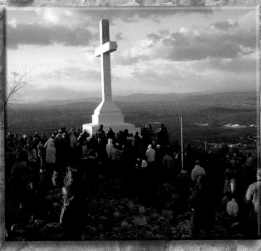

The Cross on Mt. Krizevac that dominates and blesses the village; (chap. 79).

Marcel Van, child martyr in Vietnam, usedmto play with the Child Jesus. On the way,to Beatification; (chap. 5).

Daily life in old part of Medjugorje.

The author with an Indian child in the Canadian Northern Territories, 2005.

Marthe Robin bed ridden for 50 years. A source of great spiritual renewal; (chap.13).

Fr. Slavko Barbaric and Fr. Jozo Zovko

Seers Vicka and Ivanka, 1983.

Fr. Peter Ljubicic. Mirjana choose him to communicate her 10 secrets when the time comes.

Fr. Jozo Zovko. "You have forgotten the Bible", Our Lady said; (chap. 69).

Chrissey and Kim, assistants to the author, signed up for Mary's School in Medjugorje; (chap. 40).

"What did He say?"

"He told me…." And here I repeated word for word the message Sylvia gave to my guardian angel!

At the time, she did not reveal the "secret experiment" she was having with me, but some time later, I realized she was praying to the Angels with fervor, typical of former Protestants. She was so happy to have increased in such a substantial way the number of her friends above, in the Heavenly Kingdom! It was only one year later that she was finally able to tell me the whole story! She had received a big shock that day and from then on she became one of the best employers of Angels that I know!

Hold On, You're Going to Be Surprised!

Some time later, Sylvie and I were invited to give witness at a Clarisse monastery near Nazareth. The Sisters had invited all their benefactors, friends and family members to the main lobby. When we arrived, we found all the people gathered, engaged in very loud conversation. Sylvie looked at me, taken aback.

How were we going to transmit our message in such an atmosphere? Nobody was prepared! Hearts do not open in such a cacophony! That's when Sylvie smiled at me mischievously and whispered in my ear: "Hold on, you're going to be surprised!" She then invited me to follow her to a corner of the room. There, her back to the crowd, she confided to me her plan with obvious joy.

"The walls are made of concrete; this is very bad for the sound even if we try to hush them. We have to attack the enemy from above and ask for some heavenly help." She was taking her time to disclose her brilliant plan to me, in order to increase my anticipation. "So, here is my plan. We are going to have a meeting of Angels. We are going to ask all the Guardian Angels of the people in the room to talk to their charges and to make them silent. OK?"

"Excellent idea!," I retorted, ecstatic.

So there we were, immersed in a short but intense prayer, our eyes closed, secretly begging the Angels to bring in silence. The effect was astonishing. Only a few seconds passed and, without any obvious reason, all the agitation was gone and a very pure silence fell over the room. We could hear a pin drop. Nobody had anything to say anymore, all the little groups broke apart naturally and everyone humbly took a listening posture. Sylvie and I remained speechless. We were amazed at the speed with which our prayers had been answered.

"Thank you, dear Angels! Now we can speak about God!"

That day too, Sylvie's Protestant blood received a solid injection of Catholic faith!

Ah, I almost forgot! Sylvie[87] is a very talented artist. Her art blossomed during her stay in Nazareth, where she learned to paint icons. Today, if you look at her paintings, frescos and tapestries, you will find in them angels, angels and more angels. That was to be expected: the Angels know her very well now; they have her address memorized by heart since they have been there so often to visit her!

---

[87] Sylvie became Sister Esther when she pronounced her vows and entered the Beatitudes Community in 1980. Listen to CD "Make friends with your angel", by Sr. Emmanuel. See the appendix at the end of the book for more information.

"Dear Children! I thank all of those who have come here this year, so numerous and in spite of ice, snow and bad weather, to pray to Jesus. Continue and hold on in your suffering. You know well that when a friend asks you for something you give it to him. It is the same with Jesus. When you pray without ceasing and you come in spite of your tiredness, He will give you all that you ask from Him." (December 1, 1983)

39

THE ROSES MET WITH DISASTER

A Parable

It was Saturday. Elaine was expecting her brothers and sisters to show up from the four corners of France for an evening celebration of their mother's birthday. They all wanted to surprise her like never before and spoil her with their love. Elaine was put in charge of the flowers and, as it turned out, she had noticed that her mother has a weakness for fire-yellow roses, a very particular yellow, which was hard to find. She knew exactly where to go because she spotted a flower shop that had exactly what she was looking for. Of course such special roses were very expensive, but for her mother, Elaine wasn't about to skimp!

Her heart bounced with joy at the thought of making her mother happy. This evening would lift the heart of her mother, who had laboured all those years for her children without one complaint.

Elaine grabbed the car keys and skipped out through the door to 'do some shopping'. Her mother suspected nothing. Unfortunately, the carburettor malfunctioned and the car wouldn't start. Elaine had no choice but to take the bus which took double the length of time. When she finally arrived at the luxurious shopping mall in the centre of Paris, she headed to her favourite flower shop, only to find a sign that said, "Closed for annual inventory"! She felt a lump in her throat as she foresaw her plans falling apart. She thought, "Where else can I find such beautiful roses? There's no time to lose!"

She hurried back up Rue de Rivoli, heading for another flower shop that was usually pretty well stocked; but it was too late! A hotel had just cleaned out all its stock! Elaine began to feel sick, but she refused to give up. A glimmer of hope remained in her mind. Another shop, located conveniently near her bus stop, always had fresh roses. Of course they didn't always have the color she was looking for, but as she approached it, she saw that they had an ivory colour that would do. Her mother was turning 81, so she bought eighteen roses. There would also be eighteen candles on her cake because the children agreed to invert the numbers, making "18" the theme for the evening, in order to reflect back on her youth.

Elaine left the store with her roses wrapped in a beautiful star speckled midnight-blue paper; her inner frustration was quelled. As she headed for her bus stop a storm broke out over the city, and the sudden torrential rain turned her instantly into a pitiful looking, sopping-wet cat! As for the bouquet, the paper blistered and stuck to the roses. It was all a sorry sight!

Back on the bus, Elaine's spirits were wavering but she refused to be discouraged. As the bus pulled up to the next stop, the rain had gathered three times the normal number of passengers, and they all packed into the bus like sardines in a can. To make matters worse, a heavy lady, who was standing right next to Elaine, lost her balance in the middle of a turn and came crashing right onto the bouquet with all of her weight! What a disaster! Half the roses looked dreadful with their heads hanging over the side. "What am I going to do now?," Elaine wondered. "It's almost dinner time and all of my brothers and sister are probably waiting for me at my house! I have to get home as soon as possible. But how can I go home carrying this disaster in my arms?"

Sorrow seized her heart. She wanted to make her mom so happy, but all she had to offer her were the seven or eight white roses—not even yellow—that had escaped the slaughter! Elaine descended from the bus devastated. She still had a couple of hundred yards to walk before she reached her house. She hastened her steps on the sidewalk alongside a huge puddle of murky water, which had accumulated over a clogged storm drain. As if she hadn't had enough, an ambulance came around the corner at full speed, lights flashing and siren blaring, right through the puddle! She was covered head to toe! That truly was the icing on the cake! Elaine wanted to scream. The flowers look like they'd gone into a deep coma! Their dove-white complexion had turned to a dirty grey spotted with engine oil, mud and canine matter better left unmentioned. Her heart was wrenched. She thought, "Isn't there going to be at least one flower left for Mom tonight?"

While trying to salvage what was left of the roses, she found one that had managed to survive all the afflictions and traumas of her epic adventure. She was so much looking forward to surprising her mother with the splendid bouquet! In her heart she had a secret fear that her day would be an indication of the party's success.

Kavana

The Hebrew language holds a magnificent word, kavana, which can be translated as "intention of the heart" or "direction of the heart." He who has the kavana in prayer toward God is truly praying. He who performs an act of charity with *kavana* truly acts out of love. God looks into the heart, not at the appearance of success. "I the Lord search the mind and try the heart."[88] He knows the deepest desires that motivate us, and that's all that interests Him. In the parable of the roses, Elaine is filled with a great desire to please her mother because she loves her, and she does everything in her power to fulfil that desire. She has good *kavana*—she sets the rudder of her heart in the direction of love and courageously stays the course in spite of all the obstacles in her path. The world looks at results, efficiency, success and profitability. According to the appearance of her bouquet, Elaine flunked! But, in the eyes of God, those roses are far more beautiful than the ones she had dreamed to get her mom. Better yet, that beauty will last forever, because love never dries up. True love produces a fruit that survives eternally.

It's the same with prayer. To pray from the heart is to do what Elaine did. She wanted to love and made the decision to love by offering a present. Then she invested time, money, her judgment, her heart and all her human strength to succeed. Confronted with adversity, she persevered without getting discouraged. She could have given up on

---

[88] Jer 17:10.

her project several times, but her *kavana* was stronger. Her compass didn't waver. To love is to want to love, and to continue to love even when everything seems to be falling apart. To pray is to want to pray. It is to continue praying at any cost, especially when all odds are against us, both inside and outside, trying to reduce our efforts to nothing.[89]

As a child, the little Virgin Mary heard the Rabbis' comments on the Torah cite the Fathers of the faith. We can just imagine her, swallowing each word that could teach her how to know God: His ways and the expectations of His heart toward His people, Israel. It is remarkable to see how some of Mary's messages in Medjugorje are simply restating the secular teachings of the Talmud, or of some other traditional books like the Mishna!

In Medjugorje, Our Lady has established a three-hour prayer program that is carefully observed by the Franciscans. The program consists of a one-hour period for the Rosary followed by the Litanies of the Virgin Mary and a hymn to the Holy Spirit. Then one hour for Mass, and an additional hour to prolong giving thanks to Jesus. The purpose of this last hour is to avoid interrupting the *kavana* abruptly after the peak of all prayers: Our soul's intimate union with our God in the Eucharist. The first Hassidim (considered to be the first "charismatic" Jews in the 15th century) had a very similar practice. They waited one hour before saying their prayers, and another hour afterwards, to ensure that they would reach the *kavana*, and to make sure they would finish their prayers prolonging the intention of heart toward God. Maimonides, a famous Jewish Rabbi, said that, "Since praying without kavana isn't praying at all, he who prays without *kavana* must pray again with *kavana*. Someone who's anxious, inundated with worries, or just returning from a trip should not pray until he is able to regain the composure needed for *kavana*. True *kavana* implies that one is free from any outside thoughts and fully conscious of being in the presence of the Divine." (Yad. Tefillah 4:15,6). The Shulhan Arukh (pronounced Shulrahn Aroor) further states that, "the smallest supplication with kavana is worth much more than a great number of them without kavana" (OH 1:4).

---

[89] For more on how to pray with the heart, listen to CDs, "Prayer Obtains Everything!" and "Prayer with the Heart." See the appendix at the end of the book for more information.

Our Lady tells us to *"Let your prayer come from your heart." "It is better to pray one Our Father from the heart than hundreds without the heart."* But, it is very difficult for modern man to gather his heart and unify it without letting human preoccupations interfere. We have "popcorn" hearts jumping all over the place: scattered and all over the place! Thank God that *kavana* does not imply a total absence of distractions—even our greatest Saints had some[90]—instead, it implies a certain freedom towards them, and a sincere desire to pray, whatever the cost.[91]

---

[90] The following passage from Sister Faustina Kowalska's Diary is a good illustration of the kavana, even in the midst of the parchedness of the senses: "Thursday. Although I was very tired today, I nevertheless resolved to make a Holy Hour. I could not pray, nor could I remain kneeling, but I remained in prayer for a whole hour and united myself in spirit with those souls who are already worshiping God in the perfect way. But, towards the end of the hour, I suddenly saw Jesus, who looked at me penetratingly and said with ineffable sweetness, 'Your prayer is extremely pleasing to Me.' After hearing these words, an unusual power and spiritual joy entered my soul. God's presence continued to pervade my soul. Oh, what happens to a soul who meets the Lord face to face, no pen has ever expressed or ever will express." (Diary §691)

[91] Ivan, the visionary, gave this answer to a pilgrim who had asked him how to pray from the heart: "We must begin our prayer on the right foot. When you call someone on the phone, you have to pick up the phone, listen for the dial tone, dial the number, etc., or nothing will happen. It's the same thing when we want to engage in a conversation with God. We must go through the necessary motions in order to bring our heart into the condition required for calling and listening, and then be alert to the presence."

"Dear children! Today I look in your hearts and looking at them my heart seizes with pain. My children! I ask of you unconditional, pure love for God. You will know that you are on the right path when you will be on earth with your body and with your soul always with God. Through this unconditional and pure love you will see my Son in every person. You will feel oneness in God. As a Mother I will be happy because I will have your holy and unified hearts. My children, I will have your salvation. Thank you." (To Mirjana, August 2, 2007)

40

NO TIME TO PRAY?

One day in 2006, Father Jozo Zovko received a group of American pilgrims at his monastery of Siroki Brijeg. He said to them:

"Your family is a desert. It lacks water. You have Human Rights, you have jobs, many of you have money but you do not have the blessing of God. Why is there such pain in your families? Why is there no joy? When did this desert come?"

He continued, "It came when you said you had no time to pray, the light inside your families turned off!"

If you could only see my schedule!

I often hear people say, "OK sister, we agree prayer is important, but for us it's so hard to find time together to pray. We have so many pressures"

Well, as dear Father Slavko would reply, "It's rather a matter of love! When we love, we find means. When we don't love, we find excuses!"

Speaking of prayer, I always remember Father Michel, a pastor of a big parish in Paris. On a pilgrimage to Medjugorje, he had the misfortune to ask me what special messages Our Lady had given to priests. I cited several of them and added, "Our Lady is also asking priests to live all of her messages, especially that on the daily Rosary."

"Let all priests pray the three parts of the Rosary everyday", she said. But Father Michel immediately cried out, "How can you ask such a thing, Sister! I can't! It's impossible! If you could only see my schedule!"

"But it's not me Father, who is asking you. It is the Mother of God!

"Impossible!" he said. So I said "OK Father, perhaps I am mistaken, maybe she actually said, "Let all priests pray the three parts of the Rosary everyday, except Father Michel who is way too busy!"

He then gave me a brittle smile, so in an effort to help, I suggested:

"OK Father I have an idea! Why don't you just try it for two or three weeks? After all, it is the Mother of God speaking, and your own Mother, you don't want to ignore her, do you? So before you brush her request aside, just give it a try! And if you see that it makes your life impossible, well then you can think again."

Father Michel agreed to give it a go. Two years later, I saw him again in Medjugorje with a group of pilgrims. Timidly I asked him, "Hi Father! So, how is it going with the Rosary?"

Beaming with happiness, he put his thumbs up and said, "It works!" To which I responded, "Great, Father! Please tell me more!"

"Well Sister, I stuck to our deal. As soon as I arrived back in Paris, I made space for the rosary. That first night I felt an unusual sense of calm. The next day, I was not only calm but I found myself with spare time to read before going to sleep. The third day, I felt the same peace and found even more time to do other things as well. As the days went on I realized that Our Lady was actually walking before me, opening doors for me and preparing my ministry. I was no longer alone, instead I had an awesome partner by my side, working with me and guiding me. Now I live with much more peace and no longer rebuff my parishioners as I used to. Basically, I am now a much happier priest."

Father Michel is no exception. Coming to the conclusion that one has no time to pray, is just false arithmetic! Why? Because when Our

Lady sees us gathered in prayer and receiving graces, her motherly heart leaps for joy. She then makes a point of walking ahead of us, opening the doors that need to be opened. She guides our thoughts and choices and helps us avoid so many mistakes. Put simply, she saves so much time for us, much more time than we take to pray!

If you still have the courage to tell me that you have no time to pray in your families, don't be surprised by my answer –"If you don't have time, pray, and you will have time!"

"Dear Children! Pray, because in prayer each one of you will be able to achieve complete love." (October 25, 1987)

41

THREE LEVELS DEEP

Facing the bronze plaque of the Nativity, not far from the great wooden Cross of Apparition Hill, I picked out my own little private spot beyond the bushes and among the weeds. The Cross is a representation of what the visionary Marija saw on, June 26, 1981. It was the third day of the apparitions and Marija was walking home after the 6:40 p.m. apparition, when Our Lady appeared to her for the second time that day, but privately. According to Marija, the Gospa was standing in front of a wooden Cross, crying. Her tears streamed down her cheeks, down her dress and disappeared into the ground. Our Lady said, *"World peace is in danger".* [92]

My little hideout was just a stone's throw from that Cross because, as Marija explained, the actual spot of that apparition was off the current path. [93] So whenever I need to speak to my Heavenly Mother one-to-one, this is where I go, among the rocks and the brambles, because this is the place she visited and drenched with her own tears.

One day I learned that I was to give a talk on prayer during a Marian Conference in the United States. The Gospa has taught us so much about prayer! I didn't know what pearl to choose from such a large treasure trove of messages! How could I accurately target the innermost needs of people I'd never met? Faced with this problem, I went up to the hill to ask my Heavenly Mother and from the recess of my little hiding place, tucked in between two rocks and blest with the strong perfume of wild thyme, I opened up my heart to her and said,

---

[92] "World peace is in danger! Peace, make peace, reconcile! Peace, only! Make peace with God and one-another! To do this, you must believe, pray, fast and confess."

[93] Marija hadn't gone down with the rest of the group because her home was just at the base of the hill. Instead, she took a shortcut to her house that day.

"I will pass on to them whatever you inspire me to say. The ball is in your court, dear Mother!"

I didn't receive an inner locution, vision, or apparition. In fact I have never received one. (I am holding back until I get to Heaven!). But what my soul received was a sort of indescribable insight that I can't describe but from it I began to understand a small part of her famous *"Pray, pray, pray."* It was Mary's answer for the Conference.

I understood that there were three levels of depth to prayer. My task was to invite my audience to explore the deepest of these levels. To discover their full capacity for prayer and to help them to live it, with the hope of touching and one day attaining the highest level of holiness that God has in store for each one of us.

I further recognized that, as a mother, Mary has a drama, really a tragedy, playing out in her heart. She sees clearly the degree of our holiness as well as the splendor of the beauty that God has intended for us. When we make choices that limit the degree of our holiness, often out of simple ignorance, our Heavenly Mother is saddened because she can see how it traps us at the beginners' level.

Her words *"Pray, pray, pray!"* brings to mind Jesus' words from the Cross, "All is accomplished," because, like Jesus, she herself desires fulfillment. She doesn't leave things half done and she isn't satisfied with only the first level of prayer or even the second. She wants all three— the complete package. As our Mother she wants the same for us. She wants to take us to a place that we can't even imagine. And if we could, if we had any idea of the beauty in store for us, we would be delirious with joy! Why does she so often repeat her invitation to prayer over and over again? Why does she never hesitate to repeat her request to, "Pray, pray, pray," sometimes two months in a row and in spite of those sophisticates who look down on such repetition? It is because she is not afraid of their sneers! "In prayer, Dear Children, you will reach perfect love." That's what she wants for us and she will spare nothing when our happiness is at stake.[94]

---

[94] Someone from Paris once told me: "I don't believe in Medjugorje's apparitions, the messages are too repetitive!" In reply, I asked him this question: "When you were a kid, how many times did your mom have to tell you: 'Don't pick your nose'?" He replied: "Oh, many times!" "And when did she stop telling you?," I asked. "Well, when I stopped doing it!" "There you go…." When we start really praying, she won't need to tell us anymore!

The First Level of Prayer

In the first level of prayer we have shed our atheism or spiritual indolence. We now believe in one all-powerful and all-loving God and we are pleased to have such a God. When we have a problem, when we're suffering or in trouble, when we feel a great need for something, we like to pray to Him. Our prayer can be really passionate:

"Lord, please heal me!"

"Lord, make this person stop hurting me!"

"Lord, help me out of this miserable situation. Help me find a job!"

"Lord, please help me find my soul mate!"

How sincerely and fervently we pray then! And this is a good thing because God is our Father and He wants us to share our needs with Him. If our prayer is answered, we feel satisfied. We may even put God aside until the next need surfaces. Yet too often, if we don't obtain what we desire, we tend to feel put out and begin to question everything, sometimes to the point where we might even give up on "that God who doesn't listen."

In this first level of prayer I have a one-way relationship with God. My prayer is a monologue: I painstakingly explain to God what I'm expecting of Him, carefully making it clear how my demand is justified and how much good will come out of it. In other words, I'm asking God to serve my own design! Even if my plan appears to be the best thing in the world (a healing, success in an exam, resolution of a conflict, etc.), it is nonetheless *my* plan. I develop it according to what I perceive, albeit sincerely, to be necessary.

So many Christians remain at this first level of prayer throughout their life. They never go beyond a monologue prayer, which is so limiting. They miss the immense joy that a true heart-to-heart exchange provides. It's so sad!

How can we move to the next level?

The Second Level of Prayer

The second level of prayer introduces us to a true relationship with God. To attain it, all we need is to want it! God offers Himself to us. It's up to us to allow Him to give and communicate Himself to us. At this point our freedom plays a major role.[95] In fact, God acts in us according to what we decide to let Him do. After having pleaded with Him to realize our desires (first level), the time comes when we ask ourselves the question: "What about God? How does He feel about all this? He's alive, after all, and He has a heart. What if His ideas are different from mine?"

At this point our prayer and our life can be turned upside down. We have a choice: either we open our hearts to listen to God's view about our life? (and get ready to act on it), or we close ourselves away from Him for fear of a conflict!

To shift to the second level, I must make a firm decision to place my heart in listening mode and to do all I can to be in tune to God's heartbeat.[96] As a sentinel, I will listen to the murmurs of Jesus in the silence of my heart. God is Word. He waits for this goodwill gesture to communicate Himself to us – starting with a drop at a time and, with infinite care, He slowly increases and measures it to our ability to receive.

Now the soul can begin her trek on the path of holiness towards unsuspected horizons. There's a secret code for this passage that Jesus himself whispers to us in the Gospel, "Father, may Your will be done and not mine." The code isn't a secret because it is to be hidden away, but instead because it is only activated when I say it in the silence of my heart. This secret or silent code gives me true access to all the richness of my God. In complete wonder, I am taken from one surprise to another because I can touch my God and taste His goodness. I now discover how much better His ways are than my own and how right I was when I decided to abandon myself to Him. I now realize how, in the past, when I was hanging on to my own logic, my own judgment,

---

[95] "Dear children: God has given each of you freedom. I kneel down in front of the freedom God has given you!"

[96] Jesus told Sister Faustina: "If souls would only want to listen to My voice when I am speaking in the depths of their hearts, they would reach the peak of holiness in a short time." (Diary §584)

and my own plans, I was unknowingly depriving myself of such great inner freedom and instead confining myself to a hole.

Since I have turned my fate over to someone else, I have found a brand new kind of peace. This "someone else" is my greatest friend. This "someone else" is Love itself, and I'm safe with Him. Before, like an orphan with only himself to count on, I had to hold onto the helm of my small raft and face the storms of life alone. But now, I have handed the helm over to my Father and my heart is at peace. What a relief! He amazes me in how He traverses the winds and the waves, and all the worldly elements. I could never have done that alone. It is truly divine!

Now I just hop onto His lap, and together we plot just like two best friends. In this loving intimacy, He forms and teaches me. He feeds me with His wisdom; He corrects me and refines me. Put simply, He remodels my true identity: "This is my beloved Son, with whom I am well pleased."[97]

This secret code never fails to be fruitful, and its fruit is a taste of holiness. One day, Jesus told Saint Faustina:

"My child, make the resolution never to rely on people. Entrust yourself completely to My will, saying: 'Not as I want, but according to Your will, O God, let it be done unto me.' These words, spoken from the depths of one's heart, can raise a soul to the summit of sanctity in a short time. In such a soul I delight. Such a soul gives Me glory. Such a soul fills heaven with the fragrance of her virtue. But understand that the strength by which you bear sufferings comes from frequent Communions. So, approach this fountain of mercy often, to draw with the vessel of trust whatever you need." (Diary §1487)

What wonderful news! The summit of Holiness? With such promises who would turn down the second level of prayer?

Of course, there's a major obstacle to overcome before we reach that level. It is one of the toughest: fear! The fear to let go of the helm; fear of the unknown; the fear of public opinion ("What will they say?"); and a wealth of other fears all fabricated by our imagination ("What

---

[97] Mt 3:17.

if God asked me to.... How horrible, I could never do it!"), and finally the greatest fear of all, the fear of suffering.

One day in Sarajevo, Mirjana was waiting for Our Lady's apparition as she did everyday around 6:40 p.m. However, that day, at the exact time, it wasn't Our Lady who appeared, but a very handsome young man, "dressed to kill." He said to her, "Mirjana, you shouldn't follow the Gospa! It will cause you much trouble and suffering. You should follow me instead."

On hearing this Mirjana stepped back. "No!" she answered, vehemently.

At this "no" the young man screamed and disappeared. It was Satan! Although he had disguised himself as a very attractive young man in an attempt to seduce her, Mirjana had noticed the pupils of his eyes were red.[98] Seeking to trap Mirjana, Satan had chosen the most powerful poison in his cabinet - a very subtle poison, but one that often works because it targets the wounds in our hearts: "If you walk with God, He'll send you trials and tribulation and you will always be unhappy! But if you come with me, you'll have the happiest love life.

What a joke! Who could be happy in their life with a love inspired by Satan—a being that doesn't have even an iota of love in him? "He is a liar and the father of lies" (Jn 8:44). Unfortunately, so many Christians swallow that lie without even noticing when Satan has injected his fear into them.

Satan fears God and seeks to infect us with his virus. He imposes on our mind an image of a God who doles out misfortune! But the truth is exactly the opposite: God is the source of true happiness, a happiness that does not deceive, unlike Satan who, if we listen to him, will suck

---

[98] Mirjana was left horrified, but the Gospa appeared at that time and calmed her down: "I'm sorry, Mirjana, to have let that happen, but you have to know that Satan does exists. Once, he came in front of God's throne and asked permission to test the Church for a period of time. God allowed him to test her during one century. This century is submitted to the power of evil, but when the secrets that you have received come to pass, his power will be destroyed. Already now his power is dwindling and he's getting more aggressive. Satan wrecks marriages, pits priests against one another, foments obsessions and murders. You must protect yourselves with fasting and prayer, especially group prayer. Carry with you blessed objects, keep some at home and start using blessed water again."

us into his misery.[99] If we find that we are afraid of God, or of His will, we are probably still carriers of some residue of this lie. The Great Liar is the one who inspires mistrust in God.

Being aware of this lie will help us renounce it and throw it into the ardent furnace of Christ's heart. Fear vanishes as soon as the lie is rejected. We can then move on from being afraid of God to that marvelous virtue of having a holy fear of God which proceeds from love,100 and through which the Holy Spirit always reminds us to love more, lest we should wound Love!

The tangible sign of the second level of prayer is peace. At that level, we have settled into a peace that nothing can shake. It's a gift from God. Our happiness no longer depends on this world, but on God, who has committed to communicate His peace to us. We become carriers of this immense fruit because this peace flows from our heart like a "river flowing throughout the world."[101]

Is it possible to go further? Can there be another level of prayer?

---

[99] Mother Yvonne-Aimee de Malestroit said: "People are not afraid of Satan enough. If they could only see how ugly he is, they would stop sinning!" (From Yvonne Aimée de Jésus, Fr. Labutte, Guibert Editor, France.)

[100] Blessed Charles de Foucauld exquisitely expressed this attitude of the heart in his famous prayer:

"Father, I abandon myself into your hands; do with me what you will.

Whatever you may do, I thank you. I am ready for all. I accept all.

Let only your will be done in me and in all your creatures.

I wish no more than this, O Lord. Into your hands I commend my soul;

I offer it to you with all the love of my heart, for I love you Lord,

and so need to give of myself, to surrender myself into your hands,

without reservation and with boundless confidence, for you are my Father."

[101] "Dear children! Today, I am inviting you to decide for God, because distance from God is the fruit of lack of peace in your hearts. God is only peace. Therefore, approach Him through your personal prayer and then live peace in your hearts. In this way peace will flow from your hearts like a river into the whole world. Do not talk about peace, but make peace. I am blessing each of you and each good decision of yours. Thank you for having responded to my call."

The Third Level of Prayer

The third level of prayer can be desired, but it cannot be reached by our own volition. God dispenses it on His own initiative. After having searched so ardently for God's will and having embraced it with our whole heart,[102] the time arrives when we are ripe to receive the grace of all graces: identifying with Christ.[103] As St Paul said, "It is no longer I who lives but Christ who lives in me!"[104] It is almost as if a substitution has been made because the soul begins to burn with such an intense love for Christ and His brothers that Jesus visits that soul mysteriously and installs in that person His own Heart. The most tangible and sensitive consequence of this divine intervention, called transverberation, is that the person now lives the life of Christ, thinks His thoughts,[105] endures His suffering, rejoices in His joys and burns with His very own divine desires.

I know several people who have attained this level of prayer but, out of discretion, I cannot name them. The great French mystic, Filiola, lived in such a sublime union with Christ that she saw all the horrific secret deeds performed against Christ in the Eucharist. This caused her great internal agony. However, she was also able to foresee the "Church

---

[102] Saint Maximilian Kolbe had a beautiful formula to describe this: [w=W (union of the wills)].

[103] "O, my beloved Christ, crucified by love, I wish to be a bride for your Heart, I wish to cover you with glory, I wish to love you. . . until I die of it! But I feel my weakness, and I ask you to 'clothe me with yourself,' to identify my soul with all the movements of your soul, to overwhelm me, invade me, substitute yourself for me so that my life might be but a radiance of your Life. Come into me as Adorer, as Restorer, as Savior." (St Elizabeth of the Holy Trinity)

[104] Gal 2:20.

[105] Sister Faustina was worried that she might be betraying Christ in her writings on mercy. But Jesus reassured her and asked her to continue writing, saying: "My daughter, be at peace; do as I tell you. Your thoughts are united to My thoughts, so write whatever comes to your mind. You are the secretary of My mercy." (Diary §1605)

of Light", along with Jesus' apostles on fire whom He introduced to her as the "victors," after the purification of the Church, particularly in France. These visions lifted Filiola into a blissful rapture.[106]

Just looking at people like that gives us some insight into Jesus' feelings! For example, at a party where everything is apparently going well and there's a good atmosphere, such people can be plunged into an agony inside—Why? What's happening to them? They can immediately feel that among the guests there is a man in the state of mortal sin and, in spite of his polite smiles, he is on his way to being lost. Conversely, they might also become extremely happy without any apparent reason. Thanks to the heart of Jesus which beats within them, they are aware that a great victory of grace is being obtained somewhere. For Jesus, these people are "another humanity."[107] They have offered their entire being to Him as a dwelling where he can live His Mystery again.

This third level of prayer is about Christ's own prayer in the human soul. It goes without saying that this prayer is always granted as it is in perfect tune with God's will. It obtains everything!

---

[106] Filiola (1888-1976) was a simple French woman despised by the world and her husband. In her broken French, she told pieces of her highly mystical life. In a church, as she was admiring a picture of Jesus revealing His Sacred Heart to Saint Marguerite-Marie Alacoque, she was deeply touched: "Jesus opens his Heart wide to me to give me all His love that has never left me in 45 years. Really, it was in front of that painting that my heart spoke out inside me: 'Oh how much I would like to love as Sainte Marguerite-Marie!' At that very moment, Jesus touched my heart and gave me His love. Before, I had always sought true love without being able to find it in human hearts. I was so thirsty for true love and only Jesus has been able to satisfy my heart. It was done! Oh Father, how can I explain that to you? It's as if Jesus had given His heart in my heart all alive. My heart is united to His heart and His heart is united to my heart, as if it were one single heart. Father, I do not understand very much if this can be. It's as if Jesus let His heart speak in my heart and He wants me to write what the heart of Jesus inspires me, what He desires, what He reveals to me and then, I tell things through the heart of Jesus. He reveals a reality of depth of things in the full light, even the most hidden things. The heart of Jesus wants to speak to the world before it is too late." And later on she wrote: "I felt invaded by a love that was stronger, deeper, more intense, and Jesus let Himself be seen by me, always interiorly, and He opened His chest wide open for me. I looked at Him and it was as if Jesus took out His heart from His chest and placed it in my heart. Then love, the true one, invaded me. And then I understood it was as if Jesus had given me the universe. A divine universe. I have no words for it. It's too great for me. But I feel the heart of Jesus in my heart. (Filiola, Chemin de Lumière; Téqui, p. 43).

[107] An expression dear to Blessed Elizabeth of the Holy Trinity.

A tangible sign that someone has entered into this level of ardent prayer is that any suffering is no longer distressing, but on the contrary, has become joy. Naturally, this joy has nothing to do with any kind of affinity to suffering, for that would be perverse (masochistic), but rather the fact that offering it to Christ has turned it into a source of redemption. This person no longer sees his pain, but deeply rejoices in union with the Heart of the Redeemer at the thought that, through this suffering, some souls will pass from death into life.

One day in the early 1980's, Vicka's mom had fried some potatoes for her large family. She went outside their small blue house in Bijakovici to throw out the excess oil. Carrying an enormous pot of scorching oil, she didn't notice the children playing in the courtyard around Vicka. Suddenly, a 5 year old little girl ran into her legs, causing her to lose balance. Vicka, sensing that the child was about to get burning oil all over her back, jumped at the speed of lightning and managed to push the child out of the way. She found herself taking the place of the child, under the pot. The hot oil splashed over Vicka, leaving her face badly burned!

In those days rescue teams took forever to arrive. There was no phone, local clinic or ambulance and no money to pay them. Eventually someone with a car was found to take Vicka to Mostar for medical treatment. Her sister, Anna, stayed with her the whole time and recalls that on the journey Vicka, despite the great pain she was in, kept saying: "Thank you Jesus, thank you Jesus!" for sparing her little niece. Vicka wasn't even twenty years old and she had just been disfigured! With third degree burns she was going to be handicapped for the rest of her life and yet there she was saying "thank you"! (Later on, Vicka's face was healed by Our Lady's prayer, leaving no trace of burn).

This is her secret. Sometime before that incident the Gospa had spoken to the visionaries about the great sinners and about the tears of blood that she sheds seeing those souls being lost. She had then asked them, as she had asked the little shepherds of Fatima: "Who will accept to sacrifice one's self for the salvation of sinners?" Immediately Vicka volunteered. Then the Gospa showed her the amazing fruits that suffering could bear when offered up to Jesus. Our Lady said "Very few people have understood the great value of suffering when it is offered to Jesus." As soon as Vicka understood that so many people could be saved by offering our miseries and our pain to God she began to practice it with her whole heart. This is how, for her, the joy of saving began to overshadow the hurts inflicted by the crosses of her life.

Vicka came back from Rome on September 1, 2000, after having had major surgery, which left a two and half inch scar on her neck at the level of her Adam's apple. Impulsively, I asked her: "How was the operation? Not too painful I hope!"

Vicka's eyes indicated to me that there was a feast day happening in her heart. A strange joy radiated from her. "You know, Sister Emmanuel," she answered, "we love Jesus so much that we always look for occasions to give Him a present. So, you see, when we find some pain to offer Him, we're happy! It's also a present for us to have a chance to offer Him something that costs us!"

"You're right," I said, "but how did it go in the hospital?"

"Well, before the operation, the surgeon warned me and said, 'Vicka, I'll be straight with you. This surgery is not easy. The vocal cords are very delicate organs and I'm not sure you'll be able to keep your voice. So, when you wake up, I'll hold your hand, and you try to say a word to me. We'll know then if you can talk or not.'"

"When I climbed up on the operating table, I found myself telling Jesus, 'Jesus! You're not going to take my voice away! You know that I need it to transmit the messages! How would I answer the pilgrims questions if you take my voice?' Then I lay down under the operating light and all of a sudden I realized, how silly of me! What if Jesus wanted to take my voice? If he asked this sacrifice of me, was I going to refuse Him? Of course not! If He needed my voice, let Him have it! Was I that attached to my voice? So then I told Him, 'My sweet Jesus, if you want my voice, take it, I am giving it to you whole heartedly!' You see, Sister Emmanuel, how easily we can let ourselves be disturbed in an emotional moment like surgery! When I woke up and opened my eyes, I saw the doctor at my side. He asked me, 'Tutto bene?' (Is everything OK?) And I answered him, 'Tutto bene!' I still had my voice!"

The people, who have reached the third level of prayer, as I have pointed out, are the happiest people in the world, because "they have Jesus" to the full-extent that one can have Him on earth, before the Beatific Vision. They are now reaching the summit of Christian life, where the soul, purified of all self interest, transformed into a living host, raises a perpetual fiery prayer up to God! They turn thousands of hearts to Christ. They are "co-redeemers."[108]

In Medjugorje, when Mary tells us to "Pray, pray, pray," she is pointing out to us that every soul is invited to discover the depths of union with God offered by these three levels of prayer. Of course, the Blessed Mother is the most perfect completion of this identification with Christ. In the following few words, Our Lady defined to Saint Bridget of Sweden her own role as Spouse that, taken to its fullness, made her the most pure coredemptrix:[109] "Adam and Eve sold the world for a fruit. My Son and I have redeemed it with one Heart. His suffering was my suffering because His Heart was my Heart."

How is it that so few Christians attain the third level of prayer? Among a number of possible reasons, there is ignorance. May this chapter be an opening to new horizons for many![110]

Today the media is offering the little ones and older generations alike the most efficient and easy ways to sink the soul into death. These are the fastest ways down and people are rushing into them in throngs; witness the thousands of suicides and the millions of people with psychological illnesses. But who is teaching the modern man that he can find in his Creator and Savior an incredible potential for happiness? Who has the courage to bring the world to its knees?

Mary of Medjugorje, thank you! You are doing just that!

---

[108] We have but one Redeemer, Jesus Christ, and yet through Baptism, we are members of His body in the mystery of the Church and the Communion of Saints. Therefore we can all participate in His work of redemption. See Col 1:24: "Now I rejoice in my sufferings for your sake, and in my flesh I complete what is lacking in Christ's afflictions for the sake of his body, that is, the church."

[109] On the sixth centennial anniversary of Saint Bridget's canonization, October 6, 1991, Pope John Paul II declared that she "had taken Mary as a model, invoked her as the Immaculate Conception, Our Lady of Sorrows and Coredemptrix, thus extolling the unique role of Mary in the history of redemption and in the life of the Christian people." Here are assembled the three elements that characterize the Heart identified with Christ: Purity; sharing in suffering and effective collaboration in the salvation of humankind.

[110] See CD: PrayerObtains Everything, by Sr. Emmanuel. INSERT

"Dear Children! I love each one of you as much as I love my Son Jesus." (undated)

42

MARY'S TENDERNESS

How amazing are the graces and blessings being poured out over Medjugorje! What strikes me the most are the fruits received from trusting Our Lady in a dialogue with the heart, like a child who expresses great intimacy with its mother. Many pilgrims abandon their mechanical, boring devotions in order to enter an encounter of hearts that is roused by Mary, particularly in Medjugorje. It is beautiful to see so many pilgrims who arrive with tensed faces and burdened hearts, leave Medjugorje with large, worry-free smiles! They have found a kindred spirit in their Mother! Mary likes it when we speak to her frankly and expect so much from her. It gives her the opportunity to act as a mother.

In 1999, during a mission in Romania, I was blessed with the unexpected opportunity to meet Cardinal Alexandru Todea, a martyr for the faith who had spent many years in prison under the Communist regime. Afflicted with brain damage from a stroke, he was unable to speak except to say the Rosary! If anyone started, Our Father, he would continue without hesitation.

Before his health deteriorated, he loved to tell the story about the day when, during solitary confinement in a dark and sordid cell, he was starving to death like many of his companions. He knew that the way things were going he wouldn't last much longer. He had the good sense not to behave as an orphan, but instead to give a few tugs on his Mother's cloak. He knew just what to say to touch her feelings, and he spoke to her sternly, "Mom! Can't you see I'm starving to death here! Don't you care? If I ever have a chance to preach again, I certainly won't be able to give you as an example like I've so often done in the past! I am your child, and yet you are letting me die of hunger!"

A little later that morning he heard the latch of his food pass-through click, something that hadn't happen in over two days. It was a miracle! There was his food bowl with meat in it! Not only was there enough meat there for lunch, but also for dinner and even the next day. Unfortunately, all the food bowls had to be returned in the evening and there was no way Alexandru could eat all that meat. Reluctantly he handed the leftovers back to the jailer who, miraculously, told him that he could keep it for the next day. It's never too late to cry out to our Mother from the bottom of our souls.

Mary's Embrace

On her birthday, September 3rd, Vicka likes to invite her friends around in the evening. For her, it's a chance to treat those who love her. In 2000, before she was married, I attended one of her birthday parties. After a sumptuous dinner and traditional songs, I asked her if the Gospa had done the same thing as always for her birthday. Her face lit up with a smile that spoke volumes.

"Yes, of course! Like every year, she kissed me."

"How did she kiss you?"

"Like everyone else (Meaning like all local Croatian women do, not like the Americans, Swiss or Japanese. Here it's with a kiss on each cheek while holding a hand)."

Then Vicka touchingly described what the previous month had been like for her: "Look, when my birthday is coming up and I know that the Gospa is going to kiss me, I start to number the days. One more month, then twenty-five more days, soon it's ten more days. Every morning when I wake up, the first thing I think about is that moment. As the days get closer my joy increases! When finally the morning of my birthday arrives, my joy just spills over and I start counting the hours! I can't describe the happiness then. There are no words to express it! You would think that it would be like a regular kiss but oh no! My heart is turned inside out and I'm afraid I might not be able to handle that much happiness and peace."

"And then?" I asked, thinking of the apparition she had earlier that day.

"Then she thanked me. She said: 'Vicka, I thank you for receiving the pilgrims and for giving them my messages.' And I thanked her too! For the gift of life, the gift of my family, our house and the opportunity to welcome and help all those people who come here—for everything! So she thanked God for my life of service and for having created me. We just thanked each other!"

I honestly don't think I've ever seen, in my entire life, anyone as happy as Vicka was on her birthday.

I also believe that, as our Mother, the Virgin Mary comes quietly to each one of us and gives us a kiss on our birthdays. Everyone, who welcomes her into their heart in a special way, allows her to pour out her immense and unfathomable motherly love.

During one of his visits to Dublin, Ivan made this statement to the crowd: "If you saw the Blessed Mother for but one second—I repeat—if you saw the Blessed Mother for but one second, the world would hold no more attraction for you. I have to pray every day to be able to resign myself to live in this world." (Reported by Fr. John Chisholm, CSSP, who was present.)

Ivan made a similar remark during another visit to Ireland, when a woman asked him, "Ivan, you have a three year old little girl. If Our Lady offered to take you today, if you so desired, what would you tell her?" Ivan answered without hesitation, "I would leave with her immediately, because I could do so much more for my daughter from heaven than I could ever do on earth!"

"Dear Children! If you love from the bottom of your heart, you will receive much. If you hate, you will lose much. Love produces great things. The more love you have inside of you, the more you can love people around you. That is why you should pray unceasingly to Jesus for Him to fill your hearts with love." (April 12, 1987)

43

A DIAMOND IN THE ROUGH

One of Jesus' skills, which fascinate me the most, is His art for transformation. When something falls into His hands, no matter how despicable it is, He always finds a way to transform it into something good. Even our sins can become like perfume if we give them to Him with sincere repentance.[111] The killing of Jesus on the Cross, which is the gravest of all sins man has committed in the whole of history, has become the cause of our salvation! Therefore, if we are in Christ, what evil could ever dare to harm us?

That is so easy to say, but not so easy to practice when we meet the concrete, every day situations. Several times Jesus has called my attention to this issue.

I cannot stand injustice. This is a very old allergic reaction deeply rooted in my childhood. I bless the parable in the Gospel about the weeds sown by the enemy in the field of wheat because, in this situation, I would be just like the servants in wanting to go and quickly rip up all of the weeds.[112] I feel the same impatience and the same anger—but Jesus stopped them because this was to be the work of the angels when harvest time came. In giving me that example of His stopping the servants, Jesus is not asking me to swallow my anger when I see injustice, nor to chomp at the bit waiting for my hour, but rather He is showing me how to discover, through Him, the most divine and efficient

---

[111] Reference to Saint Catherine of Sienna – Dialogues.

[112] Mt 13:24-30.

way to attain true justice. I have to admit my own way would only make things worse!

Delphine, a person rather close to my Community, behaved unjustly towards us. She took advantage of the Community on every level with obvious thoughtlessness. For example, she would come and eat and sleep, without ever saying one word of gratitude. She would pile her dishes on top of the others in the sink and sit and watch everyone else wash them up. The problem was out of control, glaring, obvious, and inexcusable; on top of that it repeated every day. As she was just emerging from some rather painful teenage years, I decided to wait a bit before intervening and hoped that her eyes would open by themselves. But nothing changed and my allergy to injustice brought the situation to my mind every hour. I felt myself pressured to put an end to it by ending the relationship she had with us, gently but firmly. I continually said over and over in my mind the words I would use to make the break between us. They were logical, clear and so just! And these words satisfied my need to have justice according to my own human criteria.

Then, during Mass one day, when I was listening to a long homily in Croatian, the Lord brought back to my mind a particular situation I went through in my teenage years. I felt so ashamed! I could see myself exactly in Delphine's situation! Like so many young people who take everything for granted, I had been abusing the kindness of my parents and many other people. Some scenes and specific words that I had previously forgotten about now flashed across my mind and I started to ache from all the hurt I'd caused my family at that time with such a lack of awareness.

During those few minutes of truth—God's truth this time—my internal battle with Delphine was transformed. I started to look at her as a gift from God, an angel that Providence was sending to me out of love and mercy so that I could, in turn, express the mercy that was shown to me in the past – a mercy that I was not worthy of. In other words, this constant thorn that had me complaining, became a kiss of mercy on my heart, from the One who loves me so much that He died for me.

From that day I decided to serve and help Delphine, in spite of her behaviour. And, O surprise!—the very next day Delphine decided, out of the blue, to change her attitude and the difficulty subsided without me having to do anything.

Jesus had obtained His goal in my heart. He didn't want to leave this stumbling block in my life!

A beautiful diamond had emerged from the rough!

"Dear Children! May holy Confession be the first act of conversion for you and then, dear children, decide for holiness. May your conversion and decision for holiness begin today and not tomorrow. Little children, I call you all to the way of salvation and I desire to show you the way to Heaven. That is why, little children, be mine and decide with me for holiness." (November 25, 1998)

44

THE SEAL OF CONFESSION

Father Emiliano Tardif loved to pepper his preaching with real-life stories. He particularly liked to tell the following one which took place in a little village in Canada, between a friend of his who was a parish priest, and one of the priest's female parishioners.

This woman asserted that she was receiving revelations from Jesus Himself. She would write them down and hand them to the priest. The priest would then faithfully pile them up in his drawer without even reading them as he didn't believe a word the lady was saying. Inner locutions? Visions? Apparitions? All of that was definitely not his cup of tea! And he became increasingly annoyed with the constant visits the lady paid to him. The stack of messages was becoming more and more obtrusive, so he could hardly open the drawer. So he made a decision to burn all the papers. However, just as he was about to throw them into the fire, he felt a certain fear of the Lord and began to think, "Well, you never know!" So he decided to ask the Lord for a sign: "Lord, if you are really talking to this lady then please reveal to her all my sins. Tell her to write them down and to bring me the message."

The next day the doorbell rang. It was the same lady. She claimed that she had just received a message especially for him from Jesus, who had asked her to bring it to him. The priest was now beginning to seriously regret his choice of a sign, realizing it could be very embarrassing for him!

"Father," said the woman. "Jesus sent me to tell you that He cannot tell me your sins. You have confessed them, so he doesn't remember them!"[113]

Many Catholics would be quickly healed of being afraid of God if only they knew about this very comforting attribute of His. Jesus has amnesia when it comes to sins that have been confessed. God doesn't just pretend to forget our sins—that would make him a joker who tells us, "Everything is okay," while secretly keeping archives to convict us on the last day. God so much forgets our sins that He asks the Church, and His priests, to forget them as well, hence the "seal of Confession."

One day in Medjugorje, the Gospa taught us something remarkable about this. She was beginning to train the visionaries about the essential aspects of the Christian life. Marija often recounts this story and several people I know from the village have confirmed it.

The event happened during the summer 1981, towards the end of July when the Communist Militia had forbidden the inhabitants to go to the hill, known as Podbrdo. The Gospa asked the visionaries to gather in Jure's field, at the foot of the hill, around 10 p.m. About fifty people gathered around the visionaries that evening to say the Rosary before the apparition. Then Our Lady announced something very unusual - the people present could come and touch her. She asked the visionaries to lead them by the arm, one by one, and bring them to her, since they were the only ones able to see her.

The villagers were extremely happy to be able to touch their Gospa, but very quickly the visionaries noticed that stains were appearing on her robe. They started to cry and asked her why this was happening. (They could see that some people, after touching Our Lady, had left stains on her dress, not because their hands were dirty, but for another reason). The Gospa explained:

"These are the sins of the ones who touched me."

---

[113] Listen to CDs "The Divine Mercy Chaplet" (T3) and "The Incredible Mercy of God." (W5) see page INSERT

The visionaries could see very clearly who was leaving which stain and for what sins! That made them very angry and Marija remembers thinking: "I will remember this and take it into account."

However, once the apparition was over, the visionaries had amnesia about the sins they had seen, as if the Lord, through this experience, wanted to give them a sign about the secrecy of Confession.

It is on that particular evening that the Gospa invited everyone to go to Confession at least once a month, because "there isn't anybody on earth," she said, "who does not need monthly confession." The next day, they went to see their priest, Father Jozo, in order to "purify their hearts" through the sacrament of penance and to change what needed to be changed in their lives.

Draga Ivankovic remembers that when she touched Our Lady, she felt as though an electric bolt went through her entire body. It was something very powerful and intimate that she cannot describe in words. She also remembers that during the apparition, several groups of Croatians who were visiting Medjugorje and who were unaware of what was happening, were walking along the path and mixing, through bad habit, curse words in their conversations. She felt deeply shocked by the contrast between the immense purity of Mary and the language of those people, and she understood better the horror of sin.

I think the most important point in Draga's recollection is this one: it was not the sin in general that was staining Mary's robe, but only the sins that had not been confessed, the ones people had not yet repented of. This is because, for God, the sins that have been confessed do not exist anymore. What a profound teaching for us!

Later the Gospa said, "Dear children, I beseech you, give to the Lord your entire past, all the evil that has accumulated into your hearts."[114]

Do we want God's help? Do we want Him "to see and provide"? Do we want to be in His divine providence?

---

[114] Message of February 25, 1987

Mary still today calls us to the conversion of our hearts, to let go of the sins that defile her robe but also the world. Forgiveness in the Sacrament of Reconciliation[115] is a work from God greater than the creation of the heaven and earth![116]

---

[115] See the Catechism of the Catholic Church §§1455-58, 1468-70 (regarding the individual confession of sins).

[116] Last writing from Cardinal Ratzinger about individual Confession.

"Dear Children!   Today I beseech you to stop slandering and to pray for the unity of the parish, because I and my Son have a special plan for this parish. Thank you for having responded to my call."   (April 12, 1984)

45

THE LONG LEGS OF FATHER SLAVKO

"Do you prefer the window or the aisle?"

Father Slavko Barbaric had finished his mission in South America and was getting ready to take a long flight home. "It doesn't matter, window or aisle, but if you have a seat where I could stretch out my legs, that would be great. I have long legs and they are always very cramped on airplanes!"

"Certainly, I'll see to that! Here's your ticket. You're leaving from Gate 4 in twenty minutes."

At the counter, the attendant had recognized Fr. Slavko, and she handed him the ticket with a big grin. Once onboard the Boeing, Father looked for his seat and discovered, to his great surprise, that the charming attendant had favoured him with a seat in first class! So now he would be able to stretch out his legs in comfort and be truly at ease while he worked on his new book.

Upon his return to Medjugorje he did not escape the usual questions: "So, how did the mission go? And your trip?" Fr. Slavko jokingly recounted how he was able to lounge around like a king in first class.

Just at that moment, one passing ear caught the end of his sentence. That ear was connected to a brain which quickly informed the heart. Now that heart was, in some measure, sick. It began to produce venom in such a quantity that even the face was inundated by it: the eyes dulled, the mouth contracted. As for the tongue, that poor tongue was the most contaminated of all. At first it emitted whispering sounds but, little by little, as other ears gathered around, the pitch got higher:

"Poor Saint Francis! He must be rolling over in his grave! Think about it, the Poorest of the Poor, seeing his brothers buy first class seats for themselves! And with whose money, one might ask! So this is where pilgrims's donations go to! It's heartbreaking!"

That day, hardly without having to lift his little finger, Satan scored a huge triumph in Medjugorje. The subtle accuser had only to haul out an old trap, a trap already worn to pieces by so much use, but one that still works almost every time.

How can such a pathetic trap work? Easy!

Place a heart, sick with bitterness and frustration, in contact with a being of light. This being of light disturbs him and the bad heart will want to destroy the light. That being of light will express himself freely, without suspicion, in brotherly simplicity.

The sick heart will then extract one element of his speech and, without taking into account its context (the key part of which is ignored), he will isolate that element and treat it separately. He will then plunge this element into his gall secreted by jealousy, and the result is that this detail becomes for him a scandal, an offence, an abomination. Next, the mouth begins to spew out the whole thing, with several dramatic additions along the way, reaching ears gathered around. The news is immediately picked up, then distorted, and then amplified. It is propagated quickly thanks to the secular grapevine. The war of tongues fires up and, within 24 hours, an entire village can be contaminated.

How can one escape the trap? Treat the heart in priority. Not my neighbor's heart. No, mine!

Does my heart ooze gall? Do my thoughts focus on the negatives of my surroundings? If so, that's because I have let the Enemy sow his bad seed, and I must identify it right away: call the bad seed "poison" and declare that this poison has nothing to do with me. It's a detestable foreign substance, a corrosive element which will eat away from the inside. To give it safe harbour is out of the question!

Call upon Jesus for help, ask him to remove from your heart its corrosive contents, and declare firmly: "Lord, I spit it out!"

You put garbage in the garbage can. But since there's no real garbage can for these invisible poisons, you can use another method: deposit them at the foot of the Cross of Jesus, under the benevolent eye of

Mary. There, the Divine blood flows in abundance, and this blood has an amazing power. It transforms even sin into a positive element!

The little Arab Carmelite, Blessed Miriam of Bethlehem, joyfully invited sinners not to be afraid of their sins. In effect, she encouraged them to place their sins in front of Jesus, similarly to the way we place manure at the foot of a tree. The manure becomes a marvellous element, making the tree more fruitful, more fertile. That is the way Jesus changes even the evil into good. It's enough just to give him that evil.

With the garbage having been put aside in a reliable place, it remains to:

* Take a good tonic by benefiting from the Sacraments of Reconciliation and the Eucharist.

* Identify the areas contaminated by the poison and present them to the Mother of God, so that she can apply her maternal balm and heal them.

* Get vaccinated. Since there is no magical or definitive vaccine, as there is in medicine, we have recourse to consecration to the Immaculate Heart of Mary and to the Sacred Heart of Jesus. In living out these consecrations with all our hearts, we place ourselves under the mantle of Divine protection.

One day, Jesus gave to Sister Faustina a good key to protecting herself from the Evil One: not to get involved with that which does not directly relate to us. She wrote: "The Lord said to me, 'It should be of no concern to you how anyone else acts; you are to be My living reflection through love and mercy.... Be always merciful toward other people, and especially toward sinners.'" (Diary §1446)

Who, Then, Is This Unknown Saint?

Another great mystic of our times, Mother Yvonne-Aimée of Malestroit, France, often astonished her entourage by her impulses of mercy.

Her spiritual director, Father Labutte, recounted that one day, he asked her to accompany him to the home of a seriously ill woman, Madame Fulgence, who had recently had her foot amputated and was threatened with a possible further operation. These trials had come amidst moral suffering which had thrown her into rebellion and despair.

Everyone was grieved by her harshness. Knowing the great holiness and the amazing charisms of Mother Yvonne-Aimée, Father Labutte secretly hoped that through good spiritual conversation, she would succeed in bringing this sick person back into good spirits, thereby permitting her to prepare herself to die in peace. Once there, Mother Yvonne-Aimée leaned towards the sick woman, looked at her with profound attention and spoke to her softly. The woman drank in the gaze of Mother Yvonne-Aimée and, at the moment Mother got up to leave, the woman begged her to stay a little longer. But Mother had to leave.

Once outside, Father Labutte explained to Mother Yvonne-Aimée how very difficult this woman was. To tell the truth, he was greatly disappointed that Mother Yvonne-Aimée had kept the conversation to banalities and had said nothing about God, no exhortation of any kind, only ordinary questions: "Are you suffering? A lot? For how long?" In short, she said nothing really spiritual, as he had wished. But Mother Yvonne-Aimée interrupted his thoughts and said, "Oh, how good she is, that poor creature! While she was speaking to me, I saw her whole life."

The next day, Father Labutte went back to see the sick woman and found her completely turned around. She even asked him: "So, who was this unknown saint that you brought me? She said nothing to me out of the ordinary, but while she was looking at me, I saw my whole life pass before me. I suddenly understood that God was good and merciful to have permitted me such suffering. I had been setting myself on a path to perdition, and these sufferings have saved my soul!"

The short visit of Mother Yvonne-Aimée had been sufficient for Madame Fulgence to amend her thinking and to be able to finish her days in prayer with thanksgiving and joy.[117]

When a heart is truly infused with Jesus' mercy, He places on that being the very gaze of Our Lady. It does not stop at apparent evil, but breaking through the shadows that can surround a person, it unites with the inmost part of that soul, and there it meets the immense tenderness which rests in the heart of every person.[118]

---

[117] Yvonne-Aimée de Jesus, by Father Labutte, Editions De Guibert, p 557.

[118] "Dear children, if you could see the tenderness that lies in the heart of each man, you would love them as I love them, the good as well as the bad." (Message to the prayer group of Medjugorje)

Stop slandering!

Several months before leaving us, Father Slavko Barbaric[119] suggested a practical and effective way of reacting when one learns that an evil has been committed.

In as much as he was an apostle of Jesus, a Confessor, and an expert psychotherapist, Fr. Slavko had the skill of explaining the human soul and the unhealthy behaviours it can manifest. He said, "When we see an evil being committed, or when we hear that such and such a person has behaved badly, we are quick to telephone our friends, 'Come on over, I have a story to tell you. You won't believe your ears!' We spend a lot of time recounting this evil and exchanging all sorts of comments."

"But there is a better attitude in the face of evil or suffering. Call your friends and tell them: 'I have a story to tell you about such and such a person. You can come over, but I'm only going to tell you on the condition that you say an entire Rosary with me or that you fast with me for this person!' You will notice that a lot of your friends will no longer be interested in hearing the story! The number of your listeners will visibly diminish! But thanks to the ones who do agree to pray and fast, you will change a bad situation into something positive, and you will do some good. You will avoid many empty words, which feed curiosity and wound charity."

This is a sure way to work at our conversions and to walk towards holiness. Thank you, Father Slavko!

---

[119] Father Slavko Barbaric, a Franciscan of high esteem, arrived in Medjugorje in 1982, a year after the beginning of the apparitions. He was given charge of the pilgrims. He died on November 24, 2000.

"Dear Children! I am calling you to that love which is loyal and pleasing to God. Little children, love bears everything bitter and difficult for the sake of Jesus who is love. Therefore, dear children, pray that God come to your aid, not however according to your desire, but according to His love. Surrender yourself to God so that He may heal you, console you and forgive everything inside you which is a hindrance on the way of love. In this way God can move your life, and you will grow in love. Dear children, glorify God with a hymn of love so that God's love may be able to grow in you day by day to its fullness. Thank you for having responded to my call." (September 25, 1995)

46

FINDING THE CHILD

When the Evil One realizes that, in spite of his efforts, he is not able to poison a soul chosen by God for a special mission, he uses a technique as old as the world itself: he viciously attacks the person who is closest to that soul120, or another close one:

> For King David, it was Absalom, his son;
>
> For Jesus, it was Judas, one of the twelve;
>
> For Saint Francis of Assisi, it was Brother Elijah;
>
> For Saint Seraphim of Sarov, it was Brother Ivan;
>
> For Saint Bernadette Soubirous, it was her superior;
>
> For Sister Faustina Kowalska, it was her nurse;
>
> For Padre Pio, it was his Archbishop;
>
> For Filiola, it was her husband;
>
> For Marthe Robin, it was her neighbor. . .

At first, all of these people appeared to be "normal," and could have stayed that way. What could have motivated such a turnaround on their part, and such hatred towards those "chosen ones of God"? Why did those persecutors come to see those Saints only as a target for the release of their destructive passions? What kind of simplistic blindness had they fallen into?

Only God can search hearts and minds, and fortunately, that task does not fall to us! Woe to us if we try or even begin to judge, because then we subject ourselves to judgment! Jesus said: "Judge not, that you be not judged."[121] In fact, none of the above-mentioned saints answered back to those malicious people; they accepted their cross, they prayed, forgave them, forgave them yet again, and above all, they loved them.

Absalom tried everything he could to overthrow his father, King David, seize power and kill him.[122] However, he was the first one to die, while he was riding a mule. What tears of profound grief did King David shed when Absalom's death was announced to him! David loved his son with all his heart, with a love that resisted the aggression of animosity and hate!

In addition to the examples of the saints, there are some excellent books on the spiritual life that teach us that, on the last day, we will be judged on love. Well, that's obvious. But they also add that the degree of a person's true love is measured by the degree of love he has for his enemies, those who wish him harm and those who cause harm to him. In this area we may have reason to fear! Yet, upon reflection with the light of the Bible, we cannot help but submit to this wonderful truth. In effect, loving those who love or respect us, those who are kind to us, can cause us to delude ourselves about our own hearts. To love in this way may only require a natural sentiment, at least for a time. But to love those who cause us harm requires a love that comes from divine love—only love of a divine nature allows it. Where human sentiment wears out and disappears, divine love takes over and achieves, through grace, what flesh itself cannot produce. This divine love is the kind of love that is meant here and the kind that will be for us on the last day.

The world deals only with feelings and these feelings come and go; they weaken and wobble here and there in a dance of total confusion. The confusion becomes more and more painful. But the Disciples of

---

[120] The six visionaries of Medjugorje are no exception to this!

[121] Mt 7:1.

[122] 2 Sam 15-18.

Christ train themselves to love to the point of giving their lives just as their Master did. This requires much time and prayer.

The secret of the saints is found in their compassion. Far from judging or condemning the person who, at their side, suddenly changes into a devouring lion, or more precisely into "a minion of Satan" to torture them, they see the onetime child in that person. They do not let themselves become obsessed with the evil that is perpetrated against them. They prefer to keep foremost in their minds the soul of the child that has been torn to shreds by a cruel and merciless enemy, and they weep for this dear and torn apart child of God.

This is the miracle: negative judgment vanishes in the face of compassion. Judgment crumbles before the wave of pain that seizes the true disciple. So the disciple intercedes for his enemy; he intercedes again and again, because he sincerely hurts for him; and the more he intercedes for him, the more he loves him.

To see in his worst enemy the soul of a little child who is grievously hurt; a child who is in danger because he has been taken into the camp of this ferocious wolf who is Satan—that is the key to the compassion of the saints. That is the path to their victory over themselves, and over their nature which—like all human nature—would rather push them to exact vengeance.

Finding the child in one's enemy is possible. In her school of love, the Gospa did not spare the young people of Medjugorje from practicing some spiritual exercises which did just that. For weeks, they had to assiduously spend time with their number one enemy (or, at least, the member of the group that they did not like). By doing so, they learned to discover him, know him, perceive his needs and sorrows, help him in a thousand ways, and pray for his intentions by discovering his dreams. In short, they learned to love in a divine way! Little by little, antagonism was transformed into interest, and then into true love.

In Medjugorje, I had the opportunity to experience something beautiful in the Gospa's school. It happened that someone from the village had been causing me pain for years. I cannot count the number of times that I had to confess how I had judged him adversely. No matter how hard I prayed and tried to list his qualities, I fell into the sin of judging him almost every time I received a new blow from him.

That was until the day when, by chance, I met a person who had known this man and his family very well during his childhood.

He told me about some very painful events that this little boy had endured at the hands of the Communists, and how his family had suffered from hunger, anxiety, and injustice. He didn't spare me any details. He added that these hurts remained secretly in the heart of this man and that, probably, the bleeding would only stop in Heaven. Upon hearing this, my heart did a somersault and my attitude towards this "enemy" completely changed. Quite simply, love entered into my heart. As for my negative judgment of him, this same love immediately settled everything!

I then understood why the Blessed Mother is so insistent that we love all people, the bad as well as the good, just as she loves them.[123] Isn't her love maternal? Even if a mother had her child's most horrible crimes before her eyes, he would still remain no less her child, and she would always find a way to understand him, perhaps excuse him, hope in him, in spite of everything, in short, love him unconditionally. Maternal love can bring about the impossible. It has phenomenal power!

Finding the child in another person requires one to travel to the places that molded the other man or woman, and to meet them in their early innocence. In the face of the innocence of a child, whose heart would not melt? As for the rest, all of the outrages that might have followed as an adult, let us entrust them to God, whose only dream is to do the job of a Savior!

---

[123] Message of May 25, 1988.

"Dear Children! I wish that the Holy Mass be for you the gift of the day. Attend it and wish for it to begin. Jesus gives Himself to you during the Mass" (March 30, 1984)

47

A SHOCK TREATMENT FROM JESUS

Medjugorje, October 1999

Scott arrived in Medjugorje dragging his feet.[124] As a good Protestant, now immersed in a milieu of Catholicism of the most orthodox kind, he had a right to protest! He had warned his Catholic wife Teresa that he wouldn't stay with the group but instead would tour Mostar, Dubrovnik and all the parts around. In other words, he would have a more "sane" type of vacation! Scott managed a large computer company in England and needed to relax. He said to himself, "I'll leave the apparitions to the Catholics. To each his own, after all!" However, the hills of Medjugorje charmed him, so he decided to be the photographer and video cameraman for the group for the first few days.

By the fourth day, conversations within the group were lively. Friendships were being woven little by little and joy reigned. That day Scott threw a little barb at Father Fred, whom he liked very much:

"Up to now, the score is 2 against and 2 for."

"What do you mean by that, Scott," asked Father Fred.

"At communion time, when I went up with my arms crossed over my chest, two priests blessed me, and two priests passed by without blessing me.[125] I suppose that the latter two didn't want to stop and have to put the Host that they were holding back into the ciborium, in order to bless me."

---

[124] Scott Black from Hastings, Sussex, in England. See photo section.

[125] Because Scott was a Protestant and did not believe in the real presence in the Eucharist, under the Church's rules he could not receive Holy Communion. But, by crossing his arms over his chest, he made it known to the priest that he wished to receive the priest's blessing.

Sharing Scott's disappointment, Father Fred seized the moment to question Scott about his views on the Eucharist. "For me," Scott replied, "the Host is a symbol that allows me to receive Christ publicly. It is not the real body of Christ." He explained that, before marrying Teresa, he had carefully studied the Catholic faith. The only point that he absolutely could not accept was faith in the real presence of Christ in the Eucharist.

Father Fred challenged him: "Read John: Chapter 6, on the Bread of Life, and ask Jesus to help you understand it." Scott made an attempt to follow these directions. He went to pray at the Adoration Chapel, but nothing happened... He did not receive any enlightenment from above.

The next day, Scott realized that he had no desire to leave Medjugorje. Instead, he wanted to stay with Teresa and pursue the beautiful path of friendship within the group, which he now felt part of.

Whilst visiting the Oasis of Peace chapel where the Blessed Sacrament was exposed, Fr. Fred recommended that everyone remain silent and recollected in order to be able to enter into deep prayer, and spend some time with Jesus. But in that place, wedged in the back, Scott came up against a bizarre phenomenon within the first few minutes. He tried as hard as he could to pray to the Lord Jesus, but the only words that came to his mind were those of the Rosary: Holy Mary, Mother of God, pray for us sinners now and at the hour of our death.

These words suddenly cropped up in his mind in a steady, peaceful but insistent flow, without leaving any space for other words! Scott's mind went blank. Where were the prayers that he usually offered to Jesus? It seemed to him that someone else was praying inside him with those words which had never been his! Besides, in the preceding days, when the group had gathered to pray the Rosary, Scott had carefully kept himself apart from the group.

This was an amazing situation: all of the Catholics were adoring Jesus, and the only Protestant in the group was praying to Mary! Heaven has its funny moments...!

Then it was time for Mass at St. James Church. Scott sat down in a pew on the right side of the church, next to Teresa. When the time came for Holy Communion, the numerous concelebrants came down from the sanctuary towards the congregation, each carrying a ciborium, and they began to distribute Holy Communion to the faithful who were standing in the aisles.

Standing beside Teresa, Scott also waited, with his arms crossed over his chest. Teresa received communion, and the priest automatically took another host from his ciborium, and without even looking at Scott, raised it to him. When he noticed that Scott's arms were crossed, he didn't stop to bless Scott but simply gave the host to the next person. Scott returned to his seat and knelt down to pray.

He was disappointed, almost offended. He turned to Teresa and asked, "Did you see that?"

"Yes...."

The atmosphere was heavy. But without a warning, two other priests started down their aisle, and Scott asked Teresa: "Should I try one more time?"

"Yes, yes!"

So Scott got up and the first priest placed his hands on Scott's head and gave him a sincere blessing from the heart. Scott went back and knelt down, but then the second priest, who was none other than Father Fred, came and very slowly blessed Scott, making the Sign of the Cross with the Host.

At that very moment, Scott began to tremble. He was speechless because the priest who came to bless him, the man whom he knew, having spent five days with him, was transformed before his very eyes: Scott now saw Jesus in place of Father Fred! It was Jesus who came and blessed him with the Sign of the Cross! It was Jesus himself who held the Host and offered it to him!

Amazed, Scott received the Host and was speechless with emotion. He returned to his seat and, with his hands over his face, began to weep in silence. The people around him could see his shoulders heaving but no one could guess the extraordinary experience Scott was living. He was the only one who had seen it, the only one who knew. When the Mass ended, he left the church, supported by Teresa who, without knowing what was happening, understood that God had touched her husband in some way. The two of them sat down on a bench outside the church. A profound silence enveloped them. Scott was not able to say a word, and respecting this, Teresa waited peacefully, although her heart was beating fast.

A good ten minutes went by, as they sat under the mild October sun. The group dispersed. Seeing that they had lots of time, Scott tried to talk but was unable to complete a sentence without bursting into tears. He would need much time to be able to talk again. When Teresa finally heard Scott's secret, she was shaken to her very soul, and then understood why she herself had felt a very strong anointing at the moment of the blessing and hadn't been able to stop crying.

That evening, when discussions usually took place around the table, Teresa whispered to Scott to share his experience, but he resisted: "They won't believe me," he said. However, the next day which was the last day of the pilgrimage, Scott went to Apparition Hill by himself. He collapsed at the foot of the Cross and begged the Blessed Mother to guide him: to show him what to do, and what to say about the vision of Jesus that had been given to him in the church.[126]

It wasn't until they were at Dubrovnik Airport that Scott decided to open his heart to Father Fred, but he was nervous. As a scientist, his rather pragmatic nature was fighting with him about exposing such a secret, especially to another man. He wondered what kind of reaction he would get. Would Father Fred label him "a dreamer"?

After hearing the secret, Father Fred lowered his eyes and, in deep thought, rested his right hand on his chin for a short while. Then suddenly, as if a light had been turned on, he threw his hand in the air and exclaimed: "What a grace! What a blessing you have received! Treasure it and share this treasure with others! It's a great privilege for me to have been God's instrument for such a grace!"

The priest took Scott by the shoulders and, for a moment, prayed in silence. Then he said, with a sweet, endearing smile: "So now, do you recognize that a person truly receives the Body of Christ in Holy Communion, and not just a symbolic sign?"

---

[126] At this point in time, the metal cross had not yet been replaced with the statue of Our Lady that we see today.

Upon their return to England, Scott and Teresa got together with their friends, and Scott courageously began to witness. He shared his secret with whoever wanted to hear it. Who wouldn't have believed him? He had changed so much in just a few days! His life would never be the same.

"Each time I close my eyes," he said, "I see the face of Jesus, a face full of love and compassion. It's very moving! All of us look at pictures of Jesus and the Blessed Mother at home. But how many of us realize that Jesus and Mary are also looking at us?"

"Some people have asked me: 'Why you? You weren't even a Catholic!' I have no answer to this question. But if this vision was given to me to remind those who receive Holy Communion that they are truly receiving Christ in the Host, then the message has been passed on!"

On September 9, 2000, Scott was received into the Catholic Church.[127]

---

[127] He is now at the head of the Pastoral Committee of Holy Redeemer Church in Hastings, where he is doing excellent work. Due to the fact that he is very gifted in computer science, he takes advantage of every occasion he can to spread the messages of Medjugorje.

"Dear Children! Today I invite you to fall in love with the Most Holy Sacrament of the Altar. Adore Him, little children, in your Parishes and in this way you will be united with the entire world. Jesus will become your friend and you will not talk of Him like someone whom you barely know. Unity with Him will be a joy for you and you will become witnesses to the love of Jesus that He has for every creature. Little children, when you adore Jesus you are also close to me. Thank you for having responded to my call" (September 25, 1995)

48

A PILOT SITE FOR ADORATION

Medjugorje has sent out its colonists, and an Irish friend, Anne Marie Collins, thirty-three years old, is one of them. Her happiness was born in Medjugorje.

As an adolescent, she went to Mass out of habit, consulted fortunetellers, and, as the Blessed Mother has said about many young people, she "was looking for happiness in places where it actually gets lost."

She taught at a Montessori school and her family owned a grocery store that was not doing well. So they made a deal with the Blessed Mother. If she would help them sell their business, they would all go to Medjugorje. Our Lady revealed herself to be a wonderful businesswoman because within three weeks of the shop being on the market, she introduced them to a buyer. On August 25, 1999, the Collins family arrived in Medjugorje. It was then that the story began for Anne Marie.

At the English Mass on the first day, the homily was entirely about fortunetellers and astrologers. Anne Marie sat on the edge of her seat, deeply moved. She had the impression that the homily was addressed to her and that the priest was speaking directly to her. So, she decided to go to Confession with that priest. What a memorable confession it was! She confessed her repeated visits to fortunetellers and, as she left the confessional, she realized in her heart that she was not under the sign of Leo, as she had been encouraged to believe. Rather, she was marked with the sign of Jesus Christ! A great feeling of freedom overtook her.

That week, she felt an amazing closeness to the Blessed Mother, as if they were walking hand in hand on Apparition Hill and Mount Krizevac! On the eve of her return to Ireland, Anne Marie experienced something special with Our Lady. Seated outside the church with her mother, she prayed along with the parish while looking at her Rosary beads. Suddenly, it was as if someone had lifted her head; looking up she saw Our Lady gazing at her with a smile. Anne Marie said that she would never be able to forget the smile on her face! Not a word was spoken. Her smile said it all. What love there was in that smile! She smiled at her as if she wanted to hold her tightly in her arms at that very moment. How beautiful she was! From that moment on, Anne Marie's life was turned upside down. She had reached the point of no return.

Upon her return to Ireland, Anne Marie immediately called her fiancé and told him that she had a marvelous week. She shared with him her amazing experience, but he just shook his head. He did not believe her! So, things began to change between them. Their relationship was not the same. She prayed to the Blessed Mother: "If you want me to end this relationship, don't let my heart be broken. Then, she told her boyfriend: "I can't go on like this. I don't think you're the one that the Blessed Mother wants for me." He had also become aware they were no longer good together. After they broke up, Anne Marie felt a weight had lifted from her shoulders.

First of all Our Lady gave Ann Marie a desire for Holy Mass, and she began to go every day. She also joined a prayer group. Then gradually she experienced a desire for Eucharistic Adoration. The Gospa acts with such tact! She knew that she must feed Anne Marie by small spoonfuls at a time, because she was not yet ready to take solid food.

In 2004, when John Paul II proclaimed the Year of the Eucharist, she and several friends decided to do something special. The Blessed Mother had given them the gift of Adoration during their pilgrimage to Medjugorje. She had made them keenly aware that her Son is really present in the Blessed Sacrament and so they had only one goal, to enfold Jesus with as many adorers as possible!128 It was then that an idea sprang up in their hearts, an idea that would help Jesus in the Eucharist to launch His appeal in all directions and bring out the most isolated of His potential adorers. It was easier said than done: to create a website where everyone, no matter where they were in Ireland, would be able to know where and when Jesus was inviting them to go. By looking on the website they could find out where Adoration was available—in what church and at what time. The information could then be passed on, and it would have a ripple effect.

Anne Marie and her team went to work with the fervor of those who have found a treasure in the field, and who want to buy the field. They went to all the parishes, chapels, and other sanctuaries in Ireland, looked up telephone numbers of priests and called them. Going through the telephone directories with a fine tooth comb was one thing, but having to call back again and again; dealing with so many answering machines was another thing! Fortunately, the adorers did not lack patience and perseverance, especially as they got a good reception from most of the priests. Some priests were elated to find such providential support for their ministry from Anne Marie and her team. They were finally able to realize a dream that had seemed impossible up until then. The dream was to set up perpetual adoration 24/7 in their church or chapel![129]

---

[128] Sister Faustina saw what we do not see. She wrote this about a memorable adoration: "Holy hour –Thursday. During this hour of prayer, Jesus allowed me to enter the Cenacle, and I was a witness to what happened there. However, I was most deeply moved when, before the Consecration, Jesus raised His eyes to Heaven, and entered into a mysterious conversation with His Father. It is only in eternity that we shall really understand that moment. His eyes were like two flames; His face was radiant, white as snow; His whole personage full of majesty, His soul full of longing. At the moment of Consecration, love rested satiated—the sacrifice fully consummated. Now only the external ceremony of death will be carried out—external destruction; the essence [of it] is in the Cenacle. Never, in my whole life, had I understood this mystery so profoundly as during that hour of adoration. Oh, how ardently I desire that the whole world would come to know this unfathomable mystery! (Diary §684)

[129] This is an example in the United States of the power of establishing perpetual adoration. In the Archdiocese of Indianapolis, Msgr. Buechlein asked all parishes to set up a Holy Hour once a month in order to obtain from the Lord priestly and religious vocations. Out of the 152 parishes of the diocese, only 17 answered the appeal and organized a monthly Holy Hour. This took place in 2004. One year later, at the beginning of autumn, 17 candidates for the priesthood entered the seminary! Father Rick Eldred, a faithful Medjugorje pilgrim, is the parish priest of St. Vincent de Paul Parish in this Archdiocese of Indianapolis. He declared that, since then, things have been going well. We truly believe that vocations, adoration and Holy Hours are inextricably linked. The archbishop hopes to have 50 seminarians and, at the moment there are about 30 of them. Also, a formation center was opened.

Anne Marie's heart burst with joy at each victory. Jesus would be loved and adored more and more. He would be able to spread His divine work into a growing number of hearts. He would gradually light His fire in the silence of those Holy Hours. He would be able to win over towns and villages, and recreate from the inside out the cloth of His Church that is in an agony of love.

Anne Marie found a job in a jewelry store and her part-time hours gave her total freedom. She spent her time between Medjugorje and Dublin. She needed long, silent prayer retreats in Medjugorje under the Blessed Mother's mantle so that she could be renewed before going back into the arena. It was a hard battle for her to fight — to bring about this important work which Satan could not stand. This was expected, because with each victory she won, Anne Marie took some of his followers away from him![130]

One day, at the end of a long retreat in Medjugorje, Anne Marie did not feel well. On her return to Dublin she ended up in the hospital. She was diagnosed with Addison's disease, a serious disease that affects the suprarenal glands and requires painful medical treatment. With the daily doses of cortisone, Anne Marie would often be exhausted, even without doing anything. Unless she experienced another miracle, she knew that she would have this handicap the rest of her life.[131]

The delicious joy of her first meeting with the Blessed Mother had now changed into another kind of joy. Jesus called His little disciple to go further with Him on a path known only to Him—a mysterious path sown with thorns and dreadful insects. Anne Marie learned about true union with God. On this Way of the Cross, where each hour brought its own dose of suffering, Our Lady taught her how to love God the way He likes us to love Him: to love Him alone, with simplicity, and with all our heart. Little by little a miracle was accomplished in Anne Marie's life—a more significant miracle than any physical healing would have been. Her Way of the Cross became a way of joy, a way overflowing with good fruit. Anne Marie was radiant like never before. She had brought adorers to her beloved Jesus through the Internet

---

[130] It is phenomenal to see that the rate of suicides and accidents goes down in the places where an adoration chapel is opened.

[131] It was Addison's disease that took Blessed Elizabeth of the Holy Trinity in 1906, at the age of 26, after great suffering. At that time, there was no available cure that could have saved her.

project. Great![132] But now, there was a "plus." Her face itself became like a living monstrance! Jesus was everywhere she went. There were people who asked her: "How can you be so joyful when you have such a painful illness?"

She was surprised by the question, and willingly revealed its source: "When I am in front of the Blessed Sacrament, Jesus gives me the grace to carry this Cross and go on with my daily life. I wouldn't have the strength to endure my illness if I didn't have Jesus. Without the presence of Jesus, I am nothing. I get all my strength through adoration."

A Prayer of Adoration
"O my God, Trinity that I adore,

Help me to forget myself entirely and establish myself in you,

Immobile and peaceful, as if my soul were already in eternity.

May nothing trouble my peace,

Nor let me separate from You,

O my Changeless One,

But may each minute take me further

Into the depth of Your Mystery.

Pacify my soul; make of it Your heaven,

Your beloved home and place of rest.

May I never leave You alone,

But may I always be wholly there,

Well awake in my faith, all adoring,

Totally abandoned to Your creative Action."

(Blessed Elizabeth of the Holy Trinity)

---

[132] This Internet site is working wonders. Not a day goes by that users do not testify to graces received, and that new volunteers do not increase the number of adorers: www.watchonehour. com

"Dear children! I rejoice with you and in this time of grace I call you to spiritual renewal. Pray, little children, that the Holy Spirit may come to dwell in you in fullness, so that you may be able to witness in joy to all those who are far from faith. Especially, little children, pray for the gifts of the Holy Spirit so that in the spirit of love, every day and in each situation, you may be closer to your fellow-man; and that in wisdom and love you may overcome every difficulty. I am with you and I intercede for each of you before Jesus." *(May 25, 1987)*

49

A MASS IN JUAREZ

That day, a large crowd had gathered in Juarez, Mexico, and several well-known apostles led the long prayer that followed Holy Communion. Signs and wonders multiplied under the eyes of those who were gathered there.[133] The lame were walking, the blind could see, the deaf could hear, and inner liberations showed themselves everywhere. What joy! Christ, true to Himself, had brought to life in His children the kind of presence that the Acts of the Apostles tells us about.

Sister Briege McKenna, a young nun, was among the leaders.[134] She blessed God with all her soul for His Divine strength and compassion. Indeed hearts were wide open and attentive, and graces flowed without hindrance. Blessings flowed in torrents!

That evening Sister Briege was overjoyed! She went to her hotel room and the Lord surprised her. He had a message for her that would change the course of her life. Having entered the convent at a very young age, Briege had always paid close attention to the intimate murmurs of Jesus in her heart, but that day His voice was clearer than ever:

---

[133] The characteristic signs of an apostle, according to St. Paul, are signs, wonders and mighty works, performed with patience. (2 Cor 12:12)

[134] www.intercessionforpriests.org. For more information on Sister Briege McKenna see page 57 (footnote 23)

"I have brought you to this place to teach you where the true power of my living presence is. Your mission is to travel the world to talk to my children, reminding them of my real presence on all the altars of the world and to talk about the Eucharist and the Blessed Sacrament."

Briege also remembered that Jesus had expressed His deep sorrow, and how He was counting on her. If Francis of Assisi wept at seeing how "Love is not loved," this young nun was pierced at hearing Jesus - the living Love - talk about being abandoned by His children. This is what she wrote to me in February 2006:

"Jesus confided to me that people would come from all over the world to look for signs and wonders, they would travel from all sorts of places in the hope of receiving a message of healing or consolation. They would cross oceans and continents, and would be ready to spend fortunes to obtain help, often all in vain. They fail to recognize the greatest miracle of all, and the most marvelous wonder, His Glorious Resurrected Presence on our altars and in our tabernacles! 'I am the source of all these blessings that they need,' Jesus told me. 'And they all leave Me alone."

"Sister Emmanuel, ever since I have obeyed the order to undertake this mission and travel throughout the world, I have constantly seen and heard about very great conversions and miracles. Yesterday, when leading a day of prayer in Florida, a man told me that four years ago he was in the last stages of cancer, and then went to a Eucharistic celebration, followed by Adoration and a healing prayer. He said just at the moment when Father Kevin held Jesus in the monstrance to bless the congregation, he felt a heat go through his whole body. The next day, all traces of the cancer had disappeared."

"Dear Children! I am your Mother and therefore want to lead you to perfect holiness. I want each one of you to be happy here on earth and to be with me in Heaven. That is, dear children, my desire and purpose for coming here" (May 25, 1987)

50

HEAVEN WITHIN REACH

February 1991

Mrs. Ischia invited Vicka to France and asked me to accompany her as a translator. Since we had to take a 7:00 a.m., flight from Split (Croatia) to Paris, I carefully allowed for extra time in planning the journey, and the night before I warned Vicka:

"Tomorrow morning, be ready at two o'clock. I'll come and get you by taxi."

Vicka was punctual and that morning we rushed over the rough terrain of Herzegovina. The first part of the program in Paris was for Vicka to give her testimony to some priests. During the journey, I asked Vicka, "How are we going to organize things for your apparition this evening? Will you ask to be excused in order to see Our Lady in private, or will you let the priests pray with you?"

"Don't worry about it," she answered me, "I've already had the apparition this morning!"

"This morning... you mean last night?"

"Yes. You know, when I travel, the Gospa prefers to come early in the morning. In this way, during my mission, I don't have to worry about the how, where, and with whom I will have the apparition. So the day before, in the evening, she tells me at what time she will appear to me the next morning, and that's it!"

"If I understand correctly, she told you last night that she would come this morning before your departure?"

"Yes. She said, 'Since Sister Emmanuel is coming to get you at 2 o'clock, I will come at one o'clock....'"

"Do you mean she actually said, 'Sister Emmanuel'? And she adapted her schedule to the one that I had set?"

"Yes! That's for sure! She always takes into consideration what we decide!"

For Vicka it was obvious - this was just the way things go on in her normal everyday life, but for me it was a shock. The Mother of God had adapted her arrival to the schedule that I had set (and badly set as we had to wait three hours in a deserted, poorly heated, airport!). I remained silent for a good while in order to let my mind digest this news because, suddenly Heaven revealed itself to be within reach. So it's true - I am part of the family!

How unaware of Heaven we really are! What blindness! What a loss! What loss of happiness!

A similar fact brought my two feet back down to earth, if I dare say so! Indeed, it awakened me from this lethargy of conscience that makes us live in unreality, or rather disconnects us from half the reality and of this wonderful lot in life that is ours in God's plan. We walk on this earth encompassed in the immense reality of Heaven and the world to come; the saints are on the same level as we are! But because we are repressed by our narrow limitations of time, space, and knowledge, we quickly reduce our destiny to only what our senses tell us.

St. John of the Cross said, "Our senses deceive us." They do more than deceive us, they imprison us! Just like each of the other Medjugorje visionaries, Vicka is acutely aware of the world to come, which is already here.

"Dear Children! If you will abandon yourselves to me, you will not even feel the passage from this life to the next life. You will begin to live the life of Heaven on earth." *(Message to Jelena, 1986)*

51

HOLY DEATH, HOLY DEATH!

How could I ever forget the day when, by chance, I met Vicka in Bijakovici, and told her about the recent death of Marc, Denis Nolan's father, in California. I asked her to pray for him but to my great surprise Vicka did not say one word of condolence, nor did she appear the least bit sorry. On the contrary, her face lit up with great joy as she exclaimed:

"Holy death! Holy death!"

Her enthusiasm was so great that I had a hard time to get a word in. Then I understood that God had allowed this meeting with Vicka and Marc bereavement to teach me something - and what a lesson it was!

"When God comes to get us," Vicka explained, "what a joy it is to die! God is so merciful - unless we don't want His mercy, because He doesn't force anyone. He is so happy to be able to exercise His great mercy! God is so, so good! If only people knew that, they wouldn't be so attached to the things of this world. How can they be so attached to the things of this world when they are here today and gone tomorrow?"

"That's easy for you to say, Vicka," I said to her. "You've seen what it's like beyond the veil!"

"Exactly! And it's because I've seen heaven that I'm saying these things. It's my hope that everyone will come to know it. I want to tell everyone how good God is; they shouldn't be afraid of Him! They shouldn't be afraid of death! If every morning, as soon as you wake up, you decide to follow God, your life will become very beautiful. Each day you will grow spiritually and you will be happy forever. Forever! That's just how it is!

That evening, I informed Denis about my meeting with Vicka and he replied to me by email:

"I was able to see this mercy for myself. I've experienced it. God was truly there to give my father His love. Before that, he had been a Catholic like so many that we see today. He believed in the existence of God but he had never practiced his faith. If you were to give him a Rosary he would make it spin in the air like the blades of a helicopter instead of praying it. Sure, he was a good man, but he wasn't a saint - far from it! But, when he called on Mary, what mercy was given to him! Yes, God is really on our side! Vicka's words are true; we need not fear God."

The following is one of the Blessed Mother's most astounding messages in Medjugorje, one that Vicka told me around the time her brother-in-law, Nedjo, died: "Dear children, you should celebrate the death of those who are close to you with the same joy that you celebrate the birth of a child."

To understand the greatness and splendor of the "other life," as opposed to being unaware of it, makes all the difference in the world.

A Death Deferred

So how did the Lord set about calling Denis' father, Marc, back to him, and by what divine means did he succeed in changing this "hard nut to crack" in extremis?

Denis explained: "One night in March 1997, my family was suddenly awoken by the telephone ringing. My father, who was then 85 years old, was at that time in a hospital in California with pneumonia. The doctors had forewarned my mother he wouldn't live through the day. I immediately took the plane from Chicago and found my father dying - he was hardly breathing. The members of my family surrounded him. Suddenly, opening his eyes, he noticed the clock on the wall facing him, and murmured, 'It's 9:40.' In California, 9:40 a.m. corresponds to the time of Mary's apparition in Medjugorje (6:40 p.m.)."

"Then, I said to him, 'Dad, Our Lady is appearing right now in Medjugorje! Call her!' "

"For twenty minutes, hardly able to breathe, he called his mother: 'Mary, come! Mama, come!' This was actually the first time that I had heard my father pray aloud!"

"From that moment on, he began to regain his strength. The next day, while being transferred from Intensive Care to an ordinary room, he had improved so much that two of the nurses thought he was someone else. He took up his regular activities again and got on with his life as usual. But the Lord and the Blessed Mother had come into his life. He now went to Confession and to Mass with my mother, and he prayed the Rosary discreetly. Eighteen months later, he died suddenly of a heart attack at the age of 87."

"I don't doubt it for one second: those eighteen months were a free gift from heaven to help my father prepare for his death, and this delay was through the intercession of the Gospa, his Mother, whom he had called upon to help him."

A Ticket to Heaven?

Most people are afraid when they think about their own death, or the death of those who are close to them. In reality, the Gospa tells us, "Death does not exist"! It is simply a veil that falls, like the curtain of the temple of Jerusalem that was torn in the middle, revealing what was already there, hidden in the invisible—the Holy of Holies!

A picture came to my mind that is inadequate, as is any comparison to this: There are windows with panes that allow us to see from inside what is going on outside, but that prevent people on the outside from seeing inside. But let's suppose that the glazier makes a mistake, and installs the panes of glass in such a way that those on the inside cannot see outside! This is what happens to us! Here on earth we are like the people who don't see those who see them! This is where the tragedy of unbelief begins, because there is just one small step between not "seeing" someone, and being totally unaware of his existence. "Dear children," the Gospa tells us, "you are unaware."

The saints conquered this lack of clarity and lived as if they could see the invisible. This allowed them to embrace invisible realities without fearing the day when the pane of glass would break, when the veil would fall. The Heavenly Court was already familiar to them, and they viewed the passage through the valley of death as a long awaited kiss that would bring them forever into the company of the elect after their exile. [+]

Earth is a time of desire; Heaven is possession for eternity.[*] Here on earth, if I do not desire Heaven, I am a dying person who can still be revived. If I focus my capacity for desire on the material world, then I am a dead man and am terrified of the hour of my death, when I will lose all my false treasures. Being less attached to material things will certainly cause us to "contemplate eternal life with joy."

Marija has already been given some knowledge about this subject. The Gospa explained to her that, in Heaven, each one of the elect knows exactly what others have done for them, and how, by their prayers, sacrifices and offerings, they took part in increasing the degree of their eternal glory. Sometimes, the elect realize that the prayers of so-and-so were the reason that they were not lost! In Heaven, each one of us will be eternally grateful to each one of these people, and we will have a very special bond of love with them. This reality is marvelous and encouraging, especially when on the earth we do not yet see the fruits of our sacrifices and prayers for those we love. Here, the Gospa gives us the hope that can heal us of our discouragement! She helps us invest in real values, and in this way, "to contemplate eternal life with joy."

---

* Listen to the CDs "When Death Separates Us From Those We Love" and "Heaven? Purgatory? Hell? Choose your future!" and "The Amazing Secret of Purgatory". See the appendix at the end of the book for more information.

* During his mission to Dublin, the seer, Ivan, said to the crowd, "If you could see the Gospa for only one second, all the things of this earth would immediately lose their attraction in your eyes."

"Dear children! Today I rejoice with your patron saint and call you to be open to God's will, so that in you and through you, faith may grow in the people you meet in your everyday life. Little children, pray until prayer becomes joy for you. Ask your holy protectors to help you grow in love towards God. Thank you for having responded to my call."
(July 25, 2002)

52

O GOOD SAINT JOSEPH!

St. Joseph is the heavenly President of our Medjugorje apostolate. In order to manage well, we need an efficacious Saint who is full of love and humor!

The Little Cat

In 1998, while I was on a mission in Poland, my friends related this event to me:

"During World War II, Polish nuns were running an orphanage in Warsaw. People in that area were very poor and the nuns survived with the help of Divine Providence. One day they ran out of milk for the orphans, which seriously threatened the children's health. What could they do? In this distressing situation the Mother Superior asked the cook, Sister Ewa, to write a petition to St. Joseph and place it behind his picture, as was the community's custom. But Sister Ewa, with a sheet of white paper in front of her, was confused - how could she possibly depict milk that was as white as the paper itself? However, she did the best she could.

The next day, a man from the city knocked at the convent door. He just wanted to greet the nuns and also bring them a small gift. All the nuns were now rejoicing at the thought that the milk might have arrived. But to their great surprise and disappointment, they found that their visitor had brought them a cat as a gift - a simple little cat! What a bizarre gift! The man, perhaps noticing their look of excitement fade when seeing the cat, asked them:

"Do you need anything in particular?"

"Yes, we really need milk," the nuns replied in a single voice.

"Milk?" exclaimed the visitor. "I have plenty of it! I will bring you some as soon as possible!"

The milk was delivered that same day. However, the Superior remained intrigued by the gift of the cat, so she asked the cook to show her the petition she had left for St. Joseph. On seeing the drawing, she burst out laughing. Sister Ewa had only drawn a cat gulping down milk from a bowl! In his kindness St. Joseph had fulfilled their request. First, he supplied the cat, then, as a bonus, supplied the milk!

Blessed With Oil

Kim was not practicing her faith. She was 23 years old and appeared to have no interest in God. She was a gifted, sensible, decisive, and attractive girl. In March of 2005, she accepted her parents' proposal to accompany some family friends to Medjugorje, not to make a pilgrimage, but to simply look after their three young children. Knowing that Kim was crazy about children, her parents thought this would be a good way to get her to bathe in the graces of Medjugorje, if only for a few days. Back in their native California, both parents were praying like crazy that their daughter's heart would be touched by this Oasis of Peace.

On the last day of the pilgrimage to Medjugorje, smiling coquettishly, our dear Kim said to her friends, "I've been happy to look after the children, but I'd also like to take advantage of being in Medjugorje a little bit. Would it be possible to change my return date, so I could stay another one or two weeks? I really feel like learning more about this place, which seems kind of special." Kim had not participated in anything at all with her friends, no Mass, no climbing the hills, nor meeting with the visionaries - it had been a total blackout! So it seemed strange that Kim wanted to stay. But here, we perceive the Gospa's secret, and the skill of a mother who knows how to get through to her child, through the smallest openings. David, the group leader, asked me if Kim could remain with us for a few days. "OK," I said.

After that, Kim's return date was moved back three times! And finally, one year later, it expired! Kim fell so deeply into the graces of Medjugorje that she did not want to leave without having first received a very clear internal sign from Our Lady that it was time to go - God's time for her to go. Her heart was opened wide. Step by step, she marveled at everything, just like a young fiancée who happily discovers new characteristics of her beloved, and who savors the joy of being in his presence.

Among one of Kim's happiest discoveries was the influence of the guardian angels and saints, so present in our daily lives. I will never forget the first time that St. Joseph's tenderness touched her heart. On that particular morning, I must admit, Chrissey[135] and Kim were a bit annoyed when they arrived for Lauds, our morning prayer. In our house, there are certain foods we never buy - simply because they are expensive and St. Joseph has been given the responsibility of providing them himself! Virgin olive oil is one of those goods, and we had none left for the festive lunch planned later that day for our guests. So Chrissey and Kim had tried to convince me to make an exception just for that day and buy it, but my reply disappointed them: "You say there's no olive oil? No problem, we'll pray to St. Joseph. He sees to all that we need!" For Kim, this heavenly connection was unreal, but, that morning, when we came to address St. Joseph with our request for oil and other necessities, she did say a courageous "Amen!"

After Lauds, some good hot coffee awaited us in the kitchen; but it wasn't alone! A beautiful bottle of extra virgin olive oil from Italy was behind the front door, with a hastily scribbled note: "We don't want to disturb your prayers. We'll come back later! Your friends from Verona"

So shocked, Kim had to sit down! She shook her head, not knowing whether to laugh or cry. "You know," she ended up saying to me, "in the States, this isn't something that we know about! If people only knew! We have no idea what it's like to live with God!"

Admittedly, St. Joseph made a hit with Kim that day. He let her have a peek at the splendid mystery of the communion of Saints, through a bottle of virgin olive oil!

---

[135] Chrissey Zaums, my American assistant in Medjugorje, for the past five years.

The Carpenter in Warsaw

St. Joseph does far too much good work to be ignored! Here is a beautiful testimony from Marysia, my friend from Warsaw who is very committed to Medjugorje.

"Four years ago, Sister Emmanuel gave me a picture of St. Joseph, and she said to me: 'You never pray to him! Why not? He is such an extraordinary Saint! Take him as your friend. You'll see. He'll help you a lot!'"

"My husband, Bogdan, and I, together with our two children, needed a bigger house because our apostolate for the Gospa required more and more space. But we did not have enough money to buy one. So, following Sister Emmanuel's advice, full of hope and trust, I wrote a letter to St. Joseph, placed it behind his icon and began a novena. Months passed by, nothing happened!"

"My spiritual director then said to me, 'St. Joseph is a simple carpenter and a very practical man. You should draw him a picture of the house that you would like to find.' So, I made a precise drawing of the house, as seen from the outside, and I placed it behind the icon. Months passed by, nothing happened!"

"I told my spiritual director that obviously St. Joseph didn't like me. He answered: 'Since St. Joseph hasn't answered your prayer, no doubt it's because he is a father, and he wants to deal directly with another father about this matter. Ask your husband to pass on the request himself, to St. Joseph; between fathers of families, they will understand each other!'"

"Bogdan complied with this that same day, and within the week, we found our house! Obviously, St. Joseph wanted to encourage Bogdan in his role as head of the family. The price of the house was exactly what we had at our disposal, but it was actually worth a lot more. It had all the rooms that we had asked for, even the basement and the attic, and the exterior was the same as my drawing! Like a good carpenter, St. Joseph had chosen one made entirely of wood - and not just any kind of wood, but oak! On examining the windows and doors we noticed, with a smile, that they were ingeniously finished and in perfect condition."

"Pictures of the Sacred Heart of Jesus and the Immaculate Heart of Mary were displayed in the entrance. In fact, later I learned that in

Medjugorje Mary has asked that we put these images in our homes. There was also an old picture of Little Flower (St. Thérèse of Lisieux), a reminder of our spiritual link with France. For many years, the former owner had used one of the rooms as a prayer room. All we had to do was to take it over and light the candles! Actually this lady, who was very sick, had prayed for hours in front of the picture of Our Lady of Czestochowa, offering her sufferings day and night."

"There was also another reminder that prevented us from forgetting the messages of Mary, his spouse, about fasting. St. Joseph had provided a baker's oven! Delicious homemade bread can be a help in persevering with fasting two days a week!"

"The house itself is close to Warsaw, in the middle of nature, and the school that the children attend is better than the one in Warsaw. A priest brought us, from Jerusalem, a picture of St. Joseph watching over the Holy Family. It has a place of honor in the entrance to our home, because from now on, our family is under his protection."

Saint Joseph the Architect

In Galilee, 2000 years ago, carpenters were also architects. Despite the lack of metal frames and modern technology, carpenters would draw up viable plans to ensure the buildings would stand firm. We can imagine St. Joseph conversing with Jesus about different ways to build a house and, together, trying to find the best possible plan to satisfy a client. Furthermore, St. Joseph was the first one to place those heavy beams that carpenters had to carry on the shoulders of his Little Jesus. Although not aware, in doing this, he was in fact preparing his Son to carry the heavy beam of the Cross. The Heavenly Father had also foreseen this for Jesus because He gave this knowledgeable carpenter the job of 'project manager' during Jesus' long years of seclusion in Nazareth. We often forget that, in the unseen world, it was Joseph who helped Jesus to be able to walk the road to Calvary without collapsing, by training Him as a child.

We very rarely think of St. Joseph as a man who drew up plans. It must have been a Ben David family inherited skill because, in Medjugorje, his spouse, the Gospa, often talks of her plans for the world, and asks us for help in carrying them out. Jesus, also, has His plan of salvation for humanity. It appears that the entire Holy Family specializes in plans!

And What Plans Do We Have for Our Lives?

Saint Joseph is the saint we need to help us become enthusiastic about life itself and the gift of life. Like a good architect who is skillful, meticulous, and courageous at work, he helps us re-frame our life and adjust it according to God's dream for us. This is because he is a just one par excellence, which for the Jews of that time meant he was a man who adjusted his entire life to God. (This has nothing to do with our Department of Justice!) And today our lives have such a need to be re-adjusted towards God!

This great expert on God's plans was chosen by the Father to accompany His Son, Jesus, throughout His early life until He became a man. St. Joseph would be very happy to continue his task with each of us on this earth, especially with those who take to heart the messages of Myriam, his spouse.

The Terror of Demons

St. Catherine Labouré was dying on Rue du Bac, in Paris. The Blessed Mother had given her the Miraculous Medal. Catherine was known as the "Saint of Silence". Very few of her words have been recorded, but we know that shortly before her death her nephews and nieces asked her: "Auntie, to whom should we pray at the moment of your death?"

Quoting a title taken from the Litany of St. Joseph, she replied, "to the terror of demons!" And she added, "When the demon tries to dictate to you thoughts of impurity, hatred, envy, lies, say this little prayer: 'St. Joseph, terror of demons, protect me!' And say it on each one of your fingers and thumbs! St. Joseph will then freeze your thoughts. That's it! But they will come back. When they do, treat them again in the same way, saying: 'St. Joseph, terror of demons, protect me.' Repeat this as many times as you have fingers and thumbs on your hands. You will then gain the upper hand in the battle."

St. Joseph resembles the man who stands on the door of a nightclub, scrutinizing each newcomer closely, and deciding who he should risk allowing inside. This is how God the Father made him! It was necessary so that no one could interfere with his Son, or His favorite daughter Mary, who was His secret weapon.

He Is So Soft-Hearted

Vicka repeats often "Do not be afraid. All you need to do is ask."

St. Joseph has graces in store. It is a great joy for him to support a person who invokes him with friendliness and trust, whether it be to protect his family from a breakup, to help him understand what choices to make when faced with a tricky situation, to overcome the assaults of the evil one, to protect a child from impurity, to rebuild harmony in the person who has been hurt by life; or to help him no longer delay saying "yes" to a call from God and to persevere in prayer in the midst of a hostile world.[136] St. Joseph can also help a person to earn his living from doing work that brings about peace, giving evidence of God's charity and joy to others; to offer suffering with peace and to live a great love for our Blessed Mother. In short, to walk humbly and with certainty on the way to holiness!

What strikes me about St. Joseph is his tenderness. He falls apart like a child before a trusting heart. One day I made a novena to St. Joseph because I needed a car in Medjugorje. I explained to him: "It's to serve your spouse better where she appears." Wasn't that a strong case?! I thought that he would answer my prayer if only for love of her! The car arrived on the 9th day of the novena.

---

[136] An English priest who was passing through Medjugorje was interested in spiritual combat. He had searched the lives of the saints to find out how they had fought against the torments of temptation. The Queen of Peace must have smiled when she heard him describing to his parishioners the personal discoveries of the saints so they could overcome temptation, because she likes it when we take the saints as models. "How do you win out over distractions?" he asked. "Take a look at St. Bernadette. She only spoke the Lourdes dialect, and a certain Julie Garrow was given the task of teaching her French."

Julie asked Bernadette: 'Do you have distractions in prayer?'

'Yes,' Bernadette replied.

'Does that bother you?'

'Oh, no! I pass them on to St. Joseph and he takes care of them. No problem.'

A young woman, on hearing about this, thought she could not use the same argument to convince St. Joseph. The truth was she did need a vehicle, but just to travel to her work, for a company that had nothing particularly Christian about it. However, counting on Saint Joseph's kindness, she decided to make a novena. She couldn't believe her eyes when, providentially, the vehicle arrived and it was exactly the size she wanted! That day I discovered a new aspect of St. Joseph's personality—his tenderness for us is a free gift!

I could write a book about St. Joseph's kindnesses, but I prefer to offer this beautiful prayer of St. Francis de Sales. In this way everyone will be able to give thanks for his generosity in their own lives!

O Glorious St. Joseph, Spouse of Mary
We beg you to grant us your protection,
Through the Sacred Heart of Jesus and the Immaculate Heart of Mary.
O you, whose power encompasses all our necessities,
And who knows how to make possible the most impossible things,
Open your fatherly eyes to the concerns of your children.

We fly to you with confidence. Deign to take this great and difficult trial
That is the cause or our anxiety… (mention your needs).
Let its outcome be for the Glory of God and for the good of His devoted servants.
O amiable Saint Joseph, who has never been invoked in vain
And whose favor with God is so powerful that it has been said:
"In Heaven, Saint Joseph commands rather than pleads."

Tender father, pray to Jesus for us. Pray to Mary for us.
Be our advocate with your Divine Son
To whom you were the most loving and faithful foster-father here below.
Be our advocate with Mary to whom you were the most loving and beloved spouse.

Add to your glories that of obtaining for us a favorable answer

To the difficult problem that we entrust to you.
We truly believe that you can answer our prayers by delivering us
From the sorrows that beset us and the bitterness that overwhelms our souls.

Furthermore, we have the firm conviction
That you will not ignore the pleas of the afflicted who implore your help.
Humbly prostrate at your feet, good Saint Joseph,
We beseech you to have pity on our pleadings and tears.
Cover us with your mantle of mercy, and bless us. Amen.

(Saint Francis de Sales)

Here we could fit a simpler and shorter nice prayer to St Joseph, for people who have little time!"Dear children! Today I invite you in a special way to open yourselves to God the Creator and to become active. I invite you, little children, to see at this time who needs your spiritual or material help. By your example, little children, you will be the extended hands of God, which humanity is seeking. Only in this way will you understand that you are called to witness and to become joyful carriers of God's word and of His love. Thank you for having responded to my call." (February 25, 1997)

53

"WE ARE GOING TO PULL THE PLUG"

During the course of our mission to Malaysia, Father Tim Deeter related this incident to me:

As a seminarian during the summer of 1977, he was training to be a chaplain at St. Joseph's Hospital in Milwaukee. He visited the sick, comforting them and taking them Holy Communion. On seeing that patients in a coma had been placed in total solitude, he took it to heart to spend some time with them. He knew that when someone is in a deep coma, the last of the five senses to weaken is the sense of hearing. Therefore, he proceeded to speak aloud to those sick patients in the hope they would hear even if they couldn't reply. He would say some kind words and most certainly talk about Christ's Resurrection.

One day he was caring for one of these patients, who was still young and being kept alive by a machine that was maintaining certain essential bodily functions. Her name was Althea Turner and she had been in a coma for a long time. Fr. Tim was told that, because the hospital was short of beds, they were going to pull the plug on the machine for this woman.

On hearing this news, he went to Althea, and placing his hand on hers, he said, "I've just learned that they're going to pull the plug on the machine that's keeping you alive. If you don't want your life to be terminated, I'm ready to help you, but I'm asking you for a sign. If you squeeze my hand that is in yours, I'll understand that you want to go on living."

Althea clearly picked up his message so well that she immediately squeezed Father Tim's hand hard, holding it tight for at least a minute. It is pointless to try and describe the poignancy of this scene!

Father then said to Althea: "Thank you. Now I'm convinced that you want to live, but I'm not so sure that I can convince the hospital personnel. I'm going to go and get a nurse, and I want you to do with that nurse's hand exactly what you did to mine."

In fact, when the nurse arrived, Althea squeezed her hand so hard that no one could doubt that this woman was fighting for her life. Father Tim simply added that, about ten days later, Althea left the hospital on her own two feet, and took up her regular activities again.

It just goes to show that the real comas we need to attend to are those experienced by the people who do not have a concern for life!

"Dear Children! When you have a person who is ill pray for my intentions and offer sacrifices for my intentions and I will take care of the person who is ill." (To Marija, undated)

54

AT THE BEDSIDE OF THE SICK

Each visionary has received a special prayer mission from Our Lady. Vicka has been asked to pray for the sick. It seems that she is drawn to the sick like a magnet to metal. I have never seen her grow weary or lose patience in praying for them even when they line up by the hundreds at the foot of her small staircase in Bijakovici. She treats the hundredth visitor the same as she treated the first, and gives him the same prayer time and the same enthusiastic smile. A large part of her free time is spent visiting the sick at their homes or in the hospital. She knows that the Gospa is present at the bedside of the sick, just as she was present at the foot of the Cross, near her Son Jesus. Nothing less!

Vicka never prays aloud over people. The Gospa taught her a prayer that she says silently. This prayer is fairly long and, according to Vicka, the Gospa will allow it to be revealed to us some day.

One morning, out of the blue, she asked me to drive her to the hospital in Mostar because she wanted to visit a sick person. We made quite a round of visits because, taking advantage of having me as a chauffeur, Vicka found new visits to make on the way—the orphan's village, the Italian scouts' home—to name just a couple, and on the way back several other families near Medjugorje.

Whether she is laughing with the children, hugging them, or praying at length for the sick, or simply giving some news from Bijakovici to families experiencing hardship, she brings comforts to everyone. She radiates such happiness that people feel a little bit of heaven in her presence. I could not stop myself from thinking, "If the critics of

Medjugorje could only see what I am seeing and hearing right now, if only for two minutes, they would be won over! Conviction from the heart would remove all criticism. Heaven cannot be faked - especially for twenty-six years - it can only be lived!"

On our return, I asked Vicka: "On Sunday you had a fever of 104°, yet on Monday I saw you on your stairs with the pilgrims. How do you do it?"

"Why certainly! You can't let the pilgrims wait for nothing. They come from very far away to hear the messages. You can't stay in bed when you know they're out there waiting! You don't worry about your temperature. You get up and say: 'Gospa, help me!' You go to them, you think you're going to fall, you hold on to the railing, but they ask you a thousand questions. They have their sufferings and their intentions. They hug you, squeeze your hand, and all you can see is darkness and your vision is blurry, and you say to yourself, 'No, I mustn't fall, even if I have a fever of 102°!' Then, you see, the Gospa helps you. She cannot but help you! And it passes…. After a few minutes, it gets better, and the pilgrims receive the messages! You see, that's how it is! No one asks how you are or if you need something - no, for them, you are the "visionary" so you must give them what you have received from the Blessed Mother!"

"When Our Lady formed her prayer group, she was extremely insistent on the need for the young people to take care of the sick and on the way to pray for them. She said to Marija: 'When you have a sick person to pray for, pray for my intentions and offer sacrifices for my intention; and I will take care of the sick person.'"

"However, there is a wrong way of praying and that is when we focus only on the healing and repeat, 'Lord, heal them, heal them!'"

"The Gospa said, 'No - do not pray like that, dear children, because then your hearts are not open to God or to God's will.'"

During the summer of 1985, the Blessed Mother dictated a prayer for the sick to Jelena Vasilj where she stressed: "This is the best prayer that you can say for the sick." It is easy to recognize Our Lady's hand because God is the center of the prayer:

Prayer for a Sick Person (Dictated to Jelena)
(Three times recite the *Glory* Be followed by this prayer)[137]

O my God,
Behold this sick person before You.
He has come to ask You what he wishes and
What he considers as the most important thing for him.
You, O my God, make these words enter into his heart:
"What is important is the health of the soul."

Lord, may Your will in everything take place in his regard,
If You want him to be cured, let health be given to him;
But if Your will is something else, let him continue to bear his Cross.
I also pray to You for us, who intercede for him;
Purify our hearts, to make us worthy to convey Your holy Mercy.
Protect him and relieve his pain. That Your holy will be done in him,
That Your holy name be revealed through him.
Help him to bear his Cross with courage.

When the visionaries asked Our Lady if she was going to cure such and such a sick person, she often replied, "I cannot heal; only God can heal. But pray, my children, and I will pray with you; believe strongly, fast, and do penance. .God comes to everyone's assistance. I am not God. I need your sacrifices and your prayers."

---

[137] Glory be to the Father, and to the Son and to the Holy Spirit, as it was in the beginning, is now and ever shall be, world without end. Amen!

"Dear children! Today, in a special way, I invite you to take the cross in your hands and to meditate on the wounds of Jesus. Ask of Jesus to heal your wounds, which you, dear children, during your life sustained because of your sins or the sins of your parents. Only in this way, dear children, will you understand that the world is in need of healing of faith in God the Creator. By Jesus' passion and death on the cross, you will understand that only through prayer you too can become true apostles of faith when, in simplicity and prayer, you live faith which is a gift. Thank you for having responded to my call." (March 25, 1997)

55

BILL'S MIGRAINES

During my mission to the great North Western Territories (Canada) in May 2005, I stayed for a few days with a couple who worked for the Diocese of Mackenzie-Fort Smith. One day, at breakfast, Bill told me that he used to suffer from violent migraines but had received a wonderful healing. A woman who had been passing through Yellowknife, stopped at their home. She had the "gift of healing" and offered her services to Bill. She performed a method of healing that was unknown to him. She used hand gestures and spoke about the movement of energy. After the session was over, Bill's migraines disappeared.

Bill had barely finished his story when his wife, Linda, gave him a nudge and said, "Explain everything to Sister Emmanuel and tell her how you've been feeling since your healing."

"Um...Yes! My migraines have certainly disappeared but now I have shingles and, must admit, I don't feel good inside. To tell the truth, I've lost my peace of heart."

"Tell her everything, Bill," his wife insisted.

On hearing he had lost inner peace, I suggested that we look deeper at the problem and asked him:

"Bill, who is this woman?"

"I don't know Sister. She was a practicing Catholic. She was very nice, and she offered to pray for my health."

"Did she tell you what method she was using when she practiced this 'gift'?"

"Wait a minute while I think about it—it's on the tip of my tongue! Yes—she said that she was trained to practice Reiki."

"Reiki? Bill, do you know what that is?"

"It sounded good! The lady told us that she saw lots of sick people and it seems that she helps all sorts of people, even those who are not necessarily."

"I understand. Listen, Bill! Since you lost your inner peace at the same time as your migraines stopped, I have a question for you. If you had the choice, would you prefer to regain your sense of peace but have the migraines return, or to remain with no migraines and no peace, as it is now?"

"Oh, without question, I would choose to be at peace inside, with or without the migraines! That's by far the most important thing to me, especially as that would help restore my good relationship with Linda! And you know, I had my migraines for years, I'm used to them. I used to offer them to Jesus for His intentions and I'm ready to continue doing so!"

It was obvious to me that Bill had a good heart. He was generous; He loved the Lord, he desired to walk with Him and do some good for Him. His answer touched me and I was convinced that God would help him.

"Listen, Bill. There is a simple explanation. This woman who used Reiki for your headaches was perhaps sincere. But sincere or not, Reiki is a first class trap that brings about false healings and, in the end, you will pay a very high price for your physical and moral health![138] I

---

[138] Reiki is spreading rapidly through the English speaking countries, promoted by the New Age movement. It is a type of therapy that purports to use vital universal energy and certain powers that come from a "transcendental spirit" (certainly not the Holy Spirit!). The technique consists of invoking universal energy upon the sick person by tracing on him archetypal symbols. The therapist then visualizes the energy that enters through the "chakra" at the top of his head, fills it and overflows from his hand to enter into the patient. Actually, Reiki opens the door to occult forces. It may be that there is a temporary improvement in health in some cases, but this quickly makes way for symptoms that usually appear in the context of occult practices, even spiritualism. This practice is made up of non-verbal sounds, based on the "intent" of the

suggest that you pray to Jesus before going to bed tonight, so that He will enlighten you about what you actually received. For example, you could say to Him: 'Lord, if this healing comes from You, let me keep it and help me to also regain my peace of heart. But if this healing does not come from You and if this woman has caused me harm, then I beg you, take it back and renew my peace of heart. I am ready to accept my migraines again.'"

The next morning at breakfast, Linda, like a fellow accomplice, gave me a little sign that something new had happened. Bill came and sat down and, while drinking his coffee, he said:

"Sister Emmanuel, I have good news for you! When I woke up this morning, my migraine was waiting for me like an old traveling companion! What joy I experienced! I immediately thanked the Lord for this sign and especially for the fact that my peace has been truly restored as well! I think that from now on I'll offer my migraines to Jesus with even more fervor from now on!" Bill's joy was a delight to see.

I have no doubt that Bill's daily humble offering will help Jesus to spread His Reign of Love throughout the world,[139] and to heal many people of carditis, a condition of the heart that hinders the development of love. In any case, Bill is certainly healed and now inoculated against naivety concerning some New Age viruses that, under the guise of offering healing, bring about disastrous consequences for the soul. (for souls?)

The latest news from Bill's family is that the gift from Jesus still remains and, for Bill, the cross of his migraines has become a way of joy.

Reiki master. As is often the case with practices that the New Age movement promotes, Reiki denies the omnipotence of a personal Creative God, and works with the energies with a pantheist spirit. The fake "gift" of healing is transmitted during initiation sessions (contrary to the gifts of the Holy Spirit, which are not automatically transmitted from person to person, but which are received from on high according to God's choosing). This practice cannot co-exist with our Christian faith. With Jesus, everything is clear! The fact that some priests and nuns practice it does not mean that it is acceptable; its traps are subtle, and studies to this effect have not yet been made known to the public at large. For more information, go to Father Verlinde's site: St. Joseph's Family, 69380 Chasselay, France. Tel.:04 78 47 35 26 - Fax: 04 78 47 36 78. http://www.fsjinfo.net or http://www.final.age.net

[139] Jesus said to Sister Faustina, "Join your little sufferings to My Sorrowful Passion, so that they may have infinite value before My Majesty." (Diary §1511)

Displacing the sickness

Be careful. Today many people go to see healers, without understanding where healers get their 'gifts' from. For example, if someone has a bad back and goes to a healer, his back may be healed but he does not know that the pain has been displaced elsewhere. The problem or sickness has only been displaced. It will then affect another part of his body, perhaps a more vital organ or even his most profound being. He then returns to the healer who might cure him of this next ailment, but then a third, even worse problem, appears. Eventually he will wake up with uncontrollable anguish and possibly even suicidal thoughts. Why would a young person hang himself without any apparent reason? Often we find that, in the past, he may have been taken to a healer.

Healers often receive their gift through transmission from another person who, in turn, has received it from another. In tracing back the chain, we find that it began with a witch who received his gift from a demon! Satan can appear to heal, but as Jesus tells us in the Bible, "False christs and false prophets will arise and show great signs and wonders, so as to lead astray, if possible even the elect." (Mt 24:24)

Demons do not give gifts; but they are very adept at mimicking what God does! By displacing an illness to give the impression of healing, what they actually do is make things worse. My Community is often asked to help repair the damage from these so-called healings that have been done by healers. When the Lord Jesus heals, His healings are real and do not contain any kind of deception. There is nothing fake about them. Jesus does not only heal our bodies, but He also takes hold of our hearts, spirits, and minds, in order to bless them. He revives the whole being.

Why is it that so often those who go to healers never stop getting sick? It is because the pain goes from the body to the heart or from the body to the soul. We think we are taking care of a physical illness and then we find new, more profound illness symptoms like strange hatreds, allergies, and so on. How many witnesses have we heard! For example, all of a sudden, we cannot tolerate our husband or wife; we cannot tolerate the way he or she talks or walks. Suddenly, we cannot pray, we are blocked; we do not taste the joy of life. We are reluctant to get up in the morning or do essential work. All of a sudden, we have excruciating migraines and we become depressed. Do not sacrifice your health or your sufferings at any cost! Do not place yourself in the hands of charlatans only to end up in an even worse condition! Several times, Our Lady has recommended that we consult a doctor, but she has never recommended that we consult a healer. She knows very well why!

Healers cause many depressions and suicides, not to mention mental illnesses. It is my duty to say it: do not consult them, even if they offer free treatment, and even if they have placed a statue of Our Lady of Lourdes in their living room to attract naïve Catholics.

If you have ever consulted a healer, a fortuneteller, a medium, healing touch therapist, or reflexologist, for example, for yourself or for someone else within your family circle, I would recommend you find an experienced priest and ask Jesus for forgiveness for this, even if it was done with a good conscience or through ignorance. Ask the priest to say a prayer of liberation over you to cut off all ties that could still harm you and that are due to the words of death that the healer said over you.

Indeed, very often a good Confession is all that is needed to break this chain of evil. The Sacrament of Reconciliation is very powerful because through it we are purified by the Blood of Jesus flowing over us. However, it is not magic. We must freely renounce sin and all dark practices. When we return home, it is a good idea to renew our baptismal promises (See Chapter 71 "Oh, the Lies!") in order to repel all harmful influences. Fasting and prayer are necessary. They can heal.

Are We Going to Accuse God?

How could I keep quiet about the following story which I heard in Medjugorje and which makes so much sense?

A man was walking through the fields at the base of a hill, when he came upon a shepherd who was mistreating a lamb from his flock. The man cried out in horror because the shepherd had just, for no apparent reason, broken the leg of the innocent lamb and the poor animal was now crying out in pain and limping.

"Why are you torturing this defenseless little lamb?" shouted the man aggressively. He was ready to jump on the shepherd and inflict the same treatment on him! What blatant cruelty! "It's necessary," calmly replied the shepherd. "It's necessary? How could you cripple this animal?" "It's necessary," repeated the shepherd. "This lamb has already run away into the mountain three times, and this region is very dangerous because of the wolves. From now on, it won't run off again! I'll carry it on my shoulders until its leg heals, and this way it will get used to me. In the future, it will respond to my voice. This will save its life!" "Oh I see..."

God did not create illness, but when He allows it, He has His plan. God has only one motive— one single motive, for doing what He does for us - our eternal Salvation. In other words, He gives us unfailing assurance that we will be completely happy with Him, first in this world, and then in the next. We will not change God, and this is a good thing because His greatest attribute is mercy. On the other hand, we can change our own glasses to improve our eye sight, and then better see why He allows suffering in our lives.

God did not create illness, but when He allows it, He has His plan. God has only one motive, and only one motive for doing what He does for us - our eternal Salvation. In other words, He gives us unfailing assurance that we will be completely happy with Him, first in this world, and then in the next. We will not change God, and this is a good thing because His greatest attribute is mercy. On the other hand, we can change our own glasses to improve our eye sight, and then better see why He allows suffering in our lives.

---

* A text from the Vatican about Reiki can be found at:

http://www.vatican.va/roman_curia/pontifical_councils/interelg/documents/rc_pc_interelg_doc_20030203_new-age_en.html#Documents%20of%20the%20Catholic%20Church's%20magisterium

"Dear children! By your own peace I am calling you to help others so that they may begin to seek and find peace. You, dear children, are at peace and not able to imagine the lack of peace. Therefore, I am calling you, so that by your prayer and your life you may help to destroy everything that is evil in people and uncover Satan's deception. You should pray that the truth prevails in all hearts." (September 25, 1986)

56

A GAPING WOUND

Of course, suffering can cause rebellion or even close a heart to God. When we receive a blow, the wound that forms can make us more vulnerable and we become more susceptible to all kinds of infections. It is an open wound, a gaping, bleeding wound, and Satan - in his malevolence - is only too happy to take advantage of our vulnerability. He will lurk around trying to introduce poison into our gaping wounds. To put it plainly, he will suggest to our conscience thoughts and feelings that he draws from his own source, in order to really infect the wound. And we will think that these suggestions come from our own heart. Here are some examples of what Satan can suggest:

Despair: "Look how much you've already suffered in the past! With this added blow, you won't make it. It's too much! What's the point of continuing to live when you're constantly in pain? You might as well end it, commit suicide right now. In a minute or so, the pain will be over. Why wait?"

Hatred: "Look what that person did to you! That's Its unforgivable! Be sure to pay him back. Make every effort to destroy his reputation, his family life, his job. He must pay for it!"

Doubt or rebellion against God, and doubt: "But who is this God who allows this such evil to be done to you? And you thought He loved you! Well, now you can see He doesn't have time for you. And you don't really believe that with all the billions of people in the world that are His in the world, He's interested in your plight! Why waste your time at Mass on Sunday anymore? Let it go! Besides, does He really exist?"

Never listen to such perverse voices that reek of sulfur! Reject such violent poisons, even if they touch accord with you and seem to aim accurately. What would we gain by giving in to them? Simply more suffering and the loss of our peace! Resist them at all costs even if, through contamination or obsession, you are not able to push them away from your mind at the moment! If we live a life of prayer, it will be easy to recognize the source of such chatter; exposed by the light of the Bible, these suggestions cannot gain acceptance. They appeal to our bad tendencies and contradict the teaching of the Beatitudes. Would Jesus tell us, "You won't make it; it's too much! You'd better put an end to your life!"? There again, it is the Word of God that saves us.

Fortunately, Jesus stays very close to our gaping wound. Jesus is more than very close to us. He is one with us, united with us when we suffer. He too wants to talk to us, but what a difference there is in His dialogue! His soft, humble voice, infinitely respectful of our freedom, will let itself be recognized in prayer.

"Do not be afraid, it is Me! Look at Me! Look at My hands, My feet, and My side. You see I have suffered also! Do not be afraid of anything. I am with you. Together, we will pull through and overcome this trial."

This is precisely where Jesus is going to ask a favor of me. "Would you give me your suffering? Give me your wound?"[140] Why this request? Because Jesus makes divine everything that I give Him, everything I allow Him to have. He goes even further. In taking what I give Him, He integrates it into Himself - into His own body. My wound then becomes His, and He identifies with it so much that when the Father looks at us, He sees only one wound - mine merged with His.

Now, what was it that gushed from the wounds of Jesus on the Cross? Was it despair or hatred? Bitterness or rebellion?

---

[140] "Come to me, all who labor and are heavy laden, and I will give you rest...." (Mt 11:28); "Surely, he has borne our griefs and carried our sorrows; yet we esteemed him stricken, smitten by God, and afflicted. But he was wounded for our transgressions, he was bruised for our iniquities; upon him was the chastisement that made us whole, and with his stripes we are healed." (Is 53:4-5)

"With his stripes, we are healed," Isaiah tells us.[141] Melted into Jesus' wounds, my own wounds will also become wounds of love and a source of grace, consolation and peace. Admittedly the pain won't disappear, though it might quiet down, but the anointing of love that accompanies it will transform it into a path of joy.

The Little Flower, who endured great physical and moral suffering, wrote in The Story of a Soul: "When I get to Heaven, I will be able to contemplate, on the Glorious body of Jesus, my own wounds".

Her own wounds, hers, the Little Flower's? What is she talking about?! This great Doctor of the Church is right: With each new shock she received while on earth, each heartbreak, she hastened to give it all to Jesus. She knew that He would use them to do some good, according to His own emergencies and needs: convert a sinner; free a soul from Purgatory; bring relief to a sick person; strengthen a priest, or console a child.

With her offerings, she knew that she could quench Jesus' thirst on the Cross. Doing so, she allowed Him to carry out His work as our Savior in a wider way, transforming something bad in us into grace, or changing our miserable wounds into gushing springs of living water.

Suffering with Satan makes us his miserable targets, participants in his work of destruction; we might then become negative and bitter. But suffering with Jesus makes us co-redeemers with Mary and in Mary, the co-redemptrix par excellence. Then we might become angels of consolation and peace for others!

Just like moral suffering, sickness is a double-edged reality; it can damage us or it can glorify us, depending on which voice we choose to listen to, or which friend we give it to.

One day, Vicka had a very sore throat that was causing her lots of pain, so I asked her, "Did you pray for healing?"

"No! I never ask for my own healing. The Gospa knows what's important for me. I don't need to ask her, but I pray for the healing of others. I would like to tell all the sick that, when the Gospa appears, I pray especially for them, and then for the others." (No doubt this

---

[141] Is 53:5

explains why Vicka's apparitions last longer than those of the other visionaries!)

"I see that you remain joyful even in sickness, Vicka. It's wonderful! Many people would like to do the same. What's your secret?"

"You know, for me suffering and sicknesses are gifts and I'm happy to receive them. I thank God for these gifts with all my heart. I would like to urge the sick to pray in this way: 'O Lord, through my suffering let me have something to offer You! All I am asking now is the strength and courage to carry my cross with all the love in my heart, and with joy!'"

"Is this is how you pray, Vicka?"

"This is how the Gospa taught me. Personally, I'm happy to have suffered and to have been able to offer my sufferings to Jesus because I know that, if I offer my sufferings in this way, I help Him. The Gospa told me, 'Today, very few are the people who have understood the great value of suffering when it is offered to Jesus!' So, with all my heart, I want to say that suffering is a great gift. I talk like this because I, myself, have experienced the joy in suffering. It is a gift because through it, God's plans are fulfilled in favor of those who are close to us, and those who are far away. The best offering that we can make to God is our suffering and our sickness.[142]

---

[142] The Little Flower said, "Suffering passes, to have suffered remains [in Eternity]."

"Dear children! Today again I am calling you to complete conversion, which is difficult for those who have not chosen God. God can give you everything that you seek and yet you only seek God when sickness, problems and difficulties come to you and then you think God is far from you and does not hear your prayers. No, dear children, that is not true. When you are far from God, you are not able to receive His graces because you do not seek them with a firm faith. Day by day I am praying for you and I want to draw you ever more near to God, but I cannot do this if it is not what you want. Therefore, dear children put your life in God's hands" (January 25, 1988)

57

MATTEO'S HEALING

Vicka likes to relate the story of a certain Italian family. Matteo and Greta had two children, a boy and a girl. Money flowed freely in the family home, but there was a shortage of prayer. Months and then years went by and God remained absent from their home.

After a serious motorcycle accident, their son slipped into a deep and lengthy coma. One day their neighbor, Luciana, who often went to Medjugorje, met Greta on the street and was distressed at seeing her in such a state of despair. Greta could not stop crying; it seemed that nothing could bring her out of her depression. Greta poured out her heart to Luciana, explaining what was causing her so much unhappiness. Her family was falling to pieces. They were losing everything. They had recently arranged for their son to be transferred to a special hospital in America, but the doctors were now advising against the trip because of his condition and saying such a journey could be fatal for him. They had placed their last hope in the hospital in America! Now, it seemed, everything was crumbling (falling apart?).

"Go to Medjugorje!" Luciana cried out. "Our Lady is appearing there. She's a mother and she'll take care of you." So Matteo and Greta, together with their daughter, accompanied Luciana to Medjugorje.

On the very first day, because they were in such great despair, they asked Vicka if she could give them five minutes of her time. "OK, good! When I've finished speaking to the pilgrims I'll come and get you. Just wait for me at the bottom of the courtyard."

But Matteo said to her, "Vicka, we only have one wish—that you ask the Blessed Mother to cure our son—and to also ask her how much money I should give."

Vicka did not want to annoy him or correct him for what he had said about the money. "I'll do my best," she told him. "I'll pray for your sick son. Come back tomorrow, and in the meantime I'll talk to Our Lady."

During the apparition, the Blessed Mother said to Vicka, "Tell them that I am not looking for money. I am seeking their lives. I am calling them to come close to me and my Son."

The next day, at 10:15 a.m., their son came out of his coma in Italy and began to walk!

This family continues to pray and to visit Medjugorje. God enabled them to realize that He could have healed their son sooner without a problem, but He wanted them to come to Him with all their hearts. Today, prayer comes first in the life of this family and all the rest is secondary. Actually, the real miracle is the healing of the heart of the child's father, Matteo. The other blessings that followed were all bonuses!

"Peace and Joy Will Return to Your Families…."

Our Lady launched her appeal again to families on Podbrdo Hill on May 5, 2006. May this fundamental message be received, listened to and lived by all families that are on the edge of breaking up, or desperately searching for peace in places other than through God!

"Dear children, I am calling you to live holiness within your families. There can be no holiness without prayer. Dear children, begin praying in your families! Peace and joy will return to your families when prayer returns to your families!"

"Dear children! For these days while you are joyfully celebrating the cross, I desire that your cross also would be a joy for you. Especially, dear children, pray that you may be able to accept sickness and suffering with love the way Jesus accepted them. Only that way shall I be able with joy to give out to you the graces and healings which Jesus is permitting me." (September 11, 1986)

58

DOROTA

Medjugorje, summer of 2005

Chrissey, my assistant rushed into my office: "Come quickly, Sister! Come into the kitchen. You won't believe your eyes!"

"What's happened?"

"It's Dorota! Come and see!"

Dorota and her family had come to spend four days with us in Medjugorje.[143] That Friday morning, they had been hesitant: should they attempt to climb the Cross Mountain of Krizevac, or should they do the Stations of the Cross where it was flat?

"Dear God!" I thought. "I should never have let Dorota go to Krizevac in her condition. It was crazy! I hope nothing has happened to her!"

I literally flew down the stairs that separate the two floors, and three seconds later I pushed open the kitchen door. "Dorota! Oh, Dorota, you're dancing? And you're crying?"

Marek, her husband, seemed to be flattened against the kitchen wall to give more space to Dorota who was dancing. He too seemed to be crying—crying for joy!

---

[143] See photo section.

A Short Flashback

Warsaw, spring of 1994

We jumped off the tram and the icy wind that swept through the wide avenue stung our faces. We hurried to get to Dorota's house. It was my first mission to Poland, and the Lord spoiled me. He put me in the hands of Dorota, a wonderful young woman who had been His disciple for years.

Dorota had a kind heart, especially for the poor. She loved them tenderly and understood them.[144] She unceasingly provided for their physical and spiritual needs, and applied herself with her whole being, because she saw in them the image of Jesus—the One she loved so much!

In Poland, in 1986, she had discovered L'Arche Community for disabled people, founded by Jean Vanier, and she decided to join their "mother house" in France. She spent three years in Trosly-Breuil, situated to the north of Paris. It was at L'Arche that Dorota met Marek, who would later become her husband. Upon returning to Warsaw, while Marek was teaching mathematics, Dorota exercised her great literary skills (her father was a famous man of the theatre in Warsaw), and she became one of the pillars of a publishing house. She had translated my first book on Medjugorje into Polish; that was how we first met and became good friends.

But, let's get back to Warsaw. That evening Dorota welcomed me into her small apartment and, in front of a bowl of reviving hot soup, she happily gave me some insights into the soul of Poland, of which I am still fairly ignorant. She also confided in me about her sorrow at not having any children—or rather at losing them during pregnancy. "It's okay," I said to her. "Come to Medjugorje." Marija, the visionary, often says that it is rare that couples with no children who, after having asked Our Lady for a child when together at the top of Krizevac, do not have their prayers answered in the following months."

Marija was not mistaken. A year later to the day, after Dorota and Marek's pilgrimage to Medjugorje, their first miracle, little Agata, was

---

[144] "Blessed is he who considers the poor; the Lord delivers him in the day of trouble." (Ps 41:1)

born. The couple's joy was at its peak. It was a pure gift from Our Lady and they said to each other, "And what if another miracle child was granted to us; if we had a little brother for Agata?" But the Lord had other plans for Dorota, to whom I now pass my pen. She can fill in, in her own words, what led up to the opening of this tale:

"When my daughter was a year and a half old, I became sick with a bizarre illness. I was always tired, and my hands were so weak that I couldn't lift my daughter. I began to have more and more difficulty walking. After a year of tests and uncertainty, a diagnosis was made—Multiple Sclerosis (MS), a progressive, incurable neurological disease. Although this might seem strange: it wasn't difficult for me to accept this trial. I had given my life to God many years before this, and if He allowed such a horrible disease, I would accept it. However, I still cried for three days because I knew that I'd no longer be able to ski or climb the mountains, which I so much loved to do!"

"My friends were surprised to see that I wasn't obviously discouraged. However, inside of me I was aware that I was on a downward spiral, and I became frighteningly aware that my condition was getting worse. Actually, each month, my pain became mercilessly worse. I could barely walk and I couldn't go up stairs. When I reached the point where I could only walk 30 yards a day—just to get to the car—we decided to buy a wheelchair for longer outings."

"With the birth of my child, I had previously experienced God's healing power. I knew that a cure was possible at any time, and from the bottom of my heart I believed that. In spite of everything, months went by and I became more and more disabled. Marek prayed with me for a cure and he fasted for years! We offered our Masses for this. My friends prayed also. At the same time, I prayed very much for the Blessed Mother's intentions and, taking advantage of my sickness, I offered my weakness through her to God. I felt that it was like 'work' that I could do for the Church and I was happy about it. But for all that, I couldn't ignore the fact that the progression of my illness was taking its toll on my family. My husband was overworked. In addition to teaching at school, he had to take care of the house and our child. It was becoming more and more difficult for me to put up with the loneliness and inactivity of confinement to my house."

"At the same time, in my heart, I felt a subtle invitation from the Our Lady to return to Medjugorje and to pray for my healing there. But how could this come about? In the summer, the heat is dangerous to those with this disease, and during the school year my husband doesn't have any vacation. We finally got away at the beginning of May 2005. We left by car, my husband and I, together with my brother and my daughter, Agata, who was now aged 8 years old and for whom we wanted to give thanks to the Gospa. Our pilgrimage began in Warsaw and we went to confession so that our hearts would be fully open. The priest prepared me wonderfully for the journey: 'You are going to the source of life,' he told me. I left Poland full of confidence! Something good was going to happen to me."

"We were staying not far from the church, at Sister Emmanuel's house. On the first day, my husband carried me on his back to climb Apparition Hill. We remained silent for a long time up there, seated in front of the statue of Mary. It was nice there. In the evening, I would go to church in my wheelchair for the evening services. What happiness I felt! I had the impression of coming back home, of immersing myself in the prayer of Medjugorje which is more intense than anywhere else in the world. The peace...."

"On the second day, Sister Emmanuel accompanied us to Vicka's house. She had promised to talk to Vicka and ask her to come down from her staircase and pray for me. But how could I get to this famous staircase in a wheelchair? There was an impenetrable wall of pilgrims in front of us. In edging through this crowd, how many feet did we bumped into with our wheelchair?! We advanced inch by inch. It was a bit like a tragicomedy! Certain scenes from the Bible came to my mind. In Jesus' time, it was just like this. People were pushing and shoving each other to see Him, and here I was in the same situation. At any cost, I wanted Vicka to at least touch me. I was not ashamed. Like a child, I wanted her to approach me. Finally, Vicka prayed over me for a long time, with her hands on my head. I will never forget her wonderful smile! However, I was a bit discouraged when she left me because, after all the tension caused by the wait and the hope that something would happen, nothing happened."

"The next day, at Siroki Brijeg, Father Jozo saw me coming in my wheelchair with my little girl, and he came and prayed over me for a long time. When he left me, an indescribable PEACE came over me. Worry and tension vanished."

"Our last day in Medjugorje was a Friday. We went by car to the foot of Mount Krizevac without a plan of any kind. I couldn't imagine what we were going to do. My husband could not carry me to the top; it was much higher than Podbrdo. Perhaps I could be carried to the end of the road, and just sit in this holy place? After the car was parked, I began to walk a little bit, and then, something began to happen. I continued walking. I advanced further, and further, and further again. I was walking. I was walking! My Lord! Yes! I was walking! My husband and daughter approached me. They were stunned. They did not understand what was happening. As for me, I was laughing and walking because there was a force that was propelling me forward. A force that was both physical and spiritual, pushing me from inside. Then I thought again about the visionaries who seemed to be lifted onto the hill during the first days of the apparitions. They moved with incredible speed up the slopes of this hill that was full of thorny bushes. I climbed up as far as the first four stations and then, I felt that my legs were getting very tired, so I sat down. My husband and daughter became frightened because sometimes it happened that I walked too much during the day, and I suffered the consequences later when I had to lie down for several days."

"I tried to gather my thoughts and pray—I wondered if I was being cured. In my heart, the answer was 'yes,' even if my legs were tired. Once again my husband carried me on his back. We stopped at each station. How much longer would Marek be able to go on? I knew that he would not give up easily, but his back was in danger of breaking. We reached the steepest spot. Marek said to me, 'Wait here for me. I'm going to see if it's much further.' I sat down on a rock and waited. Suddenly I felt that my legs were rested so I began to go up again. Once again the same inexplicable force was propelling me. I began to climb the rock path rapidly and without difficulty. I looked up. The summit was very near and my brother called to me from there: 'Dorota, if you were to stop now, you would really look ridiculous!' I continued to go up."[145]

---

[145] See photo section.

"At the foot of the cross, my husband approached me. He put his arms around me and I burst into tears. We remained sitting there in total silence for a long time. Halfway through the descent, Marek took my hand and I leaned on him a little. I prayed unceasingly to God and adored Him, but I was also battling my own fear. I was afraid of waking up paralyzed the next day, afraid that something bad would happen to me. Fortunately, images of healing that are in the Bible came to my mind. For example, Peter walking on the water. If I began to doubt I would do as he did—I would sink. I fought an interior battle within myself to believe. I hung on to my faith with all my strength."

"Today, eighteen months later, I can say that I received a partial cure[146]—a great improvement in my health. It is unexplainable because, to this day, medical science can only delay the progress of this disease and stop the deterioration process, but that's all. Humanly speaking, nothing can be done."

"Now I can walk at least three hundred yards a day instead of thirty. I go up and down the stairs. I am much stronger. The wheelchair ended up in the basement. The lives of all three of us have completely changed. Our family has regained its stability. I am able to take on more work and, above all, I can take care of my daughter. I accompany her to school or to her friends' houses. The first fruit of this cure is being able to attend Mass every day. In the Eucharist, I find the same strength as the one that pushed me on Krizevac—during the week following my return, I physically felt it during the Eucharist. I feel it now in a more hidden way, but it can lift me up off the ground. It is like a piece of glory."

"At least half of the people who suffer from this disease suffer from depression. I can tell you the secret that prevented me from falling into depression, and that is prayer. 'Lord, may Your will be done, may what You desire be accomplished.' Such a prayer, said with complete trust, has great power."

---

[146] The cures that we receive on this earth are always partial and temporary because we will all have to leave this body of flesh some day, and pass between this life and the life to come. It is only there that we will receive that glorious incorruptible body, clothed in eternity that will not play tricks on us. Off course, Dorota could have received a cure that would have allowed her to go, not just 300 yards, but 3 miles. Why only 300 yards? God alone knows, and we adore His Divine Will. Father Daniel Ange, France, found the right expression, knowing that God's great plan is to make us grow in love. So he said, "God heals us enough so that we will be able to love, and He does not completely heal us so that we will be able to love."

"After my cure, my first days at home remain unforgettable. The telephone was always ringing. Some people were crying into the receiver. Without letup, we told the story of those four days, between Heaven and Earth, in Medjugorje. One of my friends cried out: 'But, that's impossible. That never happens! I must see you. When can you meet me?' I answered her, 'Let's go for a walk in the park in front of the house'—this was the same park where, for five years, my own legs could not carry me. The simplest daily tasks became great events; my first trips were to the closest supermarket, where I had previously gone in a wheelchair so many times. Now I, myself, could choose what I wanted to put in my shopping cart. From a wheelchair I saw everything from such a low level that I really saw almost nothing! I felt like I was merely an object. As for Agata, who is not very talkative by nature, she was bursting with joy, and she told her school friends about these events. She was so happy that the wheelchair days were over."

"I walk and I breathe! Before, it was like I was suffocating from lack of movement, I was lacking oxygen. Sure, I'm still handicapped, but I know that God touched me, and I adore Him. If I have a brief feeling of disappointment, I leave God free to dispose of me as He wishes—I know that He has many surprises in store for me, and I would like to have the time to work for Him a little more."

Dorota has a secret. How can I keep silent about it? "To give your life to God," she recently told me, "gives you great freedom and a feeling of security. It also changes your scale of values. Why hold on to health and earthly life at any price?"

All of that becomes of no importance when we put God first. God does not want our suffering; He wants our trust. Moments, or even years of trials, allow us to prove to Him our trust, to really abandon ourselves into His hands more and more each day. This is how we can find joy in suffering. We always have something to give to God, and as Jesus said, "There is more joy in giving than in receiving." (Acts 20:35)

"Dear children! Today I call you to prayer. I am with you and I love you each one of you. I am your Mother and I wish that your hearts be similar to my heart. Little children, without prayer you cannot live and say that you are mine. Prayer is joy. Prayer is what the human heart desires." (November 25, 1994)

59

IS GOD LATE?

Father Slavko was not without enlightening words to console sorrowful hearts. So many mothers would come to him complaining about God: "Father, the Lord doesn't listen to me. It's terrible! I've been praying every day for over three years for my son who is taking drugs, and I haven't seen any improvement. What must I do so that God will answer me?"

He was famous for giving a reply like this: "Madam, God always listens to your prayers—even the least of your prayers. But God doesn't see things like we do. He sees much further away! Look what he did with St. Monica. She cried and prayed for more than twenty years for her son, Augustine, who was behaving badly, and nothing changed. But she didn't get discouraged. She persevered in prayer and supplication. This is fortunate for us, because if her prayers had been answered right away, we would have gotten St. Augustine, but because she persevered in trust for so long, we now not only have St. Augustine but also St. Monica. Not bad, eh? Dear sister, don't be discouraged. You have not yet attained twenty years of tears!"

Hundreds of women turned up on his doorstep moaning and crying, and left totally cheered up. In their heart, frustration was replaced with the joy of walking the way of sanctity.

In Its Time, I Will Hasten It!

When I was living in Nazareth, my Community asked me to transfer our small household to Jerusalem. So, I had to find housing, something that is almost impossible in the Holy City especially when you have no regular income. Therefore, we prayed a lot and also invoked St. Joseph, the great housing specialist, as everyone knows! However, months went by and there was still nothing on the horizon. During one of those prayer times, we opened the Bible and the Lord gave us this verse: "In its time, I will hasten it." (Is 60:22)

In fact, after seeing Heaven blocked for so many months, a flurry of events suddenly took place during that summer of 1981, and in less than 24 hours, we were the owners of a small private house right in the heart of Jerusalem! The elders of the city still do not understand how this came about. Why that particular day, and why so fast? Only God knows. He had chosen this simple, modest house for us and He carefully prepared His move! If He had acted otherwise, considering the people who were involved with the contract and all the circumstances involved, we would never have been able to get that house.

On the first night after the move, we looked at each other, deeply enthused by the remarkable favor that Heaven had granted us. The wall of the small garden separated us from the Mea Shearim[147] quarter by scarcely a yard. From all the synagogues and yeshivot[148] around, arose a long plaintive cry, heartrending melodies sung in a minor key by men's deep voices. The sons of Israel were commemorating the destruction of the Temple. That day, it was Tisha Be Av.[149] We had forgotten that. The Lamentations were read from prophet Jeremiah—or rather cried—in Hebrew, filling the air, and they penetrated our hearts and very souls. It was that night, among the heartbreaking sadness of that beautiful event, that God came and sealed the vocation of our house and our lives.

"In its time, I will hasten it." Yes, we had to arrive that day, at that precise time and in that exact place, to allow God's plan for our presence in Jerusalem to be stamped on us. God's "delays" are very interesting. They always conceal a much better plan than our own.

---

[147] Mea Shearim is the quarter where the pious Jews live in Jerusalem.

[148] Schools for studying the Torah.

[149] Tisha Be Av: the 9th day of the month of Av, the day of the destruction of the Temple.

It Was Worth the Wait!

My grandmother, Annie Templier, had no equal among God's tardy ones. On January 15, 2006, she went back to the Lord. In spite of her advanced age, 103, her mind remained sharp right to the very end. She never missed saying words of gratitude or comfort to those who helped her. To help those who are afraid of growing old, I'd like to relate an episode in her spiritual life that, to me, is very comforting. At the time, she was only 101 years old.

One day, as I was passing through Paris between two missions, I had one of those unforgettable conversations with her. She opened her heart to me and confided something that was a great worry to her:

"You see, my darling, I have a sorrow—a great sorrow! Something is missing in my relationship with God and it won't leave me alone. When I see you, your mother, your brothers and all the 'little Maillards,' it's apparent to me that you like to pray. You find joy in praying, even praying for a long time. Well, for me, you see, it's not like that. It has never been like that. Yes, for sure, I say my prayers every day, as well as my Rosary and all that 'stuff,' and even 'a thought before going to bed,' but to tell you the truth, I'm glad when my prayers are over.[150] Well, for some time now, I've been telling myself that this isn't normal. God is so good, so great, surely I should find joy in praying."

Personally, I wasn't very worried about my grandmother because she had always had a wonderful heart, and she was always ready to listen, console and encourage us. She was very close to God without even knowing it. I told her, "Mamy, the most important thing in life is love, and you have it. Don't worry! However, I will pray for you in Medjugorje, and together we will ask God to let you taste the joy of prayer that you desire. It's that simple. In Medjugorje, Our Lady tells us to 'pray until prayer becomes a joy.' If she asks for this, it's because grace is given. With God, we must ask like children, with complete trust. That's what works the best.'"

"Well, my darling, I agree! You pray over there and I'll try to do the same here. We'll be united."

---

[150] In 1976, shortly after I entered the Community, she asked me to describe one of our days for her. After hearing our program, she calculated that, including Mass, we spent more than five hours in prayer. Then she said firmly: "Well you see, my darling, that's too much!"

Six months later, I went back to see her and from the outset, she said to me, "Remember our last conversation? Well, my darling, it's done! I now experience joy in praying!"

She looked like a child who was overwhelmed by the discovery of a wonderful, splendid gift that surpasses anything she could ever dream (have dreamt?) about. "Now I understand why the Lord made me wait so long on earth. Do you get it? I had to live 102 years to receive this grace! Well, I don't regret it. It was worth waiting for such a long time!"

Shortly after that, she was transferred to my Community where she lived another eighteen months. Everyone liked to come and spend some time with her. God granted her "prayer from the heart," and in the same gift package, He also slipped in some humor. She no longer feared death at all. "I'm going to throw myself into God's arms," she would say to my brother. She left this earth filled with peace.

What beautiful work God does in those that our "high performance" society too quickly judges as being "useless." In fact, those "useless" ones are the most highest performers because their invisible beauty will be an everlasting jewel for the whole Heavenly Church, while this world and its passing 'riches', will disappear.

"Dear Children! It is really a great thing when God calls men. Think how sad it would be to refuse these opportunities which God gives. So do not wait for tomorrow or the day after tomorrow. Say 'yes' to Jesus now! And may this 'yes' be forever." (May 16, 1987)

60

I ONLY HAVE TODAY TO LOVE

Father Mike from Canada had a great impact on the young people visiting Medjugorje, especially after he told them about his own experience.

He was ordained a priest at the age of 26. Six months later, he was the victim of a terrible car accident. Upon impact, he found himself below a tunnel of light, which he knew was the gate to Heaven. He then experienced an intense joy and a completeness he had never known before. When on the verge of meeting Jesus he was filled with immense peace. But then he became aware that he was being asked to return to his life on earth because his work was not yet over. He said that during his "return to earth," he had an uncontrollable desire to tell everyone he met that life is short, that God is real, and that we should not waste a moment on anything less than God. Then he woke up in the hospital.

During his recovery, which lasted almost one year, Father Mike told no one about his experience. Throughout that whole year he felt lost and out of focus. He mourned for Heaven. Then one day a parishioner invited him to go to Medjugorje. He wasn't interested but, out of courtesy, he checked his diary. Seeing that he was free at that time, he decided to go; after all a free trip to Europe! Why not?

Addressing a group of young pilgrims who had come to entrust the Gospa with their lives and vocations, he begged them, "Do not delay living your lives for Jesus. Don't say, 'When I graduate from college, I'll give my life to God and serve Him. When I get married, then I'll be able to serve God. When I am done with graduate school, then I'll be ready to do God's will.' No! Decide to live your life for Jesus right now! Starting right now, place yourselves in God's hands. Don't wait a second! Believe me; you don't know how long you have to live. I was a lukewarm priest when I came within a hair's breadth to death. If I had died at that moment, my life would have been a waste. When the end comes, only one thing counts—a life lived for God. You don't know the hour. Don't wait! Live for God, seek God, love God. Do it now, not tomorrow. You don't know if there will be a tomorrow!"

The Enemy's talk is quite different and many people fall into his trap: "Wait," he suggests to us. "You'll do this good work later. You're not ready yet."

She Loves To Drive

"What should I do?" "Which path should I take?" "Which direction should I choose?" So many young people, and those who are not so young, are tormented by these serious questions about their future.

In Medjugorje, a young French girl named Clothilde was worrying about not knowing God's plan for her life, until the day when she finally found peace, thanks to a holy priest who said to her, "In the evening when you drive your car from Avignon to Marseilles, the headlights don't light up the entire hundred kilometers of your drive. They only light up the section of the road that you need. Well, Our Lady does the same thing when she leads you! She is leading you to heaven, but rather than lighting up the whole road, she only lights up the section of the road that is necessary for you to see. Don't try to see a kilometer further. You'll not risk missing the turn that is lit up in front of you, nor should you keep your eyes fixed on the rear view mirror. Don't look back, or you'll risk running into a tree. Live in the present. Place your trust in the Blessed Mother."

Four years later, Clothilde said, "That advice changed my life. I placed my future in the hands of the Mother of God and then all my worries and fears were replaced with the profound joy of being safe with her."

"A few months after having met this priest, Jesus asked me to take a radical turn. Fortunately I was in the right frame of mind because otherwise it would have been easy for me not to hear or welcome His call or give Him my 'Yes.' I now pray for the young people, so that they will entrust their future to Mary and stop tormenting themselves, because abandoning yourself to Mary is to choose security. When you turn on the headlights of your car, renew your 'Yes' to Mary, so that you can live in the present moment."

We must acknowledge that the way Our Heavenly Mother leads us, she often proves herself to be a highly skilled driver who would make the famous Michael and Ralph Schumakers of this world become green with envy behind their Ferrari steering wheels!

Make Me a Priest!

Father Joseph Quinn travelled from Ireland to Medjugorje to give thanks to the Mother of God. At a very young age, he had begun to "turn on his headlights" under Our Lady's guidance. Little Joseph was only nine years old when his uncle, who was suffering from cancer, was preparing to make a pilgrimage to Lourdes.[151] Joseph was surprised to see friends and neighbors coming to his house to give mysterious envelopes to his uncle. His mother explained to him that these people were sending their intentions to Our Lady of Lourdes, who would read them and answer them according to God's will.

An idea then took root in the child's mind. Without saying anything to anyone, he ran to his room and wrote these words to Our Lady in his best handwriting, "Dear Mary, please make me a priest. Your son, Joseph." At that time, Joseph said his Rosary without thinking very much about it, but happily followed the family custom. He knew, from all his mother had told him, that Mary was a wonderful woman.

Our Lady took little Joseph at his word. He was ordained a priest in 1995.

Today, Father Joseph radiates such happiness being a priest. "For me," he says, "each time I change the bread into the Body of Christ, and the wine into the Blood of Christ, is a very moving experience."

---

[151] As Father Slavko used to say with humor, "Our Lady of Lourdes and the Gospa of Medjugorje are kind of cousins—they do not contradict each other!"

"Dear Children! If you want to be very happy, live a simple, humble life. Pray a great deal and do not dwell on your problems but let yourselves be guided by God. Take the simple way." (Easter Sunday, 1984)

61

TODAY, YOU'RE TAKING OUT THE GARBAGE

Maud accompanied her husband to the doctor's office (surgery?). After examining him, the doctor took Maud aside and said, "I need to talk to you." This sounded serious and alarm bells rung inside Maud. The doctor spoke plainly: "Unless you do the following things, your husband is doomed to die (death?)."

Maud was stunned. "Well, what things?" she asked.

The doctor replied, "First, every morning prepare him a good hot breakfast - No pop tarts, no cup of coffee on the run…. Have him come home from work everyday and prepare for him a good, well-balanced, nutritious lunch (meal?). And at supper time, make sure it's a good dinner every night. No take aways and no microwave dinners that undermine your health. Second, don't over-burden him with house-hold chores. Third, keep the house spotless so there are no germs around."

On the way home, Maud's husband turned to her and said, "I know the doctor talked to you. What did he say?"

"Honey, you're going to die," she replied.

Perhaps we are like Maud; we have received a prescription for the health and for the sanctity of the world. This prescription is simple but we just can't get around to doing it like the doctor ordered. We are more concerned about the private messages that have been revealed to a few, rather than the messages that are destined for the whole world. The messages that are revealed to a few are not for everyone to know. But the messages revealed to the whole world are those we are supposed to know, and yet we are not fulfilling them. We ignore them! Many Catholics make this mistake!

So, rather than committing ourselves to the daily rosary, we pour over books and newsletters about Fatima. We are determined to find out what's in that envelope locked away in the Vatican archives. Instead of fasting and doing penance, we spend our time guessing what the ten secrets of Medjugorje might be. Months go by, years go by before our next confession but we don't delay in faithfully reading The Three Days of Darkness.[152]   We are not interested in reading the Pope's encyclicals; but we are really interested in learning whether the Pope really consecrated Russia to the Immaculate Heart of Mary. We allow our personal relationships at home to suffer from a lack of prayer and interest. We waste huge amount of time trying to predict when the Medjugorje apparitions will end. And each year we find a new reason to declare that the time is imminent.

None of this is for us to know. This is why they are secrets. We are to do well what we are supposed to do today — and that is to grow in holiness!

Jesus came down to Mary and Joseph, and was obedient to them. His Mother treasured all those things in her heart. Jesus didn't say, "I am going to become the Messiah. I'm going to save the world." No.

Mary said, "Jesus today you are going to set the table for dinner, and this is how you will grow in holiness. And after that you can take out the garbage." Jesus was made flesh and showed us how to be holy in our everyday lives. He ate and He slept; He did chores. He studied and He prayed just like all of us. And yet He was the Holy One. I believe that Mary cherished these simple things, like remembering Jesus' first word, whether it was Ima (mama) or Abba (daddy). We must learn to be holy in our everyday lives and in the devastating crises that may hit our lives.

---

[152] Doubtful predictions that are making the candle merchants rich.

Blessed Pier Georgio Frassati

Some people are blessed by God, even amidst wealth and success. I am thinking of a young Italian: Blessed Pier Georgio Frassati. He lived in Turin, Italy, between 1901 and 1925. He was the son of extremely wealthy parents. His father, a senator and ambassador to Germany, owned the newspaper La Stampa. Pier Georgio grew up in mansions among maids, butlers and chauffeurs. He secretly gave all his money to the poor and the sick, not even using his own name. By the time he was 21, moved by great faith, he provided food, clothing and tuition for 125 single mothers and their children. He lived in high society and was very good looking. He was a championship skier and mountain climber. He had everything going for him. But he also made time for God and went to Mass every morning. He said morning and evening prayer, the Rosary in the evening and Holy Hour every night. Sometimes he spent the entire night in adoration before the Blessed Sacrament. He went to school and had friends, he played pool, he went swimming, he did it all.

Then one day, while visiting the sick, he contracted polio. At that time there was no cure for this illness. He died within six days of his 24th birthday. But on the eve of his death, even though he was paralyzed, he managed to scrawl out a note to one of his friends. It said, "There is a poor man named Converso. I have a prescription for needles and injections in my pocket. I forgot to have the pharmacy fill it out. Take the prescription to the drug store, have it filled out and put it on my account." That was his last act on earth. We can be wealthy and still be holy. Rich or poor, we are all called to holiness.[153]

Saint Philip Neri

He was one of the greatest priests in the history of Rome. He lived at the beginning of the 17th century. He was not only called the best priest in Rome but also the clown of Rome. He was renowned as much for his jokes and pranks as he was for his preaching. Children and

---

[153] See the CD of a talk given by Fr. Tim Deeter called: "The Most Handsome Saint in Heaven," based on the life of Pier Giorgio.

adults were drawn to him, but he was betrayed by jealousy. His fellow priests and bishops convinced the Pope that this priest was a disgrace and a clown, a showman. They accused him of immoral activities because they said a man could not have so much fun being a priest. He must certainly be doing something wrong. Philip was suspended from the priesthood. He could no longer celebrate Mass in public, hear confessions, or preach.

Despite all this, Philip kept faith. He prayed, fasted, and went to confession. He forgave his persecutors. He converted their hearts and sanctified himself through suffering. He greatly desired holiness for all his people. He ardently preached to them to go to Mass and Confession but, other than old ladies, there was no one to preach to. Everyone else had gone off to the dance halls and taverns in the evenings.

So, in an effort to convert the people, he fasted on boiled potatoes and water for five years. Some of his parishioners did not like his strictness and his invitations to repent. Some young people painted graffiti on the walls of the rectory and sang dirty songs about him, accusing him of having illicit relationships. All this was reported to the bishop and an investigation was conducted over a period of three years. This trial made him grow spiritually, and he said it was a grace. The result is worth mentioning—his fasting on potatoes and water let to the conversion not only of his parish, but of his bishop and all his fellow priests!

Saint John Bosco

He lived in Turin, Italy, in the 19th century. He is well known through his oratories. He was concerned about the large number of young people victims of abuse and left to roam the city streets. These young people were used in factories as child laborers and then sold into the sex slave trade in houses of prostitution. The Church did nothing about it. The State did nothing about it. So John Bosco decided to do something about it. He opened small oratories homes for poor children where they could learn a trade, get an education and be formed in their faith. We could have expected the Church and the State to be grateful but, on the contrary, they were jealous. Editorial cartoons soon began to make fun of John, articles were run about him in the daily papers, suggesting that someone so good had to be really bad! He was abandoned by his own Church. John Bosco laughed a lot, he played a lot of games, but he also suffered.

Each one of these saints lived the messages. They prayed, fasted, confessed their own sins, they forgave those who sinned against them and thus they found peace. Even before Medjugorje existed, the messages existed because they are rooted in the Gospel! They are to be lived by all Christians, everywhere and at all times. These messages were conceived by the Holy Spirit in the heart and the womb of the Virgin Mary, and if we live the messages, we will become holy, and share in her Triumph. When does this Triumph begin? Today, right now, while she is giving birth to us and nourishing us with her milk—us, the Mystical Body of Christ.[154] *"Dear children, may today be the day that you will begin to love."*

---

[154] This chapter was inspired by a talk given by Fr. Tim Deeter at Irvine, California (USA).

*"Dear Children! I urge you to ask everyone to pray the Rosary. With
the Rosary you will overcome all the troubles which Satan is trying to
inflict on the Catholic Church. Let all priests pray the Rosary. Allow
time for the Rosary." (June 25, 1985)*

62

THE BATTLE FOUGHT BY PRIESTS

1984

Sister Briege McKenna first discovered Medjugorje in 1984.[155] As
soon as she arrived she recognized the famous church that the Lord had
shown her in May 1981, just a month before the Gospa appeared in
Medjugorje. Briege knew that her feet were walking on sacred ground,
a land of fire, a holy land. Her excitement was great. She felt part of
the Gospa's plan for Medjugorje.

In the jam-packed church of St. James she sat with her friend, Claire,
in the midst of the people—a friendly people who had come from all
over Yugoslavia; they were singing at the top of their voices to honor
their Gospa. Father Tomislav Pervan, the parish priest at that time,
gave a long homily in Croatian. Claire did not understand a word but
noticed that Briege was crying. She wondered, "Why these tears?" but
she was too taken up with the experience to ask then and there. In fact,
Jesus was talking to Briege's heart, giving her a full interpretation of
the homily. Then He revealed to her a scene that will remain engraved
in her mind for the rest of her life.

"I can still see it vividly," she said. "There was a huge black cloud
coming down like fog, thick black fog, and as it was creeping down
into the cities and villages, all these priests were sitting in front of me.
I was desperate and I saw myself saying to them, 'Fathers, please stop
it, you have the authority.' I knew it was the evil that was taking over

---

[155] See page 57 (footnote 24)

people's lives. I was pleading with those priests to recognize their power against the forces of evil, their God given power."

In the next scene, Briege saw that many of those priests had allowed themselves to be caught up in the cloud of darkness that had blinded them. The Lord Jesus then said to Briege:

"You must tell these priests that, for them, the only way to conquer the evil forces is by the holiness of their lives, their consecration, and their willingness to let themselves be immersed in the light of Christ."

That day, the Lord revealed many things to Briege that sustain her to this day, so that she can carry out her very special ministry to priests, bishops and cardinals.[156]

At the end of this eventful Mass, she went to the sacristy to meet Fr. Tomislav, who speaks very good English. She learned that his homily, given in Croatian, had dealt precisely with the following three points:

- The power of the priesthood;

- The need for the faithful to pray for priests;

- The urgency to recognize that we are living in times when a great spiritual battle is raging, that the souls of the people of God are at stake, and that the clergy is the army to whom God has given His power.[157]

---

[156] Sister Briege is often asked to witness, and to personally pray with priests, Bishops and Cardinals. She is also a participant at symposiums in Rome on healing, deliverance and other topics of this kind where she brings valuable insight.

[157] Listen to the CD-M11, The Most Beautiful Mass of my Life. Also DVD-V46 "Pray for priests!" Part 1 and V47 Part 2 with Sr. Briege McKenna. See pages ??? - INSERT

"Dear children! I wish to call you to a living of the Holy Mass. There are many of you who have sensed the beauty of the Holy Mass, but there are also those who come unwillingly. I have chosen you, dear children, but Jesus gives you His graces in the Mass. Therefore, consciously live the Holy Mass and let your coming to it be a joyful one. Come to it with love and make the Mass your own. Thank you for having responded to my call " (April 3, 1986)

63

A HARD WON MASS

Francis is one of those people who lead an adventurous life. He is like those friends you would never want to leave your home because their stories are such a delight. Between two other official assignments, he was a bodyguard for important politicians. He couldn't stop talking about incidents where he took advantage of his position to bless an "important person" who was going through a bad time. He tried to guide them and suggest a solution. When he could, he would also whisper a word into the ear of a villain or slip a miraculous medal into the pocket of a criminal.

This disciple of Christ was fearless, and God needs people like him to reach some of his children who would not dream of setting foot inside a church. How he became hooked on Medjugorje during the 90's is already a novel in itself. However, here I would like to relate an episode from his time in Lebanon which was, in effect, a fruit of the graces he received from Medjugorje. It also brilliantly illustrates those encouraging words from Jesus: "All things are possible to him who believes!" (Mark 9:23). Here are his words:

"As an officer, I was put in charge of Security. I had to protect the American Embassy in Beirut, as well as the Ambassador himself. Upon arriving I was informed that I was forbidden to leave the Embassy, even to go to Mass. The only means of entering or leaving the compound was by helicopter. The entrance door was blocked and this was to last for one year! I was extremely annoyed, even if the reasons given were valid. For example, a church had recently been bombed, causing many deaths."

"However, as a faithful pilgrim to Medjugorje, I had acquired the habit of going to Mass every day and Mass was the most important thing in my life. The thought of being deprived of it was terrible for me. So, I called on Mary, my Mother, and, in essence, said to her: 'Mary, help me. How can I endure such deprivation? I need the Mass!'[158] As I was looking out the window from my apartment, what did I see through the barbed wire fence? A statue of the Mother of God—a beautiful white statue! On seeing this I regained my hope."

"It happened that one of the captains was a priest and he heard that I needed the Mass. Therefore he summoned me and we had a discussion. From that day on, he would come each day to my apartment to celebrate Mass just for me. As I was preparing the water and the wine I would look out the window and see the statue of Mary. I thanked her for this priest all the more because this wasn't just any priest. The Mother of God was anxious for me to really understand that she was doing this for me. In fact, this priest grew up in Nazareth. He was an altar boy in her sanctuary, the Basilica of the Assumption, that was run by his own brother who was a Franciscan. He had lived his entire life in Nazareth and he had been transferred to Lebanon just two months earlier. It was clear to me that Mary herself had sent me her priest, from her own village! Yes, this gift most certainly came from her."

"Soon after this, another priest came and joined him to celebrate Mass in my apartment, and little by little, other faithful also came and joined us. Towards the end of my tour of duty, I asked the priest for a Mass in honor of St. Francis of Assisi (October 4), one for All Saints and another one for All Souls. The priest replied: 'I'll bring you an entire church!' In fact, he brought all of his parishioners into the compound. The people had to go through a security check, and there were almost

---

[158] The holy Curé of Ars said, "All our good works cannot equal the holy sacrifice of the Mass, because they are works of men, and the Mass is the work of God. Martyrdom is nothing in comparison. It is the sacrifice of His life that man offers to God. The Mass is the sacrifice where God offers His Body and Blood to man...." And also, "After the Consecration, God is there, just as He is in Heaven. If man only understood this mystery, he would die. God spares us because of our weakness."

two hundred of them, including a Bishop, all the Franciscans, the Capuchins, along with their novices—and many young people. In short, everyone was there. There were even some Muslims and Druze. During Mass, everyone stood together around the altar."

"Therefore, I can say that, if we truly ask the Mother of God for Mass, she will answer us. How could she leave us without her Son?"

"Later on I learned that someone had given that priest the order not to let me down and to celebrate Mass for me." At this point Francis began to laugh and he added, "I never did find out who had made such a request...."

"Dear Children! The priests should visit families, especially those who do not practice anymore and those who have forgotten God. Priests should carry the Gospel of Jesus to the people, and teach them how to pray. And the priests themselves should fast and pray more. They should give to the poor what they don't need." (May 30, 1984)

64

FATHER JOZO'S SURPRISES

Father Jozo is a man full of surprises. Some say he was born with this trait, others say that it was given to him by the Gospa. When the Serbo-Croatian conflict was at its worst in the spring of 1992, I went to see him in his monastery in Siroki Brijeg, situated 22 miles away from Medjugorje. That was not a small trek in those difficult days!

Sitting on a little wall in the garden, he started talking about the courage of some of his friends who were Croatian soldiers engaged in secret rescue operations here and there. Fascinated, I suggested he write a book so all this beauty is not lost!

"Me! Write a book?! But I am illiterate! And the Gospa does not need books. She gave us THE Book!" He started to laugh. "Come," he said. "I will show you the house where I was born."

Through a complicated maze of back roads that his car seemed to know by heart, he took me to the land of his ancestors a few miles away. He showed me the house where he was born and he asked, "How about you, where were you born?"

His question brought an end to my peaceful contemplation of the vineyards and took my mind back to the streets of Paris—neat, well designed, filled with harmonious architecture. I could still see the city people running in all directions, all far too fast, as if stretching toward their own mirage of materialism in the middle of a desert. They all seemed anxious because, for all their running and searching, they could only grasp a few grains of sand, and they appeared so disconnected from creation.

I started to answer, "I was born in a big city"... but almost immediately Father interrupted saying, "So you never worked in a vineyard as a child? Then you cannot understand anything in the Eucharist! You don't understand the Gospel!"

His declaration was final but he peacefully continued our tour, as if the fact that I didn't understand the Eucharist did not bother him.

On the way back he spoke to me about the six children the Gospa had chosen in Medjugorje. "If it had been my choice, I would never have chosen these six!"

Then he went on to tell me how he himself came to believe in the apparitions, and how dear those children had become dear to him, especially because of the peaceful heroism they showed during the adversity of those first days. As we parted, enriched by that sharing in confidences, his words "You cannot understand anything in the Eucharist!" were imprinted on my mind.

He was so right! If one day I am told that I actually understand 1% of the mystery of the Eucharist, I will then be the happiest woman in the world. But the Gospa, Our Heavenly Mother, never loses heart. In fact she teaches us to live this mystery more than she teaches us to understand it. Who could ever understand it?

Often Our Lady uses Croatian words with very rich meaning. If we could understand Croatian, we would have a deeper idea of her teachings. Those who translate her messages, run up against great difficulties when they have to choose one word, whereas the Croatian language includes several possible meanings. In order to resolve the problem, they have no choice but to diminish the meaning of the words that the Gospa uses. For example, after examining more deeply in the message, "Dear Children I invite you to live the Holy Mass...," they found that the meaning of that expression in Croatian chosen by the Blessed Mother was impossible to translate. Indeed, the word itself contains different levels of meaning, through which our Mother is inviting us to become the Mass, to enter the Passion, to live the Passion, so much so that any single translation can only be a gross betrayal.

Who on earth will ever be able to understand the splendor of the Eucharist and the sacrifice of the Mass!? Who will ever be able to guess the feelings of the "Mother of the Eucharist" when we receive the Body of her Son during Holy Communion, the Body that includes also his Heart, his Soul and his Divinity? Who will ever understand the grandeur of the priesthood and why Jesus is calling to Himself this or that man? How great is our surprise in front of God's choices and callings! The priest who celebrates the holy mysteries is another Christ; therefore the best attitude of the heart in front of such a calling is a childlike trust and simplicity. Mary gives us a beautiful example: called to become the Mother of God, she did not ask, "Why me?" Rather, having inquired about the "how" in order to better partake in God's plan, she simply said, "May it be done unto me according to your word."

Living in Medjugorje, one is able to observe all the many ways, both diverse and original, that God calls priests to carry out His ministry.

Morris Wants To Know What to Do With His Life

I remember that one day Father Tim Deeter (with whom I went on several missions) met a young American on the steps of St. James church. This young man, Morris, had many, many questions and seemed quite disoriented. He had come all the way from the States as a pilgrim, hoping to receive Divine light for his life. In this world, he was doing well financially and had every prospect of a brilliant career. However, he was looking for meaning in his life. Father Tim took time to talk to him and he mentioned he was going to visit Father Jozo that afternoon. The young man jumped at this opportunity: "Great!" he said. "Please ask him what I should do with my life!"

Father Tim took the first taxi he saw and went to Tihajina, the little parish where Father Jozo was the pastor at the time. To his surprise, he found Father Jozo waiting for him in the courtyard just in front of the church (normally it's the visitors who have to wait a long time). He just had time to close the taxi door when, without any introduction whatsoever, Father Jozo told him, "So Morris wants to know what to do with his life? Tell him God is calling him to be a priest. But he must enter the seminary right away, because God can take back a vocation just as quickly as He gives it. He should not let this grace pass by!"

In December 7, 1996, Morris Harrigan was ordained a priest in the diocese of Los Angeles.

I Wanted To Be a Mechanic

Another time, I was on a plane with Father Svetozar Kraljevic, a Franciscan priest from Medjugorje. We were on our way to Pittsburg, Pennsylvania, for a Marian Conference on Medjugorje. Those long hours of traveling together allowed us to speak heart-to-heart, much more so than in Medjugorje where so often our schedules are full from morning until night.

I asked him this question: "Father, I don't want to pry but tell me how did the Lord call you to the priesthood? How did you feel the calling?"

"The Lord never called me to the priesthood!"

I stopped—completely dumfounded— and stared at him. This priest is one of the best priests I know. He radiates peace and tenderness everywhere he goes and he has such a sense of freedom! I believe he has a profound mystical life. But knowing quite well Father Svet's unique perspective on life, people, and situations, I started to smile. Then I attempted to dig a little further:

"Even so you did become priest. So how did that come about?"

So Father Svet* began to explain that when he was young he had other plans for his life. Gadgets and machines fascinated him. He wanted to be a mechanic, get married and raise a Christian family. But at the last minute, just before starting on a line of studies that would have put him on a definite path, he said to himself, "I could also choose to become a priest."

"So", he said, with much simplicity as if it were absolutely obvious, "I thought to myself, 'We have only one life on earth, so we might as well live it all for God.' I changed direction and I immediately entered the Franciscan Seminary. Today, after thirty years of priesthood, I still haven't received the call."[159]

* For Fr. Svet's book "Pilgrimage: Reflections of a Medjugorje Priest" (Paraclete Press, Brewster MA)

---

[159] It must be noted that, even as a young man, Svetozar showed a great sense of responsibility and he carried inside a great respect for vocations and all the Christian virtues, like most Croatian Catholics—and unlike many young people in the West. He was well aware that a priest had to be ready to shed his own blood, and so he was not lightly committing to this decision. It was in this terrain, well prepared through grace, that the thought of a vocation sprang up in him like a motion from the Holy Spirit. It seems that God had no need to send him another message on top of this one to make him understand he was called to be a priest.

"Dear children! Today I call on you to realize that without love you will not understand that God needs to be in the centre of your life. That is why, little children, I call you all to love, not with a human love but with God's love. In this way, your life will be more beautiful and without self interest. You will comprehend that God gives Himself to you in the simplest way out of love." *(September 25, 1997)*

65

JULIE'S LOVE KNOWS NO BOUNDS!

On the outskirts of Marseille, the little hamlet of Saint-André stands out majestically amid the wild, sweet smelling hills that are the treasure of Provence. Here the Porta family lives at nature's peaceful pace. Little Julie, then at the tender age of 14, likes playing hopscotch in the village square, and her great beauty does not go unnoticed. As she hops along the squares traced carefully on the cobblestones, her long black hair resembles a couple waltzing, bouncing up and down and waving in the breeze. Gaston, a young man of 17, just can't take his eyes off her.

"Look how beautiful she is, so graceful and attractive!" How he longs to make friends with her. So he plucks up the courage to offer her some candy and mumbles the first words of what was to become a beautiful love story. It's not long before he proposes marriage to her.

In France, back in the days before the First World War (1914-1918), young people were not rushed into intimate relationships as they are nowadays. They took time to let their hearts grow and develop at nature's slow, gentle pace. In those days, neither of those two little lovers knew about the anguish and panic of being "discarded after use" (which is so familiar today), sometimes without even knowing the identity of the other person.

Julie had ravished Gaston's heart, but 14 and 17 they were still very young. They needed time to acquire some maturity and submit their feelings to the test of time. At the request of their parents, Julie waited until she turned 21—adulthood in the eyes of the law—before pronouncing her "Yes" before the Mayor and before God, a "yes" that would make her Gaston's beloved spouse.

Gaston was a jack-of-all-trades as well as a skilled carpenter. There was always a smile on his face as he went about his household chores. And when evening time rolled around, he loved to play his accordion on the front porch for family and friends who had gathered in the fresh time of twilight.

Julie gave birth to two children in this simple and healthy atmosphere of a home where love prevailed. The newlyweds drank life as it came to them. Who could imagine the threatening cloud that loomed on the horizon of their little heaven?

In August 1914 war broke out in Europe. Thousands of young men in the area were drafted into the army, and marched up the Rhône Valley to meet the enemy on the French-German border. Gaston was among those drafted but he stayed behind. How could he possibly be expected to leave his wife and two children, to tear himself away this tightly-knit household?

Yet war is unforgiving. He was found guilty of deserting, and so one day troops barged in to their little house, handcuffed him and dragged him away by force, as his children began to bawl. Julie ran out and tried to stop them, only to be kicked so violently that she was thrown back against the wall. Tears streamed down her face.

The troops left without a word, as quickly and silently as they had come. Gone with the wind! From one moment to the next in those horrific moments, Julie's happiness was shattered; never again would life be the same.

After years of joyful, happy family life, emptiness now invaded the home, with its cold, gnawing grip, leaving behind a great void. In front of her two frightened children, Julie pulled herself to her feet. Her head felt dizzy, but even worse her heart was wrung out. "Isn't this just a bad dream?" she asked herself. "Won't Gaston come and wake me with a kiss? Won't our life together carry on as before?" But, as if nothing had happened, the clock on the mantelpiece continued to tick, marking the hours—the hours that had become agony.

Gaston was not coming back and the family was not receiving any special rations, so Julie had no choice but to work to support her family. A middle class family hired her and she was assigned the lowest, most menial chores. They treated her badly, made fun of her and tried to take advantage of her. Many a times she was forced to bite her tongue to put up with it all, but there was no other alternative.

Long months passed and Gaston did not call or write. No one knew his whereabouts for sure, though most probably he was stationed in the terrible trenches of Lorraine. Julie turned into a sentinel, her eyes and ears constantly alert to pick up the slightest tidbit of news from the Front. Unfortunately, the picture from the trenches was blacker than black, men were falling by the hundreds. Neither side was moving anywhere, the supply lines were growing thin and many of the soldiers spent days and nights in those freezing, horrible, sordid holes.

Each piece of bad news was like a knife penetrating Julie's heart. But in this her hour of greatest anguish, her unity of heart with Gaston was forged stronger than ever. Sure, she might not be able to help him materially, nor cry out words of encouragement to her beloved. Yet her simple heart, transcending the realm of words and earthly limitations, found a way to be united with him. The imagination of a lover knows no bounds!

One winter evening, as the cold northerly wind lashed against the windows of the cabin and rattled the front door on its hinges, Julie decided lie down on the cold, hard stone floor of her bedroom. Yes, this is where she would sleep from now on, here on the floor, at the foot of her cozy bed, until the day of Gaston's return. Wasn't he freezing there in the trenches under a layer of snow? She would freeze too, with him, for him! Wasn't he shivering all night? Didn't he lack everything? Wasn't he hungry? She made up her mind to deprive herself too, with him, for him. One body, one heart!

Julie's nightly routine did not go long unnoticed by the two children. Troubled by this strange behavior, they asked her, "Mamma, but…what are you doing?" Julie has never been one to talk a lot. In three words, with her humble modesty, she was able to put the children at peace. Children are too small not to understand. Children are mystics without even knowing it. Right away they understood how much love was contained in her sacrifice. And they decided on their own to follow their mother's example.

"We're doing this for Daddy," they reminded one another as they lay down to sleep on the hard floor.

The tiles that lined their bedrooms became an altar on which a daily offering, a new Mass of love was celebrated each night. An altar on which a sacrificial offering was placed, although Julie and the children were unaware of the sacrifice, because this was an act of love and where there is love, there is no sacrifice.

Finally, on November 11, 1918, the armistice was signed and the war was at last over! Yet, there were so few survivors who limped back to Provence! Truly this armistice had been written in blood! Wailing and moaning rose from many of the thatched cottages of Saint-André, where sons, fathers and brothers had been lost. They had not returned. Julie heard over and over again, "Missing in action" when the messengers came delivering news to others.

On one of those November evenings, Julie opened the doors of the great wardrobe in her room, her cheeks wet with tears, her hands trembling with emotion. She reached in to pull out the fine linen sheets and beautiful bedspread that her grandmother had embroidered for her wedding day. Carefully she ironed them, knowing that this night was unlike any other—Gaston had come home! One of the few survivors in his unit, Gaston had made it back from the Front. Yes, he was there, home at last. She could hear him playing outside with the children.

Julie's prolonged Mass had yielded its fruit. The humble offering she made every day had won favor from on high. God had protected her sweetheart. Gaston was back alive!

"Dear Children! You do not celebrate the Eucharist as you should. If you only knew what grace and what gifts you receive, you would go to Mass everyday, and you would prepare yourselves for it at least an hour before it starts." (1985)

66

THE CIBORIUM CRIED OUT!

Too often we forget that in the Eucharist Jesus is more human than any of us. He feels everything with a sensitivity that would send us reeling. He is all heart, always expectant of love, and more vulnerable than a newborn. When we receive Communion we know what we feel. But what do we know about what Jesus feels inside our hearts?

One night, when I had prolonged my time of adoration a bit in my Community's chapel, I went over to the tabernacle to close it and to blow out the candles that surround it. In France, the avowed members of the Community of the Beatitudes are able to expose the Blessed Sacrament without touching it. One only has to open the door of the tabernacle where a small monstrance is placed. A directional spotlight illuminates the Host while the other lights around it are extinguished. This allows us to focus our attention on the Body of Jesus.

Finding myself alone in the chapel, I took my time completing these little sacristan tasks around Jesus, whilst talking to Him. After all wasn't I His spouse? Here I was then, right next to Him and, key in hand, getting ready to lock Him up until the next morning. However, my heart felt a pang: so many Christians could only dream of being able to adore Him, if only for a single hour, even in the middle of the night, and here I was locking the door! It was at that moment that a little detail caught my eye: some wax from the candle had dripped onto the wooden frame of the door. So I set about removing every trace of wax, when I was startled by a sort of cry. It wasn't coming from the monstrance, but from the ciborium, containing many Hosts, placed in the back of the tabernacle. The cry wasn't audible through my bodily ears, but it resonated all the more in my heart; our hearts have the most powerful antennae.

Jesus had something to say to me. He was truly living in each one of the Hosts, although there were not three hundred thirty-seven Jesus' in this ciborium. Jesus was one, but multiplied.[160]

It was as though each Host was beginning to explain itself, describing to me the crucial moment it was preparing to live in the coming days. It seemed to me that each Host knew to which soul, to which person it was destined. Each Host was going to live a unique, loving adventure, and the breadth of possibilities was amazing! Certain Hosts were going to fall into hearts which would be for them a Heaven; for others, it would be like a descent into hell. The cry which resonated in my heart was in reality a cry of anguish.

Many Hosts are in agony. They know they will be received into unworthy dwelling places where sins, which lead to death, reign. I stood

---

[160] At Lanciano, a small Italian city in Abruzzi, a Basilian monk had doubts about the real presence of Christ in the Eucharist. He prayed ardently to be enlightened in this regard. In 1750, during a Mass, after he had pronounced the words of the Consecration, he was surprised to see the host transformed into flesh and the wine into blood. The blood presented itself in the form of five clots of different sizes. He was frightened in the face of this marvel and called upon the faithful to witness the event. Then he called the Bishop on the spot. The relics of this flesh and this blood have been preserved by the monks until this day, in a reliquary. In order to prevent the piece of flesh from shrinking as it dried out, it was nailed onto a piece of wood; but it shrank anyway, which formed a cavity in the middle of the piece of flesh.

A number of scientific analyses have been done on these specimens, the most important of which lasted ten years, between 1971 and 1981, under the direction of Professors Linoli (University of Arezzo) and Bertelli (University of Sienna). The results show that these specimens exhibit no evidence of a preservative agent. We know that human blood, like flesh, becomes powder at the end of several years. These specimens have remained intact. The flesh was that of the left ventricle of a man. It was living at the moment of the miracle. The blood is of the type AB. One can find in it the serum of fresh blood. The electrophoresis profile of the Lanciano blood was normal, all protein elements were present, and in the quantities usually found in a healthy subject.

The point that interests us most is that, despite their different sizes, each of the five clots weighs 15.85 grams and the five clots taken together weigh the same, 15.85 grams! This phenomenon reminds us that Christ is equally present in each host and that, indivisible, He gives Himself totally to us in each Holy Communion.

Another interesting point: The analyses of the Shroud of Turin establish that the blood of the man crucified was blood type AB. From that same blood type are the tears of blood-shed by the statuette of the Our Lady of Medjugorje brought to Civitavecchia, at the gates of Rome in 1997. For more information about Lanciano, see Ave Maria Center of Peace, C.P. 489. Station U. Toronto, ON. M8Z 5Y8. Canada. An article, True Flesh and True Blood, was published in the journal 30Days (No. 2, 1997).

glued to the floor, shocked. Several of these Hosts were horrified at the prospect of being consumed.[161] Jesus was crying for help! It was a silent cry, much like the one of an infant-embryo who feels his death coming and who burrows instinctively into the womb of his mother at the approach of an instrument that will violently extract him. It was the silent cry of the innocent who has no defense in his little body if, she who carries him, does not love him. It was the silent cry of God, who had willed to entrust that little body, inert, lighter than a grain of wheat, into the hands of men, with all its risks and perils.

Each Host also knows the day and the hour when it will enter into the heart of the person who will consume it. I am fascinated by the consciousness of Jesus. He knows all, sees all, foresees all, and yet He lets Himself be treated like a lamb. Thankfully, most of the Hosts rejoice in advance at being able to unite themselves with their recipients.[162]

That night, when I closed the tabernacle, I tried to take in the message that Jesus had given me – a message not yet fully received because only when I come face to face with God in Heaven will I truly understand His cry for help. For the moment, one thing is clear: Jesus invites me to adore Him in spirit, not only in all the tabernacles of the world, but in the hearts of all those who receive Communion, the good as well as the bad, so that when He suffers anew at being put to death, Jesus will receive at least one tiny visit of love, a humble bit of attention, which will console Him.[163]

---

[161] Sister Faustina recounted this episode in her Diary: "I received Holy Communion upstairs, for there was no question of my going down to the chapel since I was exhausted because of intense sweating, and when that passed, I had a fever and chills.... Today, one of the Jesuit Fathers brought us Holy Communion. He gave the Lord to three other sisters and then to me; and thinking that I was the last, he gave me two Hosts. But one of the novices was lying in bed in the next cell, and there was no Host left for her. The priest went back again and brought her the Lord, but Jesus told me, I enter that heart unwillingly. You received those two hosts because I delayed My coming into this soul who resists My grace. My visit to such a soul is not pleasant for Me." (Diary §1658)

[162] Jesus told Sister Faustina: "Write for the benefit of religious souls that it delights Me to come to their hearts in Holy Communion." (Diary §1683)

[163] "O most Holy Trinity, Father, Son, and Holy Spirit, I adore You profoundly. I offer You the most precious Body, Blood, Soul, and Divinity of Jesus Christ, present in all the tabernacles of the world, in reparation for the outrages, sacrileges, and indifferences by which He is offended. Through the infinite merits of His Sacred Heart and the Immaculate Heart of Mary, I beg you for the conversion of poor sinners." (Prayer taught to the witnesses to Fatima by the Angel of Portugal)

Stolen Hosts

Mother Yvonne-Aimée was a great French mystic, who died in 1951 at the age of forty-nine. She had many charisms. Among others, it sometimes happened that Christ warned her when Hosts were being profaned. Today, there are those who maintain that the Real Presence does not exist outside the celebration of Mass. It is a great error. Here is a letter that Yvonne-Aimée wrote from Paris to Father Crété on March 31, 1923.

"Dear Father, I am writing to you, having Jesus with me. Last night, my Beloved told me to go to look for Him at the house of a person who, since Saturday, had been keeping a Host that she had received at the Holy Table unworthily. As soon as she had returned to her seat, this poor soul had taken it out of her mouth and slipped it into her handkerchief, in order to carry it to her house and defile it. So I asked Jesus to grant me this soul, and I spoke about it to my friends at Rue Monsieur (Paris), so that they, also, might pray for this poor lost one."

"That night, following the order of the most gentle Lord Jesus, I went to the house of this very high class person. She herself came to open the door. I told her immediately that I had come to get the Host. She became very pale while telling me to follow her. She took me into her living room and opened a small box that was sitting on a table. The Host was there!"

"I took it, and then, following the inspiration of the Master, I spoke to this poor woman, who shed tears of sincere repentance."

"I returned to my residence with my Dear Treasure on my heart. It was one-thirty in the morning. Along the way, my Beloved spoke to me. 'Keep me,' He told me, 'Until I tell you to act and make known to you my will.'" (Yvonne's spiritual director asked her to consume the Host that she was carrying on her and always to do the same in any similar case!)

Yvonne continued her letter: "That evening, Jesus told me that, again that very night, I was to take Him away from another home in which He had been violated. Oh, Poor Jesus, Dear Beloved, so badly loved!"

In her subsequent searches, Yvonne sometimes returned wounded with the Eucharist that she had torn away from profaners who had beaten her. Yvonne suffered very cruelly for the souls who profaned the

Hosts and for whom she asked for conversion to the Lord. Often, on the night that followed the recovery of Hosts, Jesus united her with His own agony, so that it would atone for the sacrileges. When these events took place, Yvonne-Aimée was not yet a nun. She was only around twenty years old. Later, she entered the convent of the Augustinians, in Malestroit, France.[164]

---

[164] Only in Heaven will we discover the interventions that the Saints have carried out on Earth, in order to reconcile man to God, and their impact on history. God sends His friends to the home of such and such a person the way a strategist sends thousands of his best men to deal with the enemy and to win accords capable of changing the course of the war. Among those emissaries of God, Mother Yvonne-Aimée is the figurehead, insofar as she had the gift of bi-location and could thus encounter the most unexpected people in any part of the world. At any given moment, she could speak fluently the language of those to whom God was sending her, even when it came to reading their newspapers!

Several years before his death in 2002, Father Labutte, who had been Yvonne-Aimée's spiritual director, visited my community of Iffendic in Brittany and recounted many episodes from her life. One of them struck me as it revealed a little how, in secret, Our Father in Heaven multiplied the attempts to bring back His children to His Heart.

At the end of World War II, Mother Yvonne-Aimée was in Malestroit, France. From there she bi-located and found herself in Germany, in the office of Hitler. This powerful man, surprised to see in front of him a religious whom he had not invited, opened his drawer, drew out a pistol, and fired it. It seems that in these cases of bi-location, bodies are not vulnerable, because Mother Yvonne-Aimée did not fall. Hitler fired a second time, but the sister remained just as impassive. Hitler stared at her, frozen in place. She delivered the message that she had brought him from God and which contained an explicit demand (Father Labutte did not reveal it to us). Hitler refused, at least on that particular day. Mother Yvonne-Aimée then approached the enormous map of Europe which covered a wall in the room. With her finger, she pointed out a city and said to Hitler: "When you reach there, you will have lost." And that is what happened.

Oh, fearsome liberty of man in front of the pressing interventions of God!

"Dear Children! I invite you, under this cross, to take your cross as the will of God. Just as my Son took His cross, so you should carry your cross, and my Son will be glorified through your crosses. Thank you, dear children, for answering my call and carrying your cross." (Good Friday, March 29, 1991)

67

THE BLEEDING CHILD

Andrew was lighting a fire. Emily, his wife, had no idea what was coming next. She watched, shocked and speechless, as Andrew took from his huge bag a dozen crucifixes that he had picked up here and there. With a snicker, he and his colleague began throwing them into the fire, one by one. Then, grabbing his wife by her hair, he said:

"Go get Him, your Christ, if you have the guts! Go on! Get Him out of there!"

Andrew had affair after affair with other women, leaving Emily in agony. Each time she felt the blow to their marriage. On top of that, he detested Jesus. Emily, on the contrary, loved Jesus immensely. Eventually, Andrew kicked Emily and their daughter out of their home, and bolted the door. Another woman had taken her place in their bed.

Emily found shelter in a house of prayer where she worked during the day and cried during the night. Luckily a priest gave her spiritual guidance and helped her to bear the trial. Too tired to continue the pace of working and unable to sleep, she was forced to take refuge in her car. For three months, she waited there, in prayer and solitude, to see how the Lord was going to pick up the pieces of her broken life.

The hour of Medjugorje was approaching her. In May 1982, her spiritual director, a Jesuit, sent her there. Immediately Father Slavko took her under his wing and, with much affection, he helped her organize pilgrimages from Canada. Emily felt able to easily confide in him and a beautiful communion of their souls developed.

In May 2002, during a pilgrimage, Emily experienced the first symptom of bleeding, but without any pain. Upon her return to Canada she consulted three doctors but none of them could put an end to her problem. Several X-rays showed that she had four kidneys, or rather two double-kidneys, and they were like sponges! During the following months traces of blood in her urine continued to slowly increase. Emily received the Anointing of the Sick. She remained in peace despite the dark cloud that seemed to shadow her future.

Indeed, whilst the doctors had given up, Emily allowed God to permeate her through a very profound Eucharistic experience. Each Mass, each Communion became for her, a new conquest of Love, a love that transcended and transfigured all the misery of her mortal body.

"My body was collapsing," she told me, "but the Eucharist was giving me strength from the inside! I could feel the effusion of the Divine Blood running into me, and that enabled me to keep going. No celebration of the Eucharist was ever monotonous; it was always a Divine Meal. I was sharing one-on-one with Christ. I needed that Divine strength to make it through the ordeal. I could feel the Blessed Mother putting her arms around me and saying: 'I am with you, do not fear for your health!'"

With this strength from above, Emily was able to continue her service of pilgrimages and prayer groups for Our Lady. She gave so much of herself, everybody around her pondered the uncanny amount of energy she had each day for each task!

On Christmas Day 2002, her friend Terri invited her to spend two months in Medjugorje and immediately she said, "Yes!" But Emily made a mistake. She had accepted some natural medicine from a therapist without checking the contents. While in Medjugorje, she bled more profusely each day. Emily found herself on another continent, far from home, and without any worthwhile medical help. She began to panic. One night, as she watched her body spewing out blood, she prayed despite the anxiety that gripped her: "Lord, if this is what You want, then so be it. Mary, I trust in you! You are my insurance; it is up to you to do something!"

Emily fell asleep in peace. The next day, as soon as she awoke, she was drawn to the tomb of Father Slavko, because it seemed that he was calling her. Despite the bitter cold and cutting winds of that January 2002, and despite the extreme fatigue of her bloodless body, Emily poured out her heart to her friend Slavko. With childlike simplicity, she said everything and, for the first time, dared to ask for a healing.

Who can tell how the Saints organize earthly matters for us from Heaven? What is their schedule, their timing, why this choice or that? We will understand it all when we finally pass on to the other side of the veil. But one thing is certain: our poor little words will never be able to reflect the real savor of their celestial interventions at certain key moments in our lives, and all the happiness they bring.

In her own words, Emily tries to express the splendid visitation of grace she received that January 30th:

"Around 3:00 p.m., after having prayed the Chaplet of Divine Mercy with Terri, we walked back to our lodging, where an irresistible force drew me to look towards Mount Krizevac. There I saw a blinding light at the foot of the Cross. This light grew larger and larger until it became really impressive. I asked Terri to look that way but, not wanting to influence her, didn't give her any details. She cried that she saw a light. The light kept getting bigger and bigger and, within it, I saw a figure like that of Our Lady: it moved from the left to the right, but kept coming back to the foot of the Cross. I decided to go to my room to get my camera, but something inside told me: 'Do not go!'"

"How I regret not listening to that voice, but went off to grab my camera! I came back from my room, clutching my camera, but my heart was pinched with sadness. I took two photos (a disaster) and little by little the light faded away until it was gone. I understood then that this supernatural light was active; it had penetrated each cell of my body, all of my being. It had invaded me. I am so sad I succumbed to the temptation of trying to get a photograph! If I hadn't, maybe the light would have stayed longer. Less than an hour later, I found that the blood had disappeared from my urine. And it was the same in the evening, and the next day. No more loss of blood! And it is true to this day! I am utterly convinced that Father Slavko interceded for my healing."

"On October 25, 2000, one month before he died, after the evening Adoration, he had come to Terri and me, and he blessed us. In the Confessional he had told me with great sadness, 'I don't know if I'll see you again!' Then he put his head in his hands and I could see that he was suffering. I understood only later that he knew his time remaining in Medjugorje was short."

Jesus Doesn't Choose the Best Ones

Jesus, my Spouse, has often given me the grace—and what a beautiful grace this is—to meet a few of His friends who are so dear to Him, friends He uses as choice instruments to pour out His Divine consolation. This consolation can be an example of physical, psychological or moral healing; it can be liberation, or an inspiration about a choice to make. I notice that Jesus does not choose worldly people; rather he uses hearts that have suffered a great deal. Suffering is the best book to learn about God and His secrets, especially when we live the experience of suffering with Mary.[165] It is the best training school to learn empathy towards the suffering of others, to the point where one would give his life to bring them relief. Suffering that is offered is the best ointment for healing the wounds of our broken humanity. "The stone which the builders rejected has become the head of the corner." (Ps 118:22)

Emily is one of these friends. No sooner was she healed from the disordered effusion of blood from her body, than Emily found herself in a mission as large as it was unexpected. I cannot describe here her new adventure as it would occupy the rest of this book, but I want to let one remarkable fact filter through to you: in Canada and in the USA thousands and thousands of people, through Emily's work, have been consecrating their country and themselves to the Immaculate Heart of Mary, in accordance to Heaven's request at Fatima. Who can evaluate the impact of this deed in the work of Salvation? To initiate this, God fetched a little bleeding child who, left alone in the streets of Montreal, only had the seat of a car on which to rest her head.

---

[165] See Chapter 63, "An Open Wound."

Tonight also, dear children, I am grateful to you in a special way for being here. Unceasingly adore the most Blessed Sacrament of the Altar. I am always present when the faithful are adoring. Special graces are then being received." (March 15, 1984)

68

ASK FOR ALL THAT YOU WANT!

On a warm summer night, Maria Torassa forged her way through the crowd, which was pressing towards the Rotunda situated behind the church of St. James, hoping to find three places on one of the benches. It was August 4, 2002. She was tired. She and her two friends, Sonia and Beatriz, were returning from a long procession through the streets of the village, a traditional part of the annual Youth Festival. Her friends had told her there would be a closing ceremony in the Rotunda and they didn't want to miss that part of the program. Maria had no idea what was about to happen, but simply followed along.

A violin began to play, followed by magnificent songs, coming from the Rotunda.[166] In that circular space, on the altar, the dancing flames of the candles seemed to announce a mysterious sequel to the procession. Maria could tell that something was going to happen, but she was reluctant to ask and expose her abysmal ignorance of religious matters. Then the violin changed tones and the choir broke into the song Benedictus qui venit. A priest advanced towards the altar, majestically escorted by two candle bearers. He then held out, at arm's length, something which he placed in the center of the altar. It looked like a sun with feet!

"What's that?" Maria asked Beatriz.

---

[166] It was the violin of Melinda Dumitrescu, who has resided in Medjugorje for several years as a member of the Figli del Divino Amore community. This virtuoso musician plays violin during the hours of adoration at St. James.

"It's a monstrance and in the middle is Jesus. You see the white round thing...? That's Jesus in there."

'Jesus,' thought Maria. 'God? She's telling me that God is in that sun?' Maria knew her friend Beatriz very well — she had always been a level-headed, normal woman, with her feet planted firmly on the ground. Still, Maria couldn't help thinking this is weird!

Maria had come to Medjugorje with a bit of curiosity, but without any expectations. She gently laughed at her friends who were so interested in everything related to religion. She herself had left the Church a long time ago and didn't remember ever having prayed with her heart. Maybe God did exist, but she didn't see how that concerned her. Her compass was to do what pleased her the most and to follow her own feelings.

A few weeks earlier, in Las Parejas, her home town in Argentina, some events had worked on her very gently, leading up to this trip. One evening, after leaving work, she went to visit her one year old godson, Felipe, and confided in his young mother, Beatriz, "I don't feel very well and I don't know why."

Beatriz listened without saying anything, but when Maria repeated the same thing to her a week later, she held out a picture to her. On it was written, "The Queen of Peace." Maria was taken aback. She took it and quickly put it away in her purse. That evening she took it out and began to read the messages printed on the back. Each evening, instinctively, her fingers searched for the picture, and Maria remained fixed on those words of peace and tenderness. She was unaware that the messages were little by little seeping into her and, finally, she revealed to Beatriz the depth of her turmoil: "I have no peace!"

The words had simply escaped from her. She allowed them to tumble out. Yes, that was it, she had no peace, and she just didn't want to look that reality in the face. After all, why face it if she already knew that she couldn't cope with it? She asked her husband to buy her some do-it-yourself relaxation tapes, but he had another idea: "Why don't you take a little trip to the coast of Yugoslavia? As a matter of fact, Sonia and Beatriz are going there soon. Couldn't you take advantage of it and trace your family roots in the area?"

The idea of being with her two friends was delightful and a change of scenery really appealed to Maria. So she agreed to go. But in addition to researching ancestors, her friends had another purpose: they particularly had in mind making a pilgrimage to Medjugorje. "Oh, so what," Maria told herself. "The country must be beautiful, and it's summer over there—I'm going." She rapidly scanned a little summary of the events at Medjugorje just to prepare herself and smiled when several good souls marveled at her departure.

"You are so lucky! The Blessed Mother is inviting you there!"

"No," Maria answered. "It's Sonia and Beatriz who invited me!"

Contrary to all expectations, Maria spent several unforgettable days in Medjugorje. "In my heart," she would say later, "only an indefinable peace existed, so special to Medjugorje that one feels it only there."

Maria was enjoying her vacation and had discovered with happiness a new kind of human relationship, a communion deeply simple and joyful between people. However, one important detail began to disturb those days of grace: the telephone lines in the village were not functioning properly and Maria could not reach South America; no one knew when they would be repaired. Now Maria had left behind her 81 year old father, her husband, and her children aged 21, 18 and 14 years old. Waves of inner frustration and anxiety began to upset her tranquility. Especially the worry about her son, Matias—Matias the knife; Matias the wound; Matias her failure as a mother.

His younger sister had experienced a terrible problem with her eye that cost the family most of what they earned. The sacrifice was difficult for Matias to make and as a result he had rebelled by not speaking to his mother from the age of 15. The past three years had been filled with intimate suffering for Maria. She was tormented with those nagging questions, typical of a mother who is bleeding: What did I do to make him hate me so much? What is he doing now? How is he going to come out of this? Is he going to leave home? How can I reconnect with him without being rejected?

That evening, near the Rotunda, Maria found herself in front of the Blessed Sacrament for the first time in her life. Without even trying to comprehend the rather strange words that Beatriz had conveyed to her in little dribbles, Maria now fell to her knees. In front of the "Golden

Sun" positioned on the altar, she waited. She did not know how to pray and her mind began to drift. Then Beatriz whispered a few words into her ear, like a secret reserved for a select few: "Jesus is there. Look! Right now they are worshiping Him. It's a very special moment. Ask Him for whatever you want. He will grant it to you."

Maria wasn't sure of anything. She had never spoken to Jesus, and now her best friend was telling her that there He was, and that she could ask Him for whatever she wanted, the way you ask a neighbor or a friend for something. She realized that she had nothing to lose and she didn't have to think about what she most wanted: it was Matias!

"Oh, Jesus, if You are really there, if You hear me, grant that my son Matias and I reconcile and be friendly again!"

For the first time in her life, she prayed, or rather, she cried out to God with all of her heart, from the depth of her being. She laid her burden on the heart of God, and she looked at the Host, completely white, like a beacon in the night. She looked and she leaned her face, bathed in tears, towards the Host, and ... yes, there he was—Matias!! It truly was he! The face of Matias was in the golden sun! It seemed to be inscribed on the Host, as though emanating from the Host, floating in front of the Host! Maria forgot Beatriz, the crowd, and even her own body. She was fascinated by what her eyes could perceive! Then she called her son inwardly, and what a surprise! He answered her in her heart, as if some connection had been established between her soul and the soul of Matias.

"Is this an apparition?" she wondered. Maria was seeing Matias the way he was the day she left him. Although in a state of shock, Maria spoke to Matias, and he answered. They spoke for a good moment, heart to heart. At the end, when Maria became conscious again of her surroundings, Beatriz enfolded her tenderly in her arms. She cried with joy along with her!

"Beatriz, Sonia, I saw my son, I saw Matias!!"

From that hour on, Maria was not the same person. Jesus had entered her life. She had seen Him at work. He had answered her cry. She adopted Him.

Maria received other signs during her stay in Medjugorje, among them one related to the telephone lines, which were still in a state of chronic disrepair. She was the only one to manage any communication. One evening, with her friends, she wanted to dial the number of her family, but—to this day she doesn't know how it happened—her fingers went astray and unaware she dialed Matias' number.[167] And he answered! He was there on the other end of the line, all peaceful! Out of all the pilgrims, she was the only one who was able to reach Argentina!

She returned home to find her husband, Juan Marcos, waiting for her at the airport. Maria was now full of new joy and immediately launched into telling Juan Marcos the most extraordinary of tales from her time in Medjugorje. Juan Marcos listened to her with one ear but then interrupted her. He had his own piece of news for her!

"Maria, I don't know what has happened with Matias. You'll see yourself. He hasn't stopped asking me when are you coming back, how are you doing, etc. It's bizarre! I've never seen him like that! He's been waiting for you with such impatience, as if you were his best friend in the world!"

"Really? When did this start?"

"Wait; let me think, yes, August 4th in the afternoon. All of a sudden he asked for you, and since then he has been really impatient to see you."

"What a miracle! Do you remember what time it was on August 4th?"

"It was around four in the afternoon."

On hearing this, Maria's heart turned upside down. Intuitively she knew. She remained speechless for a few seconds. At lightening speed she calculated in her mind the time difference between Bosnia and Argentina. Four o'clock was nine o'clock in Medjugorje—the time of the Holy Hour of Adoration. It was at that very moment she had cried to Jesus and she had seen Matias in the Host. Then holding back her tears, she murmured to her husband: "You said 4:00 p.m., Juan Marcos?"

"Yes, Maria, it was 4:00 p.m."

---

[167] Matias was then at the University of Rosario, where he occupied an apartment owned by his family. He used to return to his parents' home in Las Parejas for the weekends.

"Dear Children! Read Sacred Scripture, live it, and pray to understand the signs of the times. This is a special time. Therefore, I am with you to draw you close to my heart and to the heart of my Son, Jesus. Dear little children, I want you to be children of the light and not children of the darkness." (August 25, 1993)

69

MY BIBLE ON FIRE

In the land of Herzegovina, the Communist regime cast a very disapproving eye on the presence of Bibles in people's homes. For Croatian believers, owning a Bible meant being in the possession of a treasure beyond price but it had to be a well hidden treasure! In fact the persecution was so severe that most families buried their Bibles. At least once a year, in great secrecy, they took the risk of taking their Bibles out of their hiding place and would read several passages with great veneration. Sometimes, a person who knew how to read and write would hurriedly copy out several verses with which to nourish himself in the long months ahead.

One day the authorities demanded that those in possession of Bibles bring them forward. Anyone refusing to comply with their demands ran the risk of imprisonment. People were reduced to tears as their Bibles were thrown into fires and burnt in public places amidst the sounds of curses from the Communist militia.

For the circle of believers, all that remained was listening to the Word during Sunday Mass in—and this is what saved them—those long homilies by the Franciscans, who knew how to distill this Living Word for those courageous people who came to Mass. As for those who had the audacity to keep a Bible in spite of the Communist rules, they saw it as the treasure of treasures, a personal link between their family and the things of God, a Heavenly inheritance which allowed them to endure in hope.

When the apparitions began in 1981, the regime was still acting ruthlessly against the local people. Nevertheless, this is when the Queen of Peace dropped her own bomb: *"Dear Children, you have forgotten the Bible! Put the Bible in a visible place in your homes. Read several verses each day and put these verses into practice during the day. Let the people who come into your homes be able to see the Bible and read passages from it with you. In that way, you will be able to talk about God together . . ."*[168]

We must admit that none of us, who were 'foreigners', understood the revolutionary importance of this message. We were ignorant of its context! According to Father Jozo Zovko, who may be considered the seventh witness of Medjugorje, the Gospa delivered this message to him in tears, and she repeated it five times.[169]

Fr. Jozo gave witness to the profound sorrow she manifested when he said, "I have seen many mothers crying over the death of a child, but never have I seen a deep sorrow like that of the Gospa when she said, 'You have forgotten the Bible!'"

Father Jozo added: "Let the father of the family read a passage from the Gospel each day to his children before dinner. When he has finished, let him close the Book and kiss it. Because when he kisses the Gospel, it is Jesus he kisses."

Jesus is the Living Word. He is the Word through whom all was created. The Mother of God does not differentiate between Jesus and the Bible; she knows their identities. To forget the Bible is to cast Jesus aside, to scorn him. To forget the Bible is to allow our consciences to wallow in words that do not give us Divine life and which, too often, poison us. The person who absorbs the Word of Life is enriched with "antibodies" that know how to reject words of death which are fabricated by our media-driven, false gods, in order to wage war against the human soul. Through the modern media obsessions with money, violence, perversion, power-seeking, Satanism or disordered sexuality (Our Lady mentions "disordered passions"), are constantly brought into our homes and placed in a visible spot! All of our visitors can see these things,

---

[168] The fall of Communism in Yugoslavia did not take place until 1991.

[169] Father Jozo, a Franciscan, was the pastor of the parish of Medjugorje at the beginning of the apparitions.

hear them or read about them! But we have forgotten Jesus. We have forgotten the Bible!

In June 1973, three years before I entered my community, two major events opened my heart to the transcendent power of the Bible, and for this I give thanks to God, because until that point I was unaware and misled. Scarcely three days after my conversion, I found myself at the house of a couple who, in worldly terms, were very poor, but very rich in their extraordinary — almost visceral— attachment to Jesus.[170] They belonged to a Pentecostal church, and they knew their Bible almost by heart.

Seeing my Bible, the mother, Andrée, asked me to look at a certain passage in the Gospel. For her, the choice was not by chance. She had to have guessed something because, I had barely opened the book, when my eyes began to devour literally each word on those two pages I had opened. I could not even turn the pages, because a fire was leaping out from each line! Not a material fire such as we are familiar with but flames that illuminated each line, each word without burning the paper. The flames leaped up in front of my eyes and nourished me. How can a fire "nourish" a soul? I don't know but that's what came about. I devoured those Gospels with the greediness of a starving person who had found a delicious food and who could feel all his cells beginning to revive as he consumed the food!

Noticing I had paused over a page, which was not the one recommended, Andrée wanted to help me and so pulled the Bible towards her, but I kept hold of it, enable to detach my eyes from this fire. I saw the Living Jesus emerging from those lines, as if from the other side of a veil. Or rather, it was as though scales fell from my eyes and from my sealed heart, so that I could finally see the Word of God as it truly was: divine food which communicates Life!

From where did such a hunger come? That, also, was a gift of the Holy Spirit! He made me understand who I truly was, and what an immense desire for God my soul was hiding, a secret squashed and muzzled, amid the thick jumble of my miserable earthly interests.

In His mercy, the Lord sometimes allows these epiphanies of the invisible reality. This is in order to re-center us on the true purpose of

---

[170] See Chapter 4, "My Future in the Planets?"

our lives. After that experience, I had to persevere, like everyone else, in the Lectio Divina, which was sometimes dry and at other times gratifying.[171]

The second event occurred around the same time in the summer of 1973. I suppose that in order to help restore the health of my soul, the Lord needed to work overtime! The scene took place in Paris, in the little chapel of the Sisters of the Assumption. There were about thirty of us seated in a circle for a prayer meeting. It was all new to me—I felt that I had disembarked into a new world—and I had no idea how it was supposed to work. So I didn't dare open my mouth except to stammer the few songs that I knew a little. But the people amazed me with their faith, their joy, and the unbelievable familiarity they manifested towards Jesus. They related to Him as they would to their best friend! I was like a newborn who had everything to learn and who took pains to understand everything without losing a crumb.

To my right was seated Martine Lafitte, a medical doctor, who assisted the founder of the group, Pierre Goursat. Breaking out around I could hear the sincere explosion of praise for God. But suddenly a thought crossed my mind and I began to be afraid: here is joy, the heaven of brotherly communion, peace—but what if my inner nightmare returns? What if the horror of my internal hell takes hold of me again? I would die from it! Then from deep inside, like a drowning person who had just grabbed hold of a rope but was still afraid of drowning, I let out a silent cry towards God, "Oh, Lord, I beg of You! May Your Word never leave me! May I never again stray far from Your Word! Oh, Lord, promise me, promise me!"

I had scarcely uttered this silent cry towards God, when Martine, who, of course, was completely ignorant of my prayer, opened her Bible and, with majestic calm, resolutely proclaimed the following passage:

"This is my covenant with them, says the Lord: My spirit, which is upon you, and my words, which I have put in your mouth, shall not depart out of your mouth, or out of the mouth of your children, or out of the mouth of your children's children, says the Lord, from this time forth and for evermore." (Is 59:21)

---

[171] An excellent little book about this technique is: Thelona Hall's Too Deep for Words—Rediscovering Lectio Divina (Paulist Press).

I doubt that anyone in the group understood why huge tears were running down my cheeks. God used the prophet's words to answer my plea! But eight years later, almost to the day, when the Gospa cried out in sadness that we had forgotten the Bible, she knew that a tiny Parisian would cry for joy all her life in remembering the kiss of love which Jesus had given her on an evening, at Assumption Street, solely because Martine had opened her favorite book, the Bible!

They Shall Seek But Not Find It

These signs are the tangible evidence of a very profound reality, barley sugar sent by God to a soul when He judges it necessary. These signs alone however, cannot constitute the essence of our relationship to the Word of God. This relationship will have to be built up day by day, in the way that a living person allows himself, little by little, to be tamed. Each of us carries deep inside a gnawing hunger for the Word of God. How can it be that we don't feel it, or feel it so little? We carry this same hunger for the Eucharist, so why are we so indifferent? Because we are far, tragically far, from having explored the dimensions of our own living space, the fabulous landscapes of our human soul.

It is as if we lived in a narrow, two-room apartment overlooking a street. We remain confined there for fifty, seventy, eighty years as though we were in the superintendent's quarters, and we never suspect for a moment that beyond the wall, in the back, extends the rest of our property—yes, really, our property! And it's a magnificent castle! This castle of the soul is completely equipped so that we can live there in intense love. It is entirely conceived so that we can taste happiness in growing measure, and we can lodge there among marvelous friends, like the Saints, whom we have not yet met. The human soul, created in the image of God, is a world in itself, so vast and so splendid that we would dance with joy if we perceived even a tenth of it!

Each of us knows that he has a body; he feels it, he touches it, it's a tangible reality; he cares for it and maintains it according to his own principles. Every person knows that he has a heart—a sensitive heart, especially when he suffers; it is real, although invisible. We attempt to satisfy this heart, but already those personal laws of the heart are unknown to him. Each of us knows that he has a brain; he can reflect and compare his intellectual capacity with that of other brains. He attempts to enrich it with diverse knowledge in keeping with his own attractions or necessities.

But the soul? Who really knows that he has a soul? Who feels his soul? Who perceives the hunger, the thirst, the needs and desires of his soul? Who realizes that these desires are infinitely more powerful, more vital than those of his body, of his intelligence, or of his heart? Why this insensibility towards his soul, this rock-hard indifference, in a word, this ignorance?

Yes, there exists an immense, marvelous castle behind the wall of that heavy sideboard in our apartment room, where, in spite of the television, our videos, and our social life, our romances and our distractions, in spite of our well being and the fact of having "everything" we need, there is something deep inside of us that is bored to death. And we prefer not to get too close to the edge of this boredom for fear of being dizzy.

Am I dizzy in front of emptiness? In front of the intolerable absence of meaning in my life? Here I have to sit down for five minutes, take my head in my hands, and bravely ask myself the real question: "What do I want for my life?" Because, what I decide to be today, is what I will be at the end of the journey and for eternity.

Option 1: I stay as I am. I will live confine in my little tangible, fleeting world. I will try to take from it several flashes of happiness, and when time and aging have done their work and everything is taken from me, well, I don't want to know.... I'll see it soon enough!

Option 2: I sense that I am bigger than my little concrete and ephemeral world. I aspire to live an unfailing, eternal love—and, if I am capable of desiring it, it must exist! So I'm going to look for it, and I'm going to find it!

The Bible is my key for the second option, the life option: by means of the Bible, I am going to "explore God" and through that, at the same time, my own depths, my secret dimensions. I'm going to discover my friends (my enemies, also!) and know how much I am loved.

I begin very humbly to wander through this mysterious Book, because I arrived at it like a sight-impaired, hearing-impaired, motor-impaired person. I explore my Bible by trial and error, I get blocked, I get discouraged sometimes, but here and there, yes, a word touches me, a word nourishes me, a new room in my secret house is illuminated! What beauty I discover! And I didn't know it was there. I continue my exploration and I go from beauty to beauty. Then my soul finally begins to budge; it eats, it drinks, it absorbs its heavenly manna and unfolds in concert with its own harmony. My soul manifests itself to me. It exists, and it is my soul! What a revelation! In reading the Bible I feel my soul crackle like a fire deep inside me. What a marvel! So, it's true. I am really created in the image of God. This baby soul, which dances in the depths of me like a flaming fire, is my true being - the one that cannot die!

The Bible is the vital food of my soul. I want to give it pride of place and put other nourishments back into their proper positions from this day on.

"Behold, the days are coming, says the Lord God, when I will send a famine on the land; not a famine of bread, nor a thirst for water, but of hearing the word of the Lord. They shall wander from sea to sea, and from North to East, they shall run to and fro, to seek the word of the Lord, but they shall not find it." (Am 8:11-12)

Yes, Blessed Mother, I had forgotten the Bible. I had reserved no space or time for it in my existence. In doing this I had condemned my soul to die of hunger, which is why you cried so bitterly. I had eliminated any hope of my knowing your Son and walking in His path, to the sound of His voice. I was defeated from the start because, to the great joy of my enemies, I had stupidly appeared on the battlefield of this world without my sword, the Bible!

"Dear Children! Do not be afraid of Satan. It isn't worth the trouble, because with a humble prayer and an ardent love, one can disarm him." (August, 1985)

70

OPERATION JERICHO

Spring had arrived in Nice and its most beautiful flower beds were on display. The sumptuous avenues were arrayed with colorful attractions which captured the eye. The purses of tourists would be empty in no time!

Florence was hurrying to some charitable activity or other when, suddenly, she froze: an enormous poster, occupying the entire display window of a hotel, with a fluorescent title guaranteed to catch the eye: "Clairvoyance Festival." Her heart skipped a beat. Her eyes studied every detail of the poster. Obviously it had been brilliantly conceived by a skilled professional, certain to strike the passerby and provoke amazement and desire. The poster was impossible to miss and the advertising irresistible. In a single weekend you could learn your entire future and all the deepest thoughts of the people around you: your friends, your foes, and your so-called friends. And, of course, no one would leave without solid hopes for his financial, emotional, and sexual future.

Who were the speakers for this festival? Of course, they were prestigious experts with mysterious Asian-sounding names. They would make their exceptional and extraordinary gifts accessible to all! Promises of miracles, astonishing revelations, something never before seen in France!

Florence's eyes were accustomed to contemplating Jesus, Light of the World, during the long hours of adoration she set aside for herself every week before engaging in any other activity. The sight of the poster cut through her heart, and a prayer sprang from her lips immediately:

"No, Lord, no! You will not allow your children to be poisoned that way!"

Florence had noticed that this hotel, which was in most ways quite proper and even luxurious, had in the past displayed a few rather bizarre posters that she had always previously ignored. She was well aware that Nice was hosting far more than simple Disciples of Christ, but a festival like that, no, that was too much. It was the last straw. There had to be a way to prevent the enemy from striking.

Florence started praying in total confidence. She knew that for every plan from the dark side there was a plan for victory hidden in the heart of God. She also knew if we want to discover what it is, all we have to do is get down on our knees and pray. And then rise up again, with courage, to implement it!

It was in the Bible that Florence found the key to open the doors of mercy. Jericho! But, of course! What caused the walls of Jericho to fall in front of the outnumbered and poorly armed Hebrews?[172]

A very simple plan came to Florence's mind, and she immediately grabbed the phone. "Will you join me?," she asked her trusted assistant from the prayer group. "Here's the plan: Do you remember how the city of Jericho fell? How its walls came tumbling down? Let's do the same thing! We will walk around the block where the hotel is, praying and praising the Lord the whole time. We can also say the Rosary. We'll each have to take one hour during the day; we'll take turns; we have to do it for seven days in a row."

Among the members of her prayer group, ten volunteered. This number is reminiscent of the ten righteous ones Abraham mentioned to God while he was interceding for the city of Sodom.[173] He called those ten his *minyan*. To this very day, in Israel, it is forbidden to destroy a synagogue, if ten pious Jews are assembled there to ensure prayer.

So here were the ten "Walkers for God," doing their good works in this upper class area of Nice. This went on for seven days, Rosaries in hand, Psalters in their pockets, wearing out their shoes, and above all, great fervor in their hearts.

---

[172] Jos 6:1-21.

[173] Gn 18:17-32.

Some time later, Florence received a phone call: "By the way, did you notice anything at the Humphrey Hotel?"

"No, why?"

"They took the poster down."

"And the Festival?"

"Cancelled!"

"What do you mean, 'cancelled'?"

"I mean cancelled, kaput, finished, gone with the wind!"

That was twelve years ago. The Humphrey Hotel has never again engaged in any harmful activity, and there is now fresh air in the area. Dare we think that the good angels of Jericho, appreciating the mild climate of Nice, have decided to take up residence in the city?

That's Not All!

When someone comes to me and tells me that they are having a problem with the devil, and I see that it is possible to stop the situation with one action, I always respond the same way: "Just try an 'Operation Jericho'! You'll see. It works!"[174]

Florence recalled a time when, in a town in Provence, some Christian families were worried about an upcoming heavy metal concert, starring a band with a very dubious reputation. Its connections with drugs and the whole panoply of evils, which follows them, were enough to make local families fear the worst. An announced "rave party" was bound to entice thousands of young people to attend the concert.

"Let's do a 'Jericho,'" declared one of the families. "We know where the band is going to set up. We'll take turns, encircling the area, and pray for seven days."

This is what they did. On the day of the scheduled concert, under a magnificent July sun, the trucks arrived with all their equipment. The sound of hammers echoed throughout the southern part of town, and a big stage appeared in no time. A few instruments came out of their cases; the sound system was plugged in, spreading dissonant chords

---

[174] In Brazil, for the Community Covenant of Mercy which rescues street children from murderous gangs, recourse to Jericho happens often, bearing incredible fruit!

throughout the streets. Already, small groups of young people gathered around the technicians, asking a thousand questions. The night would be hot! They were going to have a blast! The prayer group was there too, silently continuing its vigil.

"Lord, we thank you already for what You are about to do to protect Your children! We trust in You."

Mikes, drum sets, and all the heavy elements of the sound system were now in place. The weather couldn't have been better: clear skies, intense heat, which would abate during the evening. These were ideal conditions for an open air concert! Stands of itinerant merchants sprang up everywhere, displaying their wares; business would be good, they thought. Drug dealers were on the lookout, and people in search of adventure were ready for action.* A few buses and some private cars took over a corner of the huge parking lot.

"Lord, infinite is Your mercy! You see all Your children, all these young people. Thank You for whatever plans Your fatherly heart is going to invent in order to spare them."

The sun was still at its zenith when one youth from the Jericho prayer group asked his neighbor: "Did you see that cloud?"

"A cloud? What cloud?"

"Look! Over there...!"

"You're right! That's funny. It looks like it doesn't belong there... the sky is so blue everywhere else."

"Wait a little. With Jesus, you'll see what you'll see!!"

---

* Some bands are particularly awful, promoting the use of drugs, promiscuity, violence and even suicide, in the people they attract and in their 'music'. But not all bands do this.)

---

[175] 1 Kings 18:41-46.

The scene was reminiscent, in a way, of the scene from the Bible, with the cloud called forth by the prophet Elijah. The skies of Israel had been closed for more than three years and the land had suffered a terrible drought, until the prophet produced rain.[175] And indeed, this tiny cloud too grew bigger and bigger, and in record time transformed into an enormous, black mass. The technicians and the rock stars shook their heads; anxiety gripped them. They had good reason to worry because, in less time than it takes to tell, a torrential rain engulfed the town. It was a genuine flood, totally unforeseeable. The weather forecast had been definite: sunny throughout the day. On stage, there was total panic. It was impossible to repack everything so quickly; all the equipment and instruments were getting drenched. What a disaster for them....

Years later, several members of the Jericho group still like to recall the episode of the "drowned-out concert." It gives them the courage to continue the fight, because the Enemy is everywhere, trying to seduce or destroy our young. The Enemy doesn't relent. At least that night, God put His foot down, and thousands of young people were spared—and that rock group never showed up again in the area.

"Dear Children! Offer novenas, making sacrifices wherein you feel the most bound. I want your life to be bound to me. I am your Mother, little children, and I do not want Satan to deceive you for He wants to lead you the wrong way, but he cannot if you do not permit him. Therefore, little children, renew prayer in your hearts, and then you will understand my call and my live desire to help you." (July 25, 1993)

71

OH, WHAT A LIE!

Louis had succeeded in creating a fine career. His membership in the Masonic Order had provided him with significant advantages. He knew how to keep secrets, and he had many secrets.

From the outside Louis looked like a regular Joe Smith, but in reality Louis was a high-ranking official in the Masons. As a child, he had received a Christian education but along the way he had cast aside, more than once, the promises of his Baptism, amongst other things.

He was nearing his sixties when an illness struck, an illness which would—barring a miracle—result in his death after months of humiliating suffering. Along with this sickness, anxiety had also seized him and Louis could feel rising from the very depths of his being a cloud that grew darker and darker, driving him into cold sweats. No tranquilizer could dull his pain.

One day, he took a boat ride. Having nothing special to do to occupy the long hours of the crossing, he agreed to share a drink with another passenger, also alone, whose name was Martin. Martin was smart and an excellent psychologist. What he later related to me about the conversation sounded quite interesting. Louis quickly realized that he was dealing with a remarkably cultured man, but one who was, also, very human, very warm. With his simple presence, his smile, Louis was profoundly comforted and began to talk to him about his life, his titles, his glories—and also his deceptions. Martin very quickly perceived the despair in his fellow passenger and skillfully and delicately led him to express what he had never before shared with anyone.

"I'm done for. I've done one bad thing after another. Now... I'm terrified of death. Especially by what may be in store for me after death."

Louis then revealed to Martin the pact which he had made and signed with his blood, surrendering his soul to Satan in exchange for a few fleeting successes. [176]

It did not faze Martin. "I'm a Catholic priest," Martin told him. "I don't wear a Cross, but I am a Missionary."

"Oh, I abandoned all that, long...long ago...!"

"God is never far away. He always waits for the return of His child. He is waiting for you, Louis—you can come back."

"No, I can't. My soul no longer belongs to me, Satan took it. That was the deal."

"You can break the pact you made with him. You can still reconcile yourself with God![177] I'm here, ready to hear your Confession."

"I can't go to Confession!"

"Tell me why not?"

"Because Satan warned me that after the pact I could never go to Confession."

"Oh the lie! And you believed him? Don't you know that Satan is a liar and the father of Lies?" [(Jn 8:44)]

This news scored a direct hit. A lie? A lie? Louis was stunned. His thoughts rose up with giddy swiftness. How could he have been so duped? Little by little, a glimmer of light seemed to filter into his

---

[176] It is forbidden for a Catholic to join a Massonic association. See www.vatican.va

[177] To little Van of Vietnam, Jesus said, "A simple look of trust in Me is enough to wrest sinful souls from the grip of the devil. Even if a soul finds itself at the gates of Hell, breathing its last before falling in—if, in this last breathe, there is a tiny bit of trust in My infinite love, that would be sufficient for that infinite love to draw this soul into the arms of the Holy Trinity... Your weaknesses, Van, far from diminishing your worth, only increase it more, because they are for you a sign of greater trust in Me, and thus our union is only more close! But, alas, the tragedy is that people don't have trust in My love. Oh, sin, sin! Never does sin offend My love; absolutely nothing offends My love except the lack of trust in that love."

heart, which he had thought was made of stone. A minuscule light, which might very well resemble hope!

"Yes, you can hear my Confession," he finally said in a muted voice.

When, a few hours later, the boat reached shore, Louis had immersed all of his poor life in the mercy of God. On the dock, the two had to leave one another. Louis went towards his destiny and Martin pursued his mission, his heart rejoicing. Jesus' words came back to him: "Your brother was dead and is alive again; he was lost and is found!" (Luke15:32) At the same time, a question haunted Martin: how many were there like him, in the streets? There, within his reach, how many who had fallen into the same sordid trap? And his missionary heart burned.

The Gospa Warns the Visionaries

From the very first years of the apparitions, in 1981, the Blessed Mother needed to educate the young visionaries herself on these topics. She knew that crowds would come to them, and that they had to be warned about what was going on in the world. If this information had not come from her, the visionaries would never have believed it. They would have been so stupefied. They, who had suffered from Communist oppression and had fought step by step to hold onto their inner freedom, how could they believe that the youth of countries that were rich and free would voluntarily surrender their lives to Satan and choose to be his slaves? The Gospa removed from them their naivety, which was then transformed into fervent prayer. Gospa told the visionaries, "Those who have made a pact with Satan can still renounce the pact and come back to God, as long as they live. You need to pray for them, so that they will have the strength to decide for God." (Early' 80's, undated)

No sooner had she warned the visionaries of this, than the practical work began for them. Many who had bonded with Satan poured into Medjugorje and rang the doorbells of the visionaries. The consequences for each of them remain God's secret, but the course of events was simple: the Queen of Peace demonstrated, there again, that she merited her title of Refuge of Sinners!

NOTE: To protect ourselves from the oppressions of the Evil One, as well as to rid ourselves of him, let us recall the Promises of Baptism, one of the most efficacious prayers which can be used by the laity. We can renew these promises often, when the Evil One roams and brings with him the temptations of sin. Above all, we must not be irresolute. The Gospa invites us "to decide for God and against Satan."

Text of Baptismal Promises

Dear friends, through the paschal mystery we have been buried with Christ in baptism, so that we may rise with him to a new life. Let us renew the promises we made at baptism when we rejected Satan and his works.

Do you reject sin, so as to live in the freedom of God's children?

—I do.

Do you reject the glamour of evil, and refuse to be mastered by sin?

—I do.

Do you reject Satan, father of sin and prince of darkness?

—I do.

Do you believe in God, the Father almighty, creator of heaven and earth?

—I do.

Do you believe in Jesus Christ, his only Son, our Lord, who was born of the Virgin Mary, was crucified, died, and was buried, rose from the dead, and is now seated at the right hand of the Father?

—I do.

Do you believe in the Holy Spirit, the Holy Catholic Church, the communion of saints, the forgiveness of sins, the resurrection of the body, and life everlasting?

—I do.

God the Father of our Lord Jesus Christ has given us a new birth by water and the Holy Spirit, and forgiven our sins. May God also keep us faithful to our Lord Jesus Christ for ever and ever.

—Amen.

"Dear children! Today I call you, through prayer and sacrifice, to prepare yourselves for the coming of the Holy Spirit. Little children, this is a time of grace and so, again, I call you to decide for God the Creator. Allow Him to transform and change you. May your heart be prepared to listen to, and live, everything which the Holy Spirit has in His plan for each of you. Little children, allow the Holy Spirit to lead you on the way of truth and salvation towards eternal life. Thank you for having responded to my call." (May 25, 1998)

72

A DANGEROUS PRAYER

The day Lance joined the Community, everyone rejoiced. Young, pleasant, good looking, well-anchored in the Lord, at first he seemed like the ideal brother. I was in charge of our foundation in Jerusalem at the time, and, like the others, I really appreciated having such a vocation in our midst. Our exchanges quickly became intense and profound.

A major theme kept coming back in his conversation, the leitmotif of his deep heart: "What are we doing to help the poor? I feel called to help the poor."

"If the Lord put that in your heart," I answered him, "He knows how to let you do it. Trust Him! But for the moment, He may want you to discover another dimension of poverty."

"Really? Which one?"

"Your own, personal, profound poverty, the one that will allow you to cry to God like the poor in the streets whom you want to help, for example...."

"Huh... but I... I have everything! Well, I have a lot, even too much! And why should I take care for 'my own' poverty? Isn't that a bit selfish?"

"Let God work, in His own time. You'll see! in His own time. He knows how to make you understand what He wants from you. In the meantime, if you want to speed things up a bit, you can always ask Him to show you your own poverty, and then take it from there…."

"Okay," answered Lance. He was a little surprised, but, with his usual gentleness, he didn't argue.

A few weeks went by and Lance's demeanor changed. He didn't talk much anymore. We could see that he was lost in his own thoughts, obviously struggling with some internal tensions. Since he was very humble, it didn't take him long to come and open his heart to me:

"I'm struggling, I'm struggling!," he began, his eyes filling up.

"I'm struggling with you. We're all in the same boat," I said, trying to, to encourage him.

"The prayer that you gave me the other day…. I know you warned me, but…wow! That was powerful stuff! I thought God was going to "show" me my poverty. I was being very naïve. I thought He would show it to me the way you show someone a map, an X-ray, or a scan. But it's much more than that! He completely rubs my nose in it, and… it doesn't smell too good, not at all!"

The Lord hadn't wasted any time getting to work on this son, who—He knew in his Divine forethought—was to become a living consolation for so many children crushed to death by the cruelty of this world.

"Lance, I would like to be able to tell you that it's going to go away, that you'll soon go back to the way you were before. But God never goes back once He starts something and I would not be surprised if, in fact, He wanted to take you even further. If so, then this will only be the prelude. Brace yourself, and thank the Lord! Now that you have abandoned yourself into His hands by giving Him full power over you, your Creator is going to be able to achieve His entire plan in you. Keep your eyes only on Him!"

Several weeks went by, and I could tell that Lance was going through interior purifications that were becoming more and more painful. On top of that, as though by accident, everything he attempted to do was failing. Humiliations were accumulating. The weirdest of thoughts kept haunting his conscience, and he felt ashamed! He no longer recognized himself. Slowly but surely, the light of God was penetrating into him, shedding light upon each and every deep and unsuspected area of his being. He had to be cared for like a child, because he had lost his moorings. The process went on for several long months. He felt so filthy inside that he started changing his glasses on life.

Then, each person around him appeared to be endowed with marvelous qualities. Even the most impoverished in the eyes of the world were subjects of his profound admiration. He saw himself as the least of the least, a shapeless mass of endless and repulsive miseries, each more horrible than the previous. He would rather have disappeared into a hole than sit with us at the table, because he thought his mere presence was defiling the atmosphere.

The timing and the duration of the interventions of God will always be a mystery to us, but it is probable that it was Lance's humble submission to the events that shortened his ordeal. When God finally released His grip on him, a joie de vivre started to bubble up in Lance's heart, tremendous, so new, so delicious! A very profound peace took hold of him, and he received awareness—at least partial awareness—of what God had achieved in him. "I am He Who Is," Jesus told St. Catherine of Sienna, "You are she who is not." What a relief to know that! What peace! What does it matter, then, if we are the ones who are not, when the One Who Is is madly in love with us, and enjoys communicating Himself to us in all His dimensions!

Now, no longer at the mercy of his books, Lance understood with every fiber of his being: "Blessed are the poor in Spirit: for theirs is the kingdom of Heaven."(Mt 5:3) A better translation might be: "Blessed are the ones stripped to nothing by the Spirit: for theirs is the kingdom of Heaven." Lance's inner descent to the very depth of his own misery, and the experience of being loved in spite of it, enriched his soul to an extraordinary degree. True, having to reach deep down inside to touch the fundamental misery that is ours, is an experience that makes us dizzy and brings on anguish. But hidden even more deeply in us is the nuptial chamber, where Jesus Himself comes to be our spouse. This is when we possess everything, because, "All that is mine is yours."(Lk 15:31)

Lance has developed an astonishing charisma for teens and youths who have been damaged by life; they are attracted like magnets to his kindness, his joy, and especially to his friendship. The blessing of God flows in the relationships he has with these young people, the truly "poor" of our generation, the ones the Gospa cries for. Before his purification, Lance wanted to "take care of the poor," like a generous man who has heard their cries and wants to share his riches with them. Now he does not need to take care of them, because he has become one of them, a poor man himself, who recognizes his peers and who lives with them, who laughs, weeps, and prays with them.

"Lord, Show Me My Poverty!"

This is one of the most dangerous prayers of all, because—you must know this—God always answers it! Isn't it the doorway to the Beatitudes, in other words, the door to happiness? But God always gives more than we ask for. He overflows, He multiplies, He drenches.... We are so petty and stingy in our requests! God has no interest in showing us things. He has something better in store for us than a slide show. His passion is to transform us and to allow us to reach our true identity. Like all of us (no exceptions), Lance was poor, but he didn't know it. And to train him as an apostle, an apostle to the poor, Jesus had to put him to the test. It is in the crucible of suffering that he found his true identity as one of the poor.

The children of divorce, juveniles of the street, victims of sexual violence, and those shipwrecked from love: all those know straight away that they are poor—but they often couple this with such rebellion, especially when they are made poor at the hands of others. (King David was right: "Let us fall into the hand of the Lord, for His mercy is great; but let me not fall into the hand of man." (2 S 24:14).

An apostle is a person who has offered himself willingly to God's training and intense transformation, to the wanderings and whims of the Artistic Creator. With God, you'd better fasten your seatbelt securely, and not just for takeoff and landing—Lance went along with Him. This, in contrast to those who balk and run away, because they are afraid to go into the deep, scared to let go of the comfortable false security of familiar landscapes or to lose the illusory control of their lives. Oh, how beautiful it is to watch Jesus mold an apostle!

The apostle, like the disciple, chooses in total freedom to enter into this extraordinary mystery of identification with Christ. Unlike the children of the street, He espouses His poverty through love, not through coercion. Then, yes, he loses control of his life. What liberation! Jesus' favorite game is called Losers Win. (Mt 19:30) He invites us all to participate, because, in this game, the more of us there are, the more exciting it is. Why are the Saints so fond of this game with Jesus? Because they have discovered that they gain priceless and everlasting treasures and all they lose are scraps! The Saints are the all-time winners of this world. But whoever clings tightly to what he has, because he is afraid to lose it, has already lost.

Marthe Robin, one of the happiest women I have ever met, had certainly lost everything for Jesus. She lived with such an intense identification with the poorest of the poor that one day she confided in a friend: "Oh, I would so much like to reach Heaven accompanied by the street urchins!"

"Dear Children! Do not be afraid to have children. The more children you will have the better. You should rather be afraid not to have them" (To Mirjana, undated).

73

A MEMORABLE CONFESSION

Mary Elizabeth, a forty-five year-old high school teacher in the USA, testifies that nothing is impossible with God for those who open their hearts in prayer and allow themselves to be led by the Holy Spirit:

"In 1990, my pilgrimage to Medjugorje required the support of my husband: I had to cross the Atlantic to reach a Communist country, find money which we did not have, and get a babysitter for the children. But the call was too strong. I had to go. My husband agreed to take care of the children. I asked myself just what I was expecting to find over there, but I knew the break from the demands of my four young children would be a welcome one. I had been thinking for some time that I was a bad mother, because I so often needed time to rest and catch my breath. I knew this trip would help me step back and take a long look at my relationships with my family, my activities, and my future."

"Towards the middle of my stay, I gave the priest my usual list of sins and continued on through the dreaded sacrament of Confession. The last evening, frustrated at not understanding a word of the homilies given in Croatian, I brought a book of English homilies to church. As soon as I opened the book, I fell upon a homily that spoke to my heart. I understood that God was calling me to return to Confession, because I needed to resolve a situation, which prevented me from having a closer relationship with Him."

"Coming out of the church, not a sound could be heard. The dark sky made the temperature seem colder and the deserted esplanade even more desolate. Strangely, I noticed that in the row of 'confession boxes,' as I call them, two lights were lit. I wanted to return to my pansion, but felt that God was drawing me to the confessional. I did not want to go, but I said to myself, 'If one of the lights indicates that English is spoken there, I'll go.' The first indicator said Polish. Phew, I thought I had escaped. But the next indicated English. I took a deep breath and opened the door."

"When I knelt down, the priest placed a Crucifix in my hands. I began to speak. The priest seemed to know why I was there, and a veil fell away. Contraception. That was the subject I had to face. Like many Catholics, my husband and I had engaged in contraception. We could not understand the Church's teaching on the subject and did not give it much thought. We were educated, responsible adults. As a matter of fact, our attitude was quite arrogant. But, by the power of the Holy Spirit, I understood that my husband and I had completely left God out of that particular element of our marriage. Our union was supposed to be based on the sacrament of marriage, and yet we gave ourselves to each other in everything but the very act which could produce life. Our relationship resembled a rope made up of three threads (the two of us and God), God being the thread which supported the sacrament of marriage. Excluding God from our union made the rope incomplete and more liable to break."

"During the Confession, my heart changed completely, and I knew that my life would also change. God was not telling me that we had to have more children, since we already had four who were sometimes difficult for me to handle, but He wanted us to open ourselves up to Him in our relationship."

"How much time I spent in the confessional, I don't know, but when I left it, I understood that God was asking me to do things that I would have never imagined possible. On the return flight home, I had the impression of having foreseen Heaven. Once home, I had to explain to my husband our change of plans. I was a little apprehensive about his reaction, knowing our financial situation at the time. When I explained to him all that had happened to me and how we were called to truly open ourselves to God in our marriage, he was in total agreement. Of course, we had much to learn, which is what we did."

"We have now celebrated twenty-three years of married life, and, after the 1990 pilgrimage, we had four more children. Even though this demanded much effort at times, I must admit that God's plan of blessings for our family was greater than I could ever have imagined. As our neighbors' nests began to empty, our house remained always full. I, too, sometimes long for solitude, but the real joy the children bring me, even in the midst of noise, confusion, and responsibilities, is truly a gift from God. We took the risk of opening ourselves up, of being generous towards God, and we found an exchange in which God never lets Himself be outdone in generosity. Each time we had another mouth to feed, God provided in an unimaginable way. Of course, we had to be good stewards of the gifts we received, but we never lacked for anything, and we have been rewarded a hundredfold."

"I had an immense thirst for learning when I returned from Medjugorje, and my husband joined me in this research for true nourishment. Today, I am the mother of eight marvelous children, from twenty-one years of age to four years of age, some of whom, I hope, have a calling to the priesthood or religious life. Two years ago I received my Master's degree in Theology. I now teach Theology of the Body (not accounting) to youngsters who are thirsting for knowledge of God, and this has become my passion.(see * page 348) I burn with a desire to share the Gospel with whoever wants to listen. I am also studying for my Master's degree in Bioethics. I, too, have to struggle. I am a sinner, and I am in need of my Redeemer. I know, however, that I can do all things in Him Who lives in me."

In Medjugorje, Xavier Testifies

"The other day, I was given the opportunity to truly understand the sacrament of Reconciliation: it is not a matter of confessing one's sins but of acknowledging God's mercy and receiving it."

"I met my spiritual director, and I said to him: 'I would be very happy to go to Confession with you, but I already did that yesterday during a weekend retreat. So I have no sins to Confess, and I feel that to confess again today, would be spiritual gluttony.'"

My spiritual director felt that I had a false perception of this sacrament, so he said something to me that I will remember all my life: 'We don't have to have something to say, because to go to Confession is, first of all, to place ourselves at the foot of Jesus' Cross to receive the mercy which flows from His heart.'"

"So, I asked him to hear my confession, even though I didn't know what to say."

"'If you feel the need to do so, why not?' he said to me. I was happy to be able to do it without having to prepare my entire list of sins, and, there on my knees, I felt I would experience something very powerful."

"I said, 'Lord, I come to the foot of Your Cross. I ask pardon for my sins, and I come to receive Your mercy!'" I was then seized by God's love to the very depths of my being and heard myself utter something I had never before thought of: 'I ask Your forgiveness for my lack of trust in You.'"

"Speaking these words, I knew at once what was wounding the heart of God the most. I had always carefully aligned my sins, one after the other but, now that I had the right to say nothing, there arose in my heart a sudden and profound understanding of what grieved the heart of God. And this is what had really caused the wound: I was not truly placing my trust in Him! About the rest, He couldn't care less. That day, I experienced what people call contrition, that is, suffering for having wounded the heart of God. I discovered my sin in the deepest part of myself. That was, without a doubt, the best confession of my life. To show me my sin, Jesus had invited me to the foot of His Cross, to the very place where my sin had pierced His heart, to the very place where He pours out His forgiveness."

---

* The Theology of the Body is our recent Pope, John Paul II's, integrated vision of the human person - body, soul, and spirit. This very inspired work encourages and nourishes many young people who are searching for a clear, profound meaning of human life on earth, a meaning that seeks to be in accord with the plan of their Creator. As darkness today is enveloping not only the laws of God, but even the laws of nature, Theology of the Body presents hope in the fight for a culture of life! John Paul II explains how the physical human body has a specific meaning and is capable of revealing answers on our relationship with ourselves and one another. By helping us understand the profound interconnection between sex and the Christian mystery of love, John Paul II's Theology of the Body not only paves the way for lasting renewal of marriage and the family; it enables everyone to rediscover the meaning of the whole of existence, and the meaning of life.

Theology of the Body Institute, Tel: 215-302-8200, (USA).

For more info, see tobinstitute.org or christopherwest.com/theologyofthebody

"Dear Children! In prayer you shall perceive the greatest joy and the way out of every situation that has no way out" (March 28, 1985)

74

GOATS WITHOUT BORDERS

The Gospa is passionately fond of little shepherds and has never hidden that love, especially considering the number of shepherds to whom she has appeared in the course of history. Why shepherds?

In Judea, during the census of Caesar Augustus, when Jesus was born in Bethlehem, the shepherds who slept in the fields represented the most despised class in the Jewish population. People thought of as bad news or nobodies. God truly chose the least of the least as the first witnesses of the birth of His Son. A shrewd, well-advised person would have chosen notable personages in Bethlehem, people respected by all. Oh the marvellous mystery of the freedom of God!

Why shepherds? It seems to me that among their many gifts they excelled in living this mysterious instruction which Christ gave in sending his disciples out on a mission: "Be as wise as serpents and innocent as doves." (Mt 10:16) In order to protect the lives of the sheep, and thereby the food of humans, they spent long hours of the day and night in Nature's school. Their souls were provided with exceptional antennae, capable of capturing the most secret communications from the Creator. The shepherd was a man of life, a survivor, a man of deliverance when the plans of others, elaborate as they might be, failed.

In Bosnia Herzegovina, in 1991 the war was raging. Entire villages suffered from starvation. The bombings came one after another. The Serbs overran an entire region near Konic, burning houses and killing all of the animals. In the United States, people who had made a pilgrimage to Medjugorje heard that children in the area had no milk. They decided to restock farm animals, and offered a large sum of money to buy goats.[178] But where could anyone even find three goats

---

[178] A goat gives three quarts of milk per day, and this milk is healthier than that of cows.

in a Bosnia so ravaged by fire and blood? Nearby Croatia was able to furnish the goats at the modest price of $160 per goat. Local Americans, who were facilitating the buying of the goats, rented trucks to transport the animals, fifty goats per truck. There were hundreds of goats to be dispersed among several villages in Bosnia. But, of course, there had to be a catch to it all—a wolf waiting for the goats: between Croatia and Bosnia-Herzegovina, one must pass through Customs, and there the first truck was stopped. In order to pass, the officers demanded a customs duty for the animals. The duty would nearly double the duty of the goats! Would the Lord allow the poor villagers in Bosnia Herzegovina to be deprived of half their goats?

A shepherd standing nearby heard what was happening. He, himself, was from Herzegovina. He was no longer an innocent twenty year-old having suffered the hardships of the arid zones adjoining that border. He smiled. Even before a distress signal could reach the USA, causing anxiety and confusion, the shepherd perfectly sized up the situation, and without fanfare, he offered to help. He signalled the drivers to turn around and to follow him along a narrow, hazardous route. He guided them through the middle of nowhere. The view was magnificent. The wild hills lay bare their shrubs and rocks and hinted at mysterious hiding places. This territory was a paradise for goats. The shepherd continued to smile. He had his plan and an air of tranquillity. He let the Americans know that he was going ahead and would station himself on a hill facing them. As soon as they saw him on the other hill, they would just have to open the doors of the trucks.

It was then that our friends, products of the best American universities, had the sight of their lives.[179] From afar, the shepherd began to whistle, and, in perfect unison, the goats jumped from the truck five at a time and hastened to him, crossing the border into Herzegovina! It's obvious that borders are for men, not for goats.

---

[179] This reminds me of an anecdote told by Msgr. MacDonald, a bishop from Canada, during his pilgrimage here in Medjugorje in November, 2005. In the seminary, he had a spiritual director who had five doctoral degrees: theology, literature, canon law, philosophy, and Sacred Scripture, plus two master's degrees. His parents were from a very simple background. They barely knew how to read and write, and lived on their small farm. However, this scholar confided one day to his protégé: "I can't wait to go on vacation to my family. I need to listen to my father, he has wisdom!"

That day, there was celebration in the villages; the goats had arrived! The villagers would survive, because there was milk for the children.

It Is Mercy That I Desire

Vain scruples made me hesitate to recounting the above anecdote, but they did not get the upper hand. In fact, a similar event comes to my mind. On a Sabbath day, while the disciples of Jesus were walking through the fields, they were plucking heads of grain. They were hungry! With Jesus, the mission comes first: the zeal for souls surpasses the needs of the stomach. One eats when time allows, and, when time does not allow, one continues the mission without eating. On this occasion, they had a chance to "eat on the run," but it was forbidden to harvest during the Sabbath. The Pharisees, only too happy to catch Jesus on this point of the Law, reproached him for allowing his disciples to violate the Sabbath. How marvellous Jesus is who, like the shepherd of our goats, places things in a proper perspective, in front of all these legal experts who are so handicapped in their heart: "If you had known what this means, 'I desire mercy, and not sacrifice,' you would not have condemned the guiltless. For the Son of Man is lord of the Sabbath." (Mt 12:1-8)[180]

Thank God, the law is made for man and not man for the law. The law that exists in time of war, amid bombings, is the law of survival!

---

[180] See also the story of David obtaining for his hungry troops the special bread which only priests could eat (1 S 21:1-6)—a story Jesus which reminded the Pharisees about (Mt 12:3-4).

"Dear Children! Believe that by simple prayer miracles can be worked. Through your prayer you open your heart to God and He works miracles in your life. By looking at the fruits your heart fills with joy and gratitude to God for everything He does in your life and, through you, also to others. Pray and believe little children, God gives you graces and you do not see them. Pray and you will see them. May your day be filled with prayer and thanksgiving for everything that God gives you. (October 25, 2002)

75

THE GOD OF MULTIPLICATIONS

The number of dinner guests had begun to dwindle because it was getting quite late. Chrissey poked me with her elbow and whispered in my ear: "Did you see the pot of chicken?"

I looked carefully at the pot, and inhaled its wonderful aroma. A delicious smell came from the curry sauce, which contained large pieces of chicken grilled to perfection.

"Yes, it's the most delicious chicken that I've ever eaten. They didn't skimp on the curry. You'd think we were in India!"

"Take another look, Sister Emmanuel! Haven't you noticed anything?"

This took place in Medjugorje. Chrissey, my assistant, had arrived in the afternoon to help this family of friends prepare a festive meal for about thirty people. A variety of dishes: raw vegetables, meats, cooked vegetables and sweets. As for the chicken, they had prepared enough to satisfy about forty healthy appetites. But, in Medjugorje, it is unwise to ignore a phenomenon that occurs when some members of the local community are invited. They sometimes turn up with other friends who also bring guests they cannot leave home alone. Anyway, for this festive 2003 Christmas party, the thirty invited guests who showed up for dinner, were augmented by at least forty extra people! Chrissey began to look askance, not at the guests, but at the serving dishes.

"They are going to run out of food! This will be a catastrophe—what a shame during the octave of Christmas!"

However, she was surprised to see that the lady of the house was perfectly at ease, welcoming everyone warmly, and taking them to the buffet with lots of exhortations to help themselves! In reply to Andrea's worried question, she raised her arms to heaven, made a face, and replied without an ounce of worry: "That's Our Lady's problem, not mine! This evening, she's the one doing the inviting!" The Gospa always thinks big, that's what makes her famous! But, like her Son, Jesus, she gives according to what she plans. That's important too. All you have to do is let things be, once you have done everything in your power with love. That's obvious.

That evening—thanks to the Gospa and thanks to Baby Jesus—the joy of Christmas burst forth in our conversations, singing, and testimonies. Everything went well, and no one noticed how the meat, roasted potatoes, beans and all the rest of the food multiplied. Everyone ate until they were satisfied, as it is written in the Gospel (in reality, a little more than just satisfied—it was Christmas after all!). Perhaps there were not a dozen baskets left over, but somehow, there were enough leftovers to make up bags for the most destitute. Only those who had prepared everything knew what the Lord had just done, and we know from the Gospel, that He will do it again in the future, until He comes to Earth again in glory.

When the prophet Elijah asked the widow of Zarephath to prepare him something to eat, she had just enough oil and flour for herself and her son, and no provisions for the coming days. The prophet entered her home unexpectedly, and it did not even occur to this woman to refuse him the little cake that he asked her to prepare for him. But, the prophet had to reassure her because she thought that when that little food was gone, she and her son would die.[181] In this regard, she was mistaken, but, in her defense, you will note that Jesus had not yet come and spoken. He would later say: "Give, and it will be given to you; good measure, pressed down, shaken together, running over, will be put into your lap."[182]

---

[181] 1 K 17:7-16.

[182] Lk 6:38. (Also see the multiplication of oil with Elijah: 2 K 4:1-7.)

I Will Share With Them!

I remember a poignant event in Medjugorje in the spring of 1992, which I wrote about at the time. The war had just begun its devastation in Herzegovina, and the entire village was without power, running water, and other things that we easily take for granted.

One day, I received a phone call from a farm in Sivric. Our dear friend Joseph begged me: "Sister, please let me borrow your electric generator. I have some food in my freezer, and I might lose it!"

I knew that a short time before this conflict, Joseph had slaughtered a little cow to feed his household of six, two members of whom were elderly. This meat had to last them several weeks. Quickly I brought the generator to him, and Joseph was able to take advantage of this providential engine that runs on gas.

About a month later, as the shortages continued to bite, I went to see Joseph and his family, and they asked me to stay for dinner. I said "Yes." "Too bad about the curfew, but since there's a full moon tonight, I will drive home without lights." At dinner, what did I see being put on the table before me but meat!

"Joseph," I exclaimed, "you must be the only one in the village who still has meat! How do you do it?"

Joseph spoke softly, and with a humility that I will never forget: "Sister, you remember that little cow that I slaughtered before the war?"

"Yes! Absolutely!"

"Well, ever since I brought refugees into our home, each evening I have gone to get some pieces of meat from the freezer for the next day and… (He opened his arms as if to say, I have no explanation) each time that I take some out, I always find the same quantity still there! That's how it is!"

Sitting there, tasting the excellent meat and taking on board what Joseph had just said, I struggled to hold back tears, thinking how his family ate, and the poor people ate. The atmosphere was serious but not heavy. Once I had managed to get my emotions under control, I whispered a question in Joseph's ear, "And you eat lots of this meat?"

"Sister, when I found these refugees in the street, with nothing—their house in Bjelo Polje had burned to the ground—I took them to my home, and I said to myself, 'These people have lost everything,[183] and I still have my house. I am going to share with them without putting anything aside for my family. When we end up with nothing, we'll all have nothing!' For a month now, I've given meat to my family and to the refugees, both at noon and in the evening. There are six of us and seven of them. That makes thirteen. But, Sister, there are also the neighbors....They know that I have this generator, so they come with plastic bags....I can't let them leave with nothing. They have children, and we are believers! So, I give them some meat. Sister, you have no idea how much meat we have taken each day since the war began. Several cows would not have been enough to supply all this meat. *Tako je, sestro!* (That's how it is, Sister!)"

And Joseph added this plea—fundamental to Croatian believers—which reveals so well the basis of this heroic charity, at a time of such scarcity: "Boze, sacuvaj!" (God, watch over us!)

---

[183] During the bombing that leveled their village, they escaped with only the clothes on their backs.

"Dear Children! I desire to draw you ever closer to Jesus and to His wounded heart that you might be able to understand the immeasurable love which gave itself for each one of you. Therefore, dear children, pray that from your heart that a fountain of love will flow to every person, both to the one who hates you and to the one who despises you. That way you will be able through Jesus' love to overcome all the misery in this world of sorrows, which is without hope for those who do not know Jesus. (November 25, 1991)

76

MARTHE ROBIN, AN ANTI-SUICIDE ANGEL

I had the privilege of personally meeting Marthe Robin four times. The last time I saw her, Father Finet took me with him to attend Marthe's weekly Holy Communion. A member of the Foyer de Charité accompanied us. In the intimacy of this magnificent event, we simply prayed one Rosary with her. After we had mentioned a few major intentions for the sake of the Church and of the world, Marthe received Holy Communion in silent adoration, and then we left. We could tell—Marthe had barely received the Host when she fell into ecstasy. It was forbidden to pray the sorrowful mysteries with her because this would cause her to fall immediately into a painful ecstasy. That day, Marthe helped me to touch another reality; it was something that would later become my daily bread in Medjugorje: the realization that the supernatural is natural for those who love God!

Sometimes, Jesus gave Father Finet a sign of His loving impatience with Marthe. He did not wait for the prayer: "Lord, I am not worthy to receive You, but only say a word, and I shall be healed," to be finished. He escaped from the hands of His priest, flew to Marthe and placed Himself on her lips!

Marthe perceived God and souls in an astonishing manner.

One day, a very rich lady entered Marthe's room. This lady was very beautiful. She expressed herself well, and enjoyed great success in the most cultured circles. She had barely put her foot in Marthe's room when Marthe cried out: "Oh Madam, you have an appalling soul!"[184]

It goes without saying that the lady received the shock of her life! Later on, thanks to Marthe's prayers, she began to change some of her ways.

Another time, one of my friends entered Marthe's room for her first visit. Marthe immediately exclaimed with unfeigned joy: "Oh, Chantal, come quickly and kiss me!" (We must remember that we had to be very, very careful not to bump Marthe's bed because the slightest hit would intensify her pain.)

Marthe set aside a special place in her heart for Chantal, and, as a result, they developed a very close friendship. Why her? That will remain the King's secret. Actually, Chantal showed remarkable charity towards the most rejected people, as well as the richest—this could be the reason.

One day, Father Finet had to travel, and he entrusted another priest with the responsibility of bringing Holy Communion to Marthe. This priest sat next to Marthe to begin the Rosary with her, but Marthe interrupted him: "Father, Jesus is not here!" The priest sought to reassure her, "Yes Marthe, Jesus is here. I brought the Communion holder."

"Jesus is not here," Marthe insisted.

So the priest removed the holder that hung around his neck, and he opened it. "Oh, Marthe, you are right! My God, I forgot to put the Host in it this morning!"

---

[184] This brings to mind Saint Catherine of Siena. One day, she met a high-class lady whom everyone in Italy praised. She arrived richly dressed, wearing much perfume, and covered in jewelry. When she entered the room, Catherine felt ill and fainted in front of the woman. Later, Saint Catherine wrote that she was not able to endure the foul odor of that woman's soul! Often St. Catherine could see the state of a person's soul and sometimes, if the soul was not in a state of grace, it had a foul odor. Jesus gave this special charisma to Catherine to allow her to help that soul be converted, change her ways and return to God. Once again, where the world so greatly admires any deadly path, a great saint allows Jesus to cry out His pain in the face of the loss of a life.

Similarly, Padre Pio could be very harsh with people who were happily wallowing in their sins. A man whom he subsequently cured of terminal cancer related that at his first meeting with Padre Pio, the latter told him that he was "very dirty" and should go away to prepare himself to die! See John A. Schug, OFM, Cap, A Padre Pio Profile, 146-47 (St. Bede's Publications 1987).

This perception of the Real Presence of Christ in the Host has always been something wonderful for me. Unfortunately, the Satanists can also tell whether or not a Host is consecrated. But, in their case, it is Satan who tells them. He has kept his angelic characteristics. Angels, whether good or bad, know where Jesus is. Satan would sneer at a Satanist who would bring him an unconsecrated host to defile. Marthe could see these hidden realities that are absent from our eyes. Each minute her heart tried to "rescue" the Eucharistic Jesus through reparation and adoration.

For my part, I have often reproached Jesus in this way: "Lord, You took me for Your bride, and I am not even able to discern whether or not You are in the tabernacle! Does the bride not know the body of her spouse? What kind of spouse am I to You, Jesus, if I cannot recognize whether it is Your body or a piece of bread?"

I know that I am not alone in this. I know many holy priests who are no further ahead than I am in discerning the consecrated Host. However it still causes me sorrow not to know where my Spouse is. I must surely need this sorrow; Jesus allows it to maintain me in humility because, otherwise, I would be quite capable of misusing this gift by falling into the sin of pride. Poor Jesus! He deprives Himself by depriving us. He prefers to protect us from the slippery slopes!

You, the Spanish Woman!

Marthe had deep compassion for people who suffered! She could feel their suffering from a distance, and she suffered with them, interceding day and night for the most afflicted, particularly those who seemed to be on the edge of blindly throwing themselves into Hell. She had even asked Jesus to stand in front of the door to Hell to convince these souls not to go there. When someone entrusted a person in distress to her, she did not let go. You could return twenty years later, and she would ask in her small, childlike voice: "And so-and-so, how are they now?"

She had a particular affection for the little ones and the poor, whom she saw as being crushed under the weight of the world's hardness, of human wickedness and of the coldness that is typical of a materialistic society. Mystically, she could see suicides happening by the thousands because of this weight. She saw especially the young people tortured by their own inner emptiness. She accompanied them in their agony, and interceded for them.

One day, she confided something that would be truly incredible—if it weren't also a charism of Padre Pio—to our wonderful friend, Estelle Sabatin, and to Father Manteau Bonamy, who are very close to my Community: "If you see someone who wants to commit suicide, tell him to call me into his heart, and I will come and help him!"

Estelle did not allow this pearl of wisdom to sink into oblivion.

Some years later, a young woman collapsed into her arms, full of despair. Having no family, juggled from one institution to another near Paris, Lorette's poor heart had been bleeding since her birth. The word family made her dream of having one, but everything seemed to be stacked against her. Crushed by the frustration of door after door closing on her, because of her misery, she saw no reason to continue living. Estelle did her best to console her and help her. She talked to her about the Lord and revealed to Lorette her pearl of wisdom. Marthe must intervene! "You know, I have a great friend, near Valence, whose name is Marthe. She is very close to God. She is a real saint, and God gave her a very rare gift—when someone is going to commit suicide, they can call to her for help. She hears their voice in her soul, and she comes to help them. So, hold on to this, okay? If you find that you are about to do something foolish, call on her, and she will come!"

This young woman had no religious upbringing, but like the true poor, her unfettered heart knew how to respond to the characteristics of God: goodness, beauty, the desire to help someone in distress. In her own way, she made a mental note of this information, and with a little more courage, she continued on her difficult life's journey. One day, misled by the false promises of a man, no doubt scarcely any better off then she was, Lorette found herself pregnant and abandoned. However, she fought to keep her child in spite of all the pressures that we can guess were heaped upon her, because, she thought, this would be the beginning of her real family, a tiny little being of her own—her own child! But, here again, she was struck a blow. She was judged too destitute to raise the child. They took her little girl away from her and placed her in an institution, in the district of Oise. Visiting rights were very limited. Her "little one" would be brought up—and not very well brought up at that—by strangers.

Two years went by. Lorette had hoped to get her daughter back, but her chronic unemployment and lack of a fixed address did not help.

When she made a new application for custody of her child, she was told that there was very little hope. Too much was too much, and Lorette snapped. At night, sleep eluded her, and during the day, she wandered aimlessly, torn, broken and desperate. One morning, at dawn, she made her way towards the Arts Bridge like a robot. Paris was still asleep. There was no one in sight. Lorette started to climb the railing to throw herself into the River Seine. She had not yet lifted her other foot when her conversation with Estelle suddenly popped into her memory like a flash.

"Oh, Estelle's lady," she thought. "The saint, what if I called her?" But Lorette had forgotten her name. Her insomnia had betrayed her. However, one detail came to her mind: The lady lived near Valence! Mistaking that little French village for a city in Spain, Lorette cried out with all her heart: "You, the Spanish woman from Valencia, come and help me!"

Suddenly, Marthe was there! Although she was invisible to Lorette, with maternal care, Marthe put her on her two feet and made her sit down. Lorette was calming down. Suddenly, her child's picture came into her mind. "Die? No, that's not the solution," she thought. "Well, what if I were to go to see my little girl in Compiègne instead? It's Saturday. That would take my mind off things."

Lorette didn't have a dime to her name, and the subway was too expensive for her anyway. So, she started walking. She walked towards the north of Paris, and the more she walked, the more her strength came back. "Yes," she thought with unusual peace, "it's a good idea to go and see my little one!"

At the limits of Paris, she tried hitchhiking and a car stopped. Lorette smiled at the man: "The road to Compiègne?"

"Yes! Get in!"

There was an intimidating silence. The man seemed to be kind and unaffected. After some time had gone by, he asked, "Are you going to the center of Compiègne?"

"Um…no, just a mile or so from there, but you can drop me off in Compiègne. That will do. I'll manage!"

"Well, I'm going to Mortefontaine."

"Mortefontaine? I'm going right next to there!"

"Good. I'll let you off there. It's no problem for me!"

Lorette wound up telling her secret to this kind man. She was going to spend the day with her little girl who had been taken away from her. Life was not easy, but this little one meant everything to her.

"And this evening, are you going back to Paris," asked the man.

"Oh, this evening? The same thing. I'll hitchhike before night falls. I'm used to it!"

"No! I must also go back to Paris, around 7:00 p.m. I will come and pick you up. That would be easier."

It was several years later before Lorette ran into Estelle by chance on a Paris boulevard—one of those days of grace that only Heaven knows how to plan. Lorette told her about that trip and what had prompted it.

"Well," said Estelle. "So, that evening, Miss Lucky had a driver to take her home! And what happened after that?"

"And then....we felt comfortable together. He had also had a rough time in his life. He was really nice to me."

"And then....?"

"Then, we got married. I was able to get my little girl back. Here, look, I have some pictures."

A few months later, when Estelle visited Marthe, she told her the whole story about Lorette, and Marthe remembered that particular dawn, on the Arts Bridge very well. Obviously this bleeding sheep who had cried out about the pains of her life, and who had much better things to do with her life than be swallowed up in the River Seine!

There are thousands of Lorettes in the world, especially in the pre-suicide phase. But there are so few Marthes. Who among us will rise up to work with Marthe, and thus multiply the number of survivors of despair![185]

---

[185] Thousands of testimonies received after Marthe's death, testify to her incredible intercession with Heaven. A shower of graces to tap into!

"Dear children! These are the days in which the Father grants special graces to all who open their hearts. I bless you and I desire that you too, dear children, will become alive to the graces and place everything at God's disposal so that He may be glorified through you. My heart carefully follows your progress. " (December 25, 1986)

77

THE LAST STEP

Kathleen's body had used up its last ounce of energy. It was a wonder how she could still stand! While on her way to church, to attend the evening program, she multiplied her prayers, reciting acts of faith, hope and charity because, from a human perspective, it was impossible to go on. She would not have the necessary strength to climb the high hill of Krizevac with Father Luciano's Community again that night. But she knew that, "God gives us what we need to carry out His will."[186] She abandoned herself to Him, so that she would not be defeated.

It was the winter of 1991. At 8:00 p.m. the last Rosary finished and the church began to empty. Kathleen and the brothers from the Community regrouped around the tireless Father Luciano. Once again he would lead them in the nightly routine of the Way of the Cross. This climb was familiar to them: it was part of their formation. They would have to wait until one o'clock in the morning before reaching their beds. And then, the bell would ring for prayers at six o'clock. But—oh miracle—Father turned to Kathleen and said to her: "You don't need to climb the mountain with us tonight. You're tired! If you wish, you may go to bed early!"

Kathleen's heart melted with relief. Not only could she finally get to bed, but she could do it with the blessing of obedience! She would finally have some time for herself, all alone in the house! It was for her, a dream come true.

---

[186] Saint John of the Cross.

Kathleen had been living in Anka Jerkovic's small pension, which Father Luciano had rented. This very jovial Franciscan priest from Italy was forming a little community with young men, offering them a place to stay while they spent six months in Medjugorje discerning their vocation through prayer. Some felt called to marriage, others the priesthood, and still others different vocations. Kathleen filled the role of "house mother," for this little group.

"What does a mom of ten or twelve young adults do?," I asked her one day. It seems that before "doing," one has, first of all, to offer the presence of a heart—an attentive and available heart, because many of these young people needed to be listened to, consoled and encouraged. Kathleen also played a part in the smooth running of the material aspects of the house which, at a time when the Communists controlled the country, presented a real headache. For some months, Kathleen had only been able to sleep three or four hours a night, but she was not counting.

That evening, Kathleen arrived at the Jerkovic pension, which had three floors. The Community occupied the first and second floors, with Kathleen's room on the latter. The chapel was located on the third floor, along with the rooms reserved for pilgrims.

"Is it the thought of bed that's making all my tiredness come to the surface," she wondered. Kathleen dragged herself up the little staircase. Each step seemed like a huge rock to conquer, and she wanted to give up. It was only the enticing thought of her dear bed that gave her the energy to reach the first floor. In her exhaustion, she literally crawled up the stairs. Then, she tackled the stairway that led to her room. She had only a few more steps to climb, when a thought went through her mind. It was the words that the Blessed Mother had recently given to the prayer group: "When you are exhausted, and you cannot do another thing, fall on your knees and ask your Father in Heaven to recreate you. He will do it."

When these words imposed themselves on her heart, she began to argue with the Blessed Mother: "Mother! You know that I really believe these words, but, you see, this evening they do not concern me! My bed is waiting for me, and I'm going to lie down!"

Kathleen tried to keep the message far from her mind, and stay focused on the goal of reaching her bed. But the message would not leave her heart. Instead it ensconced itself there! Kathleen then began to implore the Blessed Mother: "Mother, I really want to go to bed! I want to sleep. We'll see tomorrow!"

No matter how much Kathleen turned a deaf ear, she knew in her heart that the Blessed Mother was inviting her. Could she refuse her with a radical "No" for very long? The dialogue then became very heated, because the Mother of God is not a pushover who allows us to do as we will. She loves us too much to minimize God's beautiful plan for us. When Kathleen realized that the Blessed Mother was insisting so strongly, it was she who gave in. Her love for the Blessed Mother made her let go. So, she decided to go up one more flight of stairs to the chapel, and there, as the message stated, she planned to ask her Father in Heaven to recreate her—but she figured she would give Him an out: "Father, if you don't want to recreate me this evening, that's fine. I still have my bed waiting for me!"

Kathleen collapsed in front of the Blessed Sacrament, and she immediately understood that her Father would renew her strength. Yes! He wanted to renew her strength! It only took Kathleen's tiny prayer with all of her heart, without reserve, and with complete sincerity. In allowing each word to go very slowly, she pushed on the heavy door of her desire, and said to her Father: "O Heavenly Father, You know that I have been given permission to go to bed early tonight, but in my heart, I keep remembering Mother's words about what to do when we feel exhausted and just can't go on. So, Father, here I am on my knees, and I humbly ask You, if it is Your will, please recreate me!"

Kathleen had not even finished this prayer when her exhaustion vanished like a light fog in the sun! She was filled with new life! At six o'clock the next morning, when the Lauds bell sounded throughout all the floors of the house, our little sentinel was still at her guard post, watching and praying for the world before the Eucharistic Jesus, full of gratitude and song. She had gotten through the night with no trouble at all. It was as if she had slept for ten hours straight! For several days, she did not feel the weight of her body nor any weakness at all. That night, again, the grace she had received surpassed all her expectations!

He Should Have Collapsed!

This episode brings to mind other walks especially that of Jesus on the Via Crucis in the street of Jerusalem, the walk forced on Jesus when He was in a state of indescribable exhaustion from the scourging. From a human perspective, He should have collapsed—indeed died—long before reaching Mount Golgotha. How had He been able to go on? He placed Himself in the hands of His Father, who sent Him angels and the supernatural strength to take the next step. This infusion of supernatural strength in times of our greatest weakness is not automatic. It is a grace! It assumes that we entrust ourselves in the hands of our Heavenly Father, who always gives us the means to accomplish what He expects of us in His plan of love. That evening, without doubt, the Father needed Kathleen's intercession for His children! If she had based her decision on her own strength, Kathleen would have missed this marvelous gift! The saints possess the art of not missing any gift. That is their secret!

"Dear Children! Today also I am inviting you to a complete surrender to God. Dear children, you are not conscious of how God loves you with such a great love because He permits me to be with you so I can instruct you and help you to find the way of peace. However, you cannot discover the way if you do not pray. Therefore, dear children, forsake everything and consecrate your time to God and God will bestow gifts upon you and bless you.

78

THE STOREHOUSES OF DIVINE PROVIDENCE

When I was living in Paris, my job was to import handicrafts from India, Nepal, and other Asian countries. These trips often allowed me to bask in the striking simplicity of life in the East, which was restful to my soul, and to escape the materialistic oppression of Paris. Scarcely three days after my "conversion" in 1973, while I was still floating on the spiritual high of having the living Jesus with me, I sent Him this very sincere prayer: "Lord, if there is something in my life that is not in accordance with Your will, show it to me clearly, and I will remove it immediately!"

Innocent as I was then about the things of God, in spite of my twenty-five years, I was not aware that God was crazy about this type of prayer, and that He always answered it. We might even be bold enough to think that He Himself inspires this type of prayer when something within us hinders Him. In this way, He lets us believe that we, ourselves, have asked for the rotting branch to be pruned. How good Jesus is, and how well He knew how to take me at my word, in order to get around my pride and do me some good!

His reply was not long in coming. The very next day, my sister, Marie-Pia, came to see me. She had no sooner entered the living room than she noticed some objects that were displayed on the wall, and she exclaimed, "I don't see how you can actually sell those false gods and, at the same time, bring the light of Jesus to others! If I were in your shoes I would throw them out, pronto!"

"But…you must understand, it's, um…."

Too late! The blow hit me hard, and even my mumblings in my own defense about my need to earn a living seemed ridiculous to me. She was right. They were incompatible.

Having herself been converted some weeks before me, and being several steps ahead of me in the science of managing conversion in a concrete manner, my little sister saw there was no possible compromise. An apostle must not be adulterated, but 100% pure.

After she left, I sat down in the living-room, with my head between my hands, feeling completely distraught. I had just come back from Katmandu and New Delhi and was delighted to have found such beautiful and original objects that no one else had put on the market in France. A pinch of Parisian snobbery had also taken a hold of me in the process, I must admit! Were my precious "finds" now to be jettisoned, like (garbage jetsam?) from a ship? An interior battle was being fought. I tried hard to find a loophole that would allow me to combine the irreconcilable: to promote the masks of false gods and magnificent posters on Tibetan Tantrism, while at the same time, to bring the light of Christ to those around me. The clincher came when my prayer from the previous day came to my mind. Obviously, the Lord had sent Marie-Pia to me in answer to that prayer, to show me what was displeasing to Him and had to be removed from my life."

My spirits sank! With bleakness in my mind, I made the decision to have my newly acquired collection that I had purchased in India, destroyed. The items were still en route to Orly airport and had to be cleared through customs within a few days. So I phoned the customs agent in charge of this collection, and instructed him to burn the merchandise before it cleared Customs. I knew that the financial loss resulting from this action would be fatal to my small business, and this sacrifice would put an end to my livelihood. I spent the next few hours doing various damage control calculations but the conclusion was clear: Financially, I was going under.

That evening, with a sullen face, I arrived at Saint Sulpice Church, and met up with my prayer group—those marvelous brothers and sisters who were the instruments of my conversion. Martine Lafitte[187] greeted me with a big smile, but upon seeing my morose demeanor, she became worried.

"I'm in an impossible situation," I explained to her. "The Lord has shown me that I must let go of something, and...." I hadn't finished telling her my problem when she burst out laughing.

"But Emmanuelle, how can you lose your peace of mind over such a thing! The Lord will not abandon you! You are doing this for Him. Now the ball is in His court, and He will help you out! Where is your trust? Is He not God?"

The word trust hit me hard, and I realized to my great shame that I had forgotten this fundamental aspect of life with God. So, I took the plunge and said to Jesus, "Okay, Jesus, it was for Your Name that I had my things burned. My fate is in Your hands. You know that I must still earn my living. It's up to You to act on my behalf! And I thank You in advance!"

From that moment on, the feeling of oppression no longer weighed down on me and I found peace and joy once again. How sweet trust is to the heart! For His part, Jesus was just waiting for this in order to act in a divine way. Actually, during the next two days, I got so many orders from stores for other items, previously thought to be minor things, that I was reimbursed three times over for the loss that I had sustained.

In other words, the pruning was a net gain for me! With God's blessing, I was able to continue my job, until Jesus called me to follow Him radically three years later. At that point, I left Paris and entered the Community of the Beatitudes.

Jesus said to Saint Catherine of Sienna: " Take care of Me, and I will take care of you!" This discovery of God's power, through Divine Providence, had a profound effect on me. Since I often share my awe at the power of God with others, it has caused a chain reac-

---

[187] Co-founder, in 1972, of the Emmanuel Prayer Group, which became a Catholic lay community in 1977.

tion. Subsequently, many people have experienced the Living God acting powerfully in their daily lives. They have discovered that, in the storehouses of Heaven, many treasures are there waiting to slip into their hearts, their psyche, their relationships, and even their pockets—and the key to these storehouses is TRUST.

The sincere desire to please God in everything and carry out His will is fundamental, but it is not always enough to uproot the anguish that sometimes seizes us when faced with life. For that, trust in the goodness of God is the best 'tranquilizer'!

Oh, if the world would only make this move of trusting God! It is so simple and childlike! Of all those who are lined up at psychiatrists' offices with crushed hearts, mournfully contemplating the carpet in waiting rooms and no longer expecting anything, how many would then stand up straight and dance for joy!

"Dear Children! All these signs are designed to strengthen your faith until I leave you the visible and permanent sign." (October 22, 1981)

79

A BALL OF WARMTH ON KRIZEVAC

In the heart of winter, night falls shortly after four o'clock in the afternoon. As the pilgrims are fewer in number, Our Lady makes good use of this time.

One day in the '80s, as Kathleen came out of the church tower after evening prayers, and she wondered whether she had time to go to the house and put something on before going to Krizevac. It was Friday, and the Gospa had invited the prayer group to go to the top, promising to appear there at 11:30 p.m. But, the group had to be there two hours earlier, in order to prepare for her arrival. Kathleen was chilled to the bone. Since morning, the cold had penetrated right through to her skin. Her clothes were wet. The wind plastered her with that freezing rain that makes you long for a good hearth fire, and some quiet time, at home. But tonight, there would be no fire, no hearth, no quiet time for Kathleen. There would be something better, much better!

Kathleen loved the Blessed Mother with all her heart and she secretly cherished in her heart the thought that later that night, the Gospa would be there on the mountain. Yes, the Mother would descend from Heaven to be with her children, in order to bless them, transform them, and guide them. Kathleen hastened her step toward the Pavlovic house where she was living. Marija walked in front of her in silence. The two young women crossed the fields without flashlights. They knew each stone and each pothole on the road.

When they arrived at the house, Marija greeted her parents and then immediately left again with Kathleen to go to the mountain.[188] They

---

[188] In Medjugorje, there are still many homes like the Pavlovic home, simple but rich in that spirit of prayer and love that attracts the Blessed Mother. But these village houses are not on the lists of travel agencies (they don't have air conditioning). So, in order to stay in them, you have to first discover them during your pilgrimage!

hardly had time to snatch a piece of bread. They had not eaten anything since morning—there was no time! The groups of pilgrims did not stop invading the family home, which was always open, because, for every one of them, "to go and see Marija" was a bit like touching the Gospa, inhaling her perfume. Their clothes were still soaking wet and icy from the rain and the wind that blew in gusts. This was the kind of night when an ordinary person would not have the preposterous idea of going out, except in an emergency.

Divine Providence gave them a little help. Ivan, the visionary, passed by in his car and offered to take them to the foot of the mountain. The group began its ascent while making the Way of the Cross. The weather was becoming increasingly bad, and a layer of ice covered the freshly fallen snow; each step crunched beneath their feet. Soon even hail began to fall down upon them. At each Station, they stopped and sang as if they were enjoying the most delightful summer night. They knew that the Mother of God was waiting for them at the top. In her presence, there was something that transformed them so much inside that the only thing they longed for was to be with her. What did it matter about the rest? What did it matter what price the body would pay?

When they arrived at the summit, near the fourteenth station, the wind was so violent that no one could advance upright without falling down. So the group battled against the rain and the squalls of wind, crawling along the rocks to reach the foot of the large cement cross so that they could sit on the stairs and hang on to each other. Their prayers and hymns did not cease, while the violence of the elements seemed to rage more furiously with each minute leading up to the apparition. Kathleen hid her face between her knees in order to lessen the impact of the hail on her face. But her joy defied the winds: "Mother, in a few minutes, you will be here!"

That night, when Our Lady appeared, the wind that was beating the mountain began to form a circle around the group, as if it were hurling itself at an impenetrable wall. It spun around and around, and the young people found themselves within a soft ball of heat. It was as if the Blessed Virgin's mantle were invisibly wrapped around them. There it was, a soft, intimate, warm, hearth. There it was, not in the shelter of a comfortable dwelling, but at the summit of a mountain beaten by these wild, inhuman, December winds. The children could hardly believe it.

Their clothes were dry. This happened in the blink of an eye! And what peace! The singing was silenced. They all let themselves be wrapped, inside as well as outside, by this indefinable touch that belongs only to the Queen of Peace, and that makes us feel—if only for a moment—that the hostilities of this earth are nothing, nothing at all, in comparison to the fire of love.

Marija was beaming when she delivered the message given by the Blessed Mother that night: "When the Gospa arrived, she was full of joy. She stretched her arms wide open, and it was like we were engulfed in a ball of light. She gave this message: 'My dear children, I thank you for the love with which you have accepted to make these sacrifices. With your joy and your love, I have been able to realize part of my plan!'"

Then the Gospa gave them a gift. She gave them her joy. The young people then understood why they had felt such an intimacy with her during the apparition. When they were taken inside this ball of light that had warmed them and dried them out, it was as if they were being hugged interiorly. This peace came to them from above. They were bursting with joy! They tore down the mountain, unmindful of the patches of ice, the snow and the winds! It usually took Kathleen two hours to get down the mountain at night because she could not see the landscape when it was dark. That night, there was no moon, no stars and no flashlights! But Marija made this suggestion: "If you don't know how to get down, then take my hand. I'll show you how. Simply put one foot in front of the other!"

Then Marija began to run, and Kathleen could only run with her, forgetting her fears of the dark and her handicaps. In less than nineteen minutes, they were at the foot of the mountain. There are moments in life when only abandonment can save. For Kathleen, it was one of the most joyful descents of her life, and it was done in record time! It could be that her guardian angel had pulled his weight since he had no choice!

Today, Kathleen sees all these details of life in Medjugorje in the '80s as if they were yesterday: "Our Lady taught us by means of lessons like this one," she told me. "With her, we never had the impression of making sacrifices. The idea that these conditions were very harsh only hit us when we looked back. Sure, there were difficulties, but at the time, I can say that I did not live them as if they were hardships. We experienced what the Gospa wanted to make us live, what she asked of us. She supported us because we all made the choice to go to her school, and to do everything she asked of us. We were ready to do anything for her, and we still are to this day!"

"Dear children! Today I desire to tell you that I love you. I love you with my maternal love and I invite you to open yourselves completely to me so that, through each one of you, I can convert and save this world which is full of sin and bad things. That is why, my dear little children, you should open yourselves completely to me so that I may carry you always further toward the marvelous love of God the Creator who reveals Himself to you from day to day. I am with you and I wish to reveal to you and show you the God who loves you. Thank you for having responded to my call. " *(August 25, 1992)*

80

PRIVATE QUESTIONS FOR THE GOSPA

Our car, full of people, was bursting at the seams as we drove slowly toward the green tent of the Cenacolo, in Medjugorje. In less than an hour, Our Lady would appear to Mirjana Soldo, and as we did on the second of every month, we would pray with her for all those who do not yet know the love of God.

Among the young Americans piled in the back of the car, there was Helen, 25 years old, a sensitive heart, super brilliant mind, beautiful, but already contaminated by the rampant materialism that reigns in the U.S.A. She had not yet been able to give her all to life, and the thirst for more profound, wider, horizons secretly gnawed at her heart. She was starting her third week in our house in Medjugorje; the sadness that she arrived with was disappearing, furthering an inner peace. Patience was called for—the Divine ripening takes time.

As we drove along the hill of Podbrdo, we started on the loop that takes us to Bijakovici. Despite the early hour, the July sun was already fierce. A deep silence enveloped us.

"Hey! My friend Dina is getting married tomorrow," exclaimed Helen all of a sudden. "She's getting married to a girl. They've been together for years."

"She is getting married to a girl?" a few of us asked, astounded.

"Well, it's her path. I, myself, wouldn't do that, but it's her choice. She's free to choose. And I honor her choice."

"You honor her choice?" I asked.

"Yes."

"Oh boy!" I thought. "In two minutes I have to park the car, and this bomb just exploded at the last minute."

Awkwardly, I attempted a question: "How can you honor her choice when you know through the Bible that God has created us 'man and woman' and that the practice of homosexuality is not in His plan for humanity?"[189]

"C'mon Sister, you know the Bible. It all depends how you want to read it and interpret it. You can defend any position."

"Oops!" I thought to myself. "We are really going down a slippery slope here. I only have thirty seconds left to attempt to find a way out. I can't let these young people loose in the Cenacolo in this tainted frame of mind."

Fortunately, Chrissey hastened to my aid. "Listen," she said. "We will talk about the Bible later, but in the meantime, I have an idea: the Gospa is going to appear. She will be in our midst for a few minutes. Even if our own eyes cannot see her, we can always talk to her! We can tell her everything. She is a mother! So why not simply ask her what she thinks about it. For example you can ask her: 'Mom, would you honor that choice, that type of homosexual 'marriage'?'"

"OK, good idea!"

So we parked the car, and wiggled our way through the colorful crowd which was singing the Ave Maria as they waited for their Mother. We welcomed Our Lady, and prayed deeply with her. Then we returned to the house. It was completely silent. Helen seemed pensive and she

---

[189] Among the Biblical citations for this proposition is Lv 20:13. Catholic teaching is that homosexual acts are intrinsically disordered and contrary to natural law, and under no circumstances can they be approved. See Catechism of the Catholic Church §2357. The church has been at great pains to elucidate not only that position, but two other related, pastoral, positions, which are set forth in a statement adopted by the U.S. Conference of Catholic Bishops: "Ministry to Persons With a Homosexual Inclination: Guidelines for Pastoral Care" (published in Origins, vol., 36, no. 24 (Nov. 23, 2006).

did not mention her question. The next morning Helen awoke early and found me in the kitchen. After our coffee had brewed we stepped outside to sit in the morning sun before prayers.

"You know yesterday, Our Lady answered me and it is very clear to me now!"

"What do you mean, it's clear?" I asked.

"Well, something happened yesterday at the apparition and I just had the feeling that something isn't right about homosexuality. Suddenly, it felt awkward to me."

"So, Our Lady talked to you?"

"I don't know! I didn't see anything, didn't hear anything—but when I left the green tent, I was like convinced that it wasn't God's plan for humanity. It was crystal clear to me! For the first time, I understood why. Because you can be united, but not united in having babies. What's the point in being united if you can't have babies and give back to God the humanity He created? If we are the same sex, we can't participate in His plan as a married couple, in the same way. Our bodies don't fit together."

Today Helen has an important job in politics, where she sees the best and the worst. She has deepened her prayer life and she tries to see things the way Christ does, by receiving Him almost everyday through the Eucharist. Her prisms of judgment, her concepts and convictions have changed radically. The peace that bathes her face is like a lighthouse in the middle of the troubled and dangerous waters of American intellectual life.

Helen has learned to listen. Since this episode regarding homosexual marriage, when Helen has a deep question, she knows who to turn to.

"Dear children! At this time of grace, I call you to prayer. Little children, you work much but without God's blessing. Bless and seek the wisdom of the Holy Spirit to lead you at this time so that you may comprehend and live in the grace of this time. Convert, little children, and kneel in the silence of your hearts. Put God in the center of your being so that, in that way, you can witness in joy the beauty that God continually gives in your life." (May 25, 2001)

81

A PROPHET IN BIJAKOVICI?

Mate Sego was born in 1901. He lived at the foot of Podbrdo, the hill very close to Vicka's family home and to the Ivankovic clan, in the hamlet of Bijakovici, where the visionaries were born. He never attended school and could neither read nor write. He worked hard his entire life cultivating the small plot of land that he had inherited from his parents, a very stony plot that yielded little. Like his friends and neighbors, he made a living mainly from his vineyards and his tobacco field, from one cow and a few goats. Rather than going abroad to Germany for work, like so many of the locals had done, he chose to remain in his village. "It is better to live poor and with the family intact," he thought.

Once his children had grown up, he could afford to wander and take life easy while waiting for his great departure. Like all winemakers, he loved to share his wine with his friends, and now that he had grown older and weaker, this gave him a chance to fill those long hours before nightfall. His tiny stone house had neither water nor electricity and its inhabitants measured their lives by the passage of the sun and the seasons. No one knew if there would be bread on the table the next day. They all used to sleep next to one another on the floor. Beds were unheard of! And anyway, there was no room to fit them in. Every morning, Mate's wife, Nada, would fold up the blankets and store them away in a corner of the single room that was the family's only living space.

Mate Sego! A man with such intriguing and wild stories! He sometimes crisscrossed the valley of Medjugorje spreading his nonsensical tales to the four winds. Some thought it was the wine. People used to smile as he passed by and sometimes even laughed out loud, so out of this world were his visions!

"I'm not handsome," he often said. "But, everybody loves me! Everyone welcomes me with joy!"

Mate was right. He was welcomed everywhere he went. The people of Medjugorje were greatly in need of his uplifting presence and had grown much attached to him. They would say with a smile, "If we go to a wedding and Mate isn't there, it has no zing."

In winter, when it was time to make rakija (a local distilled liquor) on the farm, Mate had to be there. Otherwise everyone would get bored—Mate's warmth and joy were so attractive and contagious. There was no movie theater there, no TV or radio, but Mate more than made up for both. He was the life of their evening gatherings; he would ease the saddened hearts of his friends, burdened down by the lack of freedom. In his presence, listening to his stories, it was easy to escape. After making an enquiry among the elders of the village I learned that everyone remembers Mate with a spot of tenderness.

Mate couldn't help it: he just couldn't stop once he started talking about the future of his village, this confined little world that he never left. "Some day," he promised to whoever was willing to listen, "there will be a staircase going up the hill, behind my house, with as many steps as there are days in a year!"

"Go on, Dedo (Grandpa), keep dreaming; there's nothing wrong with that," they would answer him.

"Listen to me! Listen to me, my children! Medjugorje will be very important! People will come here by the thousands from all corners of the world, people of all colors. You'll see black people, yellow people, and white people. They'll come here to pray. The church will no longer be this little church I grew up with. There will be a new one, much bigger, and it will be full. It will not even be able to contain all the people who will come! Some day they will dynamite the church of my childhood, and that will be the day I die." *(And that is exactly what happened: damage from an earthquake caused the steeple of the old church, where Mate worshipped, to collapse. The church was dynamited and razed to the ground in 1978. Mate passed away on that exact date. The current church was completed in 1979, two years before the beginning of the apparitions.)*

"My Gospa will come—blessed are those who believe and remain in prayer! I'm telling you this now! I won't see any of this, but you, my children, you will! There will be lots of streets, lots of buildings, not like the little houses we have nowadays—some of the buildings will be huge."

At this point in his tale, Mate would become nostalgic and sad, as if he were watching the departure of a loved one. "Our folks will sell their land to foreigners who will build hotels. Medjugorje and the surrounding hills will be a holy place. There will be so many people on my Crnica[190] that you won't be able to sleep at night. They will come for my Gospa! My children, you will see this. Be kind and hospitable to them and all will go well for you."

"Dedo, you had a little too much rakija tonight; don't you think it's time for bed?"

"Pay attention! Don't let your traditions be lost! Pray to God for everyone, and for yourselves."[191]

Of course, there would be plenty of smirks and comments all around. "All that suffering and privation has gone to his head, and the rakija sure hasn't helped," some whispered.

Mate knew full well that not one of his friends believed a word of his tales. He noticed the grins, but nothing could hold him back. With a stern look he warned them, "Don't make me call on Jesus!"

Their snide comments would fall on deaf ears, since he was never one to water down his message just to fit in. He had the aura of a

---

[190] Original name of Podbrdo Hill, or "Hill of Apparitions".

[191] I was told about these conversations by a few of the older people who remembered their neighbor, Mate, well. Their testimonies confirm one another. Some of these friends were Ivan Ivankovic, who lived with Mate for 50 years before his death in 1978, Nado Cilic, and Pavica. Mate lived from 1901 to 1978. He is buried in the cemetery of Bijakovici.

prophet, a man with the sight of an eagle, unmoved in the face of the hidden realities he beheld as naturally as we watch the rising of the sun! He had the stature of a man of God; his heart was just and free. He was not threatened by what others thought of him. When he had something to say, he said it. He could neither read nor write, but he had access to some of God's secret plans for his village and through his village, for the world!

He had a friend, Jozo Ivankovic, who was younger than him and who stayed away from alcohol on principle. Since Mate liked to indulge on occasions, Jozo used to tease him about the risks of drinking wine, and advised him to quit drinking altogether for the sake of his health. But Mate knew something he didn't know.

"Jozo, I'll be there for your funeral!"

"Careful Mate, you could fall and hurt yourself ahead of me!"

"Keep talking Jozo, but I'll be at your funeral!"

Once again, Jozo, who was much younger, thought Mate was delirious, but his prediction was correct.

However, some of Mate's words are still a little unclear. "Listen, listen to me my children!" he once said. "There will be a spring right around here. A spring with lots of water! So much water that it will make a lake and our folks will own boats that they will tie to a big rock."

As far back as anyone could remember, water shortage had been the worst problem for the poor peasants of Medjugorje, whose equipment had hardly improved since the Middle Ages. They had done everything possible to locate an underground water table, drilling deep holes at several locations in the village, but to no avail! Only rocks and more rocks! There wasn't a single well in the valley and families would dig out cisterns to collect rainwater. But the heat waves of summer were hard and long, and the cisterns were not enough to provide the water needed by man for watering the animals in the mornings and the tobacco plants at night. So the villagers hitched their horses to their carts and rode all the way to Citluk, Ljubuski or sometimes even Mostar to find water! How could anyone in the village believe that this crushing burden of a lack of water could one day make way for the blessing of a gushing spring?

"Come on Mate, what are you talking about? Water, in Medjugorje? You've got to be kidding!"

Their faces fell as they listened to such fantasies. "If only it were true! Oh God, watch over us!"

But, Mate wouldn't back down. His visions permeated him as the sun permeates the sky!

Saint Paul recommended that the Corinthians yearn for the gifts of the Spirit, especially the gift of prophecy, but he also declared that "our prophecy is imperfect." [192]

Could Mate Sego's prophecy about the abundant spring of water belong to those inevitable imperfect prophecies that Saint Paul warned about? Everything else came true within the first ten years of the apparitions. Or is this element being kept in reserve for some unknown date in the future? Did his vision concern the water pipeline that brings millions of gallons of water to the pilgrims of Medjugorje? Could a natural seismic event cause such a spring to surface out of this unchangeably dry soil, or are we going to witness a truly supernatural phenomenon—which wouldn't be the first one for this blessed land of Medjugorje? Didn't the people of Lourdes see springs of flowing water with their own eyes when little Bernadette Soubirous scratched the ground near the grotto as instructed by the Lady?

But that isn't the most important point: God is in charge—as we will truly see! In the mean time, this extraordinary person, Mate, has unveiled for us a wonderful dimension of God's teachings. Allow me to end this Chapter with a simple prayer which I would like to address to my brother, Mate Sego, who has grown so dear to me that I long for the day I can sit next to him in Heaven and listen to his version of the events of Medjugorje—God willing!

Dragi Mate, MIR s tobom! (Dear Mate, Peace be with you!)

Every day I thank God for you, Mate. Here on earth, while you were subjected to all kinds of trials, you probably weren't aware of all your blessings, and to what extent you were under the protection of Heaven.

---

[192] 1 Cor 13:9.

You were born just a few yards away from the spot where your Gospa was to make her appearance, and without even knowing it, you were preparing the minds of your friends. When she did appear, and Communist soldiers began a mortal assault on believers and visionaries alike, everyone thought back to your stories and from out of the past you comforted them.

Because of the calm and steadfast courage that led you to express your visions, people were later able to understand that this was God's plan for their village, and they were able to cooperate with Him in spite of the oppression, threats and outrages rained down by hostile enemies. They remembered your words: "Be kind and hospitable to those who will come. They will come to pray."

Mate, I thank you for carrying your cross without whimpering, your eyes always fixed on the world to come. But I thank God even more for calling you back to Him before any of these things started to happen. He wanted to protect you as you carried out your mission in all simplicity, I even think that you were not aware that you were a prophet. Am I mistaken? It seems to me that you were just casually sharing your visions as others share their thoughts. You spoke with the powerful spontaneity of a pure heart, not stopping to analyzing the pros and cons.

I spoke with your friends, the survivors of that era, and each encounter filled me with greater joy. I believe that God planted you at the foot of this hill like a little tree, too modest to catch the fancy of men, yet destined to bear delicious fruit for Him one day. He kept you in conditions so crude and austere that most contemplative monks and nuns these days couldn't bear it.

In the midst of your weaknesses, He allowed you to remain unaware of your own importance, and perhaps, of your holiness. He did this to let it sprout and blossom in secret, protected from the steamrollers of human flattery and overwhelming materialism. You have been spared all this! What a blessing! Do you have any idea what could have happened to you? What if throngs of pilgrims had descended on your house just to touch you, to take pictures of you and to interview you, asking thousands of questions about their own future and the future of the world? Imagine if you were on the front page of all the magazines and papers in Medjugorje, and were given royal treatment on every continent, all the while being subjected to every imaginable type of flattery, distractions and temptations! Imagine! You have no idea what a nightmare this could have been for you, Mate! How blessed you were to have remained hidden in your busy little life, like the Mother of God in the humble home of the Ben David family in Nazareth.

Pray for your dear Bijakovici, Mate, you wouldn't recognize it any more! Intercede for your people! The viruses of the West have overrun them. They've been assaulted by all kinds of temptations totally unknown in your days. All this came down on them by surprise; they weren't ready for this! Pray to your Gospa for their protection, so that she may realize in them fully her beautiful plan for peace.

The stairs that you talked about haven't been built yet. The bottom section of the trail has already been paved, and while it was being done, your neighbors didn't stop talking about you. You have become their pride! As for me, I'd like to make you a deal: I will pray for your grandchildren, as long as you attach a special prayer to each new brick that has been set behind your house, so that everyone who steps on them—whether pilgrim, merchant, or just a curious soul—will receive one of the graces that you were known for in this life: the grace of remaining small and trusting like a child; the grace to persevere with God in the face of the howling winds and strong tides! Could you make this prayer to the one whom you so lovingly called my Gospa? Thank you so much!

"Dear children! Today I invite you to comprehend your Christian vocation. Little children, I led and am leading you through this time of grace, that you may become conscious of your Christian vocation. Holy martyrs died witnessing: I am a Christian and love God over everything. Little children, today also I invite you to rejoice and be joyful Christians, responsible and conscious that God called you in a special way to be joyfully extended hands toward those who do not believe, and that through the example of your life, they may receive faith and love for God." *(November 25, 1997)*

82

LITTLE LI

When God called his servant Fulton Sheen back to Himself, in 1979, millions of Americans mourned his death as if they had been left orphans.[193] For years, he used every possible means to reach hearts through the media, and soaking in every word of his, the people were fascinated. Gifted with a rare charisma, he was a blend of natural eloquence and the power of the Holy Spirit. Yes, through his witness, people knew that God was alive, magnificent and desirable. Archbishop Sheen shone so brightly that TV channels were fighting over him, knowing that his broadcast would shatter all ratings on record. His popular show, "Life Is Worth Living," reached around thirty million viewers every week.[194]

This great Archbishop, master of evangelization, had a secret. Like all truly great men of God, he privately cherished a chance revelation in his life. It was an episode when an abundance of grace had floored him, and set him on a path from which he would not deviate for anything in the world. To understand that experience, we have to transport ourselves back to China in the 1950's, at the peak of the Communist crackdown....

---

[193] See photo album.

[194] He would say: "If you believe the unbelievable, you will end up doing the impossible."

The Tiny Steps of a Child

In a parochial school, children diligently recited their prayers. Sister Euphrasia was pleased because two months ago, many of the children had received their First Communion, and took it very seriously; from the bottom of their hearts. She smiled as ten year old little Li asked: "Why didn't the Lord Jesus teach us to say 'Give us this day our daily rice?'" It was a very difficult question to answer, since these children ate rice morning, noon and night.

"Well, it's that 'bread' means 'Eucharist'," answered Sr. Euphrasia, whose heart radiated much brighter than her theology. "You ask the good Jesus for daily Communion. It's true that for your body, you need rice. But for your soul, which is worth much more than your body, you need bread. That is the Bread of Life!"

In May 1953, when Li made her First Communion, she had asked Jesus in her heart: "Always give me that daily bread so that my soul can live and be healthy!" Since then, Li had received Holy Communion everyday, but she was aware of the fact that the "bad people" (the Godless Communists) could prevent her from receiving Christ at any time. So she prayed ardently that it would never happen.

She would never forget the day they entered the classroom and screamed at the children: "Right now—give us all of your idols!" Li knew very well what they meant. Terrified, the children gave up their pious, carefully hand-painted images of Jesus, Mary and the Saints. Then, in a fit of anger, the Captain pulled the Crucifix off the wall, threw it down to the ground and trampled it screaming: "The New China will not tolerate these grotesque superstitions!"

Little Li, who loved her picture of the Good Shepherd so much, attempted to conceal it in her blouse. It was the special image given to her for her First Holy Communion. But a loud slap on her cheek sent her crashing to the floor. The Captain called Li's father and humiliated him before tying him up with a rope.

That same day, the police made a sweep of the village, cramming all the inhabitants they could find into the tiny church. The Captain proceeded to bark out a new kind of "sermon" ridiculing the missionaries and the "agents of American imperialism." Then, with a thundering voice, he ordered the soldiers to fire at the tabernacle. All together and

385

at once, the congregation drew a long breath and increased the intensity of their prayers.

The Captain turned back to the crowd and screamed: "Let's see how your Christ can defend Himself—here's what I think of your 'Real Presence'—the Vatican's trick to exploit all you people!" Saying this, he grabbed the ciborium and threw all the Hosts onto the tile-floor. Stunned, the faithful shrank away from his gaze and choked their cry. Little Li frozen in horror.

"Oh, no," she thought. "Look what happened to the Bread!" Her innocent and righteous little heart bled for the Hosts strewn all over the ground. "Isn't anyone going to help Jesus?" she wondered in amazement. The Captain continued his tirade of insults, interrupting his blasphemy only to let out spurts of guttural laughter. Li silently wept.

"Now, get out!," yelled the Captain, "and woe to the one who dares to return to this den of superstition! He'll answer to me!"

The church quickly emptied. But besides the angels always present around Jesus in the Blessed Sacrament to adore Him, there stood another witness who had not missed a moment of the drama. It was Father Luke from the Missions Etrangères (Foreign Missions). One month previously, foreseeing the takeover of the village, the parishioners had hidden him in a small recess of the choir, which gave him a view of the church. He sank into prayers of atonement for the sacrileges committed against Jesus and suffered because he was not able to come to Jesus' defense: one wrong move on his part, and the parishioners who had hidden him would be arrested for treason.

"Lord, have mercy on Yourself," he prayed in anguish. "Stop this sacrilege! Lord Jesus!"

Suddenly, a creaking sound broke the heavy silence in the church. Slowly, softly, the door opened. It was little Li! Barely ten years old, there she was, approaching the altar with the tiny steps of a Chinese girl. Father Luke trembled: she could be killed at any moment! Unable to communicate with her, he could only watch and beg all the saints in Heaven to spare this child. The little girl bowed for a moment and adored in silence, just as Sr. Euphrasia had taught her. She knew that she was supposed to prepare her heart before receiving Jesus. Her hands joined together, she whispered a mysterious prayer to her dear

Jesus—mistreated and abandoned. His eyes glued to her, Fr. Luke stared as she lowered herself down to her hands and knees; and with her tongue, took up one of the Hosts. She remained there on her knees, eyes closed, turned inward face to face with her Heavenly Friend.

Each second seemed an eternity to Father Luke. He feared the worst. If only he could speak to her! But soon the child went out just as quietly as she had come in, almost hopping along.

The purging continued as the volunteer brigade searched the entire village and surrounding area. This type of terror was happening all across "New China." The peasants didn't dare to move. Hiding in their bamboo homes, they knew nothing about the future and couldn't take tomorrow for granted. Yet, every morning our little Li slipped away to find her Living Bread in the church. Reproducing the same scenario from the previous day, each time she took up a Host with her tongue and disappeared. Father Luke was chomping at the bit: Why didn't she take them all? He knew exactly how many there were: thirty-two. "Doesn't she know that she could pick up several of them at once?" he thought.

No, she didn't know. Sr. Euphrasia had been very clear about that: "One Host per day is enough. And never touch the Host; we receive it on the tongue!" The little girl perfectly conformed to the rules.

One day there remained on the ground only one more Host. At daybreak, the child scurried into the church as usual and drew near to the altar. She knelt to the ground to pray, very close to the Host. Father Luke had to muffle a cry. Suddenly a soldier, standing in the doorway, aimed his gun at her. A single dry pop was heard, followed by a loud burst of laughter. The child immediately collapsed. Fr. Luke thought that she was dead, but no! He watched her struggle and crawl up to the Host, he saw her put her tongue over it. Then, a few convulsions shook her body, before it finally relaxed.

Little Li was dead—but not before she had rescued all the Hosts![195]

---

[195] The story of the little Chinese girl is told in The Thieves of God, by Maria Winowska. Having had close ties with the Russian, Polish and Chinese intelligence during the worst years of persecution, Maria was able to keep treasures from the lives of Polish Saints (Fr. Albert, Sr. Faustina, Fr. Maximilian Kolbe) from being lost.

Holy Hour, Every Day

Archbishop Fulton Sheen revealed a secret at the age of 84, two months before he passed away, during an interview on national television.

"Your Excellency," began the interviewer, "you have inspired millions of people world-wide; what about you, who has inspired you? Was it a Pope?"

"It was neither a pope, nor a cardinal or any other bishop—not even a priest or a nun! The one who has inspired me was a small, ten year-old Chinese girl."

It was then that Archbishop Sheen revealed his intimate secret by telling the story of Little Li. He explained how the love this little child had for Jesus in the Eucharist so impressed him that, on the day he first heard it, he made a promise to the Lord that every day of his life, until death, come what may, he would spend one hour in adoration in front of the Blessed Sacrament.

The Archbishop not only kept his promise, but he never missed a chance to promote the Love of Jesus in the Eucharist. Tirelessly, he invited the faithful to spend a daily Holy Hour with the Blessed Sacrament. For him, there wasn't a shadow of doubt: it was this unknown and poor child from remote, rural China who was the spark that had ignited this immensely fruitful apostolate.

On that day, in front of their TV screens, all America understood that millions of hearts touched by this great preacher had also been touched by little Li. It was this innocent child with her thirty-two heroic visits to Jesus scattered all over the floor, who paved the way for him to lead millions to adoration in front of the Blessed Sacrament. Behind the blossoming of many consecrations, vows and vocations inspired by the most popular American prelate there was the little Chinese martyr and her union in blood with the Lamb.

*****

Dearest Little Li, if I have dedicated this book to you, it is because you are my favorite hero! But I have to admit that I have another interest in doing so: you are not finished yet! Look, there aren't just thirty-two Hosts lying on the tiles any more, but thousands and millions!

Every day Jesus is shot at, laughed at and trampled upon. The number of sects that profane the Eucharist is growing. In almost every parish, every Sunday, there are a few Catholics who receive Communion even as they live in grave sin, those sins that the Bible refers to as "abominations" and that kill the soul. Jesus is tortured today as never before, Little Li. (Not to mention the indifference of so many "chosen ones" who become absorbed in the world's affairs, oblivious of the immense love that Jesus has for them.) In France, so many tabernacles have been abandoned, covered in dust! And sometimes, if someone wants to spend time in front of the Blessed Sacrament, a locked door meets him. In America, tabernacles have often been banished to some corner of the church, if not into the sacristy. Sometimes, we can't even find a kneeler, and woe to him who dares go down on his knees during Consecration; it's unacceptable and may be grounds for exclusion from some churches.

How many Sr. Euphrasias do we still find teaching Catechism? Most children are so ill-prepared to know and love Jesus. It is so rare in families to hear parents speak openly of Jesus as they would of their greatest friend. On the contrary, they ignore Him, and so, children believe that He does not really exist and get lost in atheism.

I could go on and on but, surely from Heaven, you can see so much better than I can. You aren't done Little Li! The truth is when you lived your martyrdom in China, you were just beginning! Come help us! As you stood by Archbishop Sheen, come and stand by every priest today, every bishop, every ordained minister and each Christian persons. Reveal to us the hidden Child, your great friend! Transmit to us your unadulterated love for Jesus, that radical and tender love of your innocent heart.

Medjugorje, May 13, 2006
Feast of Our Lady of Fatima

APPENDIX 1

ABOUT THE AUTHOR

Sister Emmanuel Maillard was born in France in 1947. She studied theology with Cardinal Daniélou. Further studies were in the History of Fine Arts at the Sorbonne University (Paris) from which she graduated in 1970. She joined the Community of the Beatitudes in 1976, and has been living in Medjugorje since 1989. In order to help the Blessed Mother realize her plans of Peace, she founded the apostolate "Children of Medjugorje"

"I wish to thank all the individuals who furnished me with their witness, so that love of Mary will increase in people's hearts. But history marches on, and so I launch here an appeal to all those others who might have their own testimony to contribute, for nothing touches hearts more than such simple and true stories that demonstrate the finger of God in our lives. Once a grace is shared, it multiplies!"

Write to: Sister Emmanuel, Box 8,
Medjugorje 88266, Bosnia & Herzegovina.

If you wish to join the family, ask for information from:

Children of Medjugorje,
P.O. Box 18430, Denver, CO 80218-0430;
Phone: 877-647-6335 (877-MIR-MEDJ)
Website: www.childrenofmedjugorje.com

CDs PRODUCED BY CHILDREN OF MEDJUGORJE

Specials on Medjugorje:
(Sr. Emmanuel)

The Rosary with Medjugorje

Touch Your Heavenly Mother

Prayer with The Heart

How Wonderfully You Made Me!

True Consecration to Mary

Prayer Obtains Everything

Story of a Wounded Womb

Fasting, Door to God's Power

Heaven? Purgatory? Hell? Choose
  your future!

The Most Beautiful Mass of my Life

Why Fear what is to Come?

Get Mary's Message for the 3rd Millennium (on Baby Jesus)

Stressed? Oppressed? BLESS!

The Miracle of The Rosary

  -The Joyful Mysteries
  (The Luminous, Sorrowful and
  Glorious Mysteries are to come)

  Portraits of Mary

Witnesses:

The Most Handsome Saint
  (Fr. Tim Deeter.)

In Medjugorje, He Told Me the Secret
  (Fr. Tim Deeter)

The Amazing Secret Of Purgatory
  (Sr. Emmanuel)

From Astrology To God's Light
  (Sr. Emmanuel)

The Incredible Mercy Of God!
  (Sr. Emmanuel)

Prophecies For Medjugorje
  (Sr. Briege McKenna)

Witness Of A Professional Sinner!
  (David Parkes)

Fr. Donald Calloway's Incredible
  Testimony

Teachings:

Make Friends with your Angel
  (Sr. Emmanuel)

Oh Come, Let Us Adore Him!
  (Sr. Emmanuel)

Mother, Who Are You? *(Fr. Tim Deeter)*

When Death Separates us From Those
  we Love, *(Sr. Emmanuel)*

The Divine Mercy Chaplet *(spoken,
  sang and explained by Sr. Emmanuel)*

Available in:

USA: "Children of Medjugorje, USA: P.O. Box 18430, Denver, CO 80218-0430 - Tel: 877-647-6335 pray@childrenofmedjugorje.com

CANADA: "Ave Maria C.P." Tel: 800 663 MARY

NEW ZEALAND: Tel/Fax: (64) 9 41 83 428

ENGLAND: "Children of Medjugorje" Fax: 44.1.959.52.3619; r.fenlon@ntlworld.com

EGYPT: "Children of Medjugorje", bcangegardien@yahoo.fr

AUSTRALIA: "Ave Maria" Tel: 61.899.21.4365

MALAYSIA: Kuching, Tel: 60.8224 3936

HONG KONG: "Children of Medjugorje Hong Kong", com.hongkong@gmail.com

INDIA: "The Ark" Tel: 91.484.39.26.67 Fax: 484.38.00.52

SOUTH AFRICA: Margate, Alex Knox, Tel: 27.39.317.2825

MEDJUGORJE: "Phoenix" Tel: 387.36 650 917, "Devotion" Tel: 387.36 651 497

The weekly Television Programs
"MEDJUGORJE: OUR MOTHER'S LAST CALL
with Sr. Emmanuel"

Are now also available on DVD in box sets of two in one!
(PAL DVDs Also Available For All Volumes)

Volume One:
Track 1: *I Love Each One of You As Much As I Love My Son Jesus*
Track 2: *Give Me Your Worries, And Pray For My Intentions*

Volume Two:
1: *Protect The Children (With Fr. Jozo)*
2: *You Do Not Understand The Importance Of My Coming!*

Volume Three:
1: *I Am Your Mother, Welcome Me Into Your Life*
2: *I Rejoice To See You Here, (With Phillip Ryan)*

Volume Four:
1: *I've Come To Tell You That God Exists*
2: *United With Me To Pray For Those Who Do Not Believe*

Volume Five:
1: *Take The Saints As An Example*
2: *John Paul II, (With Fr. Daniel Ange)*

Volume Six:
1: *A Briefing To The Congressional Human Rights Caucus*
2: *Only By Prayer And Fasting Can Wars Be Stopped (With Fr. Slavko)*

Volume Seven:
1: *I Am The Mother Who Comes For The People*
2: *If Only You Would Abandon Yourself To Me*

Volume Eight:
1: *I Invite You To Consecration To My Immaculate Heart*
2: *Children, Help My Heart To Triumph!*

Volume Nine:
1: *Go To Confession Once Per Month*
2: *Tonight You Can Touch Me*

Volume Ten:
1: *Thank You For Having Created Me*
2: *I Am Leading You, Dear Children, Towards Love, Towards The Father*

Volume Eleven:
1: *Pray, For through Prayer, You will Know What To Do*
2: *For God, Divorce Does Not Exist*

Volume Twelve:
1: *Today, Rejoice With Me And My Angels*
2: *I Will Leave A Great Sign*

Volume Thirteen:
1: *Pray With The Heart*
2: *A Rose For Mother Teresa (With Danielle Rose)*

Volume Fourteen:
1: *Listen To My Messages With The Heart (Five Stones)*
2: *Every Thursday Re-Read Mathew 6:24-34*

Volume Fifteeen:
1: *Be Reconciled*
2: *I Desire Reconciliation Among You*

Volume Sixteen:
1: *Your Suffering Is Also Mine*
2: *Sufferings Are Really Great Gifts From God*

Volume Seventeen:
1: *I Kneel Before The Freedom That God Has Given You (With Marija, Part I)*
2: *I Kneel Before The Freedom That God Has Given You (With Marija, Part II)*

Volume Eighteen:
1: *From Astrology To God's Hands (Sr. Emmanuel's Conversion Story, Part I)*
2: *From Astrology To God's Hands (Sr. Emmanuel's Conv... Part II)*

Volume Nineteen:
1: *Do Not Fear, Trust Me Part I*
2: Do Not Fear, *Trust Me, Part II (With Fr. Svetozar Kraljevic, OFM)*

Volume Twenty:
1: *Put Holy Mass at The Center Of Your Life, Part I*
2: *Put Holy Mass... Part II*

Volume Twenty-One:
1: *Pray For Priests (With Sr. Briege McKenna, Part I)*
2: *Pray For Priests (With Sr. Briege McKenna, Part II)*

Volume Twenty-Two:
1: *Pray For Unbelievers (With Mirjana, Part I)*
2: *Pray for Unbelievers (With Mirjana, Part II)*

Volume Twenty-Three:
1: *I Wish Your Sufferings Become Joy!*
2: *Pray For The Sick*

Volume Twenty-Four:
1: *Fall In Love With The Most Holy Sacrament Of The Altar*
2: *Pray For Priests, My Most Beloved Sons*

Volume Twenty-Five:
1: *I Have Shown You Heaven to Let You Know That It Exists*
2: *I Have Shown You Purgatory to Let You Know That It Exists*
3: *After Death There Is Eternity*

These programs are being aired on television and radio stations around the world. For information on how you can air them on your local radio or television station, contact

Children of Medjugorje, USA:
877-647-6335 (877-MIR-MEDJ)

How to get the
Medjugorje Monthly Message
of the 25th

On the Internet:

English: www.childrenofmedjugorje.com
Spanish: www.mensajerosdelareinadelapaz.org
French: www.enfantsdemedjugorje.com
Information Center MIR (parish): www.medjugorje.hr

To Receive Monthly Reports
from Medjugorje by Sr. Emmanuel

In English, send your email address to: pray@childrenofmedjugorje.com
In French (original copy): wmmedjugorje@childrenofmedjugorje.com
In German: pray@childrenofmedjugorje.com
In Italian: info@vocepiu.it or vannapg@gmail.com
In Spanish: gisele_rivert@mensajerosdelareinadelapaz.org
In Croatian: rsilic@yahoo.com
In Portuguese: medjugorjeport@yahoo.com

The website **childrenofmedjugorje.com** offers these reports in other languages.

THE HIDDEN CHILD OF MEDJUGORJE

This Book is also Available in the Following Languages

French: 1. France. Edit. des Béatitudes , Burtin, 41600 Nouan-le-Fuzelier
Tel: (33) 254 88 2118, ed.beatitudes@wanadoo.fr
2. Canada. Mediaspaul, Montreal - Tel. (514) 322 7341,
mediaspaul@mediaspaul.qc.ca - www.editions-beatitudes.fr

Croatian: A.G.M. d.o.o., Mihanoviceva, 28 10000 Zagreb, Croatia
Tel (385) 148.56.307, agm@agm.hr. www.agm.hr

Spanish: 1. Argentina. Paulinas - Buenos Aires - Tel: (54) 11.4952 5924
editorial@paulinas.org.ar www.paulinas.org.ar
2. Mexico. Communidad de las Bienaventuranzas, Atlixco Medias
atlixco@beatitudes.org or sr_janet@yahoo.com.mx
3. Ecuador, Jesus de la Misericordia, PO Box 6252, CCD
Tel: (593) 2.564.519.528.519 - jesusmi@quik.com.ec
4. Spain. Hijos de Medjugorje, Tarragona. Tel: (34) 676-05-95-94
gsba15@yahoo.es
5. Chile. Foyer de Caridad Nuestra Señora del Carmen,
Tel (56) 41 651 332 - foyer@entelchile.net

English:
USA. Children of Medjugorje-USA, PO Box 18430, Denver, CO
80218-0430 - Tel: 877- 647-6335 (877-MIR-MEDJ)
pray@childrenofmedjugorje.com - www.childrenofmedjugorje.com
3. India. The Ark, Cochin, Kerela - Tel: (91) 484 392 667
eddy@vsnl.com or manojsunny@jesusyouth.org

Italian: Editrice Shalom - Tel. (39) 071 7450 440 - ordina@editriceshalom.it
www.editriceshalom.it

Polish: Wydawnictwo Marianow, Warsaw - Tel: (48) 22 651 9970,
wkm@marianie.pol.pl

Dutch: 1. Holland. Noelle Imkamp - Tel: (31) 70.355.3943
n.imkamp@tele2.nl
2. Curacao. San Vicente de Paul - Tel: (599) 9869 5382,
hcampman@cur.net or hcampman@interneeds.net

Portuguese: 1. Portugal. medjugorjeport@yahoo.com
2. Brazil. Aleanza Misericordia - pe.enrico@misericordia.com.br

Romanian: Janine, Copiii Medjugorje, copmedj@rdslink.ro or copmedj@atnr.ro

Hungarian: Nyolc Boldogsag Kozosseg - Tel: (36) 93 356 113,
homokkomarom@beatitudes.org or maria-media@freemail.hu

German: Parvis Verlag, Switzerland - Tel: (41) 269 159 393 - book@parvis.ch

Lebanese: Amis de Marie Reine de la Paix -Tel: (961) 125 9593,
office@medugorjeliban.org - liban@beatitudes.org

Korean: Charles Kim, Fax: (60) 82.425.724 - kimianprop@yahoo.com

Chinese: COM-Hong Kong - Tel - 853/812 935 - com.hongkong@gmail.com

Latvian: Shablovskis, Latvia, Lettony - Tel: (371) 7324 230 - ei@lanet.lv

Russian: Piotr Cheltsov, Moscow - pcheltsov@mail.ru or srtamara@free.fr

Slovenian: Fr. Miran Spelic, Ljubljana, Slovenia - miran.spelic@rkc.si

Slovakian, Check, Albanian and Japanese versions are in the process.

APPENDIX 2

This is the latest official statement from the Vatican about Medjugorje.

CONGREGATION FOR THE DOCTRINE OF THE FAITH
Pr. No 154/81-06419

May 26, 1998

To His Excellency Mons. Gilbert Aubry,
Bishop of Saint-Denis de la Reunion

Excellency:

In your letter of January 1, 1998, you submitted to this Dicastery several questions about the position of the Holy See and of the Bishop of Mostar in regard to the so called apparitions of Medjugorje, private pilgrimages and the pastoral care of the faithful who go there.

In regard to this matter, I think it is impossible to reply to each of the questions posed by Your Excellency. The main thing I would like to point out is that the Holy See does not ordinarily take a position of its own regarding supposed supernatural phenomena as a court of first instance. As for the credibility of the "apparitions" in question, this Dicastery respects what was decided by the bishops of the former Yugoslavia in the Declaration of Zadar, April 10, 1991: "On the basis of the investigation so far, it can not be affirmed that one is dealing with supernatural apparitions and revelations." Since the division of Yugoslavia into different independent nations it would now pertain to the members of the Episcopal Conference of Bosnia-Hercegovina to eventually reopen the examination of this case, and to make any new pronouncements that might be called for.

What Bishop Peric said in his letter to the Secretary General of "Famille Chretienne", declaring: "My conviction and my position is not only 'non constat de supernaturalitate,' but likewise, 'constat de non supernaturalitate' of the apparitions or revelations in Medjugorje", should be considered the expression of the personal conviction of the Bishop of Mostar which he has the right to express as Ordinary of the place, but which is and remains his personal opinion.

As regards pilgrimages to Medjugorje: they are permitted if conducted privately, on condition that they are not regarded as an authentification of events still taking place and which still call for an examination by the Church.

I hope that I have replied satisfactorily at least to the principal questions that you have presented to this Dicastery and I beg Your Excellency to accept the expression of my devoted sentiments.

Mons. Tarcisio Bertone
(Secretary to the Congregation, presided over by Cardinal Ratzinger at the time)

To summarize:

The declarations of the Bishop of Mostar only reflect his personal opinion. Consequently, they are not an official and definitive judgement requiring assent and obedience.

A new commission could eventually be named.

Before further investigations are made, private pilgrimages with pastoral accompaniment for the faithful are permitted by the Church. All pilgrims may go to Medjugorje in complete obedience to the Church. Only official pilgrimages are not permitted.

Cardinal Schönborn comments:

The letter of Archbishop Bertone to the Bishop of Le Reunion sufficiently makes clear what has always been the official position of the hierarchy during recent years concerning Medjugorje: namely, that it knowingly leaves the matter undecided. The supernatural character is not established; such were the words used by the former conference of bishops of Yugoslavia in Zadar in 1991. It really is a matter of wording, which knowingly leaves the matter pending. It has not been said that the supernatural character is substantially established. Furthermore, it has not been denied or discounted that the phenomena may be of a supernatural nature. There is no doubt that the magisterium of the Church does not make a definite declaration while the extraordinary phenomena are going on in the form of apparitions or other means. Indeed it is the mission of the shepherds to promote what is growing, to encourage the fruits which are appearing, to protect the, if need be, from the dangers which are obviously everywhere.

It is also necessary at Lourdes to see to it that the original gift of Lourdes not be stifled by unfortunate developments. Neither is Medjugorje invulnerable. That is why it is and will be so important that bishops also publicly take under their protection the pastoral pronouncement of Medjugorje so that the obvious fruits that are in that place might be protected from any possible unfortunate developments.

I believe that the words of Mary at Cana: "Do whatever He tells you," make up the substance of what She says throughout the centuries. Mary helps us to hear Jesus and She desires with her whole heart and with all her strength that we do what He tells us.

This is what I wish for all the communities of prayer which were formed from Medjugorje; this is what I wish for our diocese and for the Church.

Personally, I have not yet gone to Medjugorje; but in a way I have gone there through the people I know or those I have met who, themselves, have gone to Medjugorje. And I see good fruits in their lives. I should be lying if I denied that these fruits exist.

These fruits are tangible, evident. And in our diocese and in many other places, I observe graces of conversion, graces of a life of supernatural faith, of vocations, of healings, of a rediscovering of the sacraments, of confession. These are all things which do not mislead.

This is the reason why I can only say that it is these fruits which enable me, as bishop, to pass a moral judgment. And if as Jesus said, we must judge the tree by its fruits, I am obliged to say that the tree is good.

Cardinal Schönborn

Cardinal Christoph Schönborn, the Archbishop of Vienna, who gave the Holy Father and his Papal Household their 1998 Lenten Retreat, and who was the main author of the "Catechism of the Catholic Church", gave the preceeding testimony in Lourdes on July 18,1998. The Cardinal's testimony was published in "Medjugorje Gebetsakion", #50, "Stella Maris", #343, pp. 19, 20. (*This English translation is published with the Cardinal's permission.*)

Nota Bene: On January 12, 1999, Archbishop Bertone instructed the leaders of the Beatitudes Community that the Church needed their community's presence in Medjugorje in order to help serve the needs of pilgrims. On that occasion the Secretary for the Congregation of the faith stated: "For the moment one should consider Medjugorje as a Sanctuary, a Marian Shrine, in the same way as Czestochowa."

APPENDIX 3

Private Letters from Pope John Paul II regarding Medjugorje

Pope John Paul II sometimes mentioned Medjugorje in his letters to Marek and Zofia Skmarnicki, his good friends in Krakov. Keen to respect the work of the Commissions on the Medjugorje dossier, he didn't allow himself to make any official pronouncement but we are now well aware thatJohn Paul II, in a private way, sometimes whispered a word to bishops, priests or lay people, encouraging them verbally to go to Medjugorje and pray there. Today we have his letters to Marek Skmarnicki, as private documents which are personally signed by him.

Marek, a very famous Polish poet, has collaborated with Cardinal Karol Wojtyla before he ascended to the throne of Peter. He and his wife, Zofia, built up a strong friendship with him (John Paul II always made a point of seeing them whenever he visited Krakov) and they kept in regular correspondence with him until his death in 2005. I had the privilege to meet Marek and Zofia at their home in Krakov during a mission in 1995 and they allowed me to see those precious letters. However, during his lifetime it would have been inappropriate to publish those letters; but today we can now all appreciate these true treasures. Six of these letters mention Medjugorje. These documents give us an insight into John Paul's attachment to Medjugorje.

Marek first published these letters in Poland in October 2005[1]

1.(Mr. Skwarnicki's book, "John Paul II: I Send You Greetings and Bless You –The Pope's Private Letters" was published in October, 2006, by Swiat Ksiazki-Bertelsman Media, Warszawa, Poland).

2.Fragments published with the permission of Cardinal Dziwisz, former personal secretary of John Paul II now Cardinal of Krakov, and with permission of Marek Skwarnick, May 27, 2006.

Dear Sir,
(....) and that all is well regarding the journey Medjugorje-Rome.
With a heartfelt blessing,

Jan Pawel II, Vatican, March 30, 1991

Marek writes. "The phrase, 'on the journey from Medjugorje to Rome' was not an allusion to any journey. Rather, it meant a relationship between the Medjugorje Sanctuary and the Vatican. In effect, controversies regarding the Medjugorje apparitions were still persisting as was the conflict between the Franciscans of Medjugorje and the Bishop of Mostar. It was the time when Medjugorje matters were referred to Yugoslavian Episcopal authorities for consideration".

+ Drodzy Państwo!

Serdecznie dziękuję za wspólny list Skwarnickich: Zofii i Marka. Dziękuję też za życzenia wielkanocne. Z całego serca je odwzajemniam pod adresem Państwa i Młodego Pokolenia (Dzieci i Wnuków), wreszcie pod adresem "Tygodnika" i całego Społeczeństwa. Ufam, że Matka z Jasnej Góry pomoże mi na szlaku czerwcowej pielgrzymki. Wszystkich bardzo proszę o modlitwę. W modlitwie też pamiętam codziennie o Ks.Andrzeju B. A dla Moniki szczególne błogosławieństwo na dzień I Komunii św. I niech wszystko dobrze się układa na szlaku Medziugorje-Rzym.

Z serdecznym błogosławieństwem
Watykan 30 marca 1991 r.

Jan Rwtt

Pokój Chrystusowy
niech panuje w sercach waszych
kol 3, 15
alleluja

Z błogosławieństwem

Jan Paweł II papież
Wielkanoc
1991

---

* * *

Dear Mr. Marek
(...) and now, we every day return to Medjugorje in prayer.
Jan Pawel II, Vatican, May 28, 1992

According to Marek, "This reference to Medjugorje is a sign of how deeply the Holy Father felt over the Balkan fratricidal war and believed more and more in the sanctity of Medjugorje sanctuary."

```
+ Drogi Panie Marku!

  Bóg zapłać za "Misterium".
Aby wiedzieć, co w sobie kryje,
muszę naprzód przeczytać, ale
już z Pańskiego listu można coś
przeczuć. Rychło postaram się
przeczytać.
  Na razie dziękuję za tekst
(jeszcze nie przeczytany) i za
dobre słowo od Autora. Niech
Matka Boska stale czuwa nad
Markiem i Zofią, oraz Ich Rodziną.
  A teraz codziennie wracamy
modlitwą do Mediugorii

Watykan 28 maja 1992 r.
```

* * *

Dear Marek and Zofia,
(...) I thank Zofia for everything concerning Medjugorje. I too, go
there every day as a pilgrim in my prayers: I unite in my prayers with
all those who pray there or receive a calling for prayer from there.
Today we have understood this call better. I rejoice that our time does
not lack people of prayer and apostles.

According to Marek, "All that the Pope writes here about Medjugorje is of great value. It does not concern the long-term controversies regarding the authenticity of the apparitions... After all, the Pope
participates in the faith of God's people, as the Highest Priest of the
Church, so he joins the poor people of Medjugorje through prayers,
having become convinced about a special plan of God in that very
place regarding a growing devotion to the Blessed Mother. Because
the main concern in the Medjugorje messages was the Mother's warning about upcoming confusion and war, the Pope in 1992, while the
Balkans were still at war, writes, "Today we have understood this call
better..."

* * *

Dear Marek,

"(...) I know that Madam Zofia looks very much towards Medjugorje and, of late, towards Ostra Brama for the reason of her entire past. I allowedly, was in Ostra Brama, I even quoted from Mickiewicz there. I was not instead in Medjugorje but I also look in that direction. Please tell your Wife about it. I look in that direction and it seems to me that one cannot understand today's terrible events in the Balkans without Medjugorje (...)"

Jan Pawel II, December 6, 1993

Marek comments: "And again about Medjugorje. 'It seems to me that one cannot understand today's terrible events in the Balkans without Medjugorje,' writes the Holy Father at the time when the Balkan war intensifies... Over the years, the Blessed Mother had warned against hatred and sins of people leading to human calamity." (p.117)

Vatican City, February 25, 1994
Dear Sir and Madam:

I thank you very much for letters. Zofia is writting to me about the Balkans. I guess Medjugorje is better understood these days. This kind of "insisting" of our Mother is better understood today when we see with our own very eyes the enormousness of the danger. At the same time, theresponse in the way of a special prayer - and that coming from the people all around the world - fills us with hope that here, too, the good will prevail. Peace is possible - such was the motto of the day of prayer of January 23, prepared by a special session at the Vatican in which Mr. T. Mazowiecki also participated.

Perhaps it is thanks to this as well that Europe is coming back to its senses. People in Poland are getting back to their senses, too, as foloows from your writtings. Maybe it will become easier for them to come to terms with the Pope who has not preached "the victory of democracy" but has instead reminded them of the Decalogue.

(...) With my blessing,

Jan Pawel II, Febuuary 25, 1994

* * *

Dear Sir and dear Madam,
(...) The second part of te letter provides many valuable pieces of information concerning the pilgrimage to Medjugorje on August 15 in wich Zofia particpated. These are then the impressions of a first-hand witness, that is to say, they are reliable in every respect. May God reward you! It is difficult not to read those words without heartfelt compassion for those poor little orphans and all the local inhabitants of that land. No wonder that the people put their hope only in God as, there, they do not get any support from their nearest community.

I commend to the Mother of God Zofia, Marek and their whole family. I wish you to stay healthy.

With a blessing from my heart,

Jan Pawel II, Castelgandolfo, September 3, 1994

* * *

Vatican City, February 26, 1997
Dear Sir and Madam:

I thank you very much, Mr. Mark and your Wife for the letters and the attached Polish edition of 10 Ways of the Cross from the Coliseum...
If the Lord permits, the dedication of the building will be part of the program of my visit to Krakow. We are already approaching these days in great strides. It is good that they are an object of my Countrymen's prayers, as much as my immediate trip to Sarajevo which, in a special way, involves Madam Zofia in her prayers when thinking about Medjugorje. It is good that she wrote a review to the book by S. Emily on the Apocalypse, perhaps to arouse interest in it.
As we delve into the Lent season, I wish you Divine Mercies for this period of time so tightly connected to the Secret of the Suffering of Our Savior.
I greet heartily Madam Zofia, Mr. Marek and the "kids" together with little Paul.
Blessings,

John Paul II

Marek comments: "... (The Holy Father) was planning to leave for Sarajevo. Medjugorje, nearby, was not included in his itinerary during his visit to Bosnia Hercegovina." (p.146.lines 6,7)

* * *

Vatican City, April 15th, 1986
Dear Madam Zofia and Mr. Marek,
Thank you for sharing with me your observations prompted by the issuance of a little book translated by Madam Zofia, a copy of which she sent me as a gift. I thank her for this cordially, as well as you, Marek, for your postscripts to her letter. It is comforting to hear the news about the reaction of God's people – and the implementation of what is the most essential in this whole event, which stimulates the zeal, the reconciliation of hearts, to worshiping the Merciful Father, to opening up hearts to the acceptance of the Divine Mercy.... JPII
The Good Shepherd is risen, Alleluia!
With Blessing,

413

Marek comments: "The 'little book' mentioned by the Pope was the very first Polish publication regarding the Medjugorje apparitions. It was translated from German into Polish by our friend, Maria Balewicz. Because the Pope received it from my wife he mistakenly assumed that Zofia had been a translator of that book. The Pope's interpretation of the apparitions is interesting. At this early time the controversies within the Church were significant. Moreover, an increasing interest in the Medjugorje events, among faithful in both the former Yugoslavia and other countries, was an impediment for the local government, because Yugoslavia was a State of atheistic communism. The Medjugorje Pastor was arrested. The Bishop of Mostar who had an ecclesiastical governance over that area, was against acceptance of the authenticity of the apparitions. Local Franciscans were of a different opinion... so the controversies kept growing... Those who believed in the apparitions (which themselves were revealing nothing contrary to the Church's doctrines) supported the local Franciscans. John Paul's reply to my wife's letter and to my note was written during that very period... He did not express a direct opinion, but he apparently was agreeable with the contents of those apparitions. After all, they focused mainly on calling for peace, for reconciliation in the disturbed world and in the Balkans, for love for Christ, repentance and incessant prayer." (p.43)